READINGS AND CASES IN

# *International Human Resource Management*

## ▬ KENT Series in Management

BARNETT/WILSTED, *Cases for Strategic Management*

BARNETT/WILSTED, *Strategic Management: Concepts and Cases*

BARNETT/WILSTED, *Strategic Management: Text and Concepts*

BERKMAN/NEIDER, *The Human Relations of Organizations*

CARLAND/CARLAND, *Small Business Management: Tools for Success*

CRANE, *Personnel: The Management of Human Resources*, Fourth Edition

DAVIS/COSENZA, *Business Research for Decision Making*, Second Edition

FINLEY, *Entrepreneurial Strategies: Text and Cases*

KEMPER/YEHUDAI, *Experiencing Operations Management: A Walk-Through*

KIRKPATRICK, *Supervision: A Situational Approach*

MENDENHALL/ODDOU, *Readings and Cases in International Human Resource Management*

MITCHELL, *Human Resource Management: An Economic Approach*

NKOMO/FOTTLER/McAFEE, *Applications in Personnel/Human Resource Management: Cases, Exercises, and Skill Builders*

PLUNKETT/ATTNER, *Introduction to Management*, Third Edition

PUNNETT, *Experiencing International Management*

ROBERTS/HUNT, *Organizational Behavior*

SCARPELLO/LEDVINKA, *Personnel/Human Resource Management: Environments and Functions*

SINGER, *Human Resource Management*

STARLING, *The Changing Environment of Business*, Third Edition

STEERS/UNGSON/MOWDAY, *Managing Effective Organizations: An Introduction*

TOSI, *Organizational Behavior and Management: A Contingency Approach*

## ▬ KENT International Dimensions of Business Series

Series Consulting Editor, David A. Ricks

ADLER, *International Dimensions of Organizational Behavior*, Second Edition

ALHASHIM/ARPAN, *International Dimensions of Accounting*, Second Edition

DOWLING/SCHULER, *International Dimensions of Human Resource Management*

FOLKS/AGGARWAL, *International Dimensions of Financial Management*

GARLAND/FARMER/TAYLOR, *International Dimensions of Business Policy and Strategy*, Second Edition

LITKA, *International Dimensions of the Legal Environment of Business*, Second Edition

PHATAK, *International Dimensions of Management*, Second Edition

TERPSTRA, *International Dimensions of Marketing*, Second Edition

# ▬ KENT Series in Human Resource Management

Series Consulting Editor, Richard W. Beatty

READINGS AND CASES IN

# *International Human Resource Management*

MARK MENDENHALL
*J. Burton Frierson Chair of Excellence
    in Business Leadership*
*University of Tennessee at Chattanooga*

GARY ODDOU
*San Jose State University*

PWS-KENT PUBLISHING COMPANY
BOSTON

# PWS-KENT
## Publishing Company

*Sponsoring Editor:* Rolf A. Janke
*Assistant Editor:* Kathleen M. Tibbetts
*Production Editor:* Chris Crochetière
*Cover Photographer:* Ralph Mercer
*Interior/Cover Designer:* Chris Crochetière
*Manufacturing Coordinator:* Marcia A. Locke
*Typesetter:* David E. Seham Associates, Inc.
*Printer/Binder:* The Maple-Vail Book Manufacturing Group
*Cover Printer:* Henry N. Sawyer Co., Inc.

PWS-KENT Publishing Company is a division of Wadsworth, Inc.

Printed in the United States of America.

2 3 4 5 6 7 8 9 - 95 94 93 92

**Library of Congress Cataloging-in-Publication Data**

Readings and cases in international human resource management /
  [edited] by Mark E. Mendenhall, Gary R. Oddou.
     p.   cm.
  Includes bibliographical references.
  ISBN 0-534-92332-1
  1. Personnel management—Cross-cultural studies.  2. Intercultural communication—Case studies.  3. International business enterprises—Personnel management—Cross-cultural studies.  4. Corporate culture—Cross-cultural studies.  I. Mendenhall, Mark E.
  II. Oddou, Gary R.
  HF5549.R3813  1991
  658.3—dc20

90-47880
CIP

# Contributing Authors

NANCY J. ADLER
*McGill University*
*CANADA*

RAE ANDRE
*Northeastern University*

SCHON BEECHLER
*Columbia University*

BHAL BHATT
*University of Toledo*

J. STEWART BLACK
*Dartmouth College*

NAKIYE BOYACIGILLER
*San Jose State University*

ROBERT E. COLE
*University of Michigan*

WILLIAM H. DAVIDSON
*University of Southern California*

C. BROOKLYN DERR
*IMD/University of Utah*
*SWITZERLAND/USA*

PETER J. DOWLING
*Monash University*
*AUSTRALIA*

YVES DOZ
*INSEAD*
*FRANCE*

FARIBORZ GHADAR
*George Washington University*

MARILYN HELMS
*University of Tennessee, Chattanooga*

MARTIN HILB
*University of St. Gallen*
*SWITZERLAND*

SUSAN E. JACKSON
*New York University*

MERRICK L. JONES
*University of Manchester*
*UNITED KINGDOM*

STEPHEN J. KOBRIN
*University of Pennsylvania*

HENRY W. LANE
*University of Western Ontario*
*CANADA*

MARK E. MENDENHALL
*University of Tennessee, Chattanooga*

EDWIN L. MILLER
*University of Michigan*

TOMASZ MROCZKOWSKI
*American University*

RAGHU NATH
*University of Pittsburgh*

GARY R. ODDOU
*San Jose State University*

JOHN F. PREBLE
*University of Delaware*

ARIE REICHEL
*Ben Gurion University*
*ISRAEL*

MARTIN SAILER
*Daimler-Benz*
*FEDERAL REPUBLIC OF GERMANY*

SUSAN C. SCHNEIDER
*INSEAD*
*FRANCE*

RANDALL S. SCHULER
*New York University*

JAMES G. SCOVILLE
*University of Minnesota*

MARY B. TEAGARDEN
*San Diego State University*

ROSALIE L. TUNG
*University of Wisconsin, Milwaukee*

CHARLES M. VANCE
*Loyola Marymount University*

MARY ANN VON GLINOW
*University of Southern California*

WARNER P. WOODWORTH
*Brigham Young University*

LORNA WRIGHT
*Queens University*
*CANADA*

ALBERTO ZANZI
*Suffolk University*

# *Preface*

The interdependencies of economies, political systems, and cultures have created a state of affairs in which businesspeople can ill afford not to be well-versed in the finer points of international business practices. Many business-people are well-versed in the areas of international finance, marketing, and accounting. However, the impact of the global village or, more specifically, the "global store," has often been overlooked and poorly understood in relation to its impact in the area of human resource management (HRM). It was not until the mid-1970s that researchers began to investigate the challenges, problems, and paradoxes that human resource managers face in a global context.

To date, few cases and readings have been available to both practitioners and educators in the human resource management area that explore, in depth, the complexities of a new subfield in the discipline of human resource management: international human resource management. No journals are devoted to this field; therefore, it is difficult for those who desire to "internationalize" a course (or themselves) to construct a solid reading list in this area. Furthermore, a scanning of case clearinghouses reveals a dearth of cases that specifically address human resource issues in a global context.

Thus, the purpose of this book is to bring together for practitioners and educators alike a group of readings and cases that will allow them to more fully explore this emerging field with students, managers, expatriates, and executives. We invited prominent researchers in the field to submit readings and cases for publication in this book. We also scoured all sources known to us where articles and cases might, by chance, exist. The culmination of this effort, we believe, is a book that makes for interesting reading for both undergraduates and graduates; this is a collection of readings and cases that will significantly challenge their thinking. Some of the cases are currently used at top-ten business schools, whereas others are new and were written especially for this book. Because the field is young, large numbers of cases do not yet exist. We hope that this book will encourage many of you to write cases in this area and add to the body of knowledge in the international human resource management field.

The book is organized according to traditional subareas within the human resource management discipline: human resource strategy, personnel selection, training, management development, motivation and productivity, performance appraisal and compensation, and labor relations. All these, of course, are explored in a global context. In a unique section of the book, "Culture and International Human Resource Management," we explore culture as a variable that significantly affects human resource management practices at a variety of levels in the firm. We place this section at the beginning of the book, after the introduction, for we feel that unless one develops a sense of how culture influences behavior within organizations, it will be difficult to understand why problems occur in firms doing business abroad.

## AACSB, Creativity, and Course Design

This book can be used in a variety of ways in human resource management courses. It can stand alone, if the instructor's preference is to teach predominately a case course. It can be used in tandem with other books in the Kent International Business Series (*International Dimensions of Human Resource Management* by Peter J. Dowling and Randall S. Schuler or *International Dimensions of Organizational Behavior* by Nancy J. Adler) or as a supplement to them. Or it can be used as a main text in a human resource management course and supplemented with other readings and texts with which the instructor is comfortable.

Perhaps its most compelling use is that of helping to satisfy AACSB requirements in course offerings; it can be used with a traditional introductory text as a supplement in order to insert an international dimension into the course. This would facilitate matrixing into a traditional human resource management course an international dimension. However the text is used, we feel that it will spice up one's course, mainly because students find international problems fascinating and complex and unique, as we do.

## Acknowledgments

We would like to thank all those who have contributed to this book. Many of the authors willingly sent us cases, articles, manuscripts in progress, and bibliographies that they had developed over the years. We regret that we could not include all the sources offered to us. Our thanks go primarily to Rolf Janke and Kathleen Tibbetts—to Rolf for his belief and desire to see a book like this become available to practitioners and academics because of the importance of the concept, and to Kathy for being helpful, patient, and enthusiastic as she guided us through the editorial process. Our thanks also go to the reviewers of the book, whose constructive suggestions made the book better than it would have been had we relied solely on our own wisdom in assembling it: Rae Andre of Northeastern University, Elaine K. Bailey of the University of Hawaii at Manoa, Kenneth P. Carson of Arizona State University, and Stella M. Nkomo of the University of North Carolina at Charlotte. A special thanks goes to Nilene Hopkins, whose help was vital in the actual "real time" editing of the book. Stewart Black's comments and feedback regarding portions of the book were also timely and helpful, and we thank him for this assistance. Finally, we would like to dedicate this book to our wives, Janet and Jane, for tolerating our cross-cultural meanderings and wanderlust to travel to foreign places. They make it all possible.

MARK MENDENHALL
Signal Mountain, Tennessee

GARY ODDOU
Paladru, France

# Contents

READINGS AND CASES IN

*International Human
Resource Management*

P A R T   1

# Introduction

# The White Water Rapids of International Human Resource Management

## MARK MENDENHALL
## GARY ODDOU

At the time of this writing (April 12, 1990), the world of politics and business had just been turned upside down. The democratization movement in the People's Republic of China (PRC) was snuffed out by the bloody massacre at Tiananmen Square. Currently, the leadership of the People's Republic of China is looking to the past for economic and management models and is downplaying and slowly eradicating Western influences in the country's economy. Whether the capitalist-oriented free-trade zones in the PRC will go along with this is anyone's guess. What will happen in the go-go capitalist mecca of Hong Kong in 1997 is anyone's guess.

Additionally, the Eastern bloc nations have revolted against over forty years of Communist control, and long-suppressed democratic and capitalistic tendencies are flowering. East and West Germany are rapidly moving toward a political and economic reunification; Hungary and Poland are well on their way to reinstitutionalizing market systems into their economies; and even Romania has thrown off a narcissistic dictator and is wrestling with the social, economic, and political problems of remodeling a totalitarian nation into one more democratic.

The European Economic Community (EEC) is moving toward integration on all fronts presently, though the Eastern bloc nations' defection to democratic socialism and capitalism has thrown a stick in the spokes of the 1992 plan. Currently, no one knows how this will affect the EEC's plans—especially if West and East Germany reunify (as they seem to be doing with breathtaking speed). What will Europe really look like, be like, and act like, socially as well as in the business realm, when all barriers between the countries are eradicated? What are the economic threats and opportunities to countries and companies that want to do business there?

*Source:* This article was written especially for this book.

Even Japan, a country visualized by many in the Western world as being stable and conformist within its own boundaries, was rocked by political and business scandals that sent the monolithic ruling party (LDP) into a tailspin. Though the LDP managed to retain its power in the recent elections, the turmoil perhaps presages possible shifts and changes in the continental shelf of Japanese government and business policies. The cover of the April 23, 1990 edition of *Business Week* proclaims, "Suddenly, a series of shocks is buffeting the mighty Japanese economy. The stock market plunged 30%. The yen is weakening. Inflation and interest rates are both on the rise. Political leadership is weak. And now some strains are appearing in the nation's normally harmonious social structure. Japan has proved remarkably adaptable to adversity in the past. This time, it may be harder." Even Japan seems to be in the throes of social change.

If this introduction seems outdated to you, owing to changes that have taken place since its writing, then our point is proved all the more: We live in a world where the only thing we can count on is that change will take place.

Business leaders of the present—let alone the future—need to possess international business skills par excellence in order to deal with the chaotic world of international business. It goes without saying that human resource managers also will be faced with new, unforeseen obstacles. Peter Vaill uses the metaphor of "permanent white water" to describe the unpredictable, dynamic nature of doing business in the latter part of the twentieth century.

> Most managers are taught to think of themselves as paddling their canoes on calm, still lakes. . . . They're led to believe that they should be pretty much able to go where they want, when they want, using the means that are under their control. Sure there will be temporary disruptions during changes of various sorts—periods when they will have to shoot the rapids in their canoes—but the disruptions will be temporary, and when things settle back down, they'll be back in a calm, still lake mode. But it has been my experience . . . that you never get out of the rapids! No sooner do you begin to digest one change than another one comes along to keep things unstuck. In fact, there are usually lots of changes going on at once. The feeling is one of continuous upset and chaos (Vaill, 1989, p. 2).

This metaphor aptly illustrates the world of international business. As Vaill notes, in the world of international business, "things are only very partially under control, yet the effective navigator of the rapids is not behaving randomly or aimlessly. Intelligence, experience, and skill are being exercised, albeit in ways that we hardly know how to perceive, let alone describe" (1989, p. 2). This book deals with the challenges that human resource managers will face in the 1990s and beyond. What will be the nature of those challenges? Perhaps an example of a firm or an individual would help illustrate these challenges; let's consider the case of Robin Earl.

## ■ *Robin Earl's White Water Rapids*

Robin is director of human resources for BCN, a firm that, among other things, manufactures a line of semiconductors. BCN has been very successful in the last ten years. Sales have increased at an annual rate of 13 percent, and profits have correspondingly grown.

BCN has had overseas sales offices for the last seven years, exporting its products from its local manufacturing operations to South America and Asia. Recently, BCN's top management has been mulling over the possibility of developing manufacturing capabilities in both South America and Asia, and possibly even in Europe. Doing so would allow BCN to take advantage of cheaper labor rates and avoid export barriers. In addition, it could be more responsive to local demand for its products.

Robin was asked by the CEO to put together an analysis (due on his desk in two weeks) of the human resource impact such moves would have on the firm. As Robin sat down at her desk, she began to jot down ideas. She found herself somewhat baffled by this international angle of HRM since she had no experience or training in managing human resources internationally. The following were some of her thoughts as she attempted to create an outline for her report.

### *How Will International Assignments Fit Into BCN's Business Strategy to Become A Multinational Firm?*

Do we really have a clearly focused business strategy for becoming a multinational firm? She made a mental note to call up John Fukumoto, the v.p. of finance, to see how far the thinking of the top management team had progressed on that front. How will the development of BCN's human resources fit into such a plan? I wonder why I am not on that planning team? Robin wondered how she could insert herself into that process without being perceived as having ulterior motives.

What kind of perspective and experience should BCN's future top management have if they will be leading a true multinational firm? How will that experience be best obtained? Through international assignments or by the use of consultants? Am I going to be responsible for educating them about international issues? If so, it's the blind leading the blind, she thought, for she would not even be sure how to best evaluate the validity of external consultants' proposals. I could always hire experts to evaluate the bid proposals of consulting firms, she thought, but that would run into serious budget squeezes for my department.

Will local managers, if we use local managers, desire to be promoted to U.S. headquarters? Will top management desire that? Fifteen years from now, what will, and what should, BCN's top management look like: an Asian managing a South American plant or a mixture of South Americans, Asians, Europeans, and Americans at headquarters? The cost of hiring the new workers—

not to mention well-qualified managers—is not going to be "loose change." I hope they aren't ignoring the cost of hiring well-qualified managers and retaining them in their financial analyses, Robin thought. How will we retain the best and the brightest? What do Asians want in rewards? What do South Americans want? Is a good salary enough, or are other factors involved?

### Which Countries Have Cultures That Best Fit BCN's Needs?

Robin remembered reading in the *Los Angeles Times* that one of the site-location factors important to Japanese firms in the United States was that of regional cultural norms. The Japanese liked the Southern culture because of its norms regarding interpersonal relations in business settings, tradition, and the respect that elders and those in positions are given. Which countries have educational systems that would best support the knowledge base that our personnel will need? Which countries have social systems that favor unions more than management? Which cultures within these regions are most favorable to American expatriates and their families? Most important, which cultures promote a strong work ethic?

Which countries have governments that are stable and are not likely to change and upset the equilibrium of our workers' and managers' work schedules? What about the possibility of terrorism? Will I have to devise a terrorism-prevention training program? Which countries are friendly to us, not just regarding business but in their perceptions of Americans and their right to manage the local residents? I wonder how much kidnap insurance costs? Robin's mind began to wander and she envisioned herself in a small, boxlike hole with rusty, iron bars over the top of it. When would her kidnappers give her water? Her reverie was broken by a more practical concern that flashed across her mind.

### Should We Send Our Own Personnel Overseas or Hire Locally?

Which countries in Asia, South America, or Europe have qualified personnel to staff manufacturing operations from top to bottom? Are there laws in specific countries that require hiring a certain percentage of local workers? She remembered meeting someone once at a professional convention who had worked for a mining company in Africa. He said he had to hire all workers locally below middle management level with the promise to phase-out all Americans within ten years.

Can or should the subsidiary management be from headquarters? If not, where would we hire local managers from? The universities? Robin recalled reading once that in France the norm was to hire managers from the "grandes écoles" and not from the universities.

If we send our personnel, who should go? For how long should the assignment be? How expensive will it be to house an American family at their accustomed standard of living in the new country? How should we select the

Americans to send? Should we base our decisions on years of experience in the company, adaptability potential, or desire to relocate? What if nobody wants to go?

### How Will We Train Them For Such Assignments?

How much training will they need before they go? Do they need language training or is English good enough? Robin thought that most business-people around the world speak English, so maybe this was not an issue. Will the firm budget the resources necessary for me to do effective training, or will I be left with a budget that will be able to do nothing more than bring in a few local professors for a couple of hours each to do area briefings? Who can I call on to do the training?

Robin felt somewhat relieved when she remembered reading of some cross-cultural training firms in the ad section of an HRM newsletter she sub-scribes to. But her confidence ebbed when the following thought came to her: How will I know if the training these external consultants give is valid and helpful or if it's only a dog and pony show? Can I, with my staff develop our own training program? What kind of time and money will such an endeavor take? As Robin began mentally planning a strategy to develop training pro-grams with her staff, her mind switched to yet another problem.

### What Are the Career Implications of Foreign Assignments?

Should the assignments be developmental or simply be used to fill a slot as it opens up, regardless of whether or not it will develop the employee? Robin realized that companies such as IBM, CIBA-GEIGY, and Philips view international assignments as an integral part of their management develop-ment for senior posts. If the assignment is developmental, what will we do when the employee returns? Robin wondered if they would give her author-ity to determine what position returning managers should receive. She doubted they would give her that authority.

So, how will we reintegrate these employees into BCN's home opera-tions? How will the HR department keep track and informed of the needs, concerns, performance, and evaluation of the overseas employees? By phone? Telex? Fax? Site visits? (Robin wondered whether she could justify some nice visits to the Orient, maybe, as site visits. They may be necessary but might be viewed by others as a new perk for the HR department.)

### How Productive Will the Cheap Labor Be?

If we do opt to set up in a country where the labor rates are inexpensive, can we introduce our management systems into the manufacturing plants? Will those systems be in harmony with the work culture of that country? I wonder if we will run into transfer of technology problems? Probably. Okay, so, how do we train local workers to understand how we do things at BCN? Will I have to design those training programs too?

I wonder if our managers will have to develop unique incentive systems for their subordinates in order to get them to work? No, probably, not . . . well, then again, maybe so. After all, the people under me have different "buttons" that make them work harder, and those "buttons" surely are not the same for everyone here in the United States. Is it possible, Robin wondered, for some cultures to have work norms that are antithetical to promotion and pay inducements? I would think those would be universal motivators. Maybe this won't be a major problem. Maybe it will be more of a fine-tuning issue in terms of adapting our job design, incentive systems, and motivational techniques to whichever country where we decide to set up shop. Then the thought occurred to her: What about motivating and evaluating the Americans overseas?

### How Should We Do Performance Evaluation?

Can we just use the same forms, procedures, and criteria, or is there something unique about a foreign assignment that requires unique performance evaluation systems? When should we evaluate them? (Robin remembered reading in a professional newsletter that expatriate employees require at least six months to settle into their overseas assignment.) Would it be fair to evaluate them before six months? But when would it be valid? After eight, ten, or twelve months? This is getting very messy, Robin mused.

Should the criteria by which to judge performance in Asia and other places be relative to the country, or should we keep our same evaluation criteria? The last thing Robin felt like doing was overseeing the development of a new performance evaluation system. We can get by with our current one, she mentally noted to herself. Well, who should do the evaluating? Headquarters, the regional subsidiary superiors, peers, a mixture of superiors and subordinates? Should the criteria revolve around bottom-line figures or personnel objectives? If financial performance criteria are emphasized, what happens if the dollar depreciates significantly against the local currency and wipes out the expatriate manager's cost savings, profits, and the like? How can the expatriate manager be evaluated, motivated, and rewarded under such conditions?

What about nationality differences in performance evaluation? What if an American manager is being evaluated by a Peruvian subsidiary manager—will the evaluation be fair, or is there potential for some sort of cultural bias to enter in? What if the American manager is a woman? Will we be able to put together an attractive, but not too costly, compensation package for our expatriates? Robin wondered what such a package would look like.

### Will The Unions Be Trouble?

Robin's thoughts were now racing from problem to problem. What about unions? I remember reading somewhere, she mused, that in order to shut down a manufacturing facility in France (or was it West Germany or Sweden?), management had to give the workers a full year's notice, retrain them, and then find them new jobs. She knew the top management of her firm would find such a contingency troubling at best. Well, maybe the Asian labor markets are less unionized and won't be as problematic, but then Robin recalled the public relations spokeswoman for a toy firm that she had met at a party and the nightmare she had described to Robin.

It seemed that the U.S. management had put pressure on the contract manufacturers in Hong Kong and the PRC to increase production dramatically in order to fill their unforeseen needs during the Christmas season. The press had gotten hold of stories about female workers who were working sixteen-hour days with no breaks; if they complained, they were terminated on the spot. Some of the women had even miscarried. It was a public relations nightmare. Maybe dealing with unions wouldn't be all bad. Maybe unions would protect us from questionable ethical nightmares, Robin thought. But then she thought of codetermination laws in countries like West Germany and worker's representatives sitting on the local boards of directors—that would not be easy for American managers to stomach.

As Robin put down her pen, the complexities involved in preparing this report for top management loomed before her. She had just scratched the surface of the basic human-resource issues of going international and there seemed to be no end to the potential permutations of each problem. This would not be easy, she concluded. As she left her office and made her way to the parking garage, she wondered, where can I go for help with all this?

## ▬ *The Aim of This Book*

BCN's situation closely parallels the initial path on which virtually all multinational firms have had to tread. Within this international context of business operations, many business decisions become critical. Although some of those decisions pertain to a firm's financial or physical resources, the most neglected and perhaps most important decisions to be made concern the management of the firm's international human resources. One of the principal problems is that most American businesspeople lack an international perspective. As a member of one culture, the businessperson tends to see life from that perspective, judge events from that perspective, and make decisions based on that perspective. In an increasingly global business environment, such a narrow view breeds failure.

This text has been developed to fill a void that has existed for too long. Our principal objective is to sensitize you to the complex human resource issues that exist in the international business environment. With this primary objective in mind, we have attempted to represent many parts of the world in the cases and readings. However, we have made no attempt to "force fit" something into the book for the sake of regional or geographic representation. Our first concern was including in the book what we, our reviewers, and our editors felt were the best available cases and readings in the international HRM field.

Our second concern was to include a multiperspective view in the overall balance of cases and readings. In other words, we do not focus solely on any one country or on any one movement of operations (for example, a U.S. firm moving overseas). To reiterate, we wanted as true a global perspective in our text as page-length restrictions would allow us. Finally, if we can begin to develop a sensitivity to the differences in human resource systems and broaden the student's and the manager's perspective on the appropriate management of human resources in a multinational context, then we will consider ourselves to have been successful. In this book, we hope to help make the following vision a reality:

> Peer into the executive suite of the year 2000 and see a completely different person. His undergraduate degree is in French literature, but he also has a joint M.B.A./engineering degree. He started in research and was quickly picked out as a potential CEO. He zigzagged from research to marketing to finance. He proved himself in Brazil by turning around a failing joint venture. He speaks Portuguese and French and is on a first-name basis with commerce ministers in half a dozen countries. Unlike his predecessor's predecessor, he isn't a drill sergeant. He is first among equals in the five-person Office of the Chief Executive (*Wall Street Journal*, 1989).

## ▬ *References*

Bennett, A. "Going global: The Chief Executives in the Year 2000 will be Experienced Abroad." *Wall Street Journal*, February 27, 1989, A1, A4.

Vaill, P. *Managing as a Performing Art: New Ideas for a World of Chaotic Change.* San Francisco: Jossey-Bass, 1989.

# Culture and International Human Resource Management

# National vs. Corporate Culture: Implications for Human Resource Management

## SUSAN C. SCHNEIDER*

Corporate culture has received a great deal of attention in the last five years. Popular books such as *In Search of Excellence* (Peters and Waterman, 1982) and *Corporate Cultures* (Deal and Kennedy, 1982), have sold millions of copies to eager executives in many countries. Although the academic community has taken a more cautious approach, they too are interested (Schein, 1985; Smircich, 1983; see also *ASQ*, September, 1983). While the popular press has implied that excellent companies have strong corporate cultures, the link between strong culture and performance can be challenged. Different environments require different strategies; the corporate culture needs to fit that strategy (Schwartz and Davis, 1981). In the case of the MNC, there is the need to address the fit of corporate culture with the different national cultures of their subsidiaries to assure strategy implementation, particularly HRM strategy.

Corporate culture has been discussed as a means of control for headquarters over their subsidiaries (see special issue of *JIBS*, 1984; in particular, Baliga and Jaeger; Doz and Prahalad). In this view, corporate culture serves as a behavioral control, instilling norms and values that result in following "the way things are done around here." The methods by which this is accomplished are: recruiting "like-minded" individuals, i.e., those that share the values of the company; socialization through training and personal interaction; and developing strong organizational commitment through various other HR policies such as life time employment, stock option plans, recreational and housing facilities, and expatriate rotation. These methods are fre-

*The author would like to thank Paul Evans, Andre Laurent, Randall Schuler and the anonymous reviewers for their helpful suggestions.

*Source:* Susan Schneider. "National vs. Corporate Culture: Implications for Human Resource Management." *Human Resource Management,* 1988, 27(2), 231–246. Reprinted by permission.

quently used by Japanese firms but also the so-called excellent companies such as IBM, Hewlett-Packard, Digital Equipment known for their strong corporate cultures (Pascale, 1984).

Corporate culture is in part managed through the HRM practices (Evans, 1986). Some of these practices, however, may not be appropriate given the beliefs, values, and norms of the local environment, i.e., the national culture wherein the subsidiary is embedded. Problems arise in transferring corporate culture through these practices in an effort to achieve globalization. More attention needs to be paid to the possible clash of assumptions underlying national and corporate cultures (Laurent, 1986; Adler and Jelinek, 1986).

The purpose of this article is to explore the potential clash of the corporate culture of a multinational organization and the national culture of the local subsidiary, paying particular attention to human resource practices. First, the construct of culture will be reviewed. Then the assumptions underlying human resource management practices will be discussed, questioning their fit within different national cultures. Specific attention will be paid to the implications for human resource management practices such as career planning, performance appraisal and reward systems, selection and socialization, and expatriate assignments. Case examples are used to illustrate the problem. Finally, the article will raise an issue often expressed by multinational companies—what does it mean to be a truly international company? What does "global" really look like? It will also question the use of corporate culture as a homogenizing force and as a mechanism of control.

## ▄▄ *Culture*

The construct of culture has caused much confusion. While there are multiple definitions, they tend to be vague and overly general. This confusion is added to by the multiple disciplines interested in this topic, which while increasing richness, does not necessarily increase clarity. Anthropologists, sociologists, psychologists, and others bring with them their specific paradigms and research methodologies. This creates difficulties in reaching consensus on construct definitions as well as their measurement or operationalization.

The model developed by Schein (1985) helps to organize the pieces of the culture puzzle. According to this model, culture is represented at three levels: 1) behaviors and artifacts; 2) beliefs and values; and 3) underlying assumptions. These levels are arranged according to their visibility such that behavior and artifacts are the easiest to observe, while the underlying assumptions need to be inferred. To understand what the behaviors or beliefs actually mean to the participants, the underlying assumptions have to be surfaced. This is most difficult as assumptions are considered to be taken for granted and out of awareness.

This model can be applied to both corporate and national cultures. Laurent (1986) argues, however, that corporate culture may modify the first two levels but will have little impact on the underlying assumptions that are embedded in the national culture. This raises the issue as to whether the behaviors, values, and beliefs prescribed by corporate culture are merely complied with or truly incorporated (Sathe, 1983). This is particularly relevant to concerns regarding motivation, commitment, and the possibility of employees sharing a common "worldview," i.e., the very reasons for promoting a strong corporate culture. Although it can be argued that changes in behavior may result in changes in underlying assumptions over time, the unconscious nature of these assumptions makes this unlikely (Schein, 1985).

The underlying assumptions prescribe ways of perceiving, thinking, and evaluating the world, self, and others. These assumptions include views of the relationship with nature and of human relationships (Schein, 1985; Kluckholn and Strodtbeck, 1961; Wallin, 1972; Hall, 1960; Hofstede, 1980; Laurent, 1983). The relationship with nature reflects several dimensions: 1) control over the environment; 2) activity vs. passivity or doing vs. being; 3) attitudes towards uncertainty; 4) notions of time; 5) attitudes towards change; and 6) what determines "truth." Views about the nature of human relationships include: 1) task vs. social orientation; 2) the importance of hierarchy; 3) the importance of individual vs. group. For example, some cultures, often Western, view man as the master of nature, which can be harnessed and exploited to suit man's needs; time, change, and uncertainty can be actively managed. "Truth" is determined by facts and measurement. Other cultures, often Eastern, view man as subservient to or in harmony with nature. Time, change, and uncertainty are accepted as given. "Truth" is determined by spiritual and philosophical principles. This attitude is often referred to as "fatalistic" or "adaptive."

Assumptions regarding the nature of human relationships are also different. The importance of social concerns over task, of the hierarchy, and of the individual vs. the group are clearly different not only between the East and West, but also within Western cultures. In Eastern cultures, for example, importance is placed on social vs. task concerns, on the hierarchy, and on the group or collective (Hofstede, 1980). By contrast, in Western cultures, the focus is more on task, on the individual and the hierarchy is considered to be of less importance. However, research by Hofstede (1980) and Laurent (1983) demonstrate that along these dimensions there is variance between the U.S. and Europe as well as within Europe.

## ▬ *Human Resource Practices in MNCs*

The differences described above have implications for human resource policies that are developed at headquarters and that reflect not only the corporate culture but the national culture of the MNC. Problems may arise when these policies are to be implemented abroad. According to Schuler (1987), MNCs can choose from a menu of human resource practices that concern: planning and staffing, appraising and compensating, and selection and socialization. Within this menu there are several options which need to be in line with the overall corporate strategy and culture. They also need to take into account the differences in the national cultures of the subsidiaries where they are to be implemented. This section will describe how national culture may affect these choices. In many cases, the description and examples of both corporate and national culture are exaggerated and/or oversimplified. As this is done for purposes of demonstration, it must be remembered that there remains variance within as well as between national and corporate cultures.

### Planning and Staffing

Planning can be considered along several dimensions such as formal/informal, and short term/long term. Career management systems represent formal, long term human resource planning. These systems may be inappropriate in cultures where man's control over nature or the future is considered minimal if not sacrilege, e.g., as in the Islamic belief, "Inshallah" (if God wills). Derr (1987) found that national culture was a key determinant of the type of career management systems found within Europe.

Some career management systems assume that people can be evaluated, that their abilities, skills, and traits (i.e., their *net worth* to the company) can be quantified, measured, and fed into a computer. As one British HR manager said, "A lot of that material is highly sensitive; You just don't put it into a computer." On the other hand, Derr (1987) found that the French used highly complex and sophisticated computerized systems. This may reflect a humanistic vs. engineering approach (social vs. task orientation).

Secondly, it may assume that evaluation reflects past performance and predicts future performance, which means that evaluation is based on DOING rather than BEING (active vs. passive). In other words, evaluation is based on *what* you achieve and *what* you know (achievement), and *not* on *who* you are (a person of character and integrity) and *who* you know (ascription). In the U.S., concrete results are the criteria for selection and promotion (Derr, 1987). An American general manager of the U.K. region complained that people around there got promoted because of the schools they went to and their family background, not on what they accomplished. This is also common in France, where ties with the "grandes écoles" and the "grands corps" are important for career advancement.

Third, it may assume that data banks can be created of "skills" that can then be matched to "jobs," that jobs can be clearly defined and that specific skills exist to fit them. One Dutch HR manager said that the major problems of long term planning in high technology industries is that the nature of the job in three to five years is unpredictable. IBM says it hires for careers, not jobs; Olivetti says "potential," not "skills" is most important. These differences may reflect underlying assumptions regarding uncertainty and the relationship between the individual and the group (here, organization), e.g., careers vs. jobs. For example, in Japan job descriptions are left vague and flexible to fit uncertainty and to strengthen the bond between the individual and the company. In the U.S. and France, job descriptions tend to be more specific, which may reduce uncertainty but which permits more job mobility between organizations.

Also, the nature of the skills acquired is a function of the national educational system. In many European countries, particularly France, mathematics and science diplomas have status and engineering is the preferred program of further study. This system encourages highly technical, narrowly focused specialists which may make functional mobility more difficult. In the U.S. and the U.K., psychology and human relations is valued and more generalists are welcomed. Derr (1987) found that in identifying high potentials, the French valued technical and engineering expertise whereas the British preferred "the classical generalist" with a "broad humanistic perspective." Knife and fork tests, assessment of table manners and conversation skills, as well as personal appearance were considered to be important criteria for selection in the U.K.

Many career management systems also assume geographic mobility of the work force. Geographic mobility may reflect assumptions regarding the task vs. social orientation, and the group vs. the individual. Europeans are considered more internationally oriented than Americans, as they tend to stay longer in each country and move to another country assignment rather than return home (Tung, 1987). Yet, one Belgian general manager stated that the biggest problem in developing leadership was getting people to move; "Belgians would rather commute 2 hours a day to Brussels than to leave their roots. How can you get them to go abroad?" In a survey done in one MNC, the British were most likely to be willing to relocate, while the Spanish were less so, perhaps reflecting economic considerations in Britain and importance of family in Spain. Derr (1987) found 70% of Swedish sample reporting it difficult to relocate geographically due to wives' careers. This is similar to Hofstede's (1980) findings that Sweden has the least differentiation between male and female roles, increasing the likelihood that women would have careers.

Finally, these systems may assume that people want to be promoted. While self-actualization needs are supposedly the same in all countries (Haire et al., 1966), it is not clear that self-actualization means promotion. Nor is it certain that Maslow's hierarchy of needs is universal, as McClelland (1961) found different levels of need for achievement in different societies. In collective societies, wherein the emphasis is on the group over the individual, need for affiliation may be much more important (Hofstede, 1980). In Sweden, egalitarianism as well as the desire to keep a low profile to avoid "royal Swedish envy" (i.e., others coveting your position) may make promotion less desirable. Also, promotion may mean more time must be devoted to work, which means less time for family and leisure, or quality of life. If promotion includes a raise, this may not be desirable due to the Swedish tax structure.

Overall, the notion of career management systems in which people are evaluated in terms of skills, abilities, and traits that will be tested, scored, and computerized may appear impersonal, cold, and objective. These systems may be seen as treating human beings as things, instrumental towards achieving company goals, with no concern for their welfare or for their "soul." Employees should be like family and friends, you don't evaluate them, they are to be unconditionally loved. Even seeing them as "human resources" may be considered questionable.

### Appraisal and Compensation

Performance appraisal and compensation systems are also examples of cultural artifacts that are built upon underlying assumptions. As mentioned before, performance appraisal implies that "performance," i.e., what is "done" or "achieved," is important and that it can be appraised," i.e., measured objectively. What is appraised is thus behavior and not traits. In Japanese firms, however, there is more concern with judging a person's integrity, morality, loyalty, and cooperative spirit than on getting high sales volume. Furthermore, for the Japanese, the notion of "objective" truth is usually neither important nor useful; "objectivity" refers to the foreigners' point of view while "subjectivity" refers to the host's viewpoint (Maruyama, 1984).

Giving direct feedback does not take into account "saving face" so crucial to many Eastern cultures where confronting an employee with "failure" in an open, direct manner would be considered to be "very tactless." The intervention of a third party may be necessary. Appraisal also assumes that the feedback given will be used to correct or improve upon past performance. This requires that individuals receiving the feedback are willing to evaluate themselves instead of blaming others or external conditions for their performance (or lack thereof). This assumes a view of man as having control over the environment and able to change the course of events. It also assumes that what will happen in the future is of importance, that the present provides opportunity, and/or that the past can be used as a guide for future behavior.

Appraisal and compensation systems are often considered to be linked in Western management thinking, as in the case of management by objectives (MBO). Here it is espoused that people should be rewarded based on their performance, what they do or achieve, or for their abilities and skills and not on their traits or personal characteristics. Management by objective (MBO) assumes the following.

1. goals can be set (man has control over the environment);
2. with 3, 6, 12, or 18 month objectives (time can be managed);
3. their attainment can be measured (reality is objective);
4. the boss and the subordinate can engage in a two-way dialogue to agree on what is to be done, when, and how (hierarchy is minimized);
5. the subordinate assumes responsibility to meet the agreed upon goals (control and activity); and
6. the reward is set contingent upon this evaluation (doing vs. being).

Problems with the transfer of MBO to other cultures have been discussed before (Hofstede, 1980; Laurent, 1983; Trepo, 1973). In Germany, MBO was favorably received because of preference for decentralization, less emphasis on the hierarchy (allowing two-way dialogue), and formalization (clear goals, time frames, measurement and contingent rewards). In France, however, this technique was less successfully transferred (Trepo, 1973). Due to the ambivalent views towards authority, MBO was viewed suspiciously as an exercise of arbitrary power and a manipulative ploy of management. Given that power is concentrated in the hands of the boss (importance of hierarchy), subordinates would be held responsible without having the power to accomplish goals. Within this perspective, the notion of the boss and subordinate participating in reaching a decision together is quite foreign. Also, although the French have a preference for formalization, e.g., bureaucratic systems, things tend to get accomplished outside the system rather than through it—"systeme D" or management by circumvention (Trepo, 1973). Other European managers complain that use of MBO is particularly American as it encourages a short term focus and, as it is tied to rewards, encourages setting lower, more easily attainable goals than necessarily desirable ones.

Tying performance to rewards is also suspect. It would be difficult for most Western managers to consider implementing a system at home whereby the amount that family members are given to eat is related to their contribution to the family income. Yet in the workplace the notion of pay for performance seems quite logical. In African societies, which tend to be more collective, the principles applied to family members apply to employees as well; nepotism is a natural outcome of this logic. One multinational, in an effort to improve the productivity of the work force by providing nutritious lunches, met with resistance and the demand that the cost of the meal be paid directly to the workers so that they could feed their families. The attitude was one of "how can we eat while our families go hungry?"

Preferences for compensation systems and bonuses are clearly linked to cultural attitudes. In one MNC's Danish subsidiary, a proposal for incentives for salespeople was turned down because it favored specific groups, i.e., ran counter to their egalitarian spirit. Furthermore, it was felt that everyone should get the same amount of bonus, not 5% of salary; in fact, there should be no differences in pay. In Africa, savings are managed or bonuses conferred by the group in a "tontine" system wherein everyone gives part of their weekly salary to one group member. Although each member would get the same if they saved themselves, it is preferred that the group perform this function.

The relative importance of status, money, or vacation time varies across countries and affects the motivating potential of these systems. One compensation and benefits manager explained that for the Germans, the big Mercedes wasn't enough; a chauffeur was also needed (status concerns). In Sweden, monetary rewards were less motivating than providing vacation villages (quality of life vs. task orientation). Also, there were different expectations regarding pensions, in part a function of the government and inflation. In Southern European countries the pension expected was 40% of salary, while in the Nordic countries up to 85%, which may reflect different roles of government in society as embedded in the "civic culture" (Almond and Verba, 1963).

### Selection and Socialization

One of the major concerns of many multinational companies is the training and development of their human resources. This includes concern for the level of skills at the operating levels, the development of indigenous managerial capability, and the identification and nurturing of "high potentials," i.e., those who will play major future leadership roles. At every level, this requires not only acquiring specific skills, e.g., technical, interpersonal, or conceptual (Katz, 1974), but also acquiring the "way things are done around here"—the behaviors, values, and beliefs and underlying assumptions of that company, i.e., the corporate culture.

*Selection* is one of the major tools for developing and promoting corporate culture (Schein, 1985). Candidates are carefully screened to "fit in" to the existing corporate culture, assessed for their behavioral styles, beliefs, and values. IBM, for example, may be less concerned with hiring the "typical Italian" than hiring an Italian who fits within the IBM way of doing things. For example, IBM attempts to avoid power accumulation of managers by moving them every two years (it's said that IBM stands for "I've Been Moved"), which may not suit the Italian culture wherein organizations are seen as more "political" than "instrumental" (Laurent, 1983).

One HR manager from Olivetti said that those Italians who want more autonomy go to Olivetti instead of IBM. He described the culture of Olivetti as being informal and non-structured, and as having more freedom, fewer constraints, and low discipline. Recruitment is based on personality and not "too good grades" (taken to reflect not being in touch with the environment). This encouraged hiring of strong personalities, i.e., impatient, more risk-taking and innovative people, making confrontation more likely and managing more difficult.

*Socialization* is another powerful mechanism of promoting corporate culture. In-house company programs and intense interaction during off-site training can create an "esprit de corps," a shared experience, an interpersonal or informal network, a company language or jargon, as well as develop technical competencies. These training events often include songs, picnics, and sporting events that provide feelings of togetherness. These rites of integration may also be accompanied by initiation rites wherein personal culture is stripped, company uniforms are donned (t-shirts), and humiliation tactics employed, e.g., "pie-in-the-face" and "tie-clipping" (Trice and Beyer, 1984). This is supposed to strengthen the identification with the company (reinforce the group vs. the individual).

Other examples are to be found in Japanese management development "Hell Camps" wherein "ribbons of shame" must be worn and instruction must be taken from "young females" (*International Management*, January 1985). IBM management training programs often involve demanding, tension-filled, strictly prescribed presentations to "probing" senior managers (Pascale, 1984). These "boot camp" tactics are designed to create professional armies of corporate soldiers. These military metaphors may not be well accepted, particularly in Europe or other politically sensitive regions.

Artifacts of corporate culture campaigns (stickers, posters, cards, and pins) remind members of the visions, values, and corporate goals, e.g., "Smile" campaigns at SAS, Phillips's "1 Billion" goal buttons, and G.M. corporate culture cards carried by managers in their breast pockets. Many Europeans view this "hoopla" cynically. It is seen as terribly "American" in its naiveté, enthusiasm, and childishness. It is also seen as controlling and as an intrusion into the private or personal realm of the individual. Statements of company principles on the walls are often referred to sceptically. One HR manager thought that it was "pretty pathetic to have to refer to them." Others feel that it is very American in its exaggeration and lack of subtlety.

Expatriate transfers are also used for socialization and development of an international "cadre" (Edstrom and Galbraith, 1977). The rotation of expatriates from headquarters through subsidiaries and the shipping of local nationals from the subsidiaries to headquarters occur for different reasons, such as staffing, management development, and organization development. These reasons tend to reflect different orientations of headquarters towards their subsidiaries: ethnocentric, polycentric, and geocentric (Ondrack, 1985; Edstrom and Galbraith, 1977; Heenan and Perlmutter, 1979; Evans, 1986).

Differences between American, European, and Japanese firms have been found in the use of transfers for purposes of socialization or as a system of control. U.S. firms rely more on local managers using more formal, impersonal numbers controls, while the European firms rely on the use of the international cadre of managers using more informal, personal control (La Palombara and Blank, 1977; Ondrack, 1985). The Japanese rely heavily on frequent visits of home and host country managers between headquarters and subsidiaries, using both socialization and formalization (Ghoshal and Bartlett, 1987).

Some external conditions affect the use of expatriates, such as local regulations requiring indigenous management and increasingly limited mobility due to the rise of dual career and family constraints. Also, willingness to make work vs. family tradeoffs differ between countries, the Europeans less likely to do so than the Americans (Schmidt and Posner, 1983). It is also reported that the young Japanese managers are less willing to make the same sacrifices to work than their parents were. Therefore, there may be convergence in these trends but for different reasons, e.g., task vs. social orientation or individual vs. group orientation.

This section discussed the assumptions underlying various HRM practices and explored their possible clash with the assumptions of the national cultures of subsidiaries. This clash can cause problems in implementing HRM practices designed at headquarters. The differences in underlying assumptions, however, may provide only the excuse. The extent to which these practices are seen as flowing in one direction, down from headquarters to subsidiaries, may influence the extent to which these practices are adopted and to what extent the behavior, beliefs, and values of the corporate culture are incorporated or even complied with. Ethnocentric vs. geocentric attitudes determine whether there is hope for going global and whether "truly international" is really possible. The next section will discuss some important concerns regarding the use of corporate culture in realizing this global vision.

## ■ *Going Global*

Many American multinationals are moving from having international divisions to embracing a "global" or "worldwide" perspective, i.e., stage II to stage III development (Scott, 1973). Even European multinationals having longer histories of international business due to smaller domestic markets, a colonial heritage and greater proximity of "foreign" countries, are asking, "How can we become more international?"

What does international or global really look like? Do they mean the same thing? Some companies point to the reduced number of expatriates in local subsidiaries, the use of third country nationals, and multi-national composition of their top management team as evidence of their "internationalization" (Berenbeim, 1982). Many are clamoring for "corporate culture" to provide the coordination and coherence sought. In one American MNC, the European regional headquarters president saw himself vis-à-vis the national affiliates as "a shepherd that needs to let the flock wander and eat grass but get them all going in one direction—to the barn. You don't want to end up alone in the barn at the end of the day." Is corporate culture necessary for global integration? Will socialization work as a control strategy? Several issues are raised that need careful consideration: need for differentiation vs. integration; autonomy vs. control; and national vs. corporate boundaries.

### *Differentiation vs. Integration*

To what extent can corporate culture override national culture differences to create a global company? Is that desirable or even possible? This raises the issue of the extent to which global vs. local HRM practices are needed to integrate a global company. In the case of global practices, care must be taken so that "geocentric" looks different from "ethnocentric" while remaining sensitive to needs for differentiation. In the case of local, it means determining what needs to be done differently in the context of requirements for integration.

Marketing and HRM have traditionally been functions left decentralized in multinational-subsidiary relationships. Yet, global marketing has been proclaimed the wave of the future (Levitt, 1983) despite obvious local market and customer differences. Global HRM runs along similar logic with similar risks. Is HRM necessarily culture-bound? Does competitive advantage derive from global HRM? Homogenized HRM may weaken competitive advantage by trying to ignore or minimize cultural differences instead of trying to utilize them (Adler, 1986).

Contingency arguments abound. Doz and Prahalad (1984) argue that the simultaneous need for global integration and local responsiveness must be managed. Evans (1986) argues for the product/ market logic to determine the socio-cultural strategy for adaptation. Ghoshal and Nohria (1987) argue that the level of environmental complexity and the level of local resources should determine the levels of centralization, formalization, or socialization used for control in headquarters-subsidiary relationships. These prescriptions are all quite rational but may overlook important resistances arising from the following issues regarding autonomy and boundaries.

### Control vs. Autonomy

Visions of going global with corporate culture as a strategy for control may have some unforeseen consequences. While Schein (1968) has likened socialization to brainwashing, Pascale (1984) says the maligned "organization man" of the 1960s is now "in." At what point will the push to conform be met with an equal if not stronger push to preserve uniqueness? Dostoyevsky (1960) said that man would even behave self destructively to reaffirm his autonomy. What reactance may be provoked by socialization efforts? Those managers selected out or who "drop out" may be valuable not only by providing their expertise but also by providing an alternative perspective. Certain cultures, both national and corporate, that value conformity over individuality may be better able to use corporate culture as a mechanism for control but may lose the advantage of individual initiative.

Hofstede's (1980) research demonstrates that even within a large multinational, famous for its strong culture and socialization efforts, national culture continues to play a major role in differentiating work values. Laurent (1983) has demonstrated that there is greater evidence for national differences regarding beliefs about organizations in samples of single MNCs than in multicompany samples. These findings may point to a paradox that national culture may play a stronger role in the face of a strong corporate culture. The pressures to conform may create the need to reassert autonomy and identity, creating a cultural mosaic rather than a melting pot.

The convergence/divergence argument (Webber, 1969) states that economic development, technology, and education would make possible globalization whereas differential levels of available resources and national cultures would work against this. A simple comparison of U.S. and Japanese management practices demonstrates that the level of economic development, industrialization, or education is not going to bring about convergence. According to Fujisawa, Founder of Honda, "Japanese and U.S. management is 95% alike and differs in all important aspects."

Equal and opposing forces for unification and fragmentation coexist (Fayerweather, 1975) as seen within and between countries. The ongoing case of trade policies between Canada and the U.S. (Holsti, 1980) and the hopes for the future of the EEC trade agreements in 1992 rest precariously on this tension. Issues of asymmetry and interdependence between multinationals and host country governments (Gladwin, 1982) and between multinational headquarters and their subsidiaries (Ghoshal and Nohria, 1987) make globalization efforts precarious. Therefore, attempts by headquarters to control subsidiaries through more "subtle" methods, such as corporate culture, should take into account the dependency concerns and autonomy needs of the subsidiary and anticipate their resistance.

For example, efforts to educate Western managers to "understand" Japan met with local resistance (Pucik, personal communication) as ignorance may provide the autonomy zone desired by the local managers. Socialization as a power equalizer as argued by Ghoshal and Nohria (1987) is suspect and will be rejected for precisely this reason. As one general manager of a national subsidiary said regarding the European regional headquarters of a U.S. based MNC, "As long as we give them the numbers they leave us alone." And U.S. headquarters? "They don't have the foggiest idea about what's going on really. They get the numbers. They get 100 million dollars a year in profit and that's probably about as much as they want to know about." Perhaps formal reporting preserves autonomy and will thus be preferred regardless of the logic of globalization.

### Boundaries: National vs. Corporate

In the 1960s, multinationals threatened to take over the world; host country governments' sovereignty was risk (Vernon, 1971; 1977). However, through the transfer of technology and managerial capacity, the power became more symmetrical, even tipping the scale in the other direction as seen at one point in the rash of nationalizations that occurred in the 1970s (Kobrin, 1982). While the balance has subsequently restabilized, larger forces, such as the rise of religious fundamentalism in some areas, threaten this stability.

National boundaries are again threatened. Economic victory in lieu of military victory seems to have created "occupation douce." This is reflected in the anxieties of Americans as they see their country becoming owned by "foreigners" and the Japanese invasion of Wall Street. Mitterand, President of France, said recently that in the future the French might become the museum keepers, relying on tips from Japanese tourists.

The vision of developing an international cadre of executives through frequent and multiple transfers designed to encourage the loss of identification with their country of origin and its transfer to the corporation (Edstrom and Galbraith, 1977) is frightening. In these global "clans," corporate identification may come to override community and even family identification (Ouchi and Jaeger, 1978). These citizens of the world, men and women without countries, only companies, become corporate mercenaries. One story has it that a French IBM executive arriving at JFK airport in New York while searching for his entry visa pulled out his IBM identification card. The customs official, seeing it said, "Oh, it's O.K., you're IBM, you can go ahead." Business schools train these corporate soldiers, dispatching them to multinationals to control the world through finance and management consulting. Perhaps now is the time for academics and practitioners to sit back and reflect about the implications.

## ■ *References*

Adler, N. J. *International dimensions of organizational behavior.* Belmont, Calif.: Kent, 1986.

Adler, N. J., and Jelinek, M. "Is 'Organizational Culture' culture bound?" *Human Resource Management,* 1986, 25(1), 73–90.

*Administrative Science Quarterly,* 1983, 28(3).

Almond, G. A., and Verba, S. *The civic culture: Political attitudes and democracy in five nations.* Princeton, N.J.: Princeton University Press, 1963.

Baliga, B. R., and Jaeger, A. M. "Multinational corporations: Control systems and delegation issues." *Journal of International Business Studies,* 1984, 15(2), 25–40.

Berenbeim, R. *Managing the international company: Building a global perspective.* New York: The Conference Board, Inc., Report no. 814, 1982.

Deal, T., and Kennedy, A. *Corporate cultures: The rites and rituals of corporate life.* Reading, Mass.: Addison-Wesley, 1982.

Derr, C. "Managing high potentials in Europe." *European Management Journal,* 1987, 5(2), 72–80.

Dostoyevsky. *Notes from the underground.* New York: Dell, 1960.

Doz, Y., and Prahalad, C. "Patterns of strategic control within multinational corporations." *Journal of International Business Studies,* 1984, 15(2), 55–72.

Edstrom, A., and Galbraith J. "Transfer of managers as a coordination and control strategy in multinational organizations." *Administrative Science Quarterly,* 1977, 22, 248–263.

Evans, P. "The context of strategic human resource management policy in complex firms." *Management Forum,* 1986, 6, 105–117.

Fayerweather, J. "A conceptual scheme of the interaction of the multinational firm and nationalism." *Journal of Business Administration,* 1975, 7, 67–89.

Ghoshal, S., and Bartlett A. "Organizing for innovations: Case of the multinational corporation." WP INSEAD No. 87/04, 1987.

Ghoshal, S., and Nohria, N. "Multinational corporations as differentiated networks." WP INSEAD No. 87/13. 1987.

Gladwin, T. "Environmental interdependence and organizational design: The case of the multinational corporation." WP NYU No. 82-13, 1982.

Haire, M., Ghiselli, E., and Porter, L. *Managerial thinking—An international study.* New York: John Wiley & Sons, 1966.

Hall, E. T. "The silent language of overseas business." *Harvard Business Review*, 1960, 38(3), 87–95.

Heenan, D. A., and Perlmutter, H. V. *Multinational organization development: A social architectural perspective.* Phillippines: Addison-Wesley, 1979.

Hofstede, G. *Culture's consequences.* Beverly Hills, Calif.: Sage Publications, 1980.

Holsti, J. "Change in the international system: Integration and fragmentation." In R. Holsti, R. Siverson, and A. George (eds.), *Change in the International System.* Boulder, Colo.: Westview Press, 1980, 23–53.

*Journal of International Business Studies,* Fall 1984.

Katz, R. "Skills of an effective administrator." *Harvard Business Review*, 1974, 90–102.

Kluckholn, F., and Strodtbeck, F. *Variations in value orientations.* Evanston, Illo.: Row, Peterson, 1961.

Kobrin, S. *Managing political risk assessments: Strategic response to environmental change.* Berkeley, Calif.: University of California Press, 1982.

La Palombara, J., and Blank, S. *Multinational corporations in comparative perspective.* New York: The Conference Board, Report No. 725, 1977.

Laurent, A. "The cross-cultural puzzle of international human resource management." *Human Resource Management*, 1986, 25(1), 91–102.

Laurent, A. "The cultural diversity of western conceptions of management. "*International Studies of management and Organizations*, 1983, 13 (1–2), 75–96.

Levitt, T. "The globalization of markets." *Harvard Business Review*, 1983 (May–June), 92–102.

McClelland, D. *The achieving society.* New York: D. Van Nostrand, Inc., 1961.

Maruyama, M. "Alternative concepts of management: Insights from Asia and Africa." *Asia Pacific Journal of Management*, 1984, 100–110.

Ondrack, D. "International transfers of managers in North American and European MNE's." *Journal of International Business Studies*, 1985, XVI(3), 1–19.

Ouchi, W. G., and Jaeger, A. M. "Type Z organization: Stability in the midst of mobility." *Academy of Management Review*, 1978, 3(2), 305–314.

Pascale, R. "The paradox of "Corporate Culture": Reconciling ourselves to socialization." *California Management Review*, 1984, 27(2), 26–41.

Peters, T., and Waterman, R. *In search of excellence.* New York: Harper & Row, 1982.

Sathe, V. "Implications of corporate culture: A manager's guide to action." *Organizational Dynamics*, 1983 (Autumn), 5–23.

Schein, E. H. "Organizational socialization and the profession of management." *Industrial Management Review*, 1968, 9, 1–15.

Schein, E. H. *Organizational culture and leadership.* San Francisco: Jossey-Bass, 1985.

Schmidt, W., and Posner, B. *Management values in perspective.* New York: AMA, 1983.

Scott, B. "The industrial state: Old myths and new realities." *Harvard Business Review*, March–April 1973, 133–148.

Schuler, R. "Human resource management practice choices." In R. Schuler and S. Youngblood (eds.), *Readings in Personnel and Human Resource Management*, 3rd ed. St. Paul: West, 1987.

Schwartz, H., and Davis, S. "Matching corporate culture and business strategy." *Organizational Dynamics*, Summer 1981, 30–48.

Smircich, L. "Studying organizations as cultures." In G. Morgan (ed.), *Beyond Method: Strategies for Social Research*. Beverley Hills, Calif.: Sage Publications, 1983.

Trepo, G. "Management style à la Francaise." *European Business*, Autumn 1973, 71–79.

Trice, H. M., and Beyer, J. M. "Studying organizational culture through rites and ceremonials." *Academy of Management Review*, 1984, 9 (4), 653–669.

Tung, R. "Expatriate assignments: Enhancing success and minimizing failure." *Academy of Management Executive*, 1987, 1(2), 117–126.

Vernon, R. *Sovereignty at bay*. New York: Basic Books, 1971.

Vernon, R. *Storm over the multinationals*. Cambridge, Mass.: Harvard University Press, 1977.

Wallin, T. "The international executive baggage: Cultural values of the American frontier." *MSU Business Topics*, Spring 1972, 49–58.

Webber, R. "Convergence or divergence?" *Columbia Journal of Business*, 1969, 4(3).

# Human Resource Management Issues in Europe: An Interview with Dr. Martin Sailer, Human Resources Manager at Daimler-Benz

**CHARLES M. VANCE**
**MARTIN SAILER**

*Vance:* What are some of the most critical issues facing human resource management in Europe today?

*Sailer:* First of all, you have to be very careful not to automatically generalize something across all of Europe. If you talk about Europe, you talk about a diversity of cultures. Human resource management in Italy, for example, has to be quite different from human resource management in Switzerland. There is a totally different labor market situation in different European countries.

*Vance:* Could you illustrate how different labor market situations are reflected today in different HRM practices?

*Sailer:* Yes. For example, there is full employment in Switzerland, in fact, overemployment—there's no unemployment at all. There is about 6 percent unemployment in Germany. And so you get no politically influential trade unions in Switzerland, but you get tremendously influential trade unions in Germany.

*Vance:* What are some fairly consistent themes of HRM challenges that you've noted across much of Europe?

*Source:* This article was written especially for this book.

*Sailer:* One important theme is organizational commitment toward employees—management's commitment toward the work force. This essential term "commitment" should be explained. The company demonstrates its long-term commitment toward its employees through job stability and security. The security of a job is a very important factor of personnel management image and marketing for a company. If a company loses this ability to guarantee secure jobs, it loses a lot of image, and it might be very difficult to hire good employees. Part of this high value for security and stability can be explained because, generally, people in Europe are not as geographically flexible as they are in the United States. For example, let's say that you live in Austria and lose a job at the place where you are living, and you cannot find a comparable job near this place. Logically, you should now have to move to find a comparable job, but this move from your social and family ties is a very stressful experience. We have different regions in Europe where, for example, steel and local mining industries are located, and workers are laid off and companies are shut down because losses are too high, and the state cannot continue to cover those losses. In these regions, there are a lot of these same people who prefer being unemployed rather than moving just 100 or 200 miles. There are typically generous unemployment benefits guaranteed by the government, so there is a basic social net which enables people to stay where they live and not have to move for new employment. But these people would much prefer to remain employed. Employment is very important to them. Their self-identity is often closely tied to their work and profession. So secure jobs are a very, very important factor of the image of a company. Most companies mention this goal of security in their corporate philosophy and general corporate aims and goals. We still have the concept of life employment, especially in nonmanagement jobs. There's a difference if you're talking about management jobs, especially in marketing or sales jobs—those people have more mobility. But lower-level workers, engineers, and other professionals tend to desire very little job mobility and relocation. This strong desire for stability and security is especially true if people are older and have families around them. The age group between 40 and 50 is usually not very flexible.

*Vance:* Therefore, many European organizations and companies try to demonstrate and market strong commitment toward employee security because that is what the people want. In the United States, workers often want the mobility and flexibility necessary for career advancement. However, you are saying that many employees in European countries would consider such mobility to be very stressful—anxiety raising and threatening to their highly valued stable roots.

*Sailer:* Exactly. Some of my friends where I studied and where I come from in Southern Austria are actually now unemployed. They could get a job just 40 miles away. But they prefer to be unemployed rather than to move. Of course, there are differences, the Germans tend to be more flexible than the Austrians or Swiss. But generally, people don't like to move. So what I want to express with this idea of commitment is that companies are willing to spend a lot of money to secure jobs and to pay for jobs that actually could be canceled. A major reason for this is to preserve their image of commitment to employee security and stability, which greatly helps their competitiveness in recruiting the best human resource talent. Usually losses have to become very high and actually endanger the very existence of a company before there are ever any layoffs.

*Vance:* Would you say then that the reason for this demonstration of commitment is due more to the desire to market a desirable company image and attract capable talent than to a sense of social ethics or responsibility?

*Sailer:* Actually, the reasons for demonstrating strong commitment toward employees are several and on different levels. First of all is the involvement of politics. Regional politics are a very important factor. Companies can be subsidized, such as with tax breaks, for securing jobs in critical high unemployment industries and areas. There are a lot of fiscal instruments to help companies save jobs. If you get critical industries, such as the steel industry, and there are a lot of people affected, such as in a region where 10 percent of the population are affected, then regional and national politics get involved. This is no longer a business problem but a problem of the whole economy, especially if you've got social democratic parties who are in charge. So there is a strong local and national political involvement. Secondly, trade unions are fighting for jobs. In the past years, the most important issue was increasing wages. But since the beginning of the 1980s, employment—securing jobs—has become the most important issue for trade unions.

*Vance:* So besides company interest in maintaining a strong image for obtaining the most capable employees, other forces that encourage this commitment to employees are government and political bodies, as well as trade unions. Anything else?

*Sailer:* You mentioned social consciousness. Certainly, I think that unemployment is recognized to be a social problem and not only an individual problem, especially structural unemployment which affects a major industry. There is a strong social commitment in Europe which can be explained to some extent by our historical experience. We know that the tragic developments in the 1940s with the Nazi movement and Fascism were largely a consequence of severe economic crisis and high unemployment. A large part of German workers had absolutely nothing.

There were no real social welfare programs or unemployment insurance. There was extreme poverty everywhere. And so everyone here knows that unemployment is really a political problem, a social threat, a problem that affects the whole community and society. In addition to this collective sense of responsibility with regard to controlling and minimizing worker displacement and unemployment, there is a lot of legislation that restricts and limits the actions that management can take.

*Vance:* What are other significant problems or challenges in managing human resources in European countries today?

*Sailer:* One major challenge that we face is the future lack of a qualified work force in certain areas, such as electronics, engineering, and certain professionals in any field of research and development. There is going to be a severe shortage of those qualified. We found out that certain German companies are actually hiring employees who are not fully employed today, but they will be needed in the future. These employees aren't needed right now, but they are being hired right now and being prepared for the future.

*Vance:* What do you believe is causing this future lack of a qualified, competent work force?

*Sailer:* I believe that our educational systems are becoming less and less adaptive to changes in the economy. We are losing touch with what is going on in the real world. This trend is also true with subjects being taught in business administration. Owing to these shortcomings in the formal education system, the internal training function is becoming more and more broadened to provide the necessary internal knowledge, skills, and abilities for companies to remain competitive. We are beginning to see that the market for training is exploding. More and more money is being spent for external and internal training. This is a great opportunity for meaningful contribution for people in human resources management because now they can prove the importance of their job.

*Vance:* How do you mean?

*Sailer:* When production and marketing managers won't be able to find qualified employees and coworkers, they will realize how important strategic, long-term human resources planning, management, and development will be. I'm convinced that those companies who really understand that this knowledge and skill shortage will take place, who take actions early to ensure a competent work force, and who really think in strategic terms—a long-term orientation—those will be the companies with the competitive edge in the future.

*Vance:* And you believe that human resource professionals now have a great opportunity to help their company achieve that competitive edge?

*Sailer:* Yes, I'm convinced of that. However, many managers also say that they are convinced too, and everybody talks about strategic management of human resources. But if you look at what is really done, you realize that there is really nothing done. The point is, as long as every manager is just talking about the increasing importance of human resources, it is not changing anything. As long as any operative problem, regarding computers or anything else, is more important than effectively managing human resources through training and development, gaining employee commitment, and optimizing motivation of the people in the company, there will be no changes. There has got to be a change of views regarding what is important. Several years ago when the market was growing and there were no problems with the labor market, the focus was one of how to produce more, and how the needs of the market can be covered. Then in the 1970s in many areas there were increasing problems in the market. So the marketing and sales functions gained in importance. And now in the 1980s, 1990s, and the beginning of the next century, critical resources will be human resources—qualified human resources.

*Vance:* What do you think needs to happen in Europe to meet the future crisis due to a shortage of competent labor?

*Sailer:* We've got two challenges for our society. The first is a challenge for our politics. We have to somehow bring about an improvement in our educational systems. We have to adapt our educational systems to the demands of the future. Teachers have been trained for the needs of the past, and they are not forced to catch up. So you've already got in colleges and universities a severe gap between education and the contents and practices that will be demanded in the future by our economy. The second challenge will be for human resources managers. How can they acquire the necessary image of professionalism, influence, and credibility that they did not previously require in their less strategic roles? They have to be competent, professional human resources managers. We now have administrators of personnel who are the administrators of social programs, the cafeteria, and the Christmas party. But there is a change taking place now which we are perceiving among today's human resources managers, although things won't change overnight.

*Vance:* In the United States there has been in the past, and many believe currently exists, a general impression that if you've moved into a personnel department, you've been demoted. And in some companies, instead of getting rid of someone who is not competent, they will put him or her in personnel. And so, that is the kind of resulting overall impression which management, employees, and people in general have about human resource professionals. Is it somewhat the same in European companies?

*Sailer:* It is absolutely the same, but with one exception. It is often required by law that employees have union representatives. These union representatives have considerable influence with the company, including a presence on the company's board of directors. For example, if you want to change the wage system, you need the approval of the employee representatives. If you want to install a human resources information system, you need the approval of the representatives. Traditionally, it is the job of the personnel department to negotiate with the workers' representatives. This negotiation responsibility is perceived to be very important, and management knows that they just cannot put the least competent people over this area of responsibility. But all the other major functions, such as selection, training, development, and compensation and benefits, are often perceived as having a lack of professional attitude and business understanding.

*Vance:* How, if at all, do these personnel professionals contribute to this unfavorable perception?

*Sailer:* They often reflect a strong bias against hard data quantification, measurement, human resources accounting, and new high-technology advancement applications. For example, I often encounter a lot of resistance from human resource managers over the use of quantitative methods in human resource accounting that can actually be very helpful in demonstrating the important economic worth of their human resource activities when budget allocations are considered. But these human resource managers typically insist that the effects of their work are all subjective and can't be measured objectively. They often focus too heavily on ensuring the happiness and success of the employees, and miss the important link of relating their work to the necessary ultimate measurable performance and financial objectives of the company.

*Vance:* How does top management contribute to this poor perception about human resources professionals?

*Sailer:* I would say that the worst thing they do is in not recognizing the strategic potential value of effective human resources management. You often hear beautiful words and speeches from top management, such as at the annual Christmas party when they say, ''People are important and we want you to be happy. We are all a family.'' But when it comes to investment decisions and setting priorities, the human resources function will be at the bottom of the agenda. The focus in business decisions is typically just on financial investment and capital decisions, and not on human resources decisions. There's usually no strategic plan or focus for human resources. So far only a few companies require a human resources plan for investment decisions. This is a major problem, for when companies plan to order new machines, for example, they usually worry only about the installment and financing of those machines. And afterwards, without previous planning, the human resource department has to somehow provide the people who can work with the system. Only a few companies are beginning to connect the human resource aspects of investment decisions with the other aspects of the investment decisions. In the future, the human resources decisions might be the most important restriction to major investment decisions.

*Vance:* Do you see anything changing on the part of top management?

*Sailer:* Yes. The increasing new technologies are forcing management to think about the training needs of the work force, just by the immediate necessity—you've got a new machine and you need people who can handle the system and the technology. Some companies are really trying to develop manpower forecasts. If you know that you'll need, for example, certain engineers in ten years, you have to work to plan and prepare for them now because there is a real time lag in developing the necessary talent.

*Vance:* I recently talked to a human resource director in Switzerland who said that it is harder for a human resource manager to be promoted than it is for other managers. Do you believe that this perception represents an accurate trend in Switzerland and other Western European countries?

*Sailer:* Yes. Usually you won't find human resources managers in the top management level. However, in West Germany, it is required by law to have a so-called personnel director in the top management of a company. But the problem is that this is just a legislative measure. It won't change the way management is done and the perception of the relatively low priority of the human resources function. In Germany, the professional specialty of human resources management is primarily represented by the legally forced cooperation between management and the workers' union representatives.

*Vance:* Another human resources manager in Switzerland recently told me that his company has no discrimination problems with minorities and women as we have in the United States. But my impression is that problems do exist, but there is a lack of awareness of and sensitivity to these problems, much like that which existed in the United States prior to the 1960s.

*Sailer:* You're right. Management in German-speaking countries and in much of Europe not only has a problem related to discrimination but also generally doesn't realize it has a problem. We have no equal opportunity employment legislation. All those very important laws in the United States are completely unknown here, in Switzerland, Germany, everywhere. Any company really can discriminate openly with no lawsuits or legal consequences. In German-speaking areas in particular, there are no racial minorities, but there is, of course, a problem with women. If you look at corporate executives, you will note the marked absence of women. The percentage of female business executives is actually declining. One can hardly imagine a woman in a company to be more than a secretary. You really find the reaction on the part of virtually all managers that a woman cannot really succeed in a career because one day she will marry, have children, and quit her job. And so the company will lose this knowledge and know-how, which is an important investment. This argument is interesting because in all other contexts, such as in training and turnover, managers are not used to talking about human resource investments—only when it comes to trying to justify their negative decisions regarding women's career opportunities. And so it isn't credible argument.

*Vance:* What about the treatment of immigrant employees from Southern Italy, Turkey, and other areas with less-developed economics?

*Sailer:* In the 1960s and 1970s, there was tremendous economic growth in Western Europe, and in German-speaking countries in particular. There was a lack of manpower in certain industries such as mining, manufacturing, construction, and tourism, and several companies were heavily recruiting foreign workers, thousands and thousands of people from countries such as Turkey. At that time the only issue was how to provide for manpower. The other problems related to cultural differences and new culture assimilation were not considered. We know much more about those problems today, but only because there are millions of Turks living in Germany and many of them living in special areas. They want to maintain their culture, but it is now neither a German culture nor a Turkish culture. They benefit from all the governmental social programs. But there are some cultural problems, and German society tends to want to just leave those problems to the Turks. Today, there is a new generation, a lot of children from German Turks. They are not yet German, but neither are they Turks anymore. You have many people who don't know where they belong.

*Vance:* How about their opportunities for going into higher management positions?

*Sailer:* Besides some exceptions, I cannot imagine that these people would have a chance to climb up the career ladder higher than a lower-level executive or supervisor position. Maybe things are changing, partly because these people have more of a chance today if they are qualified. There is no structural discrimination within the educational system. But there is, of course, certain social discrimination. For example, in Switzerland, about 14 percent of the population are foreigners. There are many executives and qualified professionals in Swiss companies who are not Swiss but are Germans, Austrians, Italians, or French. When it comes to really important decisions, and in selecting top-level executives who will have great influence in the company and within the external political and economic environment, you won't find foreigners involved. They are respected as professionals and are certainly not discriminated against in terms of wages and so on. But when it comes to making those important decisions, they are not involved.

*Vance:* What kinds of changes related to human resource management do you foresee taking place with the establishment in 1992 of the European Common Market?

*Sailer:* The intentions for 1992 are to open the borders for a free flow of the work force. Today, someone who comes from one European country and wants to work in another needs a working license. The company has to receive this permission from the government authorities. Sometimes it is granted; sometimes, it's not. In the Common Market, those permissions won't be necessary anymore. So, for example, a German employer can employ anyone from any country in the European Common Market community, and the government authorities cannot intervene.

*Vance:* So you see the development of the Common Market after 1992 leading to increased employee mobility between the countries that are members of the community?

*Sailer:* Yes, but more important than the increased mobility of the individual members of the work force will be the increased mobility of companies. After 1992, any company based in a European country that is a member of the community may put up a plant or factory in any other European member country. So there will be the opportunity for companies to work throughout Europe without permissions. For example, a German company's production process can be transferred to Spain, Greece, or Italy, where the work force costs are cheaper. And so human resources management will become more international, and the important issues of managing work force diversity will become much more present in top-management thinking. There will be less of a need politically for joint ventures, and production and manufacturing will become much more flexible.

*Vance:* How will the Common Market affect the often self-serving influence of regional and national politics?

*Sailer:* Today, there is a lot of influence from politics. But after 1992, the national company has no advantage over the foreign company. Today, if you are a national company near an educational institution—a university, for example—which provides qualified engineers, you have an advantage in obtaining this qualified work force. After 1992, another foreign competitor might just put up a plant right there and compete for those qualified engineers. So personnel marketing and recruitment will become much more important in European companies.

*Vance:* What about the strong interest that you talked about earlier for high job security to minimize mobility and geographic displacement?

*Sailer:* That interest is now strong. However, another important development with the 1992 Common Market will be a change in people's attitudes toward mobility. I believe that more and more people will begin to regard the whole of Europe as their potential national, regional, and local community. And human resources managers will certainly face more strongly such challenging issues as recruiting and managing foreign employees, and employing their own native workers in foreign countries. It is a development that will take years and years to mature, but the political framework and economic context will be provided by the Common Market.

# Management Culture and the Accelerated Product Life Cycle

## FARIBORZ GHADAR
## NANCY J. ADLER

One way to understand the evolution of international firms is through the international product life cycle, which was described by Raymond Vernon of Harvard in 1966.[1] The position of a product in the life cycle has several important implications for the firm's relationship with the external environment as well as its internal functioning. Generally speaking, the international product life cycle for trade and investment can be divided into three principal stages: high tech, growth and internationalization, and maturity.

## Phase One: A Product Orientation

Phase One products are new and unique and are the fruit of extensive research and development (R&D). They have never been produced before and only a handful of companies are capable of producing them. These high tech products are purchased by a highly specialized and limited market. Not surprisingly, given their uniqueness and the few companies capable of pro-

---

[1]While originally espoused by Vernon in 1966, this argument has been picked up by many commentators. See Raymond Vernon, "International Investment and International Trade in the Product Cycle," *Quarterly Journal of Economics* 80:2 (1966), 180–207; Sovereignty at Bay Ten Years After," *International Organization* 35:5 (1981), 517–29; *Sovereignty at Bay: The Multinational Spread of U.S. Enterprises* (New York: Basic Books, 1971). See also Fariborz Ghadar, *The Evolution of OPEC Strategy* (Lexington, Mass.: Lexington Books, 1977); "Political Risk and the Erosion of Control: The Case of the Oil Industry, in T. Brewer (ed.), *Political Risks in International Business: New Directions for Research, Management, and Public Policy* (New York: Praeger, 1985); and "Strategic Considerations in the Financing of International Investment," in P. Grub et al. (eds.), *The Multinational Enterprise in Transition*, 3rd ed., (Princeton, N.J.: The Darwin Press, 1986).

*Source:* Fariborz Ghadar and Nancy J. Adler. "Management Culture and the Accelerated Product Life Cycle." *Human Resource Planning*, 1989, 12(1), 37–42. Reprinted by permission.

ducing them, Phase One products generally command a high price relative to direct costs.

The conditions needed for nurturing products differ depending on the phase they are in. In particular, a Phase One product can be created only if several important conditions are met. The development of new technology requires an environment in which technical skills and information are relatively abundant. New products tend to be developed in industrialized, wealthier countries. The materials and laboratories necessary for research and development are themselves costly, as is the training of engineers and scientists. New products tend to be developed in industrialized, advanced countries. Wealthier countries also supply an outlet for these products because they can afford the high price tag of new technology.

## ▬ Phase Two: A Market Orientation

The entrance of competition marks the beginning of Phase Two, growth and internationalization. All firms producing Phase Two products must now focus on expanding their markets and producing overseas. Initially, the firm supplies new foreign markets from the home country. Gradually, production shifts to those countries with the largest domestic markets as firms erect foreign plants and assembly lines to supply local demand. As foreign markets grow, more is produced locally, and exports from the original home country diminish.

Thus, as products reach Phase Two, market penetration and control replace research and development as the most important functions. Because the product technology has been perfected in Phase One, R&D as a percentage of sales decreases. The firm's activity need no longer center on developing the product, but rather on refining the means of production. Consequently, the focus moves from product engineering to process engineering, although the firm still may address specialized engineering problems associated with design modifications for specific international markets. With other firms continuing to enter the market as producers, competition increases and drives down both price and the proportion of price to cost.

## ▬ Phase Three: A Price Orientation

Products enter Phase Three, maturity, when standardization of the production process makes further reductions in production costs impossible. The technology inherent both in the product itself and in the production process has become widely available; hence R&D drops off almost completely. Moreover, the market, while large, is completely saturated with competitors. The potential for growth in either market or market share becomes severely limited, and price often falls to a bare minimum above cost.

Given these conditions, Phase Three firms can gain a competitive advantage only by managing factor costs, that is, by shifting production to those countries in which the factors of production are least expensive. Because product development occurs in countries with a high standard of living and relatively high labor costs, by Phase Three, home country production usually ceases to be competitive. As a result, the home country market now is supplied primarily by production imported from offshore plants.

## The Accelerated Product Life Cycle

During the years following World War II, the changes which marked a product's progression through the entire life cycle were gradual, taking between fifteen and twenty years. These changes seemed as inevitable as the passage of time itself, and the international product life cycle provided a reliable guide to business strategy. Gradually, however, the European and Japanese economies developed to such a point that they became capable of supporting their own product development and providing an ample market for their own new products. In addition, the worldwide dissemination of technical information has improved. Today, the United States no longer has a hegemony on research and development or on skilled engineers and scientists. As a result, the Europeans and the Japanese have challenged, and in some cases, surpassed the U.S. in the origination of new products.

A consequence of this development is that the time it took for a product to progress through the product life cycle decreased. By the early 1970s, the acceleration of the product life cycle made the need for new strategies and new models imminent. By the 1980s, instead of taking fifteen to twenty years for a product to make its way through the cycle, it took from three to five years. For a growing number of products, it now takes less than six months.

## The Trans-Global Phase

As the progression from Phase One to Phase Three has quickened, we have achieved more unified world markets. Now a single, Trans-Global Phase describes the life cycle of many products.[2] To compete effectively, trans-global products must be flexible, capable of being shaped to meet individual needs, and yet assembled from components sourced worldwide. We are seeing the beginnings of mass customization. In today's environment, when trans-global approaches more and more frequently substitute for those which only a decade ago were appropriate to Phases One, Two, and Three, successful firms must be responsive, that is they must listen to their clients, accurately identify trends, and act quickly.

To succeed in such a trans-global environment, firms must become si-

[2]See J. Naisbitt, *Megatrends* (New York: Warner Books, 1982) and Stan Davis, *Future Perfect* (Reading, Mass.: Addison-Wesley, 1987).

multaneously more highly differentiated and more integrated. Structurally, successful firms pass far beyond the organizational strategies of Phase Two and Phase Three firms, with their international divisions and their global lines of business, to form what could be called trans-global hierarchies: a web of joint ventures, wholly-owned subsidiaries, and organizational and project-defined alliances. The rapid rise of global alliances appearing in the automotive, aerospace, computer, biotechnology, and telecommunications industry is a trend few can dispute.[3] To maintain responsiveness in this type of environment, successful firms are developing global corporate cultures that recognize cultural diversity and its impact on the organization, allowing them to integrate culture specific strategic choices within a global vision of the firm. Appropriate approaches to human resource management in trans-global ventures are, consequently, rapidly being redefined.[4]

How important are cultural differences to the success of the firm? Can't such ethnic and national differences just be ignored? The answer is no. The importance of cultural differences depends on the phase of the life cycle in which the firm operates. Phase One firms can operate appropriately from an ethnocentric perspective and ignore most cultural differences they encounter. These firms produce a unique product that they offer primarily to their domestic market. If the firm exports the product, it does so without altering it for foreign consumption.

By Phase Two, competition brings the need to market and to produce overseas. Consequently, sensitivity to cultural differences becomes critical. As Phase One's product orientation shifts to Phase Two's marketing orientation, the firm must address each foreign market separately. Successful Phase Two firms can no longer expect foreigners to absorb cross-cultural mismatches between buyers and sellers, but rather must modify their own style to fit with that of their foreign clients and colleagues.

As firms enter Phase Three, the environment again changes and with it the demands for cultural sensitivity. By Phase Three, many firms produce an almost undifferentiated product. Interestingly, companies in this phase need to place little emphasis on cross-cultural differences. Firms gain competitive advantage almost exclusively by reducing cost, and thus reducing price, through sourcing factors on a worldwide basis, and benefitting from the resultant economies of scale.

In the Trans-Global Phase, however, top-quality, global products and services become the minimally accepted standard. Competitive advantage

---

[3]Numerous articles have described the rise of global alliances in the automotive, telecommunications, and computer industries. For a general description, see Gunnar Hedlund, "The Hypermodern MNC—A Heterarchy?" *Human Resource Management* 25:1 (1986), 9–36.

[4]See Nancy J. Adler and M. Jelinek, "Is 'Organization Culture' Culture Bound?" Human Resource Management 25:1 (1986), 73–90 and P. Lorange, "Human Resource Management in Multinational Cooperative Ventures," Human Resource Management 25:1 (1986), 133–48.

comes from sophisticated global strategies based on mass customization. Firms draw product ideas, as well as the factors and locations of production, from worldwide sources. However, firms tailor final products and their relationship to clients to very discrete market niches. Culture becomes of paramount importance. Successful firms understand their potential clients' needs, quickly translate them into products and services, produce those products and services on a least possible cost basis, and deliver them back to the client in a culturally appropriate and timely fashion. Moreover, firms continually scan the globe, often including geographically dispersed and culturally diverse alliance partners. Alliances bring cross-cultural dynamics within the "organization culture" and, more significantly, within the very uppermost executive committees. In the trans-global corporation, cultural diversity is no longer something to be ignored, nor something to be relegated to low-level sales people and assembly workers.

## International Human Resource Management

Is there a best international human resource management policy? No, again "best" is relative—relative to the phase in which the firm is operating. Excellent firms search for the best fit between their external environment and overall strategy and their human resource management policy. Unfortunately, many firms continue to use Phase One approaches to managing human resources, while operating in Phases Two, Three or even in trans-global environments. This does not work. Human resource management, rather than being a key component of competitive strategy, becomes marginal, a mere afterthought in the firm's cultural decision making.

Let's look at each phase separately. Given the domestic focus of Phase One firms and the absence of competition, the firm has little need for people experienced in international business. The firm generally sends few employees on international business trips and none on expatriate assignments. Those few are almost always home country nationals, sent abroad on marketing assignments. For them, neither cross cultural management nor language training is essential, because potential buyers have few options other than the particular firm for purchasing Phase One products.[5] Furthermore, since domestic sales dominate Phase One profits, firms generally do not assign their best people to international positions.

Unlike Phase One firms, Phase Two firms face competition and respond by expanding from domestic to international operations. Phase Two firms frequently select and send home country sales representatives to market products overseas, technical experts to transfer technology to overseas production sites, and managing directors and financial officers to control overseas operations. Because most R&D, and thus most innovation, still takes

[5]See M.E. Mendenhall, E. Dunbar, and G.R. Oddou, "Expatriate Selection, Training and Career-Pathing: A Review and Critique," *Human Resource Management* 26:3 (1987), 331–45.

place at home, firms view foreign operations primarily as sites for replicating that which has already been done at home. International service is rarely considered central or of primary importance. Therefore, while not selecting marginal performers, Phase Two firms rarely send their very best people abroad. In practice, companies often continue to use Phase One's primary criterion—technical competence—when selecting employees for overseas assignments.[6] Furthermore, their colleagues in the firm's home country offices view returning expatriates as out of the mainstream.[7] Although Phase Two firms often include host nationals in marketing and personnel positions, they too find their career advancement limited. Typically, they advance no higher than country managing director.

In Phase Three, the competitive environment changes again. As we have seen, price, rather than either product or market, determines Phase Three firms' ability to survive. Geographical dispersion often increases and with it the firms' need to integrate. Phase Three firms accomplish integration primarily through centralizing and standardizing as many aspects of their products, processes, and structure as possible.

Given the critical role that multinational production and operations play in corporate survival of Phase Three firms, they select their best, rather than their marginal, employees for international positions. The firm uses international positions to develop an integrated, global organization through the international career development of high potential managers and thus the creation of a global cadre of executives. But, whereas Phase Three makes international experience essential to firmwide management and career advancement, the importance of cross-cultural sensitivity and language skills diminishes. Rather than using cultural diversity, Phase Three firms often enforce similarity when attempting to integrate the global firm. Phase Three firms generally adopt English as a common language. Similarly, they assume that their organizational culture will dominate any national cultural differences.[8]

The trans-global environment requires firms to assign their best people to international positions, because the very idea of a single, dominant domestic market has become a relic of the past. Top-quality, low-cost production necessitates worldwide operations, with location dictated by strategic, politi-

---

[6]See R. Tung, Selection and Training of Personnel for Overseas Assignments, *Columbia Journal of World Business* 16:1 (1981), 68–78; S. Ronen, *Comparative and Multinational Management* (New York: John Wiley, 1986); and M.E. Mendenhall and G.R. Oddou, "Acculturaltion Profiles of Expatriate Managers: Implications for Cross-Cultural Training Programs," *Columbia Journal of World Business* 21:4 (1986), 73–79.

[7]Nancy J. Adler, "Re-entry: Managing Cross-Cultural Transitions," *Group and Organizational Studies* 6:3 (1981), 341–56.

[8]Nancy J. Adler, "Organizational Development in a Multicultural Environment," *Journal of Applied Behavioral Science* 11:3 (1983), 349–65.

cal, and economic constraints, along with the supply of inputs and market access. Key employees must be multilingual and culturally sensitive.[9] Hence, neither cultural forms of control emphasizing more homogeneous selection, socialization, and training nor more bureaucratic forms of control can independently address the simultaneous needs for integration and differentiation. One of a trans-global firm's major competitive weapons is its ability to use global human resources along both dimensions, to enhance national responsiveness and global integration.

For trans-global managers today and in the coming decade, the salient question is not if there is cultural diversity, but rather how to manage it. Trans-global managers must constantly turn to cultural diversity to balance three organizational tensions. First, they must minimize the impacts of cultural diversity when integration is needed. Second, they must use cultural diversity to differentiate products and services when culturally distinct markets or work forces must be addressed. And third, they must employ cultural diversity as a primary source of new ideas when innovation is needed.

Balancing cultural integration and differentiation affects all aspects of the human resource management system. For example, when firms promote managers from the local culture to positions of significant power in their own country, they are using cultural diversity to increase differentiation. By contrast, when they design multinational career paths for high potential managers and bring them together to create new approaches to managing innovation, production, finance, and marketing, they are using the diversity to create cultural synergy.

Trans-global firms no longer have an international division. Simply put, they are truly international. They select the best people for global assignments and continually train them in the skills necessary for national responsiveness and culturally synergistic integration. Promotions go to those managers who skillfully assess and balance the needs for differentiation and integration; those who are continually learning and therefore are capable of making new choices. In this context, international human resource management is crucial to a firm's success.

# ▄▄ *Implications*

The accelerated product life cycle and the globalization of the business environment make it imperative for firms to adjust their human resource management systems to the international marketplace. Increasingly, as trans-global development comes to replace the gradual shift from Phase One

---

[9]See F.T. Murray and A.H. Murray, "Global Managers for Global Businesses," *Sloan Management Review* 27:2 (1986), 75–80; and Y.L. Doz and C.K. Prahalad, "Controlled Variety: A Challenge for Human Resource Management in the MNC," *Human Resource Management* 25:1 (1986), 55–72.

through Phase Two to Phase Three, a progression which had dominated the international product life cycle, firms must understand cultural differences to implement global R&D, global marketing, global production, global financial and global human resource strategies successfully.

# Mitsuhoshi France, S.A.

## SUSAN SCHNEIDER
## RYUKICHI INOUE
## CHRISTINE MEAD

Satoshi Suzuki has been lost in thought for more than an hour in front of a telex from the foodstuffs division in Tokyo. Its subject was a new project proposed for France. The telex read as follows:

TO MITSUHOSHI PARIS FOODSTUFFS DEPT
COPY MITSUHOSHI LONDON FOOD DIV
FROM MITSUHOSHI TOKYO FOODSTUFFS DIV

RE HEALTHY FOOD PROJ IN FRANCE
OKAMOTO RESEARCH INSTITUTE ONE OF TOP BIOTECH COMP IN JPN PLANS TO MAKE J/V IN FRANCE TO PRODUCE HEALTHY PRODUCTS OF "TOFU" OR FOOD FROM SOY BEANS STP THEY ASKED US TO COOPERATE IN FINDING FRENCH PARTNER AS WELL AS PARTICIPATING J/V STP ACDGTO PLANS NOT ONLY "TOFU" BUT ALSO DIET FOODS BASED ON SOY BEANS AND VITAMIN FOODS BE PRODUCED STP IF RESULT OF F/S SATISFACTORY WE ARE READY TO INVEST AS MUCH AS ONE BILLION YEN STP PLS IMMEDIATELY ARRANGE FORMA-TION AT YOUR SIDE TO PROCEED ZS PROJ STP RPLY IMMEDIATELY STP RGDS

He thought through what this project would mean for him. It would be a new venture, something that he would be responsible for, which could be useful for him when he returned to Japan in a few years time.

In thinking about who to hire for this project, he remembers his recent discussions with his superior, President Tanaka, about the problems of Japanese expatriates and the French nationals working at Mitsuhoshi, France. He knows that these problems reflect a deeper concern—the internationalization of Mitsuhoshi Corporation.

*Source:* This case was prepared by Susan Schneider, Ryukichi Inoue, and Christine Mead, as a basis for class discussion rather than to illustrate either effective or ineffective handling of an administrative situation. (c) INSEAD/CEDEP. Reprinted by permission.

# Company Background

Mitsuhoshi Corp. Tokyo is one of the leading Japanese general trading houses (sogoshosha). It has more than 150 offices around the world and the volume of information it exchanges daily through its telex channel network is the equivalent of some 1,600 pages of *The New York Times*. The total turnover in 1987 was more than $90 billion. The corporation employed 8,000 Japanese staff and 5,000 local staff around the world.

Mitsuhoshi France S.A. is a wholly owned subsidiary of Mitsuhoshi Tokyo. Its activity ranges from importing Japanese steel and machinery into France and exporting French goods to Japan, to organizing a huge refinery complex in Francophone Africa. Its turnover reached 1,800 million French francs in 1987.

Mitsuhoshi France is tightly controlled by Tokyo, although legally independent in France. Mitsuhoshi's European Regional Center is in London, where Mitsuhoshi Tokyo's senior managing director acts as a general manager of Europe and Africa operations.

# Employees

Of its fifty employees, ten are expatriate Japanese managers who have been appointed by Tokyo headquarters. They are the president, two vice presidents, and seven department managers. In addition, there are fifteen locally employed Japanese, only one of whom is scheduled to be promoted to manager. The expatriate Japanese return to Tokyo after five or six years; the locally employed Japanese always stay in France. The remaining thirty-five are all French. Some of them have worked more than ten years to obtain the title of manager.

Yuuji Tanaka is the fifty-two-year-old president of Mitsuhoshi France. He has worked for Mitsuhoshi for thirty years, joining them straight after university graduation. He will retire in eight years. Through on-the-job training, he has become a specialist in chemical trading. Before Paris, he was posted in London and Dusseldorf.

Susumu Sato is the forty-five-year-old vice president of Mitsuhoshi France. He has been appointed to France for the second time because he studied French at the Tokyo University of Foreign Studies. This time he chose to come to France alone. He cannot sacrifice the future career of his only son, who is fourteen years old. His son must study in the Japanese way to win entry in a good Japanese university. His wife has remained in Tokyo with the son to help him in preparing for his difficult examinations. In four years' time, after the boy has passed his examinations and succeeded in getting a place at the university, he might reconsider calling his wife back to Paris.

He is in charge of administration in Mitsuhoshi France, including accounting and personnel, which are particularly important. His assignment is not easy. Managing the complaints of the French staff is one of his headaches; he often finds himself caught between the two fires of Tokyo headquarters and the French office.

Owing to the slow growth of the world economy, the business of Mitsuhoshi France has been stagnating recently. This means that salaries cannot be raised sharply or constantly. Mr. Sato submitted a draft proposal for a wage hike that would fit the French employees' expectations to London. London required that the French subsidiary implement the same policy as the British, German, Belgian, Italian, and Scandinavian subsidiaries, and keep the average wage hike below 2 percent. Mr. Sato understands that the motivation for keeping the French staff is largely through salary increases since it is clear that they are not promoted to posts where they have decision-making power. He was almost swallowed by complaints from the French staff when he announced the salaries for the coming year. A particular bone of contention has been the traditional Japanese Bonenkai; the equivalent of the western company Christmas party. Many of the French staff made it clear that they would rather be paid more money than have such an absurd party sponsored by the company.

Satoshi Suzuki is the thirty-eight-year-old Japanese expatriate manager in charge of the foodstuffs department of Mitsuhoshi France. He was sent by company order from Tokyo in April 1986, along with his wife Keiko (thirty-six) and two children (six and ten).

Before Paris, he spent three years (1979–1982) as the company's chief representative in Khartoum. Although regarded as the worst place to work among Mitsuhoshi's overseas offices, he had enjoyed the responsibility of being the only manager, in charge of the whole operation. If he had stayed in Tokyo, he would have waited ten years for such responsibility. In Khartoum he had performed well, getting contracts financed by the Japanese government's official aid programs.

Returning to Tokyo, he was assigned to work on imports of foodstuffs from the USA and the EEC. In addition, he was appointed vice chairman of Mitsuhoshi's employees' union, and negotiated with Mitsuhoshi Tokyo for the wage hike of some 5,000 union members. This was a vital experience in giving Mr. Suzuki a global view of the company and its activities.

Mr. Suzuki studied French for two years at the University of Tokyo, but realizes that his French is far from perfect when it comes to communicating with his French clients and subordinates. He is confident in conducting daily business in English.

He wakes up every morning at 7 a.m., has a Japanese breakfast, leaves his cozy apartment paid for by the company near the Bois de Boulogne in the 16e arrondissement in Paris, and arrives at work at 8:45 a.m. He reads telexes—mostly in Japanese—until 10 a.m., and then he plans and suggests to his subordinates what to do for the day.

Satoshi Suzuki has three subordinates: Mr. Vincent and two secretaries. Mr. Vincent is a senior member of the staff who has worked there for twelve years. After finishing high school, he worked as a salesman for a leading French foodstuffs company, but he decided to change to Mitsuhoshi France in order to practice his English. Working in a Japanese company was a bit like living on a different planet for him, but he learned through his twelve years of experience in the company how to be patient with his bosses. He is considered a reliable member of the staff in his field of trading French wines, brandies, and cookies.

## ■ *Overseas Assignments*

At last year's Bonenkai party, President Tanaka and Mr. Suzuki discussed the differences in the older and younger Japanese managers' attitudes toward international assignments—hardship or privilege? President Tanaka reminisces about the days when he was sent to London in 1961. The Japanese economy had then just recovered from the effects of World War II and was concentrating on the development of heavy industry and chemicals. As very few companies had overseas activities, any person who went abroad was considered part of an elite, called "glorious representative abroad," and sought after by young girls as an ideal husband.

*Tanaka:* I heard that there have come to be more employees, especially in the younger generation in Tokyo headquarters, who do not want to work abroad. This might indicate the devaluation of the status of overseas representatives of sogoshosha. Mr. Suzuki, what do you think of this tendency?

*Suzuki:* Well, frankly speaking, I think we cannot find anything better than Tokyo, even in the cities of the U.S. or Europe. It is true that in Tokyo the cost of living is higher than anywhere else in the world, but we can enjoy life without the horror of terrorism or holdups in the street. Goods are abundant, service is quick and precise. For the younger generation, candidly speaking, not only Paris but also New York is ranked below Tokyo.

*Tanaka:* But can't you recognize the superior quality of life in Paris? In Tokyo, we have no Louvre and no opera. Those who enjoy the classical arts are regarded as a privileged minority, whereas in Paris, everyone is very much accustomed to enjoying the artistic life after work.

*Suzuki:* In my opinion, that is the evidence that French culture has entered a period of decline—longing for the good old days. Your generation, President Tanaka, may understand the feeling of adoring the "made in France" products, but we know that most of them are not of better quality than Japanese goods.

*Tanaka:* By the way, what do you think of sogoshosha's young employees who no longer wish to work abroad?

*Suzuki:* Working abroad is not reserved for the elites today. In fact, if we think of the importance of good education for our children, working abroad as a representative might not be an advantage for us any more. Vice President Sato seems to be clear that he is living here apart from his family just because he has a boy who has to study in Japan preparing for entering the better universities.

What is worse is that even an independent subsidiary like Mitsuhoshi France is not allowed to initiate action. It is always Tokyo that makes the final decision. Even though we have a hard time abroad, it is said that people who remain in Tokyo have more chance of being promoted more quickly. For a rational person, his heart is not in working abroad, even if it is in the developed countries.

## The Role of the Local Staff

At Mitsuhoshi Tokyo headquarters, a new strategy regarding HRM abroad became one of the main issues to be addressed immediately. Mr. Takahashi, the General Manager of the Overseas Coordinating Division, came to Paris on the way back to Tokyo from his visit to the offices in Africa to discuss his plan—that excellent local staff should play a more important role. Mr. Takahashi asked President Tanaka to talk more informally after office hours, at the Japanese restaurant Takara near the opera.

*Takahashi:* In the 1960s when you first went to London, the English who applied for jobs with Mitsuhoshi had a high school education. We were obviously a second choice for those who could not find work in a good English company. Now, as the Japanese economy grows and Mitsuhoshi's reputation increases, even Oxbridge boys are coming knocking on our doors. We cannot, of course, make their salaries equal to those with a high-school level education. It is moreover much more economical for us if they do the work previously done by Japanese representatives. I believe that in the future we should make the most of the power of local employees. Or we might abolish the differentiation between Japanese representatives who were employed in Tokyo and others.

*Tanaka:* General Manager Mr. Takahashi, I understand what you say as a theory; however, there would be a lot of troubles when this new policy is introduced in practice. For example, if we employed a graduate of the top grandes écoles, I cannot believe they would work for us for a long time. How then would they function as well as the Japanese expatriate managers in the very hierarchical Japanese organization?

In addition, they probably do not understand Japanese. You know that 90 percent of our telexes are in Japanese. It is out of the question that directors could use an interpreter to communicate with Tokyo.

*Takahashi:* Language problems can be solved if Tokyo headquarters would change. As you know, until we acquired a worldwide network in the late 1960s, we traded by telegram in English. Why can't the younger generation do as we did?

*Tanaka:* What about the relations between Tokyo and offices abroad? Do you think the local manager would understand the limit of his power, even though he was general manager of Mitsuhoshi France? Although we are an independent company by law, we cannot undertake any business without Tokyo's full assistance.

It happened quite recently that the general merchandising division in Tokyo decided not to work in France any more. We, therefore, have to do our own risk assessment and accounting if we want to keep in that line of business. But it is almost impossible with our limited number of staff to assess the reliability of each client and to manage the shipments one by one. I am considering abandoning all the business we have in the general merchandising field, but it will be very troublesome to persuade the French staff to change their assignment or to quit Mitsuhoshi.

*Takahashi:* At Tokyo headquarters, we are facing a critical situation. We should be flexible enough to adapt to fundamental changes in the structure of Japanese industry. We hope that as a means of survival in the twenty-first century, every subsidiary company in the U.S. and in Europe should act independently without any help from Tokyo. As you know, we have established the President's Prize for the overseas subsidiary who has performed well in these fields of off-shore or local transactions.

*Tanaka:* The mentality of the Japanese will not change so quickly. This month I had twenty guests from Japan, many of whom were not clients of Mitsuhoshi France but were somehow related to the corporation as a whole. When asked by Tokyo to "Please attend to them carefully," I could not find any other way but to do it. Can you imagine that there are times when I have two guests in one night, manage to have dinner twice, and after dinner take them to the Moulin Rouge? Yesterday, too, I came home at 2 a.m., and this morning I went to my office at half past eight. I cannot imagine that any French manager would be willing to do this.

*Takahashi:* I am sure that sooner or later the Japanese mentality will change. At least I can say that it will be internationalized, as we have to survive in the international business world and cannot keep our company closed. The labor environment should be much more open to anyone who is capable. This will be a key success factor for sogoshosha very soon.

## ▬ A New Challenge

Coming back to the telex, Suzuki believes that to be successful in this project requires the hiring of a business elite—a highly qualified French manager who had attended the top schools (grandes écoles), with a degree in bioengineering and experience in management as well as marketing. Before proposing his plan to President Tanaka, he decides to talk to the vice president in charge to personnel affairs, Mr. Sato:

*Sato:* It seems to me that your plan to employ a French manager in the new project would incur great risks for us. The salary of the new manager would be double that of the current staff. This would lead to great dissatisfaction among the current staff. In your department, Mr. Vincent, who has worked with us for twelve years, would surely claim that he should get as high a salary as the new manager.

As you know, it is almost impossible to fire a man once employed in France. If Mr. Vincent undertakes legal proceedings to support his claim—or even hints at them—President Tanaka cannot help accepting his claim, because Tokyo headquarters does not like any legal proceedings, especially in personnel affairs. It would be a black mark against President Tanaka. Do you think that President Tanaka would risk his future post in Tokyo, his promotion, for such a project?

*Suzuki:* I don't believe it is all so bad. I heard that the overseas coordination division in Tokyo recently adopted a new strategy of encouraging local managers. Besides this, I can say that Mr. Vincent is not qualified enough to run this new project. He is lacking in knowledge of biotechnology, and he is not from the grandes écoles nor from a university. Do you imagine that Mr. Vincent, considering his background, could promote the project successfully with top management in French companies who are all from the grandes écoles?

*Sato:* If you worry like that, you should do it yourself.

*Suzuki:* We cannot expect to encourage local staff by continuing in our traditional way. I am sure that even Mr. Vincent would accept the difference in salaries because the new director is from the grandes écoles.

EXHIBIT 1

*Mitsuhoshi France Organization Chart*

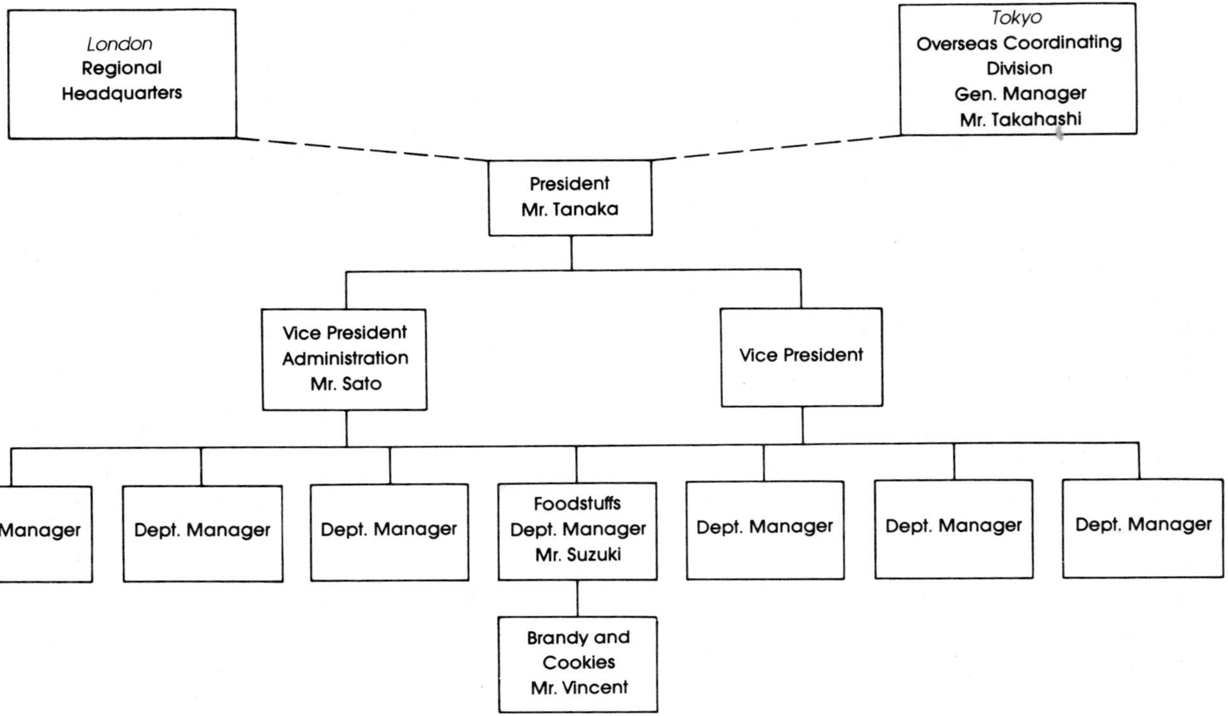

*London*
Regional
Headquarters

*Tokyo*
Overseas Coordinating
Division
Gen. Manager
Mr. Takahashi

President
Mr. Tanaka

Vice President
Administration
Mr. Sato

Vice President

Dept. Manager

Dept. Manager

Dept. Manager

Foodstuffs
Dept. Manager
Mr. Suzuki

Brandy and
Cookies
Mr. Vincent

Dept. Manager

Dept. Manager

Dept. Manager

*Sato:* After employing someone from the grandes écoles, imagine that we will find out that this new project is not feasible. What will you do with him? We cannot dismiss him, except at huge cost to us, and he would not accept being in charge of say the machinery department. We would have to keep him employed for life without any suitable assignment!

*Suzuki:* Perhaps you are referring to the case of Mr. Dupont of the general merchandise department. But once we decide to abandon the department, we should dismiss him at any cost. Whether President Tanaka might be regarded as incapable by Tokyo headquarters is not relevant if we consider the benefit of the whole Mitsuhoshi group.

Anyway, even without your consent, I shall ask President Tanaka to employ a manager from the grandes écoles, as I already have a favorable opinion from Tokyo's foodstuffs division, who are very strongly pushing this project.

Mr. Suzuki leaves the conversation thinking that it is unlikely that President Tanaka will agree immediately. However, the Tokyo foodstuffs division considers the success of this project critical to their continued good relationship with the Okamoto Research Institute in other business fields, and have already approved the appointment of an elite French manager. If need be, he can appeal directly to the managing director of the Mitsuhoshi Corporation in London. This is not the traditional Japanese way of respect for seniors. But he must also consider his duty to the foodstuffs division in Tokyo. He knocks on President Tanaka's door with qualms of conscience, as well as confidence in his plan.

# The Anstrichehof Infrared Coating Corporation—AICC

## ALBERTO ZANZI
## PAUL LEMIEUX

"Well, I'm really not surprised," Ron Wheeler thought to himself as he looked in disgust at SwissAir's monitor. The "Arrivals" display video terminal read as follows:

11 MAR 1988   FLIGHT 402 - ZURICH   1 HOUR DELAY

It had been that kind of a day. More than the usual amount of bull at work, the Friday night traffic jam in the Sumner Tunnel, and now that he was finally inside the terminal, the flight from Zurich was late. If there was one thing he hated more than a trip to Logan Airport, it was a trip to pick up Dr. Buerlanger at Logan.

"I guess it comes with the territory," he sputtered barely under his breath. As executive vice president of AICC, he felt responsible to personally pick up the directors from AICC's parent company, Masseverk AG. The visits were becoming more frequent and more tense; this time Dr. Vogtgartener was also coming.

Ron found a corner table in the Skyway Lounge, ordered a Lite (an American beer!), and set out his workpapers in front of him. He had a right to be in such a foul mood. AICC was in major trouble. That trouble was traveling toward him at 1,100 miles per hour at 30,000 feet.

He sat back and thought about his beloved AICC. Started in 1968, its growth had been steady but not earthshaking. They actually shipped over $18 million worth of infrared products in 1986. Their current employment of 225 people was their highest level ever. AICC manufactured infrared band-pass filters and antireflection coatings for use in a wide variety of biochemical, military, and aerospace applications. AICC filters were on the job in commu-

Source: Alberto Zanzi and Paul Lemieux. "The Anstrichehof Infared Coating Corporation." Suffolk University, 1989. Reprinted by permission.

**55**

nications satellites, blood analyzers, burglar alarms, and literally hundreds of other places. The growing worldwide market for commercial applications currently exceeded $250 million. Since the largest competitor only had 25 percent of the market, AICC's potential for continued growth was quite good.

Ron marveled at the contrast to Masseverk AG, the parent firm. With 1986 revenues of over four billion Swiss francs ($2.8 billion), Masseverk was a significant force in European industry. Although over 60 percent of their production was military, their optics division, which included AICC, accounted for 12 percent of their total sales. AICC's president, currently a Dr. Mueller, reported directly to Dr. Buerlanger at the optics division headquarters in Zurich.

For the first five years after Masseverk had bought the company, AICC had lost money. Although they had managed to make a small profit last year, this year they barely broke even, and the trend at year end was down, with a bullet. To make things worse, all the good technical people were leaving just when the competition was getting tougher.

There was the memo from Dr. Buerlanger in front of him. As he began to reread it for the sixth time, he felt his ulcer kick up.

MEMORANDUM
TO: Dr. W. Mueller, Pres. AICC
CC: Mr. R. Wheeler, Exec. V.P.
FROM: Dr. J. Buerlanger, Mgr. Masseverk AG., Dir. AICC
SUBJECT: 1987 Performance

---

Needless to say we are extremely disappointed in your recently reported year end figures, especially after our repeated exhortations that you make improvements. We continue to fail to understand why your technical efficiency remains weak in spite of continued capital equipment investments on our part.

We thought it was sufficiently clear in our memo of 22 FEB 1986 that the new capital of nearly 3.8 Million SFr (2 Million US$) that we invested at that time was supposed to cure whatever was needed, and your predecessor readily agreed. It seems unlikely that the . . .

"Ladies and gentlemen! Your attention please! SwissAir Flight 402 from Zurich has been delayed one additional half hour."

"Waitress, another Lite, please. There goes any hope of making it home in time for the Celtics game. Now, where was I," he mused, as his agitation increased.

. . . seems unlikely that the present management team will ever reach the minimum level of success which Masseverk AG demands from all it subsidiary companies.

As some immediate and direct action on our part seems desirable, in fact unavoidable, I ask you to prepare in advance of our meeting on 12

MARCH 1988 at your location any defenses you wish to raise. Dr. Vogtgartener and myself have some thoughts on structural changes at AICC which may prove effective, but may not be your preference.

As always and best regards,

Dr. J. Buerlanger

Ron bottomed-up his second beer and wandered over to the plate glass windows overlooking the runway. A light rain was starting to fall. He allowed his mind to wander back to his early days at AICC. In retrospect, they were beginning to look like the good old days. "I'm starting to sound like my father," he thought wryly to himself.

When Ron started in 1973, proudly toting his new Suffolk M.B.A. under his arm (a nice supplement to his B.S. in chemistry from Northeastern), AICC hadn't been invented yet. It was a nice, fresh, American company, with a pleasantly high tech name, Infra-Tech. The founder, George Mason, was the man for all seasons, the life of the party, the perennial entrepreneur who was fully involved in everything and made everything work. Infra-Tech was vibrant, growing, alive, and exciting. Direct communication between employees was unhampered by rigid rules and regulations. Each employee felt a sense of involvement and contribution. People worked hard and derived satisfaction from their jobs. Productivity and creativity were high. Under Mason's informal style of leadership, the company flourished.

In the late 1970s, though, Infra-Tech started to lose its edge. Infrared technology was developing at a lightning pace. State-of-the-art equipment was expensive, and margins were slim. Infra-Tech's growth became stifled by lack of investment capital. They had good ideas, but they did not have the resources to bring those ideas to the market. Gradually, as the competition got the edge with better equipment, Infra-Tech tried to buy back its market share by cutting prices. Shortly after the margins disappeared, so did the cash. When Masseverk AG began looking for an American base for its infrared coating business in 1980, the match looked like a natural. The Swiss firm was a world recognized name in infrared technology; they would add their financial and technical strength to Infra-Tech. It had to be a winning combination.

Back in the lounge, Ron thought to himself how the vanishing foam on his beer was like his evaporating hopes over the AICC years. He had been a strong and early supporter of the buyout. But almost immediately things started to go wrong.

Dr. Buerlanger arrived with the contracts, the capital, and a new organization chart. George Mason was replaced with a Swiss national, who proceeded to alienate most of the Infra-Tech managers. By the end of the second year, most of the creative people had quit or been fired. Mason had run his firm in a loose, freewheeling manner, but he had encouraged close, frequent, and direct communication. No organization chart. No memo. No bull. Now all that was changed.

*[margin note: Very different structures from loose to rigid]*

Dr. Buerlanger came from a different world. At Masseverk AG, where he had worked his whole long and successful career, company structure was hierarchical and very rigid. Employees were loyal and hardworking, and they knew their place. The working environment was strict and formal.

Wheeler was reminded of a meeting two years ago in Zurich. He recalled how he was out of sorts because all he could get with his meal was dark Swiss beer, no Lite. To his right, he had overhead Dr. Buerlanger make a comment to Dr. Vogtgartener under his breath about how the American's bad taste in beer was only surpassed by his childish impatience, disloyalty, and lack of organization. Dr. Buerlanger must have sensed Wheeler's attention because he turned his back slightly and continued in his native Suisse-Deutsche[1]:

*[margin note: He wants order and formality]*

**Dr. B:** Seriously, Herr Doctor, I cannot understand these Americans. They are bright, but they don't have any regard for the way things should be done. Everyone wants to be in charge. The technicians want to tell the scientists about ion exchange. The salesmen want to tell the supervisors how to run the plant. No one has any respect for order and control.

*[margin note: He agrees]*

**Dr. V:** Believe me, I understand your disappointment. We have given them the opportunity to come here and learn from our success, but it is no use. They are hopelessly uncivilized. They carry their democratic ideas into the workplace; it is no surprise that the structure collapses.[2]

*[margin note: Want to inflict very different ideas on U.S.]*

**Dr. B:** I would be content to deal with the EC [European Economic Community—ed.] countries; these are people I can understand. But the American market is too lucrative to ignore. I suppose we will have to continue to try to educate them to the correct way of doing things.

"Organization! Organization! Organization!" Wheeler thought over and over. "Ever since they have tried to make us an organization, we have stopped being an enterprise." Just that afternoon an angry exchange had taken place between Dave Howard, Manufacturing Manager, and Michael Steiner, Director of R&D. The stark contrast between now and Infra-Tech was foremost in Ron's mind as he recalled the scene in the corridor.

**Howard:** Where were you when Jonesie started up the 1500 Hi-Vac! He blew away almost $80,000 worth of germanium in two runs before Larry from QC shut him down!

---

[1]Translated by the editor.

[2]Dr. Vogtgartener used the word *gefallenundversagenvollig,* a colloquialism which I have translated as "collapse." The literal meaning has a sense of total failure—ed.

*Steiner:* What do you mean "Where was I?" Where were you? You're the manufacturing manager, not me. Look on the wall in Wheeler's office next to manufacturing. That's you there, not me.

*Howard:* Listen, Mike. You know as well as I do that chart is Dr. B's little fantasy. You're the only one here who knows the right way to start up the 1500 Hi-Vac. We can't afford to foul up like this, or the Swiss will take their francs and go home. I got a kid in college and orthodontist bills to pay!

*Steiner:* Look Dave, it's nothing personal. But I've got to play it safe at least until I can get my résumé out on the street.

*Howard:* Well, do what you have to. But I'll tell you this much. This business is too complicated to run like the army. If we're gonna survive, we gotta learn to talk. And then we gotta learn to help each other out . . . not just hide behind the organization chart.

"Ladies and gentlemen! Your attention please! SwissAir Flight 402 from Zurich is now arriving at gate 12. Disembarking passengers can be met at the U.S. Customs exit in the lower lobby in approximately 30 minutes."

"Well, here they are. Buerlanger and Vogtgartener with another organization chart, and . . .," thought Wheeler, "I don't even know if I'm on it!" The possibility of another president, the fourth in seven years, made Ron's ulcer kick up again. He pulled out the manilla folder which held tentative plans for a management leveraged buyout; he had been toying with the idea for six months, but it wasn't quite ready.

"Half an hour for customs? Waitress! I'll have another Lite, please."

EXHIBIT 1

## Anstrichehof Infrared Coating Corporation Comparative Balance Sheet

| | 1981 | 1982 | 1983 | 1984 | 1985 | 1986 | 1987 |
|---|---|---|---|---|---|---|---|
| **Assets** | | | | | | | |
| Current assets | | | | | | | |
| Cash | 822,042 | 83,893 | 34,794 | 60,453 | 33,526 | 42,534 | 55,979 |
| Accounts receivable | 544,860 | 862,158 | 1,620,623 | 1,224,444 | 1,798,451 | 2,414,426 | 2,138,830 |
| Inventories | 363,029 | 641,220 | 1,772,533 | 1,988,948 | 1,508,320 | 1,813,490 | 1,757,092 |
| Prepaid expenses | 36,764 | 10,840 | 43,399 | 36,804 | 26,384 | 61,403 | 43,195 |
| Total current assets | 1,766,695 | 1,598,111 | 3,471,349 | 3,310,649 | 3,366,681 | 4,331,853 | 3,995,096 |
| Equipment and Leaseholds, Net | 1,610,522 | 4,119,974 | 3,686,767 | 3,598,186 | 3,543,186 | 3,589,534 | 3,995,455 |
| Intangible Assets | 92,340 | 81,262 | 58,774 | 30,028 | | | |
| Total Assets | 3,469,557 | 5,799,347 | 7,216,890 | 6,938,863 | 6,909,867 | 7,921,387 | 7,990,551 |
| **Liabilities & Equity** | | | | | | | |
| Current Liabilities | | | | | | | |
| Notes Payable | | | 1,100,000 | 2,600,000 | 2,100,000 | 1,750,000 | 3,400,000 |
| Accounts payable accruals | 256,122 | 719,511 | 1,763,529 | 1,607,329 | 548,434 | 1,564,220 | 614,781 |
| Salaries, wages, taxes | 139,864 | 42,610 | 69,871 | 48,805 | 59,592 | 134,536 | 127,568 |
| Income taxes payable | | | | | | 450,288 | |
| Deferred tax, current | | | | | | | 10,710 |
| Due to affiliates | 36,802 | | | 589,210 | 2,000,000 | | 92,141 |
| Current portion, LTD | | | | 315,625 | 315,625 | 315,625 | 315,625 |
| Total Current Liabilities | 432,788 | 762,121 | 2,933,400 | 5,160,969 | 5,023,651 | 4,214,669 | 4,560,825 |
| Deferred Taxes | | | | | | | 4,590 |
| Long Term Debt | | 2,525,000 | 2,525,000 | 2,209,375 | 1,893,750 | 1,578,127 | 1,262,502 |
| Equity | | | | | | | |
| Capital | 3,300,000 | 3,300,000 | 3,300,000 | 3,300,000 | 4,300,000 | 2,015,601 | 2,015,601 |
| Retained earnings (deficit) | (263,231) | (787,774) | (1,541,510) | (3,731,481) | (4,307,534) | 112,990 | 147,033 |
| Total Equity | 3,036,769 | 2,512,226 | 1,758,490 | (431,481) | (7,534) | 2,128,591 | 2,162,634 |
| Total Liabilities | 3,469,557 | 5,799,347 | 7,216,890 | 6,938,863 | 6,909,867 | 7,921,387 | 7,990,551 |

*Anstrichehof Infrared Coating Corporation Comparative Statement of Income*

| | 1981 | 1982 | 1983 | 1984 | 1985 | 1986 | 1987 |
|---|---|---|---|---|---|---|---|
| *Net Sales* | 2,305,046 | 6,101,116 | 8,456,087 | 8,888,253 | 14,795,246 | 18,275,256 | 17,916,961 |
| *Cost of Sales* | 1,601,356 | 4,822,067 | 6,817,782 | 8,749,517 | 12,583,515 | 13,747,058 | 13,906,623 |
| | 703,690 | 1,279,050 | 1,638,305 | 138,735 | 2,211,731 | 4,528,198 | 4,010,338 |
| *General, Administrative Expense* | 590,303 | 710,670 | 775,411 | 1,098,033 | 1,049,720 | 1,519,662 | 1,504,070 |
| *Selling Expense* | 161,408 | 547,316 | 646,117 | 742,743 | 634,106 | 873,087 | 961,367 |
| *Product Development* | 88,344 | 228,534 | 204,855 | 227,656 | 98,544 | 1,320,469 | 1,177,992 |
| | 840,055 | 1,486,520 | 1,626,383 | 2,068,432 | 1,782,370 | 3,713,218 | 3,643,429 |
| *Other Expense* | 126,865 | 317,072 | 765,658 | 260,274 | 1,005,414 | 250,756 | 306,566 |
| *Income Taxes* | | | | | | 428100 | 23300 |
| *Earnings (Deficit)* | (263,231) | (524,543) | (753,736) | (2,189,971) | (576,053) | 136,125 | 37,043 |

EXHIBIT 3

## *Anstrichehof Infrared Coating Corporation Organization Chart*

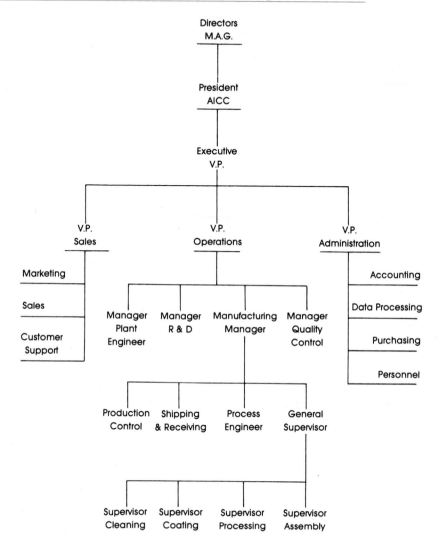

# Human Resource Strategy in the Global Context

# The Relationship Between the Global Strategic Planning Process and the Human Resource Management Function

### EDWIN L. MILLER
### SCHON BEECHLER
### BHAL BHATT
### RAGHU NATH

The rapid increase in U.S. multinational corporations' (MNCs) foreign direct investment has generated a series of intersections between MNCs' human resource management systems and their global strategic planning processes. As the MNCs strive to administer their overseas operations, the control mechanisms developed by the corporate headquarters to regulate the activities of their overseas subsidiaries impact the structure, the human resource management system and the enterprise's internal environment. Structural changes within the parent company or its overseas subsidiaries frequently lead to greater decentralization and increased emphasis on management development. Simultaneously, Human Resource Management (HRM) is placed under increased pressure to solve problems associated with promotion and management succession, measurement of performance, and issues pertaining to the distribution of power between corporate headquarters and overseas subsidiaries.

Because of the increasing importance of human resource issues in the management process of multinational corporations, a longterm research project has been undertaken to examine the nature of the linkages between HRM

*Source:* Edwin Miller, Schon Beechler, Bhal Bhatt, and Raghu Nath. "The Relationship Between the Global Strategic Planning Process and the Human Resource Management Function." *Human Resource Planning*, 1986, 9(1), 9–23. Reprinted by permission.

and the global strategic planning processes of multinational corporations. The first phase of the project has been completed, and this article presents the results of that part of the study. The purpose of this article is to describe the nature of Human Resource Management's participation in the formulation and implementation of global strategic plans of leading American multinational corporations. It also provides information about the role of HR professionals in the planning process.

A review of the strategic planning literature indicates that MNCs have adopted a strategic planning perspective as a means for helping them make rational decisions in the face of rapidly changing and complex environments. As the management teams of these corporations begin to develop and implement their firms' global strategic plans, do they concern themselves with human resource issues? Lorange reports that they do, and these issues appear in the context of discussion concerned with such topics as acquisitions or divestitures of overseas production facilities, entering or withdrawing from markets, proposed redesign of corporate structures to accommodate different cultures or nations, the means for controlling relationships between overseas subsidiaries and the parent, and the procedure for effectively managing the fundamental elements of the human resource system (Lorange and Vancil, 1977).

Bartlett's work on the evolving nature of multinational corporations supports Lorange's conclusion (Bartlett, 1983). He stresses the importance of human resource issues associated with the structural problems generated by multiple and often conflicting pressures emanating from most host country and global competitors. Bartlett writes:

> "Human resource issues become critical to the formulation and implementation of the MNC's strategic plan. It is management that must develop the perspective, viable organization structures and systems through which they can interact as well as develop an appropriate decision making apparatus" (Bartlett, 1983).

When does HRM fit into these strategic concerns of the MNCs? Is the function an active, contributing partner in the global strategic planning activities of MNCs? Or, is it viewed as contributing little of value to the strategic planning process? The strategic planning literature indicates that at least at the corporate level, human resource concerns are a collective top management responsibility rather than that of the HRM function (Hofer and Schendel, 1981). If this is so, just what is the nature of HRM's involvement? These are important questions because they deal with the future direction and contribution of HRM.

In the HRM literature, it has become fashionable to cast the human resource system into a strategic context. To add legitimacy to their conceptual frameworks, authors and scholars have provided examples of: (1) companies that have successfully linked their human resource management systems to strategic planning, (2) top human resource management executives who have been instrumental in tying the HRM function and its activities to their respec-

tive corporations' strategic plan, and (3) procedures for moving a human resource management function into the strategic arena (Tichy, Fombrun and
Devanna, 1984).

K.R. Andrews was one of the earliest advocates for linking business
strategy with human resource management (Andrews, 1957). Although he
used different terms, the essence of his argument stressed the value to be
achieved by integrating these organizational activities. After almost two decades, HRM scholars and authors have begun to express themselves about
the relevance of linking HR activities to the strategic planning process. A
plethora of articles and books have appeared, and they have concentrated on
strategic human resource management. For example, authors have written
about the relationship between staffing and product life cycles (Leontiades,
1982; Miller, 1984) performance appraisal and business strategy (Latham,
1984; Tung, 1984) management succession and stockholder wealth (Reinganum, 1973) and compensation structures and business strategy (Salter, 1973).

The HRM literature offers a picture of an important and relevant role
for the function as well as providing concrete examples of what it can be. However, Dyer has written that the interrelationship between HRM and strategic
planning represents an uncharted area (Dyer, 1984). Notwithstanding Dyer's
comments, a consensus is emerging among leading HRM scholars and professionals that the function is expanding far beyond the traditionally accepted
activities of staffing, training and development, rewards and appraisal.

A distinguishing characteristic of the developing HRM model is its strategic orientation. The HR professional and executive is a central element in
the emerging model, and it is noted that the HRM professional is confronted
by a twofold challenge: (1) to develop viable processes whereby HRM contributions can and do occur in the strategic planning process, and (2) to adopt
and promote strategic thinking within the human resource function itself.

What are the variables that differentiate strategic human resource management from previous definitions of the function? We believe that it is helpful to use Miles and Snow's strategic human resource management dimensions (Miles and Snow, 1984), and the following attributes appear to capture
the spirit of the developing model:

1. Top managers of the human resource function should possess at least
   a conceptual familiarity with all services needed to acquire, allocate
   and develop managers and employees.
2. The function should have a comprehensive understanding of the language and practices of strategic planning. Appropriate human resource representatives must continually participate in the planning
   process to assess the probable demand for their unit's services.
3. The human resource function should pursue appropriate strategies
   of its own to match the organization's business strategy.
4. The function must act as a professional consultant to the line. In addition to their expertise in strictly human resource matters, the human
   resource specialist should be knowledgeable about organization

E X H I B I T 1

## Human Resource Management Involvement in the Organizational Employee Staffing Process

| | |
|---|---|
| *Strategic Level* | Strategic Planning Relationship to Human Resource Management System |
| | "What kinds of people will be needed to lead the organization in the years to come?" |
| *Managerial Level* | Development of Activities to Satisfy Forecasted Organizational Human Resource Requirements |
| | "What programs and activities must be developed to satisfy forecasted human resource requirements?" |
| *Operational Level* | Implementation and Monitoring of Specific Human Resources Programs and Activities |
| | "What are the specific plans for this year's college recruiting? What colleges will be visited? How many college recruits must be interviewed? And what will be the college recruiting budget?" |

structure, management processes including communication and control, and organization change and development.

Given these benchmarks, how does one classify the nature of the decisions made by HRM as it goes about discharging its responsibilities? Anthony's classification of management decision making is a useful tool for classifying the nature of HRM participation in the strategic planning process (Anthony, 1964). According to his classification scheme, there are three levels of decision making: strategic, managerial, and operational. Anthony defined the levels in the following way: (1) Strategic level decisions are concerned with policy formulation and setting of overall goals, (2) Managerial level decisions are more pragmatic in orientation, and these decisions are associated with the development of programs to guarantee the availability of resources to carry out the strategic plan, and (3) Operational level decisions are concerned with the execution of day-to-day activities, and these decisions are the consequence of programs and issues developed at the managerial level.

Applying Anthony's framework to HRM's responsibility for staff, Exhibit 1 provides an example of the three levels of decision making.

### Conceptual Framework

Although there are many variables that could be considered as important determinants of HRM's contribution to the planning process, it is our opinion that three variables are central to a meaningful understanding. Based upon the strategic planning and the HRM research and literature, the following variables comprise the framework that was used in the study: Organizational Level of Strategy, Human Resource Management Functions, and Global Strategic Planning Process.

## Organizational Level of Strategy

The nature of a corporation's business strategy can be viewed in several different ways. In this study, however, strategy was limited to two organizational levels: corporate and strategic business unit. At the corporate level, strategy is concerned primarily with such issues as long-run organizational survival, domain differentiation, resource allocation and goal formulation. Strategy associated with the strategic business unit is concerned with competition in a particular industry or product market segment. Attention is centered on competencies and competitive advantage and major functional area policy decisions.

## Human Resource Management Functions

This variable is divided into the HRM activities of staffing, training and development, rewards and appraisal. In this context the Human Resource system is defined by the breadth and quality of services needed to acquire, allocate, develop and evaluate managerial personnel.

## Global Strategic Planning Process

This variable can be divided into four categories: strategy preplanning, strategy formulation, strategy implementation and strategy control and evaluation. For purposes of this research project, only strategy formulation and strategy implementation were used in the analysis. Much of the previous work on strategy has been limited to these two categories, and in the pilot phase of this study, it was found that respondents were familiar and comfortable discussing the formulation and implementation phases of strategy. The respondents found it difficult to describe their involvement in strategy preplanning and evaluation activities because they generally don't view the strategy cycle as being divided into four distinct categories.

The framework for classifying HRM involvement in the global strategic planning process is presented in Exhibit 2. As one can observe in this framework HR involvement in the strategic planning process can be divided into four different categories. First, HRM can be involved in the formulation of corporate level global strategic planning. Second, it can participate in the formulation of the SBU's global strategic plan. Third, HRM can be involved in the implementation of the MNC's corporate level global strategic plan. And fourth, HRM can participate in the implementation of the SBU's global strategy.

EXHIBIT 2

## Human Resource Management Functions

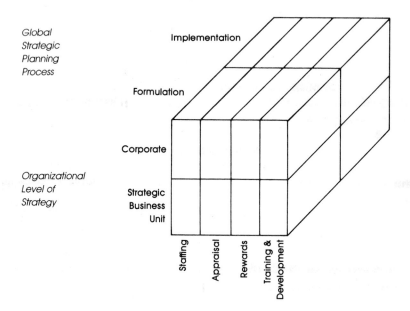

Human Resource Management Functions

## ■ Methodology

Since very little has been published about HRM linkages with MNC's global strategic planning processes, it was decided to gather data by means of the structured interview technique. The rationale for that decision flowed from the commonly acknowledged fact that structured interviews allow an investigator the freedom and flexibility to explore a wide range of topics as well as the opportunity to collect qualitative data on attitudes, values and opinions. At this stage of the research project, qualitative information was critical for successive phases of the investigation. It was imperative to obtain the subjects' cooperation, and from past experience it was known that more relevant information could be obtained by means of the interview method than by use of the questionnaires. Experience indicated that executives and staff specialists would be much more willing to spend time talking about their participation in the planning process than they would by filling out a survey instrument.

The managers and executives who participated in the study occupied positions in one of the following areas: the strategic planning function, the human resource management system, or as corporate or SBU senior-level line executive. Regardless of their official titles, each participant was involved in the overseas activities of his or her organization. As such, they were able to provide several different and relevant perspectives about the global strategic planning process and HRM involvement in it.

Five U.S. multinational corporations comprised the sample, and they represented several different types of manufacturing industries. The following criteria were used as the basis for choosing the MNC's: (1) the enterprise must have a significant overseas presence i.e., (the firm must have manufacturing, marketing or administrative facilities in at least six different countries), (2) The firm must have been engaged in international business for at least 20 years.

Net annual sales for the corporations ranged from approximately three billion to over twenty billion dollars, and foreign sales represented at least 20% of total sales for each corporation. These were large U.S. firms and their foreign sales represented a significant portion of these firms' total annual sales.

Twenty-two interviews were conducted during the data collection phase of the study. Twelve of the participants were involved in the global strategic planning process at the corporate level. The 10 remaining participants were involved in the global strategic planning process of those SBU's engaged in the production and sale of goods overseas. Consequently, interview data have been obtained on five MNC's global strategic planning processes at corporate and SBU levels.

Among the 12 participants at the corporate level, five were senior HR executives in their respective corporations, four were top-level line executives, and three were responsible for development of their corporations' global strategic plan. At the SBU level, the 10 participants were divided in the following manner: five were in charge of the SBUs' HR systems, four were general managers of the SBUs, and one was responsible for the development of business planning.

# ▄ Discussion

What was the nature of HRM involvement in the global strategic planning process? In each of the MNCs it was found that HRM was participating in the global planning process. However, the degree of participation did vary across the corporations, which was not surprising. What was interesting was where and how the HR system linked with the MNC's global strategic planning processes and the role the top HR executive played in bringing about those linkages. In this section, we will discuss some of the more interesting findings.

## *The Nature of Human Resource Management Involvement in the Global Strategic Planning Process at the Corporate Level*

Incorporation of a HRM perspective at the corporate level was informal and limited. In two of the MNCs, the senior line executives and strategic planners reported that it wasn't clear how HRM could contribute to the MNC's global strategy. In the words of one of these executives:

> "Human resource issues are considered when they are pertinent to the topic at hand, but we would never think of asking the HR people to participate in those strategic discussions. Although those guys are nice people, they are soft and they have little to contribute to the broader strategic issues of the corporation."

When there was HRM involvement in the strategic planning process, the CEO played an instrumental role in that relationship. Three of the top HR executives attributed their effectiveness to their personal relationship with the CEO. As one HR executive said:

> "I see or talk to the CEO on a daily basis, and we talk about personnel related matters. However, you must understand that he trusts me or else I wouldn't be in this job. We go back a long way together."

Involvement of HRM was fragile and subject to change given the nature of the personalities involved, and the function's effectiveness was influenced by the executive's ability to develop and maintain personal relationships with the CEO. The presence and participation of HRM at the corporate level required constant revalidation because each time there was a change of CEO or the senior HR executive, a period of testing and critical review occurred. The HR executive had to win acceptance on the basis of value added to strategy matters or else win acceptance on the basis of personal qualifications. However, it was not an either-or situation.

HRM involvement in the formulation and implementation of the MNCs global strategic planning process varied across organizations and the HR system's four basic activities of staffing, training and development, appraisal of performance, and compensation. It was the area of staffing which represented the major arena in which HR made its presence felt. Management development was another area in which there was a reasonably strong degree of HRM participation in the strategic planning process. Apparently discussions about executive compensation and performance appraisal were considered by these five MNCs to be the responsibility of top management itself, and there was little reason to include an HRM contribution.

Among several of the MNCs, HRM contributions to staffing had moved to the strategic decision-making level, and considerable time and effort were devoted to the process of choosing the very best executives for overseas positions. Many times these assignments were designed to meet three objectives: (1) to assign the very best person to the vacant post, (2) to gather evidence about the expatriate's capabilities to manage in a foreign environment, and (3) to provide the executive with an overseas experience prior to advancing to still higher and more responsible positions within the management hierarchy of the parent organization. The HRM executive was expected to help develop the criteria that an executive must possess in order to successfully perform on the overseas assignment. In two of the MNCs, the senior HR executives indicated that they participated in discussions about the selection of executives to head major geographic regions overseas. In both companies, the HR executive helped develop the slate of candidates and the HR executives offered their opinions about each candidate's qualifications to the CEO and other members of the management committee.

In several of the MNCs, the HRM function was responsible for administering the management succession and career development plans for high potential managerial personnel. These executives and managers were holding key positions within the management hierarchies of their respective firms, and they were judged to possess the potential to rise to senior management positions within the near future. The HR executives who participated in those discussions, reported their opinions were sought out with respect to the following subjects: (1) The managerial qualities required to successfully manage the MNC in the future, (2) The types of domestic as well as foreign assignments that would help the executives build the competencies that would be necessary to lead the corporation in the future, and (3) Which individuals should be considered for overseas assignments as part of their career progression. A particularly helpful insight into HR involvement was provided by the following comments of a senior HR executive:

> "I was requested to generate a slate of candidates for the position of president of the Southern Asia region. In my opinion, that geographic region no longer warranted a 'star' just because we had little market share and there were no plans to try and expand it. The job required nothing more than a figurehead, and all we needed to do was to show the flag. An executive close to retirement seemed to be the ideal type of person to assign to the job. I used the BCG framework as the basis for my argument to the management committee because I knew they were familiar with that terminology and approach. Much to my surprise they went along with my argument."

Given the nature of HR involvement in the global strategic planning process at the corporate level, it is somewhat artificial to try to force the function's involvement into formulation or implementation of strategy. It was more meaningful to state there was an HR presence at the corporate level, and the content of the HR decisions was, in Anthony's framework, essentially strategic and managerial in substance. Exhibit 3 summarizes the nature of HRM involvement in the global strategic planning process at the corporate level.

### The Nature of HR Involvement at the Strategic Business Unit Level

At the SBU level, HRM participation in the global strategy was well established, valued, and expected by management and planners alike. They reported that an HR perspective added value to the strategic planning process, and there was high regard for the professional competence of the HRM staff and, in particular, the senior HR manager. In general, the HR profes-

E X H I B I T  3

## HRM Involvement in Global Strategic Planning Process at the Corporate Level

| Decision | FORMULATION HUMAN RESOURCE MANAGEMENT ACTIVITIES | | | | IMPLEMENTATION HUMAN RESOURCE MANAGEMENT ACTIVITIES | | | |
|---|---|---|---|---|---|---|---|---|
| | Staffing | Development | Appraisal | Rewards | Staffing | Development | Appraisal | Rewards |
| Strategic | Participation in the development of qualifications necessary for success in an overseas position. | | | | | | | |
| Managerial | Participation in the development of management | Participation in the development of management | | | Administration of management succession program. | Administration of management development program. | | |

| | |
|---|---|
| | |
| | |
| Integration of management development and management succession programs. | Determination of other type of development assignments for executives and high potential managerial personnel. |
| | Development of state of candidates for overseas. Participation in the selection and assignment of executives to overseas assignments. |
| | |
| | |
| development programs. | |
| succession program. | |
| *Operational* | |

sionals were considered to be sensitive to the environmental pressures on the SBU, they understood the dynamics of the business and they brought a long-term orientation to the strategic problems facing the business. In the words of one senior SBU HR manager:

> "Management and the business planners trust me, and they look for ways to take advantage of my expertise. On technical matters, management will routinely ask me if I see any HR issues. Let me give you an example, as part of our global strategy we began thinking about going into Mexico and opening up a manufacturing facility. As part of the feasibility study, I was asked to provide an HR input. I raised questions and provided information about the reactions of our union if we outsourced part of production, I provided information about the skill level of the potential workforce, its commitment to work and its stance relative to outside management."

Among this sample of companies, HRM was deeply involved in the strategic planning process, and its participation crossed all four HRM functional activities. Perhaps one of the most dramatic statements pertaining to HRM involvement in the planning process was made by one of the HR managers in the following way:

> "I have an excellent staff, and it handles the day-to-day HR routine much better than I can. As for me, I'm concerned about the 21st century for this company."

Management succession and career development again represent two of the main ways in which HRM was involved in the formulation of the SBU's global strategic planning process. In two of the SBU's, the HR executives reported that a key element for tying HRM to the SBU strategic plan occurred by means of the management succession plan, and it was important for the function to play an important role in that relationship. As an example of that, HR executives indicated that they were participants in discussions about the SBU's strategy for a particular market or product and the human resource requirements needed to implement that strategy. Several of the HR officials reported they devoted a large amount of their time to locating managerial and technical professional personnel who could fill vacancies that opened up as a result of the strategic discussions about the future of the SBU's international involvement.

Relatively speaking, HRM was much more involved in the implementation rather than the formulation of the SBU's global strategic plan. One HR executive made a statement that seemed to be a common thread through many of the discussions, "I'm a doer. Give me a direction, and I'm off and running." Examples of such behavior were most evident in the area of staffing. HRM was responsible for the development and administration of programs associated with internal movement and development of managerial and professional technical personnel. In contrast, the performance appraisal and reward programs required HRM to do nothing more than administer them, and it was limited to monitoring the decisions of overseas management to determine if they were in compliance with the corporation's guidelines and stated policies and procedures. In several of the firms, the reward system had been designed by an outside consulting group, and the HRM function did little more than oversee a compensation program that had been developed by a group external to the MNC.

Classifying HRM decisions according to Anthony's classification scheme, the majority of its decision making occurred at the operational level. The HR function was responsible for preparing managerial, professional and technical personnel for impending overseas assignments. For instance, arrangements were made for language training, presentation of indoctrination programs for the soon-to-be expatriates, preparations for moving household goods overseas, making travel arrangements prior to departure from the U.S. and responding as best it could to the personal requirements of the person about to be sent abroad. While the expatriate was away from the United States, the function was in touch with the overseas employee, and it responded to personal requests ranging from seeking college application forms for college-age dependent children, to gathering information about legal issues that sometimes arise between the expatriate and the state and federal government, and finally, locating hard-to-find food and personal products. Prior to repatriation, the function prepared the expatriate and family members for their return to the U.S. This included: (1) locating an assignment within the SBU that would be similar in authority and responsibility to the expatriate's present position, and (2) helping with preparations to move the family back to the U.S. Exhibit 4 summarizes HRM involvement in the global strategic planning process at the strategic business unit level.

## Conclusion

This article has reported the results of the first phase of a long-term research project designed to examine the interrelationship between HRM and the global strategic planning processes of large multinational firms. It is our opinion that this study has helped to bridge part of the knowledge gap that has existed with respect to the linkages between HRM and the planning processes of MNCs. When considering the findings of this study, one of the most striking results is the potentially influential role that senior HR executives can play in the strategic planning process. That is, among those firms in which there was a high level of HRM involvement in the planning process, the HRM executives were viewed as the functional leaders, and they were judged by senior management as having something of value to contribute to the strategic planning discussions. The professional competence and personal characteristics of the senior HR executive were critical determinants for MNC management willingness to include HRM contributions to the planning process. This finding held true at the corporate as well as the strategic business unit levels.

Professional competence was a necessary but not sufficient condition for

EXHIBIT 4

## HRM Involvement in Global Strategic Planning Process at the Strategic Business Unit Level

**DECISION**

FORMULATION
HUMAN RESOURCE MANAGEMENT ACTIVITIES

| | Staffing | Development | Appraisal | Rewards |
|---|---|---|---|---|
| *Strategic* | Participation in discussion of qualification necessary for success in an overseas position. | | | |
| *Managerial* | | | | |
| *Operational* | | | | |

**DECISION**

IMPLEMENTATION
HUMAN RESOURCE MANAGEMENT ACTIVITIES

| | Staffing | Development | Appraisal | Rewards |
|---|---|---|---|---|
| *Strategic* | | | | |
| *Managerial* | Administration of management succession program. | Administration of management development program. | Administration of performance program. | Administration of reward program. |
| *Operational* | Identification of potential candidates for overseas assignments. Preparation of personnel for overseas assignment and repatriation to the U. S. | Individual specific development assignments | Monitor performance appraisals | Monitor individual compensation decisions |

inclusion in strategy decisions. In those companies where there were effective HRM inputs, the senior HR executive was described in the following terms: professionally competent, value added, personal confidante, trustworthy and insightful. However, there was not a direct correlation between the power and prestige of the senior HR executives and the involvement of the function, and in some cases the HR executive was involved in the strategic planning process while similar status was not enjoyed by the HRM function.

It is our conclusion that if the senior HR executive and ultimately the function is to be included in the global strategic planning process, several conditions must be met. First, the senior HR executive, as the key legitimate function leader, must be included in the strategic planning process, and legitimacy is the result of professional competence. Although there may be times when HRM contributions to the planning process will be limited, there will be other times when the function's contributions will be critical and participation active. Without inclusion, HRM contributions to the strategic planning process will be minimal and of little consequence.

Second, the senior HR executive must be competent and sensitive to the problems, needs and circumstances confronting the organization. Members of management and strategic planners alike must recognize the value added by the contributions made by the function and its senior executive. As a corollary, HRM must conscientiously strive to understand the language and practice of strategic planning, the nature of the business and a demonstrated sensitivity to the demands and circumstances impacting the manager and his or her job. It is our opinion that such an awareness is just beginning to occur, and the results of this study support such a conclusion.

As firms become more deeply involved in international business, there will be more opportunities for strategic HRM to become active and full participants in the global strategic planning process. The function must seek ways to exploit these opportunities to contribute to the planning process, and the HR professionals must prepare themselves professionally to contribute. The perspective and competence of the HR professionals will be critical for their inclusion in the strategic planning process, and the senior HR executive must provide an important example to management and to lower level HR professionals of how the interface can occur. In this regard the HR executive must be an excellent teacher, and teaching must occur by deeds not words alone. It is our opinion that more HR professionals are becoming aware of the need to prepare themselves and to develop a perspective that will be helpful for building viable and important relationships between HRM and the global strategic planning processes of MNCs.

Third, integrity and the quality of the interpersonal skills possessed by the senior HR executive are critical contextual determinants of his or her participation in the planning process. Several of the HR executives reported that being viewed as trustworthy and the confidante of the CEO were two of the most important elements contributing to the degree of influence they exerted on the MNC's global strategic planning process. However, they were quick to add that without demonstrated professional competence, being trustworthy or a good sounding board to the CEO or other members of management meant very little in terms of the likelihood of being included in the strategic planning process.

If human resource management is to begin moving out of a role of just responding to the global strategic plan, if it is to participate in the strategic arena of the multinational corporation, senior HR executives must begin to recognize and understand at least conceptually the nature of the services needed to acquire, allocate, develop, reward and evaluate managerial personnel. The HR executive must understand how the HRM function relates to other functional activities of the enterprise as well as its contribution and importance for managerial and organizational effectiveness. Finally, the executive must be sensitive to his or her personal image including integrity and interpersonal and communication skills.

It is our conclusion that if senior corporate level HR executives wish to improve upon the degree of participation in the global strategic planning process there are steps that can be taken. Several of these are as follows:

1. Design a Human Resource Management system that meets the needs of management. In part, be concerned with providing the types of services and support that enable management to do its job more efficiently and effectively. Furthermore, strive to guarantee that management consider human resource issues as they plan and implement the global strategic plan.

2. Develop a personal strategy for building a meaningful relationship with his or her CEO. It is our opinion that the strategy must be proactive in its orientation and perspective, and the executive must be committed to it.

3. Assess one's listening and communication skills. These skills are important components for building and maintaining a strong, personal relationship with the CEO. Carl Rogers' work on effective communication and the means for developing nondirective counselling skills should be helpful in this regard (Rogers and Farson, 1976).

4. Carve out an active, helping and consulting role with top management. The HR executive should be viewed as an individual of high integrity, one who will be available to listen and talk, and one who provides nonjudgmental but sound advice.

5. Interpret the organizational political signs accurately. Although the HR professional may be politically literate, it should not be construed to mean the successful HR executive is a master politician who relies solely upon political influence to achieve an HR presence in the global strategic planning process.

At the SBU level, HR managers can increase their involvement in the global strategic planning process too. Our recommendations are similar to those that we offer to corporate level HR executives interested in improving relationships with their respective CEOs. For example, SBU level HR managers can develop supportive communication skills, acquire an understanding of the organizational, political and cultural environment, demonstrate professional competence, establish links between HRM and SBU global strategic planning processes. These skills and activities are essentially short-term in their perspective. However, there are activities that will have long-term consequences that should be undertaken too. One such activity is the need to develop strong and meaningful relationships with SBU line management. These managers are the future leaders of their respective MNCs and it is important for the HR manager to establish the relevance of the function's contribution in the eyes of these managerial personnel. The findings of this study indicate that several of the corporate level HR executives indicated their influence could be traced to the strong and trusting relationships they had developed with current top level management while they both served at the SBU level.

Given the findings and our interpretation of them, the second phase of the research project will be developed, with several different dimensions to be explored. For example, one aspect of the new project will be the revalidation of the current findings in a wider sample of MNCs. More firms will be involved in the study, and there will be in-depth investigations occurring in several of those firms. Another dimension of the research project will be to study firms that have successfully integrated HRM into the global strategic planning process in contrast to those companies that have not been as successful in the integration process.

The senior HR executive was a central person in the process of linking HRM and the global strategic planning process of MNCs. As a third facet of the new research project, we are especially interested in studying the senior HR executive role and its occupant closely. Is there something that can be learned from an in-depth study of HR executives who have been successful in bringing about an effective, formal HRM presence in the global strategic planning process? We believe there is.

It is our opinion that we have much to learn about HRM participation in the management process of firms' international business activities. Just what is the scope of HRM involvement in the strategic planning process as well as its responsibilities for maintaining the HR system overseas? Is international HRM different from domestic HRM? This type of research should be of interest and value to the practitioner as well as the academic researcher concerned with the evolving nature of the field.

# References

Andrews, Kenneth R. "Is Management Training Effective?" *Harvard Business Review.* March–April 1957, 35.

Anthony, Robert. *Planning and Control Systems: A Framework for Analysis.* Division of

Research. Graduate School of Business Administration, Harvard University, 1964.

Bartlett, Christopher. "How Multinational Organizations Evolve." *Journal of Business Strategy.* Summer 1983, 10–32.

Dyer, Lee. "Studying Human Resource Strategy: An Approach and an Agenda." *Industrial Relations,* Spring, 1985, 156–169.

Hofer, Charles and Schendel, Dan. *Strategy Formulation: Analytical Concepts.* St. Paul, Minn.: West, 1986.

Gary Latham. "The Appraisal System as a Strategic Control" in Fombrun et al. *Strategic Human Resource Management.* New York: John Wiley & Sons, 1984.

Leontiades, Milton. "Choosing the Right Manager to Fit the Strategy." *Journal of Business Strategy.* Fall 1982. 3, 58–69.

Lorange, Peter and Vancil, R. *Strategic Planning Systems.* Englewood Cliffs, N.J.: Prentice-Hall, 1977.

Miles, Raymond F., and Snow, Charles C. "Designing Strategic Human Resource Systems." *Organizational Dynamics,* Summer 1984, 36–52.

Miller, Edwin L. "Strategic Staffing," in Fombrun, Charles, Tichy, Noel and Devanna, Mary Anne (eds.). *Strategic Human Resource Management.* New York: John Wiley & Sons, 1984.

Reinganum, Marc R. "The Effect of Executive Succession on Stockholder Wealth." *Administrative Science Quarterly,* 30, 1985, 46–60.

Rogers, Carl and Farson, R. *Active Listening.* Chicago: Industrial Relations Center, 1976.

Salter, Malcom S. "Tailor Incentive Compensation Strategy." *Harvard Business Review,* March–April, 1973, 94–102.

Tichy, Noel, Fombrun, Charles and Devanna, Mary Anne. "The Organizational Context of Strategic Human Resource Management," in Fombrun, Charles, Tichy, Noel and Devanna, Mary Anne (eds.) *Strategic Human Resource Management.* New York: John Wiley & Sons, 1984.

Tung, Rosalie. "Strategic Management of Human Resources in the Multinational Enterprise." *Human Resource Management,* Summer 1984, 129–144.

# The Formation of an International Joint Venture: Davidson Instrument Panel

## RANDALL S. SCHULER
## SUSAN E. JACKSON
## PETER J. DOWLING
## DENICE E. WELCH

"Ok, so you're thinking about manufacturing and selling your company's wares abroad, but you're more than a little daunted by the risks. Why not join forces with a foreign partner? That way, you can split the start-up costs and divide up any losses, not to mention gaining quicker international credibility, smoother distribution, and a better flow of information. Then again, maybe you'd rather not share your potential profits—or the secrets of your company's success—with anyone. That's fine. But don't be surprised if, after trying to crack a foreign market on your own, you develop a new enthusiasm for joint ventures" (Hyatt, 1988, p. 145).

Even without having first attempted to crack a foreign market on your own, you may be ready for an international joint venture (IJV). Such is the case with many U.S. firms today, especially since the advent of Europe 1992 and the events in Eastern Europe. In fact, there may be little real choice for firms that desire to expand globally. According to Nicholas Azonian, vice-president of finance at Nypro, an $85 million plastic injection-molding and industrial components manufacturer in Clinton, Massachusetts, with a presence in six countries and four international joint venture factories in the United States: "Without these foreign ventures, we'd be very limited in terms of our knowledge, our technology, our people, and our markets. We'd be a smaller company in every sense of the word" (Hyatt, 1989, p.145).

*Source:* Randall S. Schuler, Susan E. Jackson, Peter J. Dowling, and Denice E. Welch. "The Formation of an International Joint Venture: Davidson Instrument Panel." Forthcoming in *Human Resource Planning*. Reprinted by permission.

Of course the benefits of IJVs are not limited to small companies. Sales of companies in which Corning Glass has a joint partnership are nearly 50 percent higher than the sales of its wholly owned businesses. Says Corning's CEO James Houghton of international opportunities and joint venture alliances:

> Alliances are the way to capture that window. By marrying one party's product to the other's distribution, or one party's manufacturing skill to the other's R&D, alliances are often quicker than expanding your business overseas—and cheaper than buying one (Stewart, 1990, p. 68).

With high failure rates and increasing competitiveness, launching an international joint venture offers little guarantee of success. Some of the most significant barriers to success involve people issues—issues relating to international human resource management. This article describes many of the issues associated with forming and managing IJVs and illustrates how one international joint venture is addressing many of them. Because this venture is in the early stages of formation, this article addresses only critical start-up barriers. This article addresses the international joint venture from the view of the U.S. partner, Davidson Instrument Panel.

## ■ *Davidson Instrument Panel*

Davidson Instrument Panel is one of 33 divisions of Textron, an $8 billion conglomerate headquartered in Providence, Rhode Island. Davidson Instrument Panel and its two sister divisions, Interior Trim and Exterior Trim, make up Davidson-Textron. All three divisions are component suppliers to the automotive OEMs (original equipment manufacturers). Davidson-Textron is the largest independent supplier of instrument panels for the U.S. automobile industry.

Originally begun as a maker of rubber products for drug sundries in Boston in the early 1850s, Davidson moved its operations to Dover, New Hampshire, in the 1950s. Its headquarters are now located in Portsmouth. A staff in Portsmouth of fewer than 50 oversees the operations of two manufacturing plants, one in Port Hope, Ontario, and the second in Farmington, New Hampshire. The 1,000-person operation in Point Hope is unionized, and the 900-person operation in Farmington is not.

The nature of the U.S. automobile industry has changed drastically during the past 20 years, and the effects have been felt by all of the Big Three auto makers. As the automobile industry has become globalized, success has turned on quality products that fit right and perform smoothly and reliably. But while quality has become a major concern to the auto industry so have cost and innovation. New products and new technology are vital to the success of the Big Three, but without cost reduction new products cannot be offered at competitive prices.

The characteristics of the auto industry are, of course, reflected in all companies supplying it. Davidson Instrument Panel is no exception. To succeed, they must adapt to the demands of the new environment. Doing so will bring rewards, such as market share and even more important perhaps, an extensive, cooperative relationship with the Big Three. Essentially gone are the days of the multiple bidding system, where winning meant delivering at the lowest cost, with no assurance that the next year will be the same. Today, the automobile companies use sole sourcing for many of their supply needs. Accompanying this is a greater sense of shared destiny and mutual cooperation:

> The component suppliers are having to change with the times. The multinational car manufacturers increasingly want to deal with multinational suppliers, giving them responsibility for the design and development of sub-assemblies in return for single supplier status (*Financial Times*, March 1, 1990, p. 8).

Thus, it is not unusual to have design engineers from suppliers doing full engineering design of the components they will supply to their customers.

An important aspect of the new cooperative, sole sourcing arrangement adopted by the Big Three automotive makers is the willingness to conceptualize and form longer-term relationships. For Davidson Instrument Panel, this has meant the opportunity to establish an international joint venture. In the summer of 1989, Davidson agreed to establish an IJV to supply instrumental panels to a Ford Motor Company plant in Belgium beginning in 1992. They chose as their partner for this venture a British firm named Marley.

What seems like a good opportunity is not a guaranteed success, of course. U.S. studies estimate that the failure rate of IJVs is between 50 and 70 percent (Harrigan, 1986; Levine and Byrne, 1986). Because this IJV is in its early stages, evaluations of success would be premature. Probabilities of success can be estimated by comparing the actions of Davidson Instrument Panel with the recommendations of others and with the mistakes made by others in their early stages. These comparisons might offer guidance to firms seeking to go global through such alliances.

## ▬ *International Joint Ventures*

Although there is no agreed-upon definition of an IJV, one definition is as follows:

> A separate legal organizational entity representing the partial holdings of two or more parent firms, in which the headquarters of at least one is located outside the country of operation of the joint venture. This entity is subject to the joint control of its parent firms, each of which is economically and legally independent of the other (Shenkar and Zeira, 1987a, p. 547).

The use of an international joint venture as a mode of international business operation is not a new phenomenon (Ohame, 1989a,b,c), but economic growth in the past decade of global competition, coupled with shifts in trade dominance and the emergence of new markets, has contributed to the recent increasing use of international joint ventures. According to Peter Drucker, IJVs are likely to grow in importance in the 1990s:

> You will see a good deal of joint ventures, of strategic alliances, of cross-holdings across borders. Not because of cost, but because of information. Economists don't accept it, but it is one of the oldest experiences, that you cannot maintain market standing in a developed market unless you are in it as a producer. As an exporter, you will be out sooner or later, because you have to be in the market to have the information (Drucker, 1989, p. 23).

### Reasons for Forming an IJV

Harrigan (1987a) argues that because a joint venture draws on the strengths of its owners, it should possess superior competitive abilities that allow its sponsors to enjoy synergies. If the venture's owners cannot cope with the demands of managing the joint venture successfully, Harrigan advises the owners would do better to use nonequity forms of cooperation, such as cross-marketing and/or cross-production, licensing, and research and development consortia. Some companies shun joint ventures, preferring 100 percent ownership to the drawbacks of loss of control and profits that can accompany shared ownership (Gomes-Casseres, 1989). However, there are many reasons why a firm, regardless of previous international experience, enters into an IJV arrangement. The most common reasons cited in the literature are:

- Host government insistence (Datta, 1988; Gomes-Casseres, 1989; Shenkar and Zeira, 1987b);
- To gain rapid market entry (Berlew, 1984; Morris and Hergert, 1987; Shenkar and Zeira, 1987b; Tichy, 1988);
- Increased economies of scale (Datta, 1988; Morris and Hergert,1987; Roehl and Truitt, 1987);
- To gain local knowledge (Datta, 1988; Lasserre, 1983; O'Reilly, 1988) and local market image (Gomes-Casseres, 1989);
- To obtain vital raw materials (Shenkar and Zeira, 1987b) or technology (Gomes-Casseres, 1989);
- To spread the risks (Morris and Hergert, 1987; Shenkar and Zeira, 1987b);
- To improve competitive advantage in the face of increasing global competition; and
- Because globalization of markets forces cost-effective and efficient responses (Datta, 1988; Harrigan, 1987a and 1987b; Shenkar and Zeira, 1987b).

For many firms, several reasons apply. Some of these outcomes may be unanticipated but later recognized and welcomed, as was the case at Nypro. Nypro entered into a joint venture with Mitsui to operate a factory in Atlanta that could serve as a U.S. source for videocassette parts to Enplas, a Japanese concern. Enplas taught Nypro some lessons in both cost-saving management skills and quality control, according to Gordon Lankton, Nypro president and CEO:

> "Why did you reject this shipment?" Lankton would ask. "The label on the box," they would answer, "was crooked." "We eventually learned," says Lankton. Now, Nypro's Atlanta plant is its most productive, with sales per employee averaging $2,000. By comparison, most of Nypro's other nine plants hover around $1,250 (Hyatt, 1988, p. 148).

For Davidson Instrument Panel, gaining local knowledge, spreading risks, improving competitive advantage, and becoming more global are important reasons for their IJV. In addition, it is important for them to extend their relationship with the Ford Motor Company as much as possible. Being a sole source supplier means working with the customer as much as possible.

### Failure in IJVs

IJV failure rates (50–70 percent) reflect the difficulty of establishing a successful IJV. Reasons for failure include:

- Partners cannot get along;
- Managers from disparate partners with the venture cannot later work together;
- Managers within the venture cannot work with the owners' managers;
- Partners simply renege on their promises;
- The markets disappear; and
- The technology involved does not prove to be as good as expected.

Failure rates are difficult to measure, however. Some of the difficulty in measuring success or failure rates is due to the fact that "joint ventures can be deemed successful in spite of poor financial performance, and conversely, they can be considered unsuccessful in spite of good financial performance" (Schaan, 1988, p. 5). The criteria for defining success or failure depend on the parent companies' expectations from and motives for establishing the joint venture. For example, financial performance may take second place to profits from fees for management or royalties for technology transfer.

### It's a Marriage

Many writers compare the IJV to a marriage (Tichy, 1988). The analogy seems to spring from the factors that are necessary for success and the problems inherent in the IJV due to its contractual nature. To help manage an IJV for success, it is important to understand the joint venture process, which includes these five parts:

- Finding an appropriate partner;
- The courting and prenuptial process;
- Arranging the marriage deal;
- The launching of the venture and the honeymoon period; and
- Building a successful ongoing relationship.

Observers (Gomes-Casseres, 1987; Harrigan, 1986; Lyles, 1987) suggest that effective use of joint ventures requires managers to develop special liaison skills to cope with the mixed loyalties and conflicting goals that characterize shared ownership and shared decision making. Joint venture managers also need to have and to instill team-building values and receptivity to outsiders' ideas.

Increasingly, it is recognized that good joint venture marriages are not created with a handshake and a stroke of the pen. Instead of rushing headlong into a flurry of strategic partnering, savvy managers are now moving slowly into long-term relationships with their cross-national counterparts. They are purposefully trying to avoid many of the mistakes created by the kneejerk venturing behaviors of the early 1980s. One way to help make an IJV work is to establish equal partnerships. According to James Houghton, of Corning Glass, "To work alliances must be true marriages, not dates. A fifty-fifty deal usually works best because it commits both parties to success" (Stewart, 1990, p. 66). In addition, according to Gordon Lankton of Nypro, "Just finding a knowledgeable partner for a joint venture isn't enough, though. You have to make sure that partner's long-term goals are in sync with your own" (Hyatt, 1988, p. 145).

## Critical Issues in Managing IJVs

There is consensus that the very nature of joint ventures contributes to their failure—they are a difficult and complex form of enterprise (see Shenkar and Zeira, 1987b, p. 30) and many companies initiate IJVs without fully recognizing and addressing the major issues they are likely to confront (Morris and Hergert, 1987). Success requires adept handling of three key issues. Below, we first describe each of these key issues. Then we discuss how Davidson is preparing to deal with them.

### Control

Who actually controls the operation can depend on who is responsible for the day-to-day management of the IJV. Ownership distribution may matter less than how operating control and participation in decision making actually is apportioned (Harrigan. 1986). For a parent with minority ownership, for example, having the right to appoint key personnel can be used as a control mechanism (Schaan, 1988). Control can be achieved by appointing managers who are loyal to the parent company and its organizational ethos. Of course, loyalty to the parent cannot be guaranteed. "The ability to appoint the joint venture general manager increases the chances that the parents' interests will be observed, but it is no guarantee that the joint venture general manager will always accommodate that parent's preferences" (Schaan, 1988. p. 14).

Top managers will be expected to make decisions that deal with the simultaneous demands of the parents and their employees in the enterprise. At times, such decisions will, by necessity, meet the demands of some parties better than those of other parties. If the partners do not foresee such decisions, they may fail to build in control mechanisms to protect their interests. Weak control can also result if parent company managers spend too little time on the IJV, responding to problems only on an ad hoc basis. Finally, control-related failures are likely to occur if control practices are not re-evaluated and modified in response to changing circumstances.

### Conflict

Business and cultural differences between IJV partners often create conflict. Working relationships must be established on trust. Because a joint venture is an inherently unstable relationship, it requires a delicate set of organizational and management processes to create trust and the ongoing capacity to collaborate. This means that the senior executives must be involved in designing management processes that provide effective ways to handle joint strategy formulation, create structural linkages, provide adequate day-to-day coordination and communication, and establish a win-win climate (Tichy, 1988).

Many of the misunderstandings and problems in IJVs are rooted in cultural differences (Datta, 1988). Differing approaches to managerial style are one area that can create problems. For example, one party may favor a participative managerial style, while the other believes in a more autocratic style of management. Another area that can be problematic is acceptance of risk-taking because one parent may be prepared to take more risks than the other. Such differences often make the process of decision making slow and frustrating. The resulting conflict can be dysfunctional, if not destructive. The big challenge here is how to work through top management disagreements and avoid deadlocks (Thomas, 1987).

### Goals

The partners in an IJV often have differing goals. This is especially likely to be true when an IJV is formed as a solution for reconciling incongruent national interests. For example, a parent may be obliged to share ownership with a host government despite their preference for complete ownership and control. In such a case, the two partners are likely to be concerned with different constituencies, and business strategies may differ as a result. For example, the local partner may evaluate strategic choices based upon how effective they are likely to be in the local market, while the MNC parent would favor strategies that maintain their image and reputation in the global market (Gomes-Casseres, 1989). Cultural differences may also impact strategy. For example, Americans are alleged to have a short-term focus compared to the Japanese (Webster, 1989).

Differing levels of commitment from the two parents are yet another source of difficulty (Datta, 1988). The commitment of each partner reflects the project's importance to the partner. When there is an imbalance, the more committed partner may be frustrated by the other partner's apparent lack of concern. On the other hand, the less committed partner may feel frustrated by demands and time pressure exerted by the more committed partner. The level of commitment by the parties to the IJV can be a contributing factor to either success or failure (Bere, 1987).

## ▄▄ *Davidson's Preparation for the Critical Issues*

The management at Davidson Instrument Panel has recognized the importance of these critical issues in their IJV. To begin, they were very careful in their selection of a partner. More than twenty-five years of licensing experience in Western Europe with four different licensees gave the company an opportunity to develop close relationships with at least four potential partners. From these they chose the one, Marley in England, with whom they had the most in common. This commonality includes:

- Both use a consensus style of management;
- Both are part of a larger organization that is relatively decentralized;
- Both have the desire to move to the Continent with a manufacturing presence;
- Both have similar views on how to grow the business;
- Both have similar philosophies on how to run a business and how to manage human resources;
- Both desire a fair and open relationship.

These several dimensions of commonality should help minimize difficulties that can arise due to differing goals and objectives.

Thus far the parents have already made several strategic decisions in their establishment of the IJV, including where to locate the new plant and who will be responsible for what functions. Davidson's preferences for how these decisions would be resolved were important influences on Davidson's selection of Marley as a partner. Being located in Europe, Marley gives Davidson knowledge of the market. But far more than this, it gives them functional fit and personal contacts. Whereas Marley understands the marketplace well, Davidson has expertise in manufacturing and administrative systems. Thus while Davidson supplies the technology and the systems, Marley supplies knowledge of the markets and the contacts needed to get the plant built.

## Locating the Facility

The decision about where to locate the plant was an important decision and a very early test of the compatibility of the two parents. Together, the parents gathered extensive information and visited many sites. Of value here was Davidson's position as a division of a large conglomerate that could provide tax and legal guidance. Textron has an office in Brussels that provided this service. During the initial site selection process, Davidson collected information related to possible locations from the consulates of the nations located in the United States. According to Joe Paul, Vice President of Administration at Davidson Instrument Panel, the consulates provided extensive information about business conditions, and they provided names and telephone numbers of employment agencies, training centers, union officers, and local business organizations. Davidson also acquired information from DeutscheBank, the international banker for Textron.

The decision was made to locate in Born, The Netherlands. This decision was made after eliminating France, West Germany, and Belgium. These four nations were all possibilities because of their proximity to the Ford plant in Genk, Belgium, and because all four governments offer cash grants to firms locating in the coal region these four nations share. With relatively high unemployment, the governments of the four nations offer incentives to firms regardless of parent company nationality. The particular site in The Netherlands was selected because it is within thirty minutes of the Ford plant, a location that will facilitate compliance with Ford's just-in-time requirement.

According to Jonathan T. Hopkins, Vice President of Worldwide Business Development at Davidson Instrument Panel, the location was also selected in part because labor unions in the area indicated a willingness to consider accepting job flexibility and a relatively small number of job classifications. These features are important to both parents because they operate using principles of employee involvement and egalitarianism. Both parents want these principles to be reflected in the management style of the new plant in Born. Davidson's experience in running a unionized plant in Canada proved valuable to foreseeing some of these labor-related international issues.

Another important consideration was the availability of job applicants. The area now has a 15 percent unemployment rate. In addition, two government controlled firms are expected to privatize and downsize, thus increasing the pool of applicants with work experience. These considerations were deemed more favorable in The Netherlands than in the other three nations by both parents.

## ■ Human Resource Management: Unfolding Issues

As the establishment of the IJV between Davidson Instrument Panel and Marley continues over the next twelve months, six human resource management issues are likely to unfold (Shenkar and Zeira, 1990). In light of the shared goals and objectives of the two partners, the extent to which these issues are likely to become problem areas may be minimal. Nevertheless, the substance of the issues needs to be explicitly addressed (Lorange, 1986).

### The Assignment of Managers

Since each partner may place differing priorities on the joint venture, it is possible for a partner to assign relatively weak management resources to the venture. To be successful, the assigned managerial resources should not only have relevant capabilities and be of adequate quality, but the overall blend of these human resources must have a cultural dimension. Recognizing the importance of key personnel appointments, the parents have agreed to collaborate in the selection of the general manager. They have already agreed on the search firm that will help them identify candidates, and they are now in the process of jointly deciding the final criteria to be used in the selection process. Although the selection criteria are not yet finalized, Davidson has expressed some desire to have a person with manufacturing experience in plastics who is from The Netherlands. Once this individual is selected (scheduled for early 1991), he or she will come to Davidson's headquarters in New Hampshire for several months. During this time, the individual will become familiar with Davidson's technology, manufacturing systems, and human resource management practices and philosophies.

Specific selection, performance appraisal, and compensation practices will be left to the discretion of the new general manager, but it is expected that this individual will adopt the Davidson-Marley philosophy of employee involvement, participation, job flexibility, egalitarianism, and teamwork. These are practices both parents adopted in their own operations to facilitate high quality. Davidson and Marley feel that local labor councils are flexible and open to these practices, but the task of actually negotiating specifics will be done by the IJV's management staff. At that point, control issues are likely to become very salient.

### Transferability of Human Resources

Are the parents willing to transfer critical human resources to the new business venture? Given the long time frame of most joint ventures, strategic human resources sometimes have to be transferred from the parents on a net basis during the initial phase. In this case, because of the skills of the two partners, Davidson Instrument Panel is supplying the human resources relevant to the manufacturing systems and the administrative systems. Marley is responsible for actually building the plant, but Davidson is designing the interior of the facility to fit their technology. In addition, Davidson has already had to assign three design engineers from its facility in Walled Lake, Michigan, to be expatriates in Europe. These engineers work with fourteen contract designers recruited in Europe to design the components that will be manufactured in the plant. Marley has located a sales manager in The

Netherlands and will supply the sales and marketing support to the company.

Davidson will also be supplying the new controller, who will install the administrative systems. Textron's accounting firm, which has offices in the United States and Europe, is also ready to provide assistance to the financial officer who will eventually be selected for the IJV. (Textron's accounting firm serves Davidson as well.) Davidson's accounting procedures will have to be adapted to the European environment, which will be done through the accounting office in Europe assisting the new financial officer. Over time, the remaining human resource management decisions will become the responsibility of the IJV as it begins to operate like an independent business organization.

### Manager's Time-Spending Patterns

The IJV has to carry out a set of operating duties simultaneously with its development of new strategies. This raises the issue of the appropriate emphasis to give operating and strategic tasks. Sufficient human resources must be allocated for both strategic development and operating tasks. This situation is similar to that of an independent business organization in that the IJV must be able to draw sufficient human resources from the operating mode to further develop its strategy. If the parent organizations place strong demands for short-term results on the IJV, this might leave it with insufficient resources to staff for strategic self-renewal. In this case, the need for strategic planning and new business development is somewhat lessened due to the expected availability of a major customer, namely, Ford Motor Company. In addition, Marley's marketing expertise and knowledge of the Continent will serve as a support mechanism that minimizes the time the new IJV needs to spend initially on longer-term issues. Over time, the balance between focusing on operations versus strategic planning will shift as the IJV becomes more independent and the short-term operating tasks become more manageable.

### Human Resource Competency

Deciding how to judge how well IJV managers carry out their assignments will be another major challenge. It has been claimed that several joint ventures have failed because they have been inappropriately staffed (Lorange, 1986). Myopic, biased parent organizations may make poor selection decisions, or they may be tempted to use the IJV to offload surplus incompetent managers. Performance evaluation is therefore important. The long-term relationship and shared objectives between Davidson and Marley suggest that inappropriate staffing decisions are unlikely in this case. Further, the early decision to limit reliance on expatriates to the controller and three design engineers is likely to minimize the likelihood of problems arising from offloading surplus managers.

## Management Loyalty Issues

Management of loyalty conflicts must be considered an integral part of the human resource management of IJVs. Assigned executives, the expatriates, are usually loyal to the IJV and are expected to stay with the IJV for a long period of time. If a conflict arises between parents and the IJV, they can be expected to side with the IJV. For Davidson and Marley, the assignments of the design engineers and the controller are primarily for startup purposes. Their loyalty may remain with Davidson because of the explicitly temporary nature of their assignments.

## Career and Benefits Planning

A recent survey of expatriates found that 56 percent felt their overseas assignments were either immaterial or detrimental to their careers (*Wall Street Journal,* 1989), a finding that indicates the potential motivational problems any IJV may encounter. The motivation of executives assigned to an IJV can be enhanced by the creation of a clear linkage between the assignment and one's future career. Some assurance of job security may be needed to offset the perceived risks. Assignment to a joint venture, as with any overseas assignment, may make the manager's future career appear uncertain. In fact, if the parent company has not thought through this issue, the apparent uncertainty may be quite justified. Thus, parent organizations should offer career planning to counter the ambiguity and riskiness associated with an IJV assignment and to limit the potential for unsatisfying repatriation experiences.

Apart from career path disturbance, the assignment to an IJV post usually requires relocation to a foreign country, with all the disruption to family and social life that such a posting entails. Benefits packages must be designed to maintain the economic and social lifestyle of the manager so that the individual does not lose through the IJV assignment. In the present case, the number of expatriate employees involved is small, so these issues have not been considered major. They will become more significant with the assignment of the controller. At that time, Davidson's own experience with R&D expatriates and the experience of Textron will be helpful.

Lorange (1986) has argued that the IJVs must have their own, strong, fully fledged human resource management function. The person in charge must establish ways to work closely with each parent, particularly in the early years. The two major roles of the IJV's HRM function are (a) assign and motivate people via job skills, compatibility of styles, and communication compatibility and (b) manage human resources strategically so that the IJV is seen as a vehicle to produce not only financial rewards, but also managerial capabilities that can be used later in other strategic settings. To the extent an IJV is staffed with temporary managerial assignees, transferring people to an IJV every two years would not be likely to result in strategic continuity of management.

In addition to the two major roles noted by Lorange (1986), the new IJV will have to establish its own set of human resource practices, policies, and procedures. It will then use these immediately to staff the new operation. We are looking forward to tracking this process with the new general manager, before and after production has begun.

## ▄▄ Summary

For an increasing number of U.S. firms, regardless of size and product, going global or international is no longer a choice. The world has become far too interconnected for many products and services to be offered within a domestic market context only. Faced with this reality, U.S. firms are seeking to establish their presence in the world market. Several large U.S. firms have already attained global presence. These companies entered the global arena early and are far wealthier than most U.S. firms. Their mode of entry into the global arena—through the direct establishment of their own subsidiaries—is an option that cannot be easily entertained today by most U.S. firms.

Consequently, many firms are considering entry into global markets via partnerships with firms outside the United States. Partnership receiving much attention now are the international joint ventures (IJVs). This form of partnership, which some say is the only feasible vehicle for U.S. firms trying to enter foreign markets, can carry substantial risk. This potential risk comes from several sources, many of which are related to the quality of the relationship between the two partners, and many of which are related to a series of international human resource decisions. While the relationship between the two partners is established at the outset of the partnership, the series of international human resource decisions unfold over the life of the partnership.

## ▄▄ References

Bere, J.F. "Global partnering: Making a good match." *Directors and Boards,* 1987, 11 (2), 16.

Berlew, F.K. "The joint venture—a way into foreign markets." *Harvard Business Review,* July–August 1984, 48–54.

Datta, D.K. "International joint ventures: A framework for analysis." *Journal of General Management,* 1989, 14 (2), 78–91.

Drucker, P.F. *The New Realities.* New York: Harper & Row, 1989.

Gomes-Casseres, B. "Joint venture instability: Is it a problem?" *Columbia Journal of World Business,* 1987, 22, (2), 97–102.

Gomes-Casseres, B. "Joint ventures in the face of global competition." *Sloan Management Review,* Spring 1989, 17–25.

Harrigan, K.R. *Managing for Joint Venture Success.* Boston, Mass.: Lexington Books, 1986.

Harrigan, K.R. "Managing Joint Ventures." *Management Review,* 1987a, 76 (2), 24–42.

Harrigan, K.R. 'Strategic alliances: Their new role in global competition." *Columbia Journal of World Business*, 1987b, 22 (2), 67–69.

Hyatt, J. "The partnership route." *INC.*, December 1988, 145–148.

Lasserre, P. "Strategic assessment of international partnership in Asian countries." *Asia Pacific Journal of Management*, September 1983, 72–78.

Levine, J. B. and Byrne, J.A. "Corporate odd couples." *Business Week*, July 21, 1986, 100–105.

Lorange, P. "Human resource management in multinational cooperative ventures." *Human Resource Management*, 1986, 25, 133–148.

Lyles, M.A. "Common mistakes of joint venture experienced firms." *Columbia Journal of World Business*, 1987, 22 (2), 79–85.

Morris, D. and Hergert, M. "Trends in international collaborative agreements." *Columbia Journal of World Business*, 1987, 22 (2), 15–21.

Ohmae, K. "The global logic of strategic alliance." *Harvard Business Review*, March–April 1989a, 143–154.

Ohmae, K. "Managing in a borderless world." *Harvard Business Review*, May–June 1989b, 152–161.

Ohmae, K. "Planting for a global harvest." *Harvard Business Review*, July–August 1989c, 136–145.

O'Reilly, A.J.F. "Establishing successful joint ventures in developing nations: A CEO's perspective." *Columbia Journal of World Business*, 1988, 23 (1), 65–71.

Roehl, T.W. and Truitt, J.F. "Stormy open marriages are better: Evidence from US, Japanese and French cooperative ventures in commerical aircraft." *Columbia Journal of World Business*, 1987, 22 (2), 87–95.

Schaan, J.L. "How to control a joint venture even as a minority partner." *Journal of General Management*, 1988, 14 (1), 4–16.

Shenkar, O. and Zeira, Y. "Human resources management in international joint ventures: Direction for research." *Academy of Management Review*, 1987a, 12 (3), 546–557.

Shenkar, O. and Zeira, Y. "International joint ventures: Implications for organization development." *Personnel Review*, 1987b, 16 (1), 30–37.

Shenkar, O. and Zeira, Y. "International joint ventures: A tough test for HR." *Personnel*, January 1990, 26–31.

Stewart, T.A. "How to manage in the new era." *Fortune*, January 15, 1990, 58–72.

Thomas, T. "Keeping the friction out of joint ventures." *Business Review Weekly*, January 23, 1987, 57–59.

Tichy, N.M. "Setting the global human resource management agenda for the 1990s." *Human Resource Management*, 1988, 27 (1), 1–18.

Webster, D.R. "International joint ventures with Pacific Rim partners." *Business Horizon* 1989, 32 (2), 65–71.

# Are Multinationals Better After the Yankees Go Home?

## STEPHEN J. KOBRIN

Twenty years ago, a visitor to an overseas subsidiary of an American firm was likely to find Americans in most significant managerial positions. A return to the same subsidiary today would find the situation radically changed. The visitor often has to look hard to find an American—and those who do pop up are often on short-term assignment.

There has been a dramatic replacement of Americans abroad by local or third-country nationals. There are many positive reasons for this shift, but one important reason is less appealing: American corporate experience with overseas assignments has been disastrous.

On the whole, replacement of expatriates with locals has been seen as positive—lowering costs, increasing managerial effectiveness, minimizing conflict with both employees and the local community, and contributing to managerial and technical development in the host country. It is viewed as a reflection of the maturation of American multinational corporations. The number of "non-American" employees is often taken as a measure of internationalization.

But much of the change is due to the fact that many Americans have not been able to handle working and living in other cultures. A high failure rate has meant enormous expenses in terms of direct costs, management time and, most important, human misery. In the end, U.S. multinationals have found it easier to replace Americans with locals than to make an effort to solve the underlying problem.

In an initial 1984 study of 126 large, U.S.-based international industrial companies and banks, I found that half had reduced their number of expatriate employees in the preceding 10 years. About 26% reported no change and 23% an increase. When asked about expected trends from 1984 to 1994, 41% projected a continued reduction, 40% no change and 18% an increase. Later studies have confirmed this trend and suggest that American firms have gone

Reprinted by permission of the author.

much further in reducing the number of expatriate employees than have their European or Japanese competitors.

As managerial and technical competence in many countries has increased, proficient managers have become more available. All things being equal, a local person who speaks the language, understands the culture and the political system, and is often a member of the local elite should be more effective than an alien.

The sharp reduction in expatriate assignments, however, has important implications for the global strategic management and competitiveness of U.S. multinational corporations.

First, a surfeit of local managers can make it difficult for corporations to meet their longer-term, world-wide objectives. Few locally hired managers in U.S. multinationals identify with the global organization. To a local in a subsidiary, the corporation as a whole is an abstraction; it is local performance that matters. At the top, managers in turn find it difficult to form and implement a global strategy. Having locals in charge increases the difficulties multinationals face in creating informal organizational links across subsidiaries. Although any diversified corporation serving a large geographic area faces challenges of this sort, the multinationals' problems are exacerbated by greater distances, time changes that make communication by telephone more difficult and, especially, cultural and linguistic differences.

Take the example of Europe's plan to complete an internal market by 1992. A Belgian manager of a U.S. firm in Brussels may have a better understanding of the 1992 opening than he does of the products his company sells outside of Belgium. Without a clear understanding of the latter, he may be ill-equipped to take full advantage of the former.

Another problem has arisen with a proliferation of local managers: Corporate control of local subsidiaries has become more difficult. Strategic control in a multinational often depends on control over personnel. But geographical and cultural differences, along with political and legal jurisdictions, may limit subsidiary responsiveness. Locals may feel caught between conflicting corporate and local interests; they may find themselves allied with local policy makers against corporate headquarters.

Nevertheless, this is not a problem without solutions. Working with local managers on their career planning, development and assignments can help put them more in tune with their company's international environment.

Another solution is the creation of a core of international employees that includes "third country" nationals. This simplifies problems of strategic control through personnel and facilitates the socialization needed to build a common organizational structure world-wide. Expatriates will not (and should not) automatically identify with their home country over their host country; rather, at their best, they should be able to assess local interests in the context of global strategy and identify with the world-wide organization. Occasional assignments at headquarters would help international staffers assimilate corporate culture and objectives.

In practice, it is doubtful whether American multinationals and the U.S. economy would be willing to tolerate the logical results of this internationalist strategy. To the extent that international expertise is a prerequisite for top managerial jobs, this policy would favor non-Americans. In reality, however, U.S. companies show a strong bias toward Americans. But since fewer Americans are doing stints overseas, American executives may simply be less qualified in the future.

This is not to recommend that the old model of a quasi-permanent core of long-term U.S. expatriates be resurrected. But it must be recognized that the core of expatriates served important functions and their departure leaves a vacuum that must be filled.

# Amtar Oil Company*

## LORNA L. WRIGHT
## HENRY W. LANE

### ▬ Management Meeting (1978)
### —The Issue Discussed

Monday morning management meetings (see Exhibit 1 for an organization chart) were a tradition at Amtar Oil in Soronga. The manpower situation was of constant concern. Complicating the matter was uncertainty over the government's policy of gradually replacing foreign nationals with trained local managers and technicians. Was Amtar on the right path, or should it be doing something differently? If it did something differently, what should the changes be? Opinion was divided on the issue.

At every meeting the debate raged over whether to hire expatriate or local staff. Joe Thomas, Production Manager, always pressed to hire more expatriates. Dipo Jil, a Sorongan who was Amtar's Administration Coordinator, advocated more local hires.

*Thomas:* We are going to need more drillers and engineers if we're planning to increase production. I know a couple of people who would fit the bill. They've just come off a job in Iran. Shall I get in touch with them?

*Jil:* What about looking locally?

*Thomas:* There's no one here qualified. You know that.

*Jil:* What about our own people? Can we move more of them up?

*Jamie Haliburton (Drilling Manager):* None of them are sufficiently trained.

*Thomas:* I was hired to produce 23 million barrels of oil this year, not train a

*Names of people, locations, agencies, and companies have been disguised.

Source: Lorna L. Wright and Henry W. Lane. "Amtar Oil Company." University of Western Ontario, 1985. Reprinted by permission.

bunch of trainees. If you want me to do more training, our production is going to drop.

*Haliburton:* Right, Joe. And if I take someone off the drilling site to send for training, I lose two day's time that we'll never make up.

*Jil:* But wait a minute. Our contract stipulates an obligation to train.

*Haliburton:* We're spending $1 million on training now. What more do they want?

*Ken Johnson (Accounting):* I must admit I agree with Dipo. We have a moral obligation to be a good corporate citizen and help facilitate the development of our national employees.

*Thomas:* The government isn't serious about that. That's just to keep the newspapers happy. They're not going to go through with it. Just wait and see. Then we'll have wasted time and money for nothing. We need more expatriates in here who know the job and can produce.

*Harry Leighton (Exploration Manager):* Besides, we can't get the training department to do anything but push paper anyway.

*Andy Petu (Finance Officer):* One thing you haven't considered yet is what it costs to keep an expat here. We pay about $10,000 a month for each one, which is about ten times what a local costs us. It would pay us to invest in training now.

*Harvey Clarke (Logistics Manager):* Wait a minute. If we step up training, it's going to be expensive. Does anyone know if these costs will be covered under the contract?

*Petu:* Hmm. I'll have to look into that.

*Jim Haines (Technical Manager):* Well, we've got to do something. I can't operate either safely or efficiently with half-trained, inexperienced people. If we don't do something about the way we're conducting training now, we'll either have to bring in more expatriates or hire better locals. Whatever, let's get off our butts and do something.

*Haliburton:* Hold on there. We've been doing pretty well so far. It's only been six years since we first struck oil and we're already pulling in $20–30 million a year after cost recovery. I don't see that we have to change much.

*Tom Jones (President, Amtar):* That's the problem. Can we continue as we have with our employees or are we going to have to make a concentrated effort to fulfill the plan to replace expatriates with national employees? I wish I knew how serious the government was.

## ▄ *Background*

In 1956, Jim Tarrant was chief geologist for the Gulf Coast division of PLESOP Corporation. He grew restless and, wanting more independence, established his own oil prospecting firm. From this chancy beginning, the company grew to be a multibillion dollar business by 1982.

Impatience with government intervention in the oil and gas industry in

EXHIBIT 1

*Amtar Soronga Organization Chart (1978)*

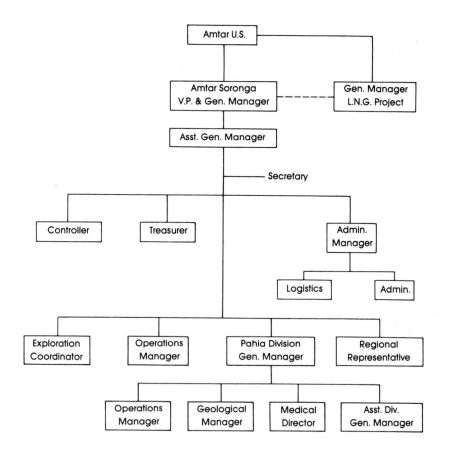

the United States prompted Jim to expand internationally to seek less regulated environments. He found what was to be his greatest success in Soronga. Amtar Soronga soon dwarfed the American parent.

The venture started in 1968 with a production contract with SOROLGA, the State oil company. Amtar bid for the drilling rights on land totalling 12,167 square kilometers. One property proved to be very rich. It was here that Amtar discovered Soronga's first major gas deposit and turned the company's main concentration from oil to gas.

Amtar's head office was in Kildona, the capital, but its main operating unit was on the island of Pahia. With over 2000 employees and $30 million in annual revenues, it would have qualified as a Fortune 500 company if it had been in the U.S. Headquarters in Oklahoma employed approximately 50 people and operated primarily as support for Amtar Soronga.

## ▬ Start-Up

Amtar was a young company which had grown very quickly. It had been hard pressed to hire the manpower needed to keep pace with this expansion.

In the start-up phase, the top priority was for people who could explore, drill, and produce oil as quickly as possible. People were hired for their technical expertise. Then, as the company grew, they had to assume more management responsibilities. Paramount concern, however, was always production.

The bulk of Amtar employees were involved in the operations on Pahia. Bachelor quarters were built at the field site. An hour's helicopter ride away in Tava, a small town which was the provincial capital, the company built a complex for workers' families. It housed 150 families and included a clinic, fire station, community center with a restaurant, snack bar, swimming pool, and tennis courts, and paved streets.

The main office in Tava included logistics, accounting, and telecommunication departments, as well as the operational sections of engineering, drilling, and exploration. The much smaller office in Kildona existed primarily as a liaison between operations and the Sorongan government. Amtar Kildona took care of work permits and communicating any operating problems to SOROLGA. They also made sure that any changes in regulations were sent immediately to the field. Personal relations were important in Sorongan business and a primary function of the Kildona office was to maintain good relations with SOROLGA.

The Kildona office also provided information to Amtar's partners who provided funds and participated in planning but not in the day-to-day operations. Prospecting was a high risk, high capital business. Amtar's current profits were the result of more than a decade of capital and technology investment. Since financing a foreign operation was extremely expensive, Amtar, a small company, found it difficult to do alone. (For example, in the past five years, exploration and production costs for Amtar Soronga had been more than $1.5 billion.) Amtar had solved this problem by forming a six company joint venture with the stipulation that Amtar was sole operator.

Prospecting consisted of drilling wells at promising sites in the hopes of striking oil or gas. It usually took seven to ten wells before oil was found. These exploration wells were called wildcats. After three and a half years of geological and seismic work, the wildcat that found the prolific field was drilled. It had proved to contain over six trillion cubic feet of recoverable gas and 132 million barrels of recoverable crude oil.

The field was in a remote jungle far from any market. Working conditions were difficult. Supplies and materials had to be airlifted in or floated upriver on barges until roads could be built. A pipeline had to be constructed to bring the oil and gas to the coast. A gas liquefaction plant had to be built. This involved not only massive amounts of capital but new technology.

Pahia was an easy area to drill in, which also made it potentially dangerous. Most disasters happened in easy areas because workers would get careless. Also, the shallower the well, the faster something could happen. The higher volatility of gas, compared with oil, also increased the danger.

Since there was no market for liquid natural gas (LNG) in Soronga, the gas had to be exported. An agreement was negotiated with the European Economic Community. Next, shipping contracts had to be developed. A new type of tanker was needed and had to be designed and built. Amtar was involved in all of this, plus much more. Liquefaction facilities, holding tanks, housing, recreational facilities, roads, etc. all had to be financed and constructed. The start-up phase was hectic and a large drain on both human and financial resources. Personnel often worked seven days a week.

There were 106 wells producing and six drilling rigs on site, and exploration continued along with production. Only a portion of the concession granted Amtar had been explored. Since Amtar would have to return some acreage on which it had not drilled to SOROLGA in 1980, the aim was to avoid giving back land with potential production.

## ▬ *Production Contracts*

A Sorongan law stated that all minerals were owned by the government and people of Soronga and, therefore, mining should be done wherever possible by Sorongans themselves. Where not possible, the work could be contracted. All oil companies worked as contractors for SOROLGA. SOROLGA took on the general management functions and the oil companies worked closely with FCCD (government coordinating agency) in SOROLGA, FCCD was the liaison between the foreign companies and the Sorongan government. It provided help in obtaining necessary permits, facilitated needed imports, and oversaw company expenditures.

These operating contracts generally were limited to a term of thirty years. Under this system, Amtar was responsible for all exploration. It provided the funding until discoveries were made. When oil or gas was found, the costs were then recoverable from the revenues generated. All exploration and operating costs were included. To be cost recoverable, however, expenditures had to conform to government rules and regulations, and had to be preapproved by FCCD.

For example, one government decree stipulated that at different levels of expenditure only certain types of vendors were approved. For purchases of under $50,000, the small, weaker local firms had priority. Only if they were unable to supply the item would the oil company be allowed to seek another vendor from a different class. Also, they could not break a $100,000 purchase down into two lots of $50,000 to use a company with a cheaper price. If these rules were not followed, the expenses would not be recoverable. Training expenses also were recoverable if the training program had been approved initially by SOROLGA.

Once oil was struck, SOROLGA and Amtar shared the production resulting from the exploration. For oil production the proportions were 80/20 respectively for SOROLGA and Amtar, but for gas, a newer business for Soronga, the split was 65/35.

## ▬ *Soronganization*

Soronga had gained independence from its colonial masters in 1958 and was trying to catch up with Western countries economically and technologically. To foster technology transfer, the government had embarked on a rapid process of replacing expatriates with national personnel. The Ministry of Labor issued a list of positions closed to expatriates and a schedule of when other positions would be closed, but this was negotiable on a company by company basis if there were extenuating circumstances.

A government decree in 1973 stated that oil companies with two years of commercial production should begin closing certain positions, starting with administration and personnel. This would be followed at the five year mark by closures of technical positions. (See Exhibit 2 for types of positions and length of time they could remain open.) The final step towards elimination of a position was relegating expatriates to the status of advisors. This could last for one year only. After that no expatriates would be allowed in those positions.

Since 1978, to facilitate orderly progress of turning over jobs to nationals in the oil industry, SOROLGA had been requiring all oil companies operating in partnership with it to submit five year plans of their organizational structure, job succession charts, and individual training. The organizational charts showed how the company planned to develop. The job succession charts showed who was holding the job at present and who was scheduled to take it over and when. The individual training charts showed the activities to prepare those scheduled to assume each position. Every employee had to be

EXHIBIT 2

## Restricted Jobs List of Foreign Employees in Mining, Soronga

| GROUP OF JOBS | JOB TITLE | CLOSED | OCCUPIABLE WITHIN A SPECIFIED PERIOD | OPEN FOR AN UNSPECIFIED PERIOD |
|---|---|---|---|---|
| 1 | 2 | 3 | 4 | 5 |
| BOARD OF DIRECTORS | 1. Member | | | X |
| | 2. Secretary | | | X |
| MANAGEMENT | 1. Executive Jobs: | | | |
| | a Representative | | | X |
| | b. President Director | | | X |
| | c. General Manager | | | X |
| | 2. Senior and Junior Staff Jobs: | | | |
| | a. within operational functions: | | | |
| | 1. Director, Manager and Superintendent | | 3 to 5 years | |
| | 2. Toolpusher | | 3 to 5 years | |
| | 3. Chemical Engineer | | 3 to 5 years | |
| | 4. Exploration Engineer | | 3 to 5 years | |
| | 5. Geologist | | 3 to 5 years | |
| | 6. Geophysicist | | 3 to 5 years | |
| | 7. And other Senior Staff jobs and such like | | 3 to 5 years | |
| | 8. Supervisor | | 3 to 5 years | |
| | 9. Driller | | 3 to 5 yers | |

10. And other such like Junior Staff Jobs — 3 to 5 years

b. in the services functions:

1. Director, Manager, Superintendent and Supervisor in: — 2 to 4 years
   - Mechanical Engineering — 2 to 4 years
   - Electrical Engineering — 2 to 4 years
   - Civil Engineering — 2 to 4 years
   - Logistics and Finance — 2 to 4 years

2. Director, Manager, Superintendent and Supervisor in:
   - Industrial Relations — X
   - Legal Affairs — X
   - Personnel Affairs — X

3. Auditor — 2 to 4 years
4. Treasurer — 2 to 4 years
5. Topographic Engineer — 2 to 4 years
6. Chief Cook — 2 to 4 years
7. And other such like Senior and Junior Staff Jobs. — 2 to 4 years

(Continued)

EXHIBIT 2
*(Continued)*

| GROUP OF JOBS | JOB TITLE | CLOSED | OCCUPIABLE WITHIN A SPECIFIED PERIOD | OPEN FOR AN UNSPECIFIED PERIOD |
|---|---|---|---|---|
| NON-STAFF | 1. Non-Staff jobs: | | | |
| | a. highly skilled/precision labor 1st, and 2nd class: | | | |
| | 1. Foreman | | 1 to 2 years | |
| | 2. Mechanic | | 1 to 2 years | |
| | 3. Machinist | | 1 to 2 years | |
| | 4. Draftsman | | 1 to 2 years | |
| | 5. Electrician | | 1 to 2 years | |
| | 6. Welder | | 1 to 2 years | |
| | 7. Machine and equipment operator | | 1 to 2 years | |
| | 8. Cook | | 1 to 2 years | |
| | 9. And other such like jobs | | 1 to 2 years | |
| | b. Skilled, semi-skilled and unskilled labor. | | | |
| | 1. Clerk | X | | |
| | 2. Typist | X | | |
| | 3. Telephone Operator | X | | |
| | 4. Plumber | X | | |
| | 5. Carpenter | X | | |
| | 6. Mess attendant | X | | |
| | 7. And other such jobs. | X | | |
| NON-INDUSTRIAL OCCUPATIONS | Advisor, Consultant, Teacher, Trainer and Instructor | | | X X X |

accounted for, which meant that the organizational charts often ran to eighty or ninety pages.

SOROLGA scrutinized these charts. If a company wanted to substitute another candidate for the one designated on the job succession chart, it had to justify the substitution. Lateral transfers of senior personnel were watched most carefully because SOROLGA was wary of companies trying to delay turning over positions to national employees.

Amtar, along with all other oil companies, prepared organizational charts, job succession charts, and individual training plans and presented them to SOROLGA every August. Discussions between SOROLGA and Amtar would follow in November. In December, there would be further discussion with MOM (Ministry of Oil and Mines). Final approval of an amended document might come the following February or March.

Each manager completed the charts for his or her own department. Because of the pressure of day-to-day operations, charts were usually ignored until the last minute and then there was a scramble to finish them on time. There was no overall corporate planning of chart preparation and the completed charts were not necessarily coordinated. Many managers had never thought about how to prepare a person to be Vice President of Exploration and Production, or to assume a position outside his department. There was little thought given to where someone would be six years from now. Managers resented the fact that each year it seemed they had to prepare the five year plan all over again. Not just an additional year to bring the plan up-to-date, but a complete, new plan.

Amtar felt it was unrealistic to be bound too tightly to the charts because many unexpected events could invalidate them. For example, a special project requiring expatriate expertise might be needed that hadn't been foreseen at the time the chart was made; someone might not respond as well to training as initially thought and, therefore, the employee's progress would not match that planned in the job succession chart; or it might become evident that someone needed broader experience in other departments before being promoted. These things were not always predictable.

## ▄▄ *Employment Passes*

Employment passes for expatriates were issued on an annual basis. Extensions had to be approved every year. This could be a long process, usually taking about four months. A request would go to FCCD for its initial approval. Then it would go to MOM, which sponsored all employment passes and on to the Ministry of Labor. It was there that the actual employment passes were issued.

The employment passes then followed this chain back down again before reaching the oil company. The process could hit a snag at any stage. Each employment pass had to be followed carefully and shepherded through. Sometimes, even though a particular position was still approved for an expatriate, the particular candidate selected to fill it was unacceptable to FCCD and hard negotiating followed.

Under a new Minister of Labor, the government was taking a harder stance on the utilization of national employees. The timetable was being accelerated and fewer exceptions were being allowed.

There were two views about the replacement of expatriates by nationals. One was that the government was going to require 100 percent of a company's positions to be taken by Sorongans. The other, more prevalent view, was that the government wanted an orderly transfer of most positions to Sorongans when they were *well-trained and qualified;* recognizing the fact that foreign companies would always require some expatriate personnel to look after their interests, since they were required to invest substantial amounts of money.

## ▬ *Staffing*

Amtar did not have any formal policies or procedures for recruiting either local or expatriate staff. Since the company had started up in a remote area, a large range of workers was needed. As well as drillers, geologists, and engineers, many support people were necessary, not just in logistics, accounting, and administration, but janitors, caterers, firemen, security guards, doctors, drivers, and maids. Amtar had built and supported a small town.

Gas technology was new to Soronga, and speed and efficiency were essential in the start-up phase, so most employees above the supervisory level were expatriates, experienced in the field. The expatriates were veterans from Vietnam as the war drew to a close, or hired from major oil companies such as Shell, Exxon, and Caltex. The latter usually brought their different policies and operating procedures with them.

Amtar was unable to offer its expatriate staff in Soronga long term job security. The head office in the U.S. was not large enough to absorb many employees and Amtar was uncertain how fast or how far the Sorongan government would go in requiring nationals to fill positions. Turnover of expatriates was therefore high.

Sorongan staff were needed quickly, so people were hired as available and qualifications were of minimal importance. Most of the workers were inexperienced and few had even finished high school. There were only three Sorongan engineers in the company.

The education system in Soronga had recently been expanded to encompass universal primary education and the resultant surge of students into the system stretched its capacity to the utmost. There was a shortage of trained teachers and classes were huge. The number of students entering university was limited by that system's capacity, so trained manpower was in short supply. There was keen competition among companies to obtain graduates to fill technical and management positions. An oil company competed not only with other oil companies, but with manufacturing, service, and mining companies.

People with experience were even scarcer than university graduates. Experience was important in the oil business, particularly in the technical areas, because each well site was unique. Principles learned in the classroom could never be applied exactly. Developing a feel for the situation was vital, and that only came with years of experience. Experience was even more critical on Pahia since it was a straightforward, easy operation. Many workers had no experience with technical problems. If something started to go wrong, they probably would not recognize the situation soon enough to prevent it, or to rectify it after the fact.

Experienced people working for other oil companies were coveted, but SOROLGA frowned on poaching. No one could be hired directly from another company. If someone was approached discretely and indicated an interest in changing jobs, he or she would first have to resign his or her present job and wait three months before applying for the new one. For special projects, Amtar often hired contractors for a specific term. At times there were as many people working on contract as there were actual Amtar employees.

In general, the working relationship between the Sorongans and the expatriates was good but there was tension. Comments such as "Just because we keep quiet, they think we are dumb," "We're not getting the best qualified expats," and "There are capable Sorongans passed over for a job just because their English is not so good" could be heard on the one side, and "We can't find qualified locals," "Sorongans don't have the drive to take responsibility," on the other side.

There were communication problems between the expatriates and the Sorongans because few expats spoke Sorongan and most of the Sorongan staff had limited English. There was also a communication problem between departments and between the head office in Kildona and the operating unit in Pahia. Lines of reporting and responsibility were not always clear.

## ▬ *Training*

Since it was extremely difficult to fire anyone in Soronga, the training department became a dumping ground for unwanted personnel. Few had any background in training. Training directors came and went in rapid succession. In one three year period, there had been more than six.

There was no training policy. Training was offered piecemeal and on an emergency basis to equip people with the skills they needed to do their current job. When an expatriate's work permit expired, a Sorongan was put into the position to "sink or swim." There was no training offered to prepare an employee to move up in the company. Amtar could not use the head office in Oklahoma or other operations for training as the major oil companies could, because the head office was so small and the company had no other operations of any significant size.

EXHIBIT 3

*Monthly Activity Report Training Department March 1978*

I.             In-House Training
- 1.      Language Programs
  - a.   English for Logistics (80 employees—ongoing)
  - b.   English for support personnel (20 employees)
  - c.   English for Secretaries (28 employees—ongoing)
  - d.   English for Production (30 participants—ongoing)
  - e.   English for Logistics Warehouse (31 employees—ongoing)
  - f.   English for Fire and Safety (22 employees—ongoing)
  - g.   Word Processor Training (4 employees—1 month program)
- 2.      Technical Training
  - a.   Solar Generator Set Phase II (18 employees—7 hours)
  - b.   Electrical Safety (5 employees—ongoing program)
  - c.   First Aid (18 employees—15 hour program)
  - d.   Welding Up-grading (7 employees—52 hours)
  - e.   Basic Electronic (2 employees—3 hours a week)
  - f.   Architectural Design (2 employees—ongoing)
  - g.   Structural Design (1 employee—ongoing)
  - h.   Motor Control (9 employees—ongoing)
  - i.   Earthworks (6 employees—ongoing)
  - j.   Electrical Safety (8 employees—ongoing)

II.           Vendor In-House
- a.   Inventory Control (SEA Management at Wapatin and Tava)
- b.   Typing (BKAS Business Services for 15 employees—3 weeks)
- c.   Secretarial Course (BKAS Business Services for 43 employees)

III.         Vendor
- a.   Training Offices Course (SOROLGA—1 employee—3 weeks)
- b.   Construction Seminar (Hako Construction Co., Kildona—2 employees—4 days)
- c.   Water Treatment Course (Soronga Utilities, Letoro—1 employee—1 month)
- d.   Problem Solving & Decision Making Certification (Kepner—Tregoe, Singapore—1 employee—3 weeks)
- e.   Vibration Surveillance Course (Solar Turbine, Singapore—1 employee—5 days)
- f.   Design of Engineering Components, Structure and System for Corrosion Prevention and Control (SISIR, Singapore—1 employee—5 days)
- g.   Stratigraphic Control for Hydrocarbon Accumulation Course (OGCI, Singapore—1 employee—5 days)
- h.   Gas and Production Technology Courses (SORGAS, Kildona—1 employee—2 months)
- i.   Electronic, Instrumentation and Gas Technology Courses (SORGAS, Kildona—2 employees—7 months)
- j.   Customs and Excises (Sorongan Management Institute, Kildona—1 employee—3 weeks)
- k.   Capital Asset Identification (SOROLGA, Kildona—2 employees—3 days)

The attitude to training was ambivalent. On the one hand, it was required to support the development of nationals, but on the other, time spent training was time taken away from production. There was great concern with operations and production. "Every barrel we lose through delay or machine breakdown is lost forever to us. Someone else will get it after our thirty years are up." The operating departments (exploration, drilling, and production) felt the training department did not understand its needs.

Training was provided at the request of individual managers. Once a certain type of training was requested, the training department would locate suitable courses. Sometimes a particular course was not available when needed. Or, it was inconvenient to release the designated person when the course was available.

Training courses varied widely in content. They included English for secretaries and drilling rig workers, Customs and Excises, mud technology, inventory control, and problem solving and decision making. (See Exhibit 3 for examples of the types of training given.) The training was conducted by in-house staff and by outside vendors, both in Soronga and abroad. It included on-the-job as well as formal classroom instructions.

Approximately $500,000–$1 million was allotted to training, but there were no guidelines as to content or the targeted participants. There were 2200 Sorongan employees in the company. A one week seminar would cost $1000, so even providing one week of training per year for 500 people would exhaust most of the budget with no great benefit for anyone.

Few records were kept of each individual's training. With the turnover in expatriate staff, it was not unknown for an individual to be sent on the same course twice.

A person could have taken forty training courses but they might not be related to the job, nor would they support a career plan. Courses could be an excuse for a holiday, or a reward for good behavior; only occasionally would they help the person do the job better.

Often the person might not have the qualifications necessary to take the training, or the training was given for the sake of training. For example, English classes were given for their own sake. Students were not grouped according to ability, nor was any thought given to whether the particular person actually needed English to do the job.

## ■ The Situation in 1982

The human resource situation and issues remained relatively unchanged to 1982 when George MacMillan, General Manager of the Pahia operation, became President of Amtar Soronga. George had been trying to convince others in the organization of the need to take the initiative on training and developing the national employees.

Amtar was at the point where it had to realize it was no longer a "cowboy outfit," but a large corporation that would have to plan its long range future. It would have to give systematic attention to its human resources. This realization stemmed from its maturing as a company and from government pressure. Expatriates were being hired with management experience rather than just operational experience. There also was continuing pressure to turn many positions over to Sorongans as fast as possible.

George remembered a recent meeting with FCCD, the Foreign Contractor Coordination Department of SOROLGA. Jipa Limbo, Amtar's Personnel Director, had faced Sar Pinto, the Director of FCCD. Pinto had held up two resumes; one of an expatriate for whom Amtar was requesting an employment pass extension, and one of a Sorongan.

"You're requesting an extension of employment pass for this man. Can you tell me any reason why the Sorongan isn't qualified to do the job? Look at them!" He pointed to the resumes. The American had four training courses listed. The Sorongan's list of courses covered three pages.

"How can you tell me that this man is less qualified than the American? You've been training him to take over the job. According to the job succession chart *you* prepared, he is scheduled to take it over now."

I'm getting tired of Amtar never sticking to the organizational charts and job succession plans they prepare. Always you come back with excuses and more requests for employment pass extensions. I'm sorry. I can't accept this any longer. You're going to be losing more employment passes from now on. We're serious about using national personnel and it's time you realized it."

It was clear to George that it was time to do some systematic, long-range thinking. He reached for the memo pad to jot down a request for all his managers to put together their ideas on the best way to prepare Amtar for the future ahead of it. He wanted ideas for a development plan for the company: what it might cost, the scope, the time frame, and how it fit with the government's plans.

# Nissan Italia, S.P.A

## AYAKO ASAKURA
## SUSAN SCHNEIDER

One afternoon in late November, 1988, Mr. Sasaki, Director of Europe Group of Nissan Motor Co., was busy signing Christmas and New Years cards in his office at the headquarters in Tokyo. He felt the pile of cards were much higher than in the previous year. "This should be because of our recent development in Europe. Now we have Nissan Motor Iberia in Barcelona and Nissan Italy in Rome. And a factory in the U.K. has just started operation. It looks as if these two years have flown away, keeping us very busy with working for those projects."

Speaking to himself with a satisfied smile, Mr. Sasaki started to look back at Nissan's European operations. Though satisfied, he worries about the future development of, and some fundamental problems in Italy, wondering what lessons could be learned for other overseas operations and what were the implications for future globalization.

### ■ The Company

Nissan Motor Co., Ltd. was established in 1933. The company has always been strongly overseas oriented and set up its first plant outside Japan in Mexico as early as 1966. Even today it is the only Japanese automobile company that has its own manufacturing base in Europe.

This is not only because the company always has been second to Toyota in the domestic market. They recognized the necessity to be close to the market in order to better satisfy customer needs, to get integrated in and to contribute to the local economy. Therefore, Nissan is aiming at a whole process localization—to be an "insider" through all operations from R&D to sales.

Nissan has dramatically increased its presence in Europe these last few years. Several international economic and market environments have pro-

*Source:* This case was prepared by Ayako Asakura and Susan Schneider as a basis for class discussion rather than to illustrate either effective or ineffective handling of an administrative situation. (c) 1989 INSEAD. The case was adapted by Mark Mendenhall for this book in 1990 by permission from INSEAD. Reprinted by permission.

moted this trend: yen appreciation, trade friction, increasing competition, and European common market integration. Reacting to those changes, Nissan has clearly positioned its strategy for internationalization and further globalization. The company intends to go beyond export and partly overseas manufacturing, to exploit cost advantage, to establish various activities abroad and to integrate them horizontally.

## ■ Corporate Culture

Nissan does not have a strong corporate culture. Since it was established through mergers of some companies during the 1910s to the 1930s, Nissan has no clear founder. This is an obvious difference from the other Japanese overseas-oriented companies like Sony, Honda, or Matsushita, whose corporate cultures are directed or affected by the strong characteristics of the founders.

This gives freedom to the organization. People are not bound by a certain philosophy, policy, or image of the founder and hence the company. That the top management positions are totally open to all the employees helps create motivation.

On the other hand, absence of a strong philosophy or visible embodiment of the founder makes it difficult to unite the whole company, to provide a clear sense of direction, and to keep moving forward. This also causes weakness in the company's external image. Nissan has enjoyed a good reputation for its high technology, but it is declining, and other competitors are catching up. Apart from this, Nissan lacks a special image in the Japanese market.

Having recognized this point, in January, 1987, Nissan, for the first time, stated a clearly written "Corporate Philosophy." On the first page of the 1987 annual report, it says, "Nissan—growing and changing to meet the needs of today's customers." The company printed this on business cards and distributed them to every employee.

This statement is translated into the languages of each country where Nissan has plants, offices, or subsidiaries (Exhibit 1). The translation is not a literal one. It is aimed to express the core policy and objectives and rewritten so that the idea would be best implemented in each situation and cultural environment.

## ■ Policy Toward Overseas Operations

Nissan's policy toward overseas operations is not rigid. Taking many different situations into consideration, the company has a "clear end and loose means" policy. There is no standardized way. As far as it is in line with the realization of Nissan's objectives, it allows a certain amount of autonomy to each plant or subsidiary and lets each seek the best way, depending on

EXHIBIT 1

*Profile of Nissan*

the situation. For example, while the Mexico plant is run in a typical Japanese style, the American one in Smyrna, Tennessee, is run in an American way with American top management. The British plant in Sunderland is run in a half-British, half-Japanese style.

This variety depends on many factors such as the location, form (greenfield investment or joint venture), history, technological level, product, human resource availability, target market, and so on.

With its long history of overseas business and operations, the company points out two issues as keys to success. One is to be an insider in the markets wherever they are present. Another is to promote globalization of the headquarters in Japan. In order to understand the development and the situation of overseas operations of Nissan, there is a good example in Europe: Nissan Italia.

## Nissan Italia, S.P.A.

Nissan Italia is a distribution and after service (repair and part sales) company. Sixty-four percent of the share is owned by Nissan Motor Co. and the rest by Nissan Motor Iberia.

### History

The company, named EBRO, was founded as a joint venture of an Italian company and Motor Iberia in February, 1978, for the commercial vehicle sales and after services.

In January 1988 Nissan Motor Co., purchased 49 percent of local share (the rest was owned by Nissan Motor Iberia) and changed its name to Nissan Italia S.P.A., and in March increased its share to 64 percent. Therefore Nissan Motor is now fully in control of Nissan Italia. The mission given to Nissan Italia in the Nissan group is to cover a very protective Italian market from the sales and service side.

It is not, however, their first footing into the Italian market. Already in 1980 Nissan started a joint venture with Alfa Romeo. But it turned out to be very difficult to control the company because Nissan had only 50 percent of the shares and the personnel decisions were made by Italian managers and the company in Italy. Therefore Nissan could not take the initiative of the business, and annulled the joint venture in 1987. So it was after this experience that Nissan set up Nissan Italia as a new base for the Italian market. Now, Nissan Italia sells cars not only imported from Japan but also those produced by Nissan Motor Iberia in Spain and, from November, 1988, also those in a new factory in Sunderland, U.K.

Concerning parts supply, there are two routes: 73 percent (in 1987) are from Barcelona (the parts manufactured by Nissan Motor Iberia) and the rest from Nissan Motor Parts Center in Amsterdam (the parts imported from Japan).

### Localization—Change to Nissan Italia

Based on Nissan's basic policy of clear end and loose means, and because of its evolution, Nissan Italia is a very Italian company. As seen in the organization (see Exhibit 2) and the communication, here Japanese have adjusted to the local way.

Even after March, 1988, when Nissan increased its share in the company, there has not been any drastic change. Mr. Arai, President of Nissan Italy, says,

> I did not give any speech to address the new president's declaration. This is not a change of that kind. I have been with them a while and nothing would suddenly change. The base of this company is Italy. Furthermore, without any formal words, the people understand Nissan's intention. In the meantime, maybe when we will move to the new office*, I will say a word.

It is obvious, however, that Nissan conveyed a clear message that it is going to be more seriously engaged in a longer-term development in the Italian market through this company. And there are also some other signals to show the company's determined will as seen below. From the part of the original company, this change is very well accepted because the company is given a chance to jump from a small business to a medium-sized one.

*Nissan Italia is now going to have a new head office with warehouse facilities.

## *Nissan Motor Iberia Organization*

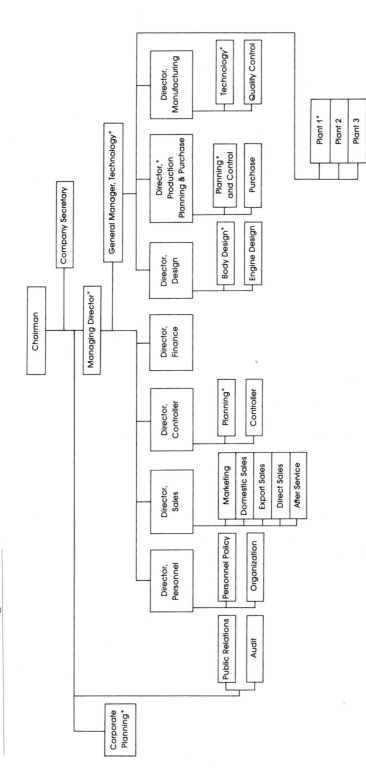

*Japanese

### Present Situation

*Organization.* The organization remains very local. Although the board consists of three Spanish directors and four Japanese, in practice only the president and his assistant are Japanese and one director and one manager are Spanish (Exhibit 3). And Mr. Oyama, the Japanese assistant, was sent over only in September, 1988.

Mr. Arai, the president, is a veteran about Italy with his 18 years of experience as a government official in the Japanese Ministry of Foreign Affairs, as a businessman in a big Japanese trading company, and in Nissan. (He has been with Nissan since the joint venture with Alfa Romeo.)

This shows the organization is not a "Japanese managers with Italian subordinates" structure but is very open to the local people up to directors. The people are given responsibilities; for example, Italian staffs fly to Amsterdam or Japan for meetings.

*Communication.* Italian is always used in the company since the Spanish managers and both Japanese are fluent in Italian. But externally the official language is English. At the moment, the communication between the headquarters and Nissan Italia is mainly done in Japanese, but it will change as English is used more by both sides, that is, headquarters and the Italian staff. In order to improve communication efficiency and to increase the internationality of the company, English lessons for the Italian staff have been started, which will also help promote the open mentality of the organization.

The company has a very open atmosphere in spite of the individually separated office style. The door of the president's office is almost always kept open and people come in to talk with Mr. Arai. He says, "I don't like to use first name to call each other because it sounds to me too casual. But of course I don't mind other people doing so among themselves." And it is true that this is only a matter of his taste, and his relationships with the Italian employees seem very warm.

*Japanization.* There is no particular effort to Japanize the company. There have, however, naturally been some changes through the history of Nissan's increasing share and hence control in the company. Mr. Arai described the change so far as Phase 1.

> Up to now, Nissan has done everything it can to help this company: invest in the facilities, send the people; finance the capital; and introduce the passenger cars (before the company was dealing only in commercial vehicles). Phase 1 is the visible change from the top. Now in Phase 2 the company should change by itself based on these preparations.

> What I expect from them is to have the participation mentality and to propose their ideas voluntarily to the company.

EXHIBIT 3

*Nissan Italia*

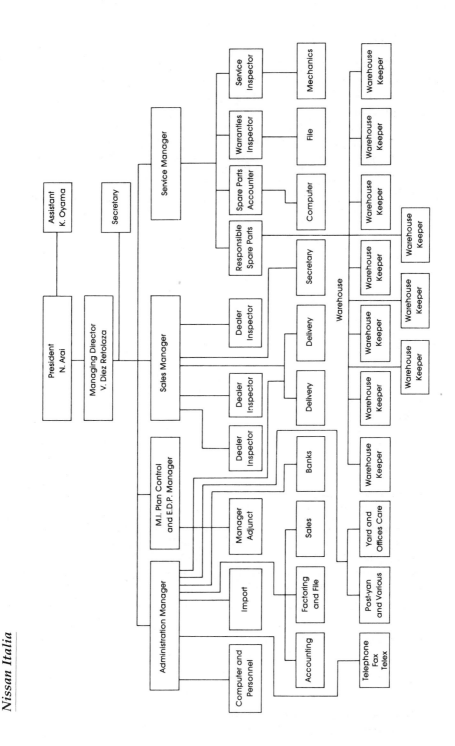

There are some variances among people's attitude depending on the department. The salespeople are quite participative and give their feedback from the field although they are paid on a salary basis and not on commissions. This is partly because sales results are, being quantitative and obvious, easier to use for control and motivation.

Compared to them, people in the office or in the warehouse are relatively passive and do not take the initiative. As their jobs are more difficult to evaluate objectively and quantitatively, this is understandable. But I would like them to change their working mind gradually.

*Dealer Relationships.* Dealer relationships in the case of sales network business are something equivalent to the supplier relationships in manufacturing. Nissan Italia's dealers are multifranchisers with contracts with several car manufacturers except Fiat. They sell various kinds of cars and being independent from Nissan, they are difficult to control. Mr. Arai says,

They are profit-oriented dealers. But I would like to change our relationships and develop a more longer-term one.

For this purpose, Nissan Italia makes efforts to improve communication with them, to make them understand Nissan's policy and product superiority and to ask for dealers' cooperation, for example, hold meetings, increase advertisement budget, and so on. And in the future, we would also like to have our own exclusive dealer network.

### Perceived Problems

*Working Style.* Mr. Arai says, "Here the manager should give every instruction to get things done. You cannot expect the employees to act positively or manage voluntary activities like QC (quality circles). Especially the people in the workshop (repair and after service) who rarely do overtime."

*Personnel.* Labor mobility is also a big problem to the human resource management. The better a manager is, he tends to move to another company, and this makes it difficult to plan in-house training, to keep good people, and to accumulate expertise. "But on the other hand, we enjoy some merits of this mobility, too. That is, we can recruit experienced people from outside whenever necessary," says a Japanese manager with a bitter smile.

### Expatriate Situation

Until September, 1988, Mr. Arai has been the only Japanese in the company, with Mr. Oyama coming to Rome sometimes for a long business trip.

Both of them do not seem to have any difficulty working and living here thanks to their language ability and personalities. Here some points are given by Mr. Arai as general comments about the expatriates' situation.

*Inconvenience About Business Schedule.* The difference of working hours, that is, the time lag and the difference in working hour length, causes the expatriates to work very long hours; for example, the early morning or late night telephone call to home, coming to the office on weekends, local holidays or during summer vacation, which is much longer here than in Japan.

Another thing is that they are expected to be attendants for Japanese managers or clients when they make a visit. They should play a role of "perfect" attendant: driver, interpreter, tourist guide, and shopping advisor all at the same time from morning to night. This is especially the case in big cities like Paris, London, or Rome.

*Japanese Circle.* In every city with more than a certain number of Japanese, there is a Japanese Association. So in Rome, but compared to Milan, where many companies locate, the Japanese population in Rome is small, and hence not many activities are going on in the Japanese circle.

According to Mr. Arai, "If you try to maintain a Japanese lifestyle or to stick together with Japanese, then you might have problems adjusting to the foreign life and people. But as far as you try to get accustomed to a new environment, there would be no problem."

And there are not many Japanese restaurants, either. "Anyway Rome is a bit different from other cities in terms of the food internationality. There are not many foreign food restaurants. For example, generally, fancy French restaurants are appreciated as the best cuisine and can be found in any big international city. But it seems that Italians mock French cooking, which damages the natural and original taste of the food with heavy sauce. People are just happy with their own Italian food," says Mr. Oyama, who also loves Italian food.

*Children's Education.* Last but not least, today perhaps the biggest issue for Japanese expatriates is the children's education.

Many foreign cities have a Japanese school with either a full-time or complementary staff depending on the Japanese population. However, since Japanese society is very education-conscious, many parents want their children to enter a good company meaning that they must enter a good university and before that a good high school. Therefore, at the critical age for high school or junior high school, many children (and their mothers) are sent back to Japan.

What is very interesting and shows a particular aspect of Japanese society is that this tendency is stronger for boys; there are many boys going back home to prepare for good universities while there are more girls going to local schools at various levels and staying abroad longer. Since the Japanese working world is still a rather male society with lifelong employment, it is thought that boys should equip themselves with a higher education for their own future happiness.

*Back at Headquarters.* Looking at the current situation in Nissan Italia, Mr. Sasaki is quite pleased with the evolution so far as the first phase. At the same time, however, he has realized some difficult problems. Most of them are not new; they come up more or less every time Nissan tries to develop business abroad. Therefore, to solve these problems would take a long time.

First, human resource management is of concern. As a whole, Nissan has kept the local identity of each subsidiary and retained almost all personnel. There seems to be no hostility or problem of adjustment. But there is a very fundamental difference among employees' working mentality, which has puzzled Japanese managers, namely, local staffs are not very participative and communication within the company (especially horizontal communication among functions and operations) is rather poor. Also high job mobility restrains them from accumulation of expertise and planning for human resource management.

"What can we do to motivate them and make them want to participate? Would the Japanese way of management with regard to motivation and incentive systems work?"

This first question leads to the second question, which is more fundamental. "How far could or should we reinforce Japanization in foreign subsidiaries? Where is the optimal balance?"

"And what is the role of Japanese expatriates and the headquarters?" Mr. Sasaki knows expatriates' frustration toward headquarters very well and recognizes the necessity of headquarter's globalization. "Expatriates' managers are sandwiched between demands from headquarters and the local subsidiary. They need our understanding and support in terms of money, people, technology, and human network and its mental support. But we cannot afford to respond to all of their needs because of shortages in resources, especially at this time of rapidly expanding overseas business. First of all, we should at least be better prepared to use English to facilitate communication between foreign subsidiaries. And more fundamentally, to raise good human resources able to cope with international operations. This will be a real long-term job."

And another question is how to train employees for globalization strategy? For example, now Nissan sends a few employees to business school, mostly in the United States. "Would we rather send someone to Europe, too, since our presence in Europe has very much increased? Then which school?"

The last question in his mind is about human resource management. How to respond to expatriates' problems both in the working situation and in the private life situation? How can headquarters support their job? How far should the company support them for their children's education or maintenance of houses they leave in Japan?

But, Mr. Sasaki was brought back to Nissan's policy at the end: clear end and loose means. "Maybe there is no right answer to be generalized, and we should try to think out each context."

# Personnel Selection for International Operations

# Pacific Basin Managers: A Gaijin, Not a Woman*

## NANCY J. ADLER

It doesn't make any difference if I am blue, green, purple or a frog. If I have the best product at the best price, the Chinese will buy!

American female manager based in Hong Kong

About the single most uncontroversial, incontrovertible statement to make about women in international management is that there are very few of them. The evidence is both subjective and objective (Caulkin, 1977, p. 58). More strikingly, think how few female managers you have come across, either in your company or elsewhere, while working in Asia. As the international personnel vice president for a North American company, would you choose to send an American or Canadian woman to Asia as an expatriate manager? Would she succeed? Would it be fair to the company and the woman to send her to Asia? Would it be wise not to send her?

International commerce has become vital to North American prosperity. Robert Frederick, chairman of the National Foreign Trade Council, states that eighty percent of United States industry now faces international competition. Already by the beginning of this decade approximately seventy percent of all U.S. firms were conducting a portion of their business abroad (Thal and Cateora, 1979). Canada provides an even more dramatic example of the importance of international business. By 1980, over 500 Canadian-based companies had foreign subsidiaries, an increase of more than 43 percent in just six years (Dun and Bradstreet, 1980). Canadians import nearly one quarter of all the goods they consume and export a slightly larger percentage of their gross national product. Moreover, foreigners own more than half of Canada's manufacturing capacity (Dhawan et al., 1981).

*A *gaijin* is a foreigner in Japan.

Source: Nancy J. Adler. "Pacific Basin Managers: A *Gaijin*, Not a Woman." *Human Resource Management*, 1987, 26(2), 169–191. Reprinted by permission.

Internationally, Pacific Rim business is the fastest growing in the world. Asian economies, most notably the "Four Tigers"—Hong Kong, Korea, Singapore, and Taiwan—have been among the most rapidly developing in recent economic history. At the same time, the People's Republic of China now commands the attention of Western economies, if for no other reason than the size of its potential market, while Japan continues to dominate global economic activity across a widening range of industries. To remain competitive, no major North American firm dare ignore Pacific Rim business.

Along with the globalization of business, stories describing women's changing role in society have gained prominence during the last decade. The United Nations' Decade of Women emphasized both what needs to be done for women to reach equality as well as the many changes now underway. Within this pattern of changes, what role do and will female managers play in Asia? Can women effectively manage in Asia? Can North American companies successfully send expatriate women to Japan? Korea? Hong Kong? And how will North American women manage in Singapore, Pakistan, India, Malaysia, Taiwan, Thailand, Indonesia, or the People's Republic of China?

One wonders if North American companies should respect Asian countries' apparent cultural norms and only send male managers overseas. Yet, with the increasing importance of international business, can North American firms afford to limit their personnel selection decisions to one gender? Women's role in international management has become one of the most important questions facing human resource managers of multinational firms. Due to the economic importance of Pacific Rim business and the apparent dearth of female managers, both local and expatriate, the question assumes particular importance. This article investigates the role of North American women working in Asia for North American firms. It begins by reviewing the context—the role of Asian women working within their own countries—and goes on to report the findings of a study investigating Canadian and American women's role as expatriate managers in Asia.

## ▬ Do Asians Discriminate Against Women in Management?

All cultures differentiate male and female roles, expecting women to behave in certain ways, men in others; for women to fill certain roles and men others. In many cultures, the traditional female role supports attitudes and behaviors contradictory to those of a manager. Therefore women in many parts of the world have failed to aspire to become managers while men have blocked their pursuit of such careers. Asia is no exception. Few Asian women are managers; fewer still have achieved prominence. Using Canada and the United States as a point of comparison, let's look at the role women play as managers in a selection of Asian countries.

Already two decades ago in the United States, more than fifteen percent (15.8%) of working women held managerial and administrative positions, while in Canada almost ten percent (9.5%) held such positions (International

Labor Office, 1970). By 1982, American women occupied over a quarter (27.9%) of all managerial and administrative positions (U.S. Dept. of Labor, 1982). Yet top management positions still elude women; even in the 1980s, American women only represent five percent of top executives (Trafford et al., 1984).

By comparison, the number of female managers in Asia remains infinitesimally small, especially those visible to the international business community. Female managers are almost nonexistent within the corporate structure and, more broadly, within the leadership ranks of the business sector. Women constitute less than one percent of the senior managers in Southeast Asian corporations (Singson, 1985, p. 4). But, our North American statistics, focusing primarily on major corporations, have missed some of the involvement of female entrepreneurs and women managing smaller and family-owned Asian companies. For example, Japan has more than 25,000 female company presidents, all of whom manage small to medium-sized firms; none are CEOs of multinationals (Steinhoff and Tanaka, 1986–1987). Similarly, a number of women control major family-owned firms in Thailand and Indonesia, while none hold top positions within corporate structures. Notwithstanding this overlooked involvement, neither the numbers nor the status of Asian women in management equals that of their male counterparts. Why? The following section reviews some of the cultural, legal, and economic dynamics explaining the role of women in management in six very different Asian countries: Indonesia, Japan, the People's Republic of China, India, Singapore, and the Philippines.

### Indonesia

In Indonesia, only one in five women (20.8%) participates in the paid labor force, as compared with 60 percent in Sweden and 53 percent in the United States, 51 percent in Canada, 46.7 percent in Japan, and 45.5 percent in Australia (Sorrentino, 1983). This compares with a male labor force participation rate of over 70 percent in the United States (77%), Canada (78.3%), Sweden (74%), Japan (80%), and Australia (79%). While a few Indonesian women hold highly prestigious leadership positions, the vast majority remain outside of the corporate and managerial hierarchy.

As in most areas of the world, Indonesian managers come from the ranks of the educated. In Indonesia, only five percent of the total population has graduated from high school and fewer than one percent from academy or university (Indonesia, 1982, pp. 47, 67 as cited in Crockett, 1987). While the proportion of those educated is rising rapidly, and considerably faster for women than for men, women remain half as likely as men to be highly educated (Crockett, 1987). Not surprisingly, these highly educated women have the highest labor force participation rate, with government administration the second most common occupation after teaching in rural areas and sales in urban areas. Yet almost twice as many educated men as women hold such positions (Crockett, 1987). In the private sector, four times as many men as women hold managerial positions (Crockett, 1987).

## *Japan*

Despite Japan's highly acclaimed advanced industrialization, private industry excludes women from most responsible managerial positions (Dahlby, 1977). In 1955, the proportion of professionals and managers in the entire female labor force was 3.5 percent, rising to only 8.5 percent by 1977 (Japan Census Bureau, 1977 as cited by Osako, 1978). By the 1980s, primarily due to women reentering the workforce after raising their families, the proportion of women working had risen to one of the world's highest, now constituting almost forty percent (39.7%) of the workforce (Women's Bureau, 1986), approximately on a par with Sweden (Hiroshi, 1982, p. 319; also see Cook, 1980). Yet, women continue to hold few managerial positions, especially in major corporations (see Steinhoff and Tanaka, 1986–1987). For example, the 1983 *Who's Who in Japanese Business,* covering the 1754 major companies listed in Japan's eight Stock Exchanges, included only 68 women among the 160,764 Japanese managers listed (Suzuki and Narapareddy, 1985). Moreover, fifty percent of all Japanese firms have no female managers, and that percent has remained constant since 1955 (Osako, 1978, p. 15). Of the Japanese women who have attained managerial status, almost all work for small and medium-sized businesses, not for multinational corporations. Despite recent legal changes, no major increase in the number of women in the latter category is predicted.

While cultural and legal constraints partially explain the role of women in Japanese management, the lifetime employment system explains their absence from major corporations. Culturally, a well-known Confucian saying states, "A woman is to obey her father as daughter, her husband as wife, and her son as aged mother" (Osako, 1978, p. 17). Not surprisingly, given this tradition, the Japanese have neither viewed women as authority figures nor as decision makers. Strong cultural norms have made it difficult for Japanese companies to send a woman on domestic or international business trips with a male colleague if not accompanied by a second man. Laws, including the Labor Standards Act, restrict certain positions to men, and preclude women from working overtime or at night in many professions. In general, Japanese society expects women to work until marriage, quit to raise children, and return, only as needed, to low level and part-time positions after age forty. Thus by 1985, women constituted seventy (70.7%) percent of all part-time workers (Women's Bureau, 1986). Clearly, in Japan, while the home has continued to be women's domain, the workplace remains the domain of men. Given this pattern, combined with major Japanese corporations' lifetime employment and promotion systems, most have not seen it as worthwhile to develop women for significant management positions. Major corporations generally place women on separate career paths from men, frequently treating them differently in wages, promotion, and retirement. Today, Japanese women seeking managerial careers often must take positions in foreign, rather than Japanese, firms (Kaminski and Paiz, 1984).

## The People's Republic of China

Although one Chinese saying states that "Women hold up half of the world," numerous other traditional folk sayings and proverbs belittle women and disparage their leadership abilities. For example, when a woman becomes a leader, some Chinese say that it is like "a donkey taking the place of a horse which can only lead to trouble" (Croll, 1977, p. 596). Since the 1970s, the anti-Confucian and Lin Piao campaigns tried to create more favorable conditions for women by identifying obstacles to redefining women's role and improving their status (Jen-min jih pao, 1974). The media reported men's and women's groups "as coming to a new awareness of an old problem through the recognition of their ideological constraints originating in the Confucian principle of male supremacy" (Croll, 1977, p. 597). However, women are still under-represented in political and leadership positions, given unequal pay in rural areas, and following traditional courtship and marriage customs that maintain work-related gender differentiation and disproportionate shares of household work (Croll, 1977, p. 596; also see Davin, 1976). Given the rapidly changing political and economic environment in China and its increasing openness to international markets, it is difficult to assess the exact proportion of women currently holding managerial and executive positions. My own interviews with female Chinese managers in 1986 confirmed the continued pattern of placing women's primary responsibility in the home, with equality at work most accessible to those in lower positions and those whose children were grown up and thus beyond the need for daily maternal care.* Whereas physical labor knows few gender boundaries in the People's Republic of China, access to top managerial positions in industry and government remains the domain of men to a substantial degree.

## India

While women have been guaranteed constitutional equality and occupied prominent positions in government since India's independence in 1947, only recently have they begun to take managerial positions in business organizations. A limited survey of thirty-three female executives across a wide range of industries concluded that while Indian women have fewer opportunities for promotion than men, once promoted they perform as well as men in executive positions. However, while these Indian women believed that they could successfully combine the roles of wife and executive, some questioned the appropriateness of continuing to work with small children (Singh, 1980).

---

*Interviews were conducted in Tianjin with female managers from throughout the People's Republic of China in a management seminar jointly sponsored by the PRC's State Economic Commission and the U.S. Department of Commerce.

### Singapore

Singapore has been one of the most rapidly developing "newly industralized countries" in the Pacific Basin. To overcome critical human resource shortages, the government launched a major campaign in the early 1980s encouraging Singaporian women to rejoin the workforce, including supporting quality child care services, flexible work scheduling and incentives, training and retraining programs, and improved societal attitudes toward career women (Report of the Task Force on Female Participation in the Labor Force, 1985, pp. ii-iii). By 1983, Singaporian women constituted more than a third (35.5%) of the labor force and more than a sixth (17.8%) of the administrators and managers (up from 7% in 1980; Chan, 1987). Chan (1987) attributes the increases to prosperous economic conditions, the government's development policies encouraging women's participation in the workforce, and women's own career aspirations. While seeing Singapore's rapid growth as an enabling condition, she also notes the 1984 economic downturn's disproportionately adverse affect on women.

### The Philippines

While women from prominent families clearly hold influential positions in Filipino political and economic life, the overall situation for women differs little from that in other Pacific Rim countries. The Philippine Labor Code prohibits discrimination against women with respect to rates of pay and conditions of employment (Foz, 1979). Yet, while women accounted for approximately a third of the labor force by 1976, less than three percent (2.7%) of the working women held administrative or managerial positions in government or business; a figure representing less than one percent of the total managerial positions (Ople, 1981). Their numbers have not increased. Philippine society still holds deeply rooted beliefs regarding the role of women at home and at work (Miralao, 1980). Social pressures in Philippine society, where both men and women frequently support strongly differentiated sex role stereotypes, make it difficult for a Filipina to choose a career instead of a family or to successfully combine marriage, career, and children (Dept. of Sociology, 1977; also see Castillo, 1977 and Gosselin, 1984).

## ▬ Women in International Management

Given the culturally mandated scarcity of local female managers in most Asian countries, can North American companies successfully send female expatriate managers to Asia? More specifically, can Canadian and American companies send women to Japan, Korea, Hong Kong, the Philippines, the People's Republic of China, Singapore, Thailand, India, Pakistan, Malaysia, or Indonesia? Is the experience of local women—i.e., their relative absence from the managerial ranks—the best predictor of success, or the lack thereof, for expatriate women?

The following research study presents the story of a "noun," "woman," that appears to have gotten mixed up with an "adjective," "female" manager. It is the unfolding of a set of assumptions predicting how Asians would treat North American female managers based on North Americans' beliefs concerning Asians' treatment of their own women. The problem with the story, and with the set of assumptions, is that it has proven to be wrong. The assumptions fail to predict reality accurately.

## ▰ *The Study*

This research on female managers in Asia is part of a four part study on the role of North American women as expatriate managers.* In the first part, 686 Canadian and American firms were surveyed to identify the number of women sent overseas as expatriate managers. The survey identified over thirteen thousand (13,338) expatriates, of whom 402, or 3%, were women—that is, 3.3% of American and 1.3% of Canadian expatriate managers are female. Overall, North American firms send thirty-two times as many male as female expatriate managers overseas (see Adler, 1984c and 1979).

Not surprisingly, larger companies send proportionately more women than do smaller companies, with financial institutions significantly leading other industries. However, the three percent, while significantly less than North American women represented in domestic management, should not be viewed as a poor showing, but rather as the beginning of a trend. The vast majority of North American female managers who have ever been sent abroad in expatriate status are currently overseas.

The second, third, and fourth parts of the study attempted to explain why so few North American women work as international managers. Each part was structured around one of the three most common "myths" about women in international management, that is:

- MYTH 1: Women do not want to be international managers.
- MYTH 2: Companies refuse to send women overseas.
- MYTH 3: Foreigners' prejudice against women renders them ineffective, even when interested and sent.

These beliefs were labelled "myths" because, while widely believed by both men and women, they had never been tested.

### *Women's Interest in International Careers*

Are women less interested than men in pursuing international careers? The second part of the study tested this myth by surveying 1129 graduating

*I would like to thank the Social Sciences of Humanities Research Council of Canada for their generous support of this research. A special thanks to Ellen Bessner and Blossom Shafer for their assistance in all phases of the research and to Dr. Homa Mahmoudi for her help, creativity, and professional insight in conducting the Asian interviews.

MBAs from seven management schools in the United States, Canada, and Europe. The overwhelming result was an impressive case of no significant difference: male and female MBAs display equal interest, or disinterest, in pursuing international careers. Eighty-four percent of the MBAs said they would like an international assignment at some time during their careers. However, both males and females agreed that the opportunities were fewer for women than for men, and fewer for women pursuing international careers vs. domestic careers. While there may have been a difference in the past, today's male and female MBAs appear equally interested in international work and expatriate positions (see Adler, 1984b and 1986).

## Corporate Resistance to Assigning Women Overseas

To test the corporate resistance "myth," personnel vice presidents and managers from sixty major North American multinationals were surveyed (see Adler, 1984a). Based on their responses, over half the companies (54%) hesitate to send women overseas. This is almost four times as many as those hesitating to select women for domestic assignments (54% as compared with 14%). Almost three-quarters believe foreigners are prejudiced against female managers (73%). Similarly, seventy percent believe that women, especially married women in dual-career marriages, would be reticent to accept a foreign assignment, if not totally uninterested. For certain locations, the personnel executives expressed concern about the women's physical safety, the hazards involved in travelling in underdeveloped countries, and, especially for single women, the isolation and potential loneliness. These results concur with those from a survey of 100 top managers in *Fortune* 500 firms operating overseas in which the majority believed that women face overwhelming resistance when seeking management positions in the international divisions of U.S. firms (Thal and Cateora, 1979).

## Foreigners' Reactions to Female Expatriates

Why do three-quarters of the North American firms believe foreigners are prejudiced against expatriate women? Perhaps, due to their lack of experience, companies predict female expatriates' success, or the lack thereof, based on the role and treatment of local women within the particular foreign culture. Perhaps the scarcity of Asian women working as managers (substantiated by statistics cited in the prior section) has led North American companies to conclude that North American women would not receive the respect necessary to succeed in managerial and professional assignments. When interviewed, more than half of the international personnel executives declared that it would neither be fair to the woman nor the company to send a female manager to Asia when it could be predicted, based on the treatment of local women, that she would have difficulty succeeding. The fundamental question was, and remains, is this a valid basis for prediction?

## ■ *Foreign Female Managers in Asia*

To investigate the third myth, foreigners' prejudice against women rendering them ineffective as international managers, fifty-two female expatriate managers were interviewed while in Asia or after returning from Asia to North America. Due to multiple foreign postings, the fifty-two women represent sixty-one Asian assignments. The greatest number resided in Hong Kong (34%), followed by Japan (25%), Singapore (16%), the Philippines and Australia (5% each), Indonesia and Thailand (4% each), and at least one each in Korea, India, Taiwan, and the People's Republic of China, Since most of the women held regional responsibility, they worked throughout Asia, rather than just in their location of foreign residence. Of those working in Asia, financial institutions sent the vast majority (71%). Other industries sending more than two women to Asia included publishing (7%) and petroleum (6%). Those sending one or two women include: advertising, film distribution, service industries (including accounting, law, executive search, and computers), retail food, electronic appliances, pharmaceuticals, office equipment, sporting goods, and soaps and cosmetics.

On average, the female expatriates' assignments lasted two and a half years (29.7 months), ranging from six months to six years. Salaries in 1983, before benefits varied from US $27,000 to US $54,000, and averaged US $34,500. The female expatriate managers supervised from zero to 25 subordinates, with the average falling below five (4.6). Their titles and levels in the organization varied considerably: some held very junior positions—"trainee" and assistant account manager—while others held quite senior positions—including one regional vice president. In no case did a female expatriate hold the company's number one position in the region or in any country.

### *Female Expatriates: Who Are They?*

As the prior description indicates, the female expatriates were fairly junior within their organizations and careers. While their ages varied from 23 to 41 years old, the average female expatriate was under thirty (28.8). Nearly two-thirds (62%) were single, with only three having children. Five of the women married while overseas—all to other expatriates. While the women are considerably younger than the typical male expatriate manager, their age probably does not reflect any systematic discrimination for or against them. Rather, it is an artifact of the relatively high proportion of women sent by financial institutions—an industry that selects fairly junior managers for overseas assignments—and the relatively low proportion in manufacturing, where international assignees are generally quite senior (e.g., country or regional director).

The women were very well educated and quite internationally experienced. Almost all held graduate degrees, with MBAs the most common. Over three-quarters had extensive international interests and experience prior to their present company sending them overseas. For example, more than three-quarters (77%) had travelled internationally and almost two-thirds (61%) had had an international focus in their studies prior to joining the company. On average, the women spoke two and a half languages, with some speaking as many as six fluently. Based on subjective observation during the interviews, the women, as a group, had excellent social skills, and, by western standards, were very good looking.

## The Decision to Go Overseas

How did the companies and the female managers decide on the overseas transfers? In the majority of cases, the female expatriates were "firsts," with only five women (10%) following another woman into the international position. Of the 90 percent who were "firsts," almost a quarter (22%) represented the first female manager the firm had ever expatriated anywhere; 14 percent were the first women sent to Asia, a quarter were the first sent to the particular country, and 20 percent were the first filling the specific position. Clearly, neither the women nor the companies had the luxury of role models; few could follow prior patterns. With the exception of a few major New York based financial institutions, both the women and the companies found themselves experimenting in hope of uncertain success.

The decision process leading the company to send a female manager to Asia could be described as one of mutual education. In more than four out of five cases (83%), the woman initially introduced the idea of an international assignment to her boss and company. For only six women (11%) did the company first suggest it to her, while for another three (6%) the suggestion was mutual.

Women used a number of strategies to "educate" their companies. Many women explored the possibility of an expatriate assignment during their original job interview and eliminated from consideration companies that were totally against the idea. In other cases, women informally introduced the idea to their bosses and continued informally mentioning it "at appropriate moments" until the company ultimately decided to offer them overseas positions. A few women formally applied for a number of expatriate positions prior to actually being selected. Some of the female managers described themselves as "strategizing their career" to be international, primarily by attempting to be in the right place at the right time. For example, one woman, who predicted that Hong Kong would be her firm's next major business center, arranged to assume responsibility for the Hong Kong desk in New York, while leaving the rest of Asia to a male colleague. The strategy paid off. Within a year, the company sent her, and not her male colleague, to Hong Kong. Overall, the women described themselves as needing to encourage their companies to consider the possibility of expatriating women in general and themselves in particular. In most cases, they described their companies as failing to recognize the possibility of expatriating women, not as having thoroughly considered the idea and having rejected it. In general, the obstacle was naiveté, not conscious rejection.

Many women confronted numerous instances of corporate resistance prior to being sent. For example:

*Malaysia.* According to one woman being considered for an assignment in Malaysia, "Management assumed that women don't have the physical stamina to survive in the tropics. They claimed I couldn't hack it."

*Thailand.* "My company didn't want to send a woman to that 'horrible part of the world.' They think Bangkok is an excellent place to send single men, but not a woman. They said they would have trouble getting a work permit, which wasn't true."

*Japan and Hong Kong.* "Everyone was more or less curious if it would work. My American boss tried to advise me, 'Don't be upset if it's difficult in Japan and Korea.' The American male manager in Tokyo was also hesitant. Finally the Chinese boss in Hong Kong said, 'We have to try!'"

*Japan.* "Although I was the best qualified, I was not offered the position in Japan until the senior Japanese manager in Tokyo said, 'We are very flexible in Japan'; then they sent me."

While only true in a few cases, some women described severe company resistance to sending female managers abroad. For those women, it appeared that their firms offered them a position only after all potential male candidates for the post had turned it down. For example:

*Thailand.* "Every advance in responsibility is because the Americans had no choice. I've never been chosen over someone else."

*Japan.* "They never would have considered me. But then the financial manager in Tokyo had a heart attack and they had to send someone. So they sent me, on a month's notice, as a temporary until they could find a man to fill the permanent position. It worked out and I stayed."

While most companies sent women in the same status as male expatriates, some showed their hesitation by offering temporary or travel assignments rather than true expatriate positions.

*Hong Kong.* "After offering me the job, they hesitated, 'Could a woman work with the Chinese?' So my job was defined as temporary, a one year position to train a Chinese man to replace me. I succeeded and became permanent."

Although this may appear to be a logically cautious strategy, in reality, it tends to create an unfortunate self-fulfilling prophecy. As a number of women reported, if the company is not convinced that you will succeed (and therefore, for example, offers you a temporary rather than a permanent position), it will communicate its lack of confidence to foreign colleagues and clients as a lack of commitment. The foreigners will then mirror the home company's behavior by also failing to take you seriously. Assignments can become very difficult or even fail altogether when the company's initial confidence and commitment are lacking. As one women in Indonesia said, "It is very important to clients that I am permanent. It increases trust, and that's critical."

Many women claimed that the most difficult hurdle in their international career involved getting sent overseas in the first place, not—as most had predicted—gaining the respect of foreigners and succeeding once there.

### Did It Work: The Impact of Being Female

When describing their actual experience working in Asia, almost all (97%) of the North American women said it had been a success. While their descriptions are strictly subjective, a number of more objective indicators suggest that most assignments did, in fact, succeed. For example, most firms—after experimenting with their first female expatriate—decided to send other women overseas. Moreover, many companies promoted the women based on their overseas performance. In addition, many companies offered the women a second international assignment following the completion of the first one. In only two cases did women describe failure experiences: one in Australia and the other in Singapore. For the first woman, it was her second international posting, following a successful experience in Latin America and followed by an equally successful assignment in Singapore. For the second woman, the Singapore assignment was her only overseas posting.

Prior to the interviews, I had expected the women to describe a series of difficulties caused by their being female and a corresponding set of creative solutions to each difficulty. This was not the case. Almost half of the women (42%) reported that "being female" served more as an advantage than a disadvantage. Sixteen percent found "being female" to have both positive and negative effects, while another 22 percent saw it as "irrelevant" or neutral. Only one woman in five (20%) found it to be primarily negative.

*Advantages.* The women reported numerous professional advantages to being female. Most frequently, they described the advantage of being highly visible. Foreign clients were curious about them, wanted to meet them, and remembered them after the first meeting. It therefore appeared easier for the women than for their male colleagues to gain access to foreign clients' time and attention. Some examples of this high visibility, accessibility, and memorability include:

> *Japan.* "It's the visibility as an expat, and even more as a woman. I stick in their minds. I know I've gotten more business than my two male colleagues. They are extra interested in me."

*Thailand.* "Being a woman is never a detriment. They remembered me better. Fantastic for a marketing position. It's better working with Asians than with the Dutch, British, or Americans."

*India and Pakistan.* "In India and Pakistan, being a woman helps for marketing and client contact. I got in to see customers because they had never seen a female banker before. . . . Having a female banker adds value to the client."

The female managers also described the advantages of good interpersonal skills and their belief that men could talk more easily about a wider range of topics with women than with other men. For example:

*Indonesia.* "I often take advantage of being a woman. I'm more supportive than my male colleagues. . . . They relax and talk more. And fifty percent of my effectiveness is based on volunteered information."

*Korea.* "Women are better at treating men sensitively, and they just like you. One of my Korean clients told me, 'I really enjoyed the lunch and working with you.' "

In addition, many of the women described the higher status accorded women in Asia and that that status was not denied them as foreign female managers. They often felt that they received special treatment that their male colleagues did not receive. Clearly, it was always salient that they were women, but being a woman did not appear to be antithetical to being a manager.

*Hong Kong.* "Single female expats travel easier and are treated better. Never hassled. No safety issues. Local offices take better care of you. They meet you, take you through customs. . . . It's the combination of treating you like a lady and a professional."

*Japan.* "It's an advantage that attracts attention. They are interested in meeting a *gaijin*, a foreign woman. Women attract more clients. On calls to clients, they elevate me, give me more rank. If anything, the problem, for men and women, is youth, not gender."

Moreover, most of the women claimed benefits from a "halo effect." As they described, most of their foreign colleagues and counterparts had never met or previously worked with a female expatriate manager. At the same time, most of the foreign community was highly aware of how unusual it was for American and Canadian firms to send female managers to Asia. Hence, the Asians tended to assume that the women would not have been sent unless they were "the best," and therefore expected them to be "very, very good."

*Japan.* "Women are better at putting people at ease. It's easier for a woman to convince a man . . . The traditional woman's role . . . inspires confidence and trust, less suspicious, not threatening. They assumed I must be good if I was sent. They become friends."

*Indonesia.* "It's easier being a women here than in any place in the world, including New York City. . . . I never get the comments I got in New York, like 'What is a nice woman like you doing in this job?' "

**No impact.**  Other women found "being female" to have no impact whatsoever on their professional life. For the most part, these were women working primarily with the Chinese:

*Hong Kong.* "There's no difference. They respect professionalism . . . including in Japan. There is no problem in Asia."

*Hong Kong.* "There are many expat and foreign women in top positions here. If you are good at what you do, they accept you. One Chinese woman told me, 'Americans are always watching you. One mistake and you are done. Chinese take a while to accept you and then stop testing you.' "

*Hong Kong.* "It doesn't make any difference if you are blue, green, purple or a frog. If you have the best product at the best price, they'll buy."

**Disadvantages.**  The women also cited a number of disadvantages caused by being female. Interestingly enough, the majority of the disadvantages involved the women's relationship to their own home companies, not their relationships with Asian clients. As discussed earlier, a major problem involved difficulty obtaining the foreign assignment in the first place. A subsequent problem involved the home company limiting opportunities and job scope once overseas. More than half the female expatriates described difficulty in persuading their home companies to give them the latitude equivalent to that given their male colleagues, especially initially. Some companies, out of concern for the women's safety, limited their travel (and thus their region), excluding very remote, rural, and underdeveloped areas. Other companies, as mentioned previously, limited the duration of the women's assignments to six months or a year, rather than the more standard two to three years. For example:

*Japan.* "My problem is overwhelmingly with Americans. They identify it as a male market . . . geisha girls . . ."

*Thailand (Petroleum company).* "The Americans wouldn't let me on the drilling rigs, because they said there were no accommodations for a woman. Everyone blames it on something else. They gave me different work. They had me working on the sidelines, not planning and communicating with drilling people. It's the expat Americans, not the Thais, who'll go to someone else before they come to me."

Another disadvantage that some companies placed on the women was limiting them to work only internally with company employees, rather than externally with clients. The companies' often implicit assumption was that their own employees were somehow less prejudiced than were outsiders. Interestingly, women often found the opposite to be true: they faced more problems within their own organization than externally with clients. As one American woman described:

> *Hong Kong.* "It was somewhat difficult internally. They feel threatened, hesitant to do what I say, resentful. They assume I don't have the credibility that a man would have. Perhaps it's harder internally than externally because client relationships are one-on-one and internally it's more of a group, or perhaps it's harder because they have to live with it longer internally, or perhaps it's because they fear that I'm setting a precedent or because they fear criticism from their peers."

Managing foreign clients' and colleagues' initial expectations proved difficult for many of the women. Some described initial meetings with Asians as tricky. Since most Asians previously had never met a North American expatriate woman holding a managerial position, there was considerable ambiguity as to who she was, her status, her level of expertise, authority, and responsibility, and therefore the appropriate form of address and demeanor toward her:

> *Hong Kong (Asia Region).* "It took extra time to establish credibility with the Japanese and Chinese. One Japanese manager said to me, 'When I first met you, I thought you would not be any good because you were a woman'. . . . The rest of Asia is OK."

> *People's Republic of China.* "I speak Chinese, which is a plus. But they'd talk to the men, not to me. They'd assume that I, as a woman, have no authority. The Chinese only want to deal with top, top, top level people, and there is always a man at a higher level."

Since most of the North American women whom Asians had met previously had been male expatriate managers' wives or secretaries, the Asians naturally assumed that "she too is not a manager." Hence, as the women claimed, initial conversations often were directed at male colleagues, not toward the newly arrived female managers. Senior male colleagues, particularly those from the head office, became very important in redirecting the focus of early discussions back toward the women. If well done, old patterns were quickly broken and smooth ongoing work relationships established. If ignored or poorly managed, such challenges to credibility, authority, and responsibility became chronic and undermined the women's potential effectiveness.

The North American women clearly had more difficulty gaining respect from North American and European men working in Asia than from the Asians themselves. Some even suggested that the expatriate community in Asia has attracted many "very traditional" men who were not particularly open to the idea of women in management—whether at home or abroad. As three of the women described:

> *Singapore.* "Colonial British don't accept women; very male. There are no women in their management levels. I got less reaction from the Chinese. The Chinese are only interested in if you can do the job."

> *Hong Kong.* "British men . . . you must continually prove yourself. You can't go to lunch with U.K. expat company men. The senior U.K. guys become uncomfortable and the younger U.K. guys get confused as to lunch being a social or business occasion. So I hesitate inviting them. Interaction is just tenuous from both sides."

> *Hong Kong.* "The older men had trouble imagining me with the bank in ten years."

As mentioned earlier, many women described the most difficult aspect of the foreign assignment as getting sent overseas in the first place. Overcoming resistance from North American head offices frequently proved more challenging than gaining foreign clients' and colleagues' respect and acceptance. In most cases, assumptions about Asians' prejudice against female expatriate managers appear to have been exaggerated. Predicted prejudice and reality did not match. Why? Perhaps foreigners are not as prejudiced as we think.

## ■ *The* Gaijin *Syndrome*

Throughout the interviews, one pattern became particularly clear. First and foremost, foreigners are seen as foreigners. Similar to their male colleagues, female expatriates are seen as foreigners, not as locals. A woman who is a foreigner (*gaijin*) is not expected to act like the locals. Therefore, the rules governing the behavior of local women which limit their access to management and managerial responsibility, do not apply to foreign women. Whereas women are considered the "culture bearers" in almost all societies, foreign women in no way assume or are expected to assume that role. As one woman in Japan said, "The Japanese are very smart, they can tell that I am not Japanese and they do not expect me to act as a Japanese woman. They will allow and condone behavior from foreign women which would be absolutely unacceptable from their own women." Similarly, as Ranae Hyer, a Tokyo-based personnel vice president of the Bank of America's Asia Division, said,

> Being a foreigner is so weird to the Japanese that the marginal impact of being a woman is nothing. If I were a Japanese woman, I couldn't be doing what I'm doing here. But they know perfectly well that I'm not (Morgenthaler, 1978).

Many interviewees related similar examples of female expatriates' unique status as "foreign women" rather than as "women" per se. For example:

*Japan and Korea.* "Japan and Korea are the hardest, but they know that I'm an American woman and they don't expect me to be like a Japanese or Korean woman. It's possible to be effective even in Japan and Korea, if you send a senior woman, with at least three to four years of experience, expecially if she's fluent in Japanese."

*Japan.* "It's the novelty, especially in Japan, Korea, and Pakistan. All of the general managers met with me . . . It was much easier for me, expecially in Osaka. They were charming. They didn't want me to feel bad. They thought I would come back if they gave me business. You see, they could separate me from the local women."

*Pakistan.* "Will I have problems? No! There is a double standard between expats and local women. The Pakistanis test you, but you enter as a respected person."

*Japan.* "I don't think the Japanese could work for a Japanese woman, . . . but they just block it out for foreigners."

*Hong Kong.* "Hong Kong is very cosmopolitan. I'm seen as an expat, not as an Asian, even though I am an Asian American."

It appears that we may have mixed up the adjective and noun in predicting Asians' reactions to North American women. We expected the primary descriptor of female expatriate managers to be "woman," and predicted their success based on the success of the Asian women in each country. In fact, the primary descriptor is "foreign," and the best predictor of success is the success of other North Americans in the country. Asians see female expatriates as foreigners who happen to be women, not as women who happen to be foreigners. The difference is crucial. Given the ambiguity involved in sending women into new areas of the world, our assumptions of the greater salience of gender (male/female) over nationality (foreign/local) has led us to make inaccurate predictions as to their potential to succeed as managers.

## ▬ *Recommendations*

It is clear from the experience of the women described and quoted in this article that North American female expatriates can succeed as managers in Asia. In considering expatriating them, both the companies and the women themselves should consider a number of aspects of the foreign assignment.

First, do not assume it will not work. Do not assume that foreigners will treat expatriate female managers the same way they treat their own women.

Our assumptions about the salience of gender over nationality have led to totally inaccurate predictions. Therefore, do not confuse adjectives and nouns; do not use the success or failure of local women to predict that of foreign women. Similarly, do not confuse the role of the spouse with the role of a manager. While the single most common reason for male expatriates' failure and early return from an overseas assignment has been dissatisfaction of the spouse, this does not mean that women cannot cope in the overseas environment. The role of the spouse (whether male or female) is much more ambiguous and consequently the cross-cultural adjustment much more demanding than for the person in the role of the employee. While wives (female spouses) have had trouble adjusting, their situation is not analogous to that of female managers and therefore not predictive.

Second, do not assume that a woman will not want to go overseas. Ask her. While both single and married women need to balance private and professional life considerations, many are highly interested in taking overseas assignments. Based on the expressed attitudes of today's graduating MBAs, the number of women interested in working overseas will increase in the 1980s and 1990s, not decrease. Given that most expatriate packages have been designed to meet the needs of traditional families (working husband, non-working wife, and children), companies should be prepared to modify benefits packages to meet the demands of single status women and dual-career couples. Such modifications might include increased lead time on announcing assignments, executive search services for the partner in dual-career couples, and payment for "staying connected"—including telephone and airfare expense—for those couples who choose to commute rather than relocating overseas.

Third, give a woman every opportunity to succeed. Send her in full status—not as a temporary or experimental expatriate—with the appropriate title to communicate the home company's commitment to her. Do not be surprised if foreign colleagues and clients direct their comments to the male managers rather than the new female expatriate in initial meetings, but do not accept such behavior. Redirect discussion, where appropriate, to the woman. Such behavior should not be interpreted as prejudice, but rather as the reaction to an ambiguous, atraditional situation.

The female expatriates had a number of suggestions for other women following in their footsteps. First, as they suggest, presume naiveté, not malice. Realize that sending women to Asia is new, perceived as risky, and still fairly poorly understood. In most cases, companies and foreigners are operating on untested assumptions, many of which are faulty, not out of a basis of prejudice. The most successful approach is to be gently persistent in educating the company to the possibility of sending a woman overseas. Second, given that expatriating women is perceived as risky, no woman will be sent if she is not seen as technically and professionally excellent. According to the women, it never hurts to arrange to be in the right place at the right time. And third, for single women, the issue of loneliness and for married women, the issue of managing a dual-career relationship, must be addressed. Contact with other expatriate women has proven helpful in both cases. For dual-career couples, most women considered it critical that they (1) discussed the possible international assignment with their husband long before it became a reality and (2) created options that would work for them as a couple. For most couples, that meant creating options that had never or rarely been tried in their particular company.

Global competition is and will continue to be intense in the 1980s and '90s. Companies need every advantage to win. The option of limiting the international area to one gender is an archaic luxury of the past. There is no doubt that the most successful North American companies will draw on both men and women to manage their international operations. The only question is how quickly and how effectively companies will manage the introduction of women into the worldwide managerial workforce.

## ▉ References

Adler, N. J. "Do MBAs want international careers?" *International Journal of Intercultural Relations*, 1986, 10 (3), 277–300.

Adler, N. J. "Expecting international success: Female managers overseas." *Columbia Journal of World Business*, Fall 1984a, XIX (3), 79–85.

Adler, N. J. "Women as androgynous managers: A conceptualization of the potential for American women in international management." *International Journal of Intercultural Relations*, 1979, 3 (4), 407–435.

Adler, N. J. "Women do not want international careers: And other myths about international management." *Organizational Dynamics*, Autumn 1984b, XIII (2), 66–79.

Adler, N. J. "Women in international management: Where are they?" *California Management Review*, Summer 1984c, XXVI (4), 78–89.

Castillo, G. T. *The Filipino woman as manpower: The image and empirical reality.* Laguna, Philippines: University of the Philippines, 1977.

Caulkin, S. "Women in management." *Management Today*, February 1977, 80–83.

Chan, A. "Women managers in Singapore: Citizen for tomorrow's economy." In Adler, N. J. and Izraeli, D. (eds.), *Women in Management Worldwide.* Armonk, N.Y.: M. E. Sharpe, 1987 (in press).

Cook, A. H. *Working women in Japan: Discrimination, resistance and reform.* Ithaca, N.Y.: School of Labor and Industrial Relations, 1980.

Crockett, V. R. "Women in management in Indonesia." In Adler, N. J. and Izraeli, D. (eds.), *Women in Management Worldwide.* Armonk, N.Y.: M. E. Sharpe, 1987 (in press).

Croll, E. "A recent movement to redefine the role and status of women." *China Quarterly*, 1977, 69, 591–597.

Dahlby, T. "In Japan, women don't climb the corporate ladder." *New York Times.* September 1977, 18, section 3, 11.

Davin, D. *Women work: Women and the party in revolutionary China.* Great Britain: Oxford University Press, 1976, 53–69, 210–213.

Department of Sociology. *Stereotype, status, and satisfaction: The Filipina among Filipinos.* Quezon City, Philippines: University of the Philippines, 1977.

Dhawan, K. C. Etemad, H., and Wright, R. W. *International business: A Canadian perspective.* Reading, Mass.: Addison-Wesley, 1981.

Dunn & Bradstreet Canada Ltd., *Canadian Key Business Directory 1980.* Toronto: Dunn & Bradstreet Canada Ltd., 1980.

Foz, V. B. *The labor code of the Philippines and its implementing rules and regulations.* Quezon City, Philippines: Philippine Law Gazette, 1979.

Galenson, M. *Women and work: An international comparison.* ILR Paperback No. 13. Ithaca, N.Y.: N.Y. State School of Industrial and Labor Relations, Cornell University, 1973.

Gosselin, M. "Situation des femmes aux Philippines." *Communiqu'elles.* Janvier 1984, 11–12.

Hiroshi, T. "Working women in business corporations: The management viewpoint (Japan)." *Japan Quarterly,* July–September 1982, 29, 319–323.

Indonesia, Biro Pusat Statistik (Central Bureau of Statistics). Population of Indonesia Series S Number 2: Results of 1980 Population Census, 1982.

International Labor Office. "Statistical Information on Women's Participation in Economic Activity." Mimeographed. Geneva: ILO, 1970, Table VIII; as cited in Galenson, 1973, Table 4, 23.

Jen-min-jih-pao (Editorial), "Let All Women Rise Up," March 8, 1974.

Kaminski, M. and Paiz, J. "Japanese women in management: Where are they?" *Human Resource Management,* Fall 1984, 23 (3), 277–292.

Miralao, V. *Women and men in development: Findings from a pilot study.* Quezon City, Philippines: Institute of Philippine Culture, 1980.

Morgenthaler, E. "Women of the world: More U.S. firms put females in key posts in foreign countries." *Wall Street Journal,* March 16, 1978, 1, 27.

Ople, B. F. *Working managers, elites: The human spectrum of development.* Manila, Philippines: Institute of Labor and Management, 1981.

Osako, M. M. "Dilemmas of Japanese professional women." *Social Problems,* 1978, 26, 15–25.

*Report of the Task Force on Female Participation in the Labor Force.* National Productivity Council Committee on Productivity in the Manufacturing Sector, Singapore, January 1985.

Singh, D. "Women executives in India." *Management International Review,* August 1980, 20, 53–60.

Singson, E. R. "Women in executive positions." Paper presented at the 1985 Congress on Women in Decision Making, The Singapore Business and Professional Women's Association, September 1985, 22–23.

Sorrentino, C. "International comparisons of labor force participation, 1960–81. *Monthly Labor Review*, February 1983, 23–36.

Steinhoff, P. G. and Tanaka, K. "Women executives in Japan." *International Studies of Management and Organization*, Fall–Winter, 1986–87 (in press).

Suzuki, N. and Narapareddy, V. "Problems and prospects for the female corporate executives: A cross-cultural perspective." Working paper, University of Illinois at Urbana-Champaign, 1985.

Thal, N. L., and Cateora, P. R. "Opportunities for women in international business." *Business Horizons*, 22 (6), December 1979, 21–27.

Trafford, A., Avery, R., Thorton, J., Carey, J., Galloway, J., and Sanoff, A. "She's Come a Long Way Or Has She?" *U.S. News & World Report*, August 6, 1984, 44–51.

U.S. Department of Labor, Bureau of Labor Statistics "Current Population Survey." *In Employment and Training Report of the President*, Washington, D.C., 1982.

*Women's Bureau, 1986. Fuin Rodo no Jitsujo, 1986* (The Actual Condition of Women Workers). Tokyo: Printing Office, Ministry of Finance, 1986.

# The International Assignment Reconsidered

## NAKIYE A. BOYACIGILLER

Close to 41% of the major U.S. multinational corporations (MNCs) plan on reducing the number of U.S. nationals assigned overseas.[1] And yet, most MNCs see an increase in the international interaction most managers will be facing. Therein lies a paradox. Just when the need for international expertise is growing, U.S. MNCs are reducing the number of Americans sent overseas, thus depriving both the country and themselves of the opportunity to increase the international experience and knowledge base of our current and future managers.

The orientation most MNCs take toward international assignments needs to be reconsidered. U.S. MNCs must view expatriation as a strategic tool, a very different perspective from that traditionally used. Historically, firms sent managers and professionals overseas to fill positions on a seemingly ad hoc basis, paying little attention either to their selection and training or to the role they could play in the overall organization. Moreover, American firms frequently sent Americans overseas because of ethnocentric attitudes ("We have to assign Americans to key positions because foreigners can't be trusted to handle the job.") Both approaches created problems. Individuals sent overseas without adequate training often failed. Indiscriminate staffing with Americans created resentment among qualified local nationals.

Fortunately, a growing number of human resource professionals and researchers in this area are beginning to speak in terms of strategic international human resource management.[2] International assignments should be utilized to develop future managers with a global orientation and to manage key organizational and country linkages.

Consider two overseas branches of the same U.S.-owned international bank opened in 1975. Both grew to equal size as measured by loans, deposits, and employment. Yet the two branches use very different personnel staffing practices. In Branch A, only 7% of the professionals and managers are U.S.

*Source:* Reprinted by permission of the author.

nationals, while in Branch B, U.S. nationals number close to 30%. Why the difference? Is it explained by location? Branch A is located in Copenhagen, Denmark, while Branch B is in Cairo, Egypt. Or can it be explained by internal organizational characteristics, such as the branches' complexity? The answer is both.

As suggested by the above example, there are a multitude of national and organizational characteristics that influence the relative utilization of U.S. and local nationals in overseas affiliates. Yet previous research in this area, while providing direction on the employee characteristics to emphasize in selection decisions, has not focused on organizational and national characteristics to consider when staffing overseas affiliates.

To fill this void in our knowledge of international staffing practices, a study was conducted of a major U.S. financial institution, here called ICB, to determine which organizational and environmental factors influence the use of U.S. nationals abroad.[3] ICB is structurally comprised of four regions: North America; Asia; Latin America and the Caribbean; and Europe, the Middle East and Africa. The present regional structure was established in 1974 to "decentralize [ICB's] approach to a coordinated global wholesale banking strategy."[4] The study includes all 84 foreign branches of ICB. Located in 43 different countries, the branches are wholly owned by ICB.

These ICB branches are involved in both wholesale (corporate) and retail (individual) banking to varying degrees. The Asian branches deal primarily in trade finance, while their European counterparts are mainly wholesale operations catering to large multinationals. In Latin America, much of the activity has been project lending and retail banking. The branches differ tremendously in size and scope of operations and the kind of businesses in which they engage. There are significant differences both across regions and within regions.

The study was designed to test the following hypotheses:

- *Political risk:* Greater levels of political risk will lead to a greater proportion of U.S. nationals in professional positions.
- *Cultural distance:* The greater the cultural distance between the host country and the U.S., the greater the proportion of U.S. nationals in professional positions.
- *Competition:* The greater the level of competition with other finance institutions, the greater the proportion of U.S. nationals in professional positions.
- *Interdependence:* The greater the interdependence between the branch and corporate headquarters, the greater the proportion of U.S. nationals in professional positions.
- *Complexity:* The more complex the branch operations, the greater the proportion of U.S. nationals in managerial and staff positions.
- *Cost:* The variance in the cost between a local national and an expatriate will not have an influence on the proportion of U.S. nationals in the branch.

# ▰▰ *Environmental (Country) Factors to Consider When Staffing Overseas Units*

This research revealed three factors—political risk, cultural distance, and competition—to be particularly important in explaining the utilization of expatriates in a foreign unit.[5]

## *Political Risk*

What is the level of political risk in the country and how can it be managed? Conventional wisdom suggests that in countries where political risk is high, it is important to have a local profile, that is, to appear to act and look like a local firm. This approach would require minimal use of U.S. personnel.

Politically risky countries are often the most difficult for managers in corporate headquarters to understand. In addition, studies have shown that inherently volatile situations (like one of high political risk) are often accompanied by decisions based on judgments rather than specific structural arrangements to deal with the uncertainty.[6]

Yet how are these judgments to be made? The knowledge and insight a well-placed U.S. national can provide to corporate executives is crucial in environments where garnering the necessary information is problematic. Understanding how to interpret economic, political, and financial signals in an alien environment is difficult even when one is located in the country in question. When one is sitting thousands of miles away in an entirely different milieu, reaching erroneous conclusions is all too possible. Parent nationals located in overseas operations can be important conduits of information. This study found that ICB utilizes more expatriate managers in countries with high political risk ratings, as was hypothesized.

## *Cultural Distance*

Cultural distance refers to the extent that two cultures differ. Key dimensions of culture include such characteristics as how collectivistic or individualistic the culture is, how time is perceived, and how rigidly sex roles are defined. When two cultures differ significantly on these and other cultural dimensions, it is more difficult for individuals from these cultures to communicate and work well together. Strategically placed U.S. nationals play an important interpretative role between the host country culture and the U.S. headquarters offices. This bridging role is clearly evident in a Scandinavian manager's description of an MNC's operations in Japan:

> Nowadays there seems to be a tendency towards "over-Japanization" of the foreign company in Japan; i.e., the top management is, after initial stages of starting up business, staffed entirely with Japanese executives. It has been observed that this can create serious problems particularly in the communication with the head office overseas. In one actual case, the Japanese president of a joint venture company got so frustrated with this

communication problem that he actually resigned and returned to the large Japanese corporation he originally came from. The occasional visitor from the head office cannot possibly understand all the complexities of carrying out business in Japan, and what the Japanese executive in the related case actually wanted was to have an able person from the head office permanently stationed in Japan and with whom he could discuss the various problems on the spot.[7]

My research found that the greater the cultural distance between the host nation and the U.S., the greater the proportion of U.S. nationals in subsidiary management.

## Competition

This research found the competition existing in the local environment of the host country to lead to fewer U.S. nationals in the foreign branches. There are two logical explanations as to why this would occur. First, greater competition indicates a greater number of firms (local and foreign) where local nationals are able to acquire banking experience. With ample situations for training in finance and banking, local nationals became more attractive to ICB.

Secondly, in a competitive market, local nationals are a critical resource in garnering more local business. Local nationals often provide critical links to local commerical communities, thus allowing the MNC to gain new business. This is especially true, given that some countries where competition was found to be the highest (e.g., Indonesia, Bahrain, and Malaysia) are also countries where good contacts with local government and business officials are very important.

## Cost

Every CEO laments the high cost of sending Americans overseas on assignment. Total expatriate compensation comes to about 2.5 times the employee's U.S. base salary, when such expenses as cost-of-living adjustments, tax equalization, housing, and education are included.[8] Yet the cost of expatriation needs to be understood in a broader framework. First, thinking about cost in averages rather than focusing on individual countries creates a fallacy. The cost of living varies greatly across international borders, thus focusing on average costs can mask real differences. For example, in 1983, the cost of a $36,000-a-year American employee was $61,500 a year in Tokyo, $41,000 in Hong Kong, $71,000 in Bahrain, and $36,000 in Argentina.

Secondly, MNCs need to address the cost issue within a broader framework of what the company seeks to gain through overseas assignments. If they use international assignments to develop future upper-level managers with a global orientation and the ability to manage key organizational issues, then absolute cost must be viewed from a very different perspective. While costly in the short term, international assignments appear more useful when perceived as a long-term investment.

Still, one important caveat must be made regarding cost. It is always an important consideration when employees sent overseas fail. Previous research suggests that the reason many U.S. firms have not sent many Americans abroad is their high failure rates overseas.[9] Another study found that when compared to Japanese and European expatriates, American expatriates tend to have significantly larger failure rates (e.g., early returns due to lack of adaptation or ineffective job performance on the job).[10] The failures are not surprising given that assignments are often made hastily, with insufficient time and care paid to selection and training. Studies show that when choosing individuals for overseas sojourns, MNCs focus on technical and managerial competence, assuming that technically competent managers will automatically function effectively overseas. Unfortunately, this is often not the case. Characteristics such as adaptability, ethnocentrism, and the family's resistance to an international sojourn are often neglected and yet frequently lead to overseas failure.[11]

## Characteristics of the Foreign Affiliate to Consider When Staffing

After considering the national factors, several characteristics of the overseas affiliate should be considered when deciding on an appropriate staffing policy. The most important are interdependence, complexity, and control mechanisms.

### Interdependence

Subsidiaries of MNCs do not operate as closed systems. Typically, they have resource links to other subunits within the MNC as well as ties to firms and customers in host, home, and other countries. This interdependence with other organizations creates important implications for staffing. For example, if a foreign affiliate maintains a high level of interdependence with the U.S. headquarters, placing some U.S. expatriates in management positions facilitates intraorganizational communication and relations. Given significant interdependence with headquarters or other U.S. affiliates, U.S. nationals perform an important role in managing the uncertainty that derives from interdependence. This is clearly evident in the comments of the non-Swedish president of a Swedish joint venture on the appointment of a Swede to the position of production manager:

> It was absolutely necessary that Mr. X was appointed. Before he came we were never able to receive any attention from the product divisions when we needed faster deliveries for some reasons or when we needed special blueprints for our own production. As a result, we sometimes had serious production delays. He [Mr. X] has improved the situation a lot in many instances just by knowing whom to contact in Sweden.[12]

Alternatively, if the foreign affiliate has its most important resource ties within the host country, then parent country managers do not provide an equivalent benefit. Intracountry, as opposed to intercountry, interdependencies are best managed by local nationals.

### Complexity

Most multinational corporations are comprised of units that differ widely in their levels of complexity. The complexity of an assembly plant in Western Europe is undoubtedly much lower than the complexity of an R&D lab in the same location. Controlling units that have disparate levels of complexity is difficult for MNCs. Complex tasks imply "an increase in information load, information diversity, or rate of information change."[13] Consequently, the amount of information processing necessary to control complex operations is much greater than the information processing required to control less complex units. Given that communication and control is facilitated among managers of the same nationality, it is not surprising that more complex units had more U.S. nationals assigned to them.[14]

### Control Mechanisms: Socialization

Given ICB's decentralized approach to global banking strategy, the firm requires several specific control mechanisms to ensure that employees in foreign affiliates act in concert with the parent organization. As an ICB executive stated:

> If your major strength is a network of global operations, you must provide that network with a strong *esprit de corps*. As operations are decentralized, we cannot tell the branches what to do. Yet if a branch turns down the loan request of a person that is a key customer for our firm, just because that particular loan does not make sense for that particular branch . . . then the company will risk losing an important customer. Yet the more you decentralize the more you localize those decisions and risk that particular loan not be made. We must make sure that the customer is managed worldwide.

Three ways an organization can achieve control are bureaucratic rules, the use of hierarchy, and socialization. Of these, socialization is the most flexible and least obtrusive. Parent country nationals can provide an invaluable role in socializing local nationals into the MNC's ways of doing business. This is especially important in MNCs where increasing rules and standards may not be possible (because of high complexity and or differentiation of operations) and increasing socialization may be the only mechanism for increasing control.

## ▬ *Conclusions: Consider Both*

Both organizational and country characteristics need to be taken into account when determining how to staff an overseas affiliate. First, and most important, one must assess the interdependencies between the subunit, the host government, local businesses, and corporate headquarters. Complexity, political risk, and cultural distance increase the inherent difficulty of doing business in the foreign country and generally require greater expatriate presence. In contrast, extensive local competition in the host country in turn increases the importance of local nationals as conduits to the local market.

International staffing decisions need to be tied to other strategic decisions. The emphasis during staffing should be on long-term organizational development and management development and above all on long-term commitment to learning about international markets. If high-potential individuals are carefully selected and trained for overseas positions, they will not only facilitate the maintenance of an international network of operations in the short term but should be allowed to continue providing informational support upon their return to the U.S. The international education that future executives could acquire in these types of assignments cannot be replicated in any classroom.

## ▬ *Endnotes*

1. Kobrin, S.J. *International Expertise in American Business: How to Learn to Play with the Kids on the Street.* New York: Institute of International Education, 1984.

2. See for example, Adler, N.J. and Ghadar, F. "Globalization and Human Resource Management." To be published in Alan Rugman (ed.), *Research in Global Strategic Management: A Canadian Perspective,* Volume One. Greenwich, Conn.: JAI Press, 1989.

3. For more detail, see Boyacigiller, N.A. "The role of expatriates in the management of interdependence, complexity and risk." Working paper 8703. San Jose State University, Department of Organization and Management.

4. An ICB internal document.

5. An expatriate refers to a parent country national assigned overseas; (e.g., an American IBM employee stationed in Japan for three years). A host national refers to a local national working for the multinational in his or her own country (e.g., a Japanese national working for IBM in Japan).

6. Leblebici, H. and Salancik, G.R. "Effects of environmental uncertainty on information and decision processes in banks." *Administrative Science Quarterly,* 1981, 578–596.

7. Delaryd, B. *The Japan Economic Journal,* May 30, 1972, 20.

8. "High cost of overseas staff." *World Business Weekly,* April 27, 1981, 4, 48.

9. Kobrin, S.J. "Expatriate reduction and strategic control in American multinational corporations." *Human Resource Management, 1988,* 27 (1), 63–76.

10. Tung, R.L. "Expatriate assignments: Enhancing success and minimizing failure." *The Academy of Management Executive,* 1987, 1, 2, 117–125.

11. Tung, R. L. "Selection and training of U.S., European, and Japanese multinational corporations." *California Management Review,* Fall 1982, 57–71.

12. Leksell, L. *Headquarter-Subsidiary Relationships in Multinational Corporations.* Stockholm School of Economics, 1981.

13. Campbell, D.J. Task complexity: A review and analysis. *Academy of Management Review,* 1988, 13 (1), 40–52.

14. On the challenges of managing a multicultural work force, see Adler, N.J. *International Dimensions of Organizational Behavior.* Boston, Mass.: Kent Publishing, 1986. For an in-depth study of the role of the manager, see Mintzberg, *The Nature of Managerial Work.* New York: Harper & Row, 1973.

# Precision Measurement of Japan: A Small Foreign Company in the Japanese Labor Market

## JAMES G. SCOVILLE

P recision Measurement of Japan (PM-J) is a joint venture company between Takezawa Electric Company (TEC),* a Japanese electrical equipment manufacturing company, and Precision Management, Inc. (PMI), a Minnesota-based manufacturer of measurement devices. Major markets for these devices are chemical processes, pipelines, aircraft, and aerospace and power generation. As a multinational corporation, PMI is faced with the problem of penetrating the Japanese market before one of its Japanese competitors perfects the various gauges and shuts the U.S. company out of the Japanese market. In order to penetrate the Japanese market, PMI has entered into a business relationship with TEC thus forming a quasi-Japanese company, PM-J. This step was intended to increase PMI's credibility with the Japanese, and to fore-

---

*All names have been changed. The company name is somewhat descriptive of its line of business; the employee names in Exhibit 2 are taken from a list of the 10 most common Japanese names collected by the Daihyaku Insurance Company. Christine Hoffman and Eliyahue Stein provided research assistance on this case.

I am also indebted to referees who commented on the case. One of their suggestions was a brief guide to pronunciation of the Japanese names in this case. In general, each vowel merits a syllable: thus, "Tah.Keh.zah.wah." The only exception is when "i" serves as a "y," as in the name of Keio ("Kayo") University. All "sh" combinations in this case are pronounced as in "shoe."

Source: This case was prepared by James G. Scoville (with the assistance of Christine Hoffman and Eliyahue Stein) as a basis for class discussion rather than to illustrate either effective or ineffective handling of an administrative situation. The U.S. Department of Education funded the preparation of this case under Grant #G00877027.

stall a Japanese competitor from using its protected domestic market to work out bugs, employ economies of scale, undercut PMI's pricing scheme, and generally take over the world instrument market. This would seriously, perhaps fatally, affect PMI's viability.

## The Problem

The problem faced by his company, according to Joe Smith, President of PM-J, is that the Japanese instrument companies are becoming more visible and are developing broader product lines, which may directly affect PM-J's market share. Corporate PMI headquarters is genuinely concerned that the Japanese long-term plan is to capture and dominate the world instrument markets just as they have taken over camera, automobile, video recorder, and other high-tech markets. The instrument market could be the next Japanese strategic industry.

Currently, the Japanese tend to dominate only their domestic instrument markets, says Smith. This could change by working their familiar strategy. This is accomplished by closing the Japanese markets to foreign competition, acquiring volume and experience in domestic markets, and basing foreign marketing on that experience.

The usual Japanese strategy is to either (1) obtain licenses for advanced technology from other companies (usually from the United States) and then improve the technology and market it alone or (2) use some company's proven distribution to establish a market base and then go it alone. Both of these approaches save considerable time and expense to the Japanese company thus freeing resources and capital for quick and effective marketing of the new and/or improved technology. Smith reports that two competitors gained real substance in this manner.

After penetrating the foreign markets with this strategy, excellent service and responsiveness from the Japanese companies is generally reported. The Japanese will, no doubt, continue their patient, persistent way of presenting high-technology, high-performance products which are backed by quality service. Even though they gain market position slowly, says Smith, once the Japanese establish accounts, their outstanding customer relations and excellent service record often mean they keep the accounts; the non-Japanese are then in a position of lost accounts and a declining market share.

## Objective

PMI wishes to establish a permanent position in the Japanese domestic market. Additionally, it would be preferable that any Japanese competition be retarded by PMI's establishment of a strong sales and manufacturing posture in Japan. To acquire and maintain a market share in the instrument industry, PMI must establish credibility as a viable company; this it sought to do by combining with TEC. By establishing PM-J, PMI is demonstrating a long-term commitment and significant investment in Japan. In its efforts to capture the Japanese market, PM-J is faced with two overriding questions:

1. Is it possible to hire a sufficient number of qualified sales engineers (preferably newly graduated) to increase sales, establish quality accounts, and achieve a reasonable profit growth?
2. In what manner might PM-J increase its market position and distribution in the Japanese market?

The answers to these questions are complicated by a variety of socioeconomic factors unique to Japan.

## ▄▄ The Country

Japan has a small amount of inhabitable land located on a number of mountainous islands, with few natural resources but abundant human resources. Pressured by the need to import almost all raw materials, including 100% of all oil, the Japanese economy grew at phenomenal rates during the 1960s and 1970s. During this period, Japanese industrial products moved from a reputation as cheap and flimsy to a position known for quality and reliability. This achievement was attained in part through protective import practices and a coordinated industrial strategy featuring cooperation between major manufacturing groups and the government, especially through activities of the Ministry of International Trade and Industry (MITI).

## ▄▄ The Company

Precision Measurement, Inc. was founded in the mid-1960s to produce a wide range of measurement and instrumentation equipment. Over the years, the company has remained at the forefront of this industry and continues to this day to pursue cutting-edge research. In recent years, the company's financial strength has been sustained by a classic "cash cow"—a gauge for measurement of flow and pressure. The success of this gauge relies on two factors: (1) very fine and precise machining of high-quality material to strict quality standards and (2) an ingenious application of elementary principles of physics. Neither of these constitutes a substantial barrier to Japanese competition: machining materials to high standard is straightforward; even the casewriter's late 1950s high school physics allows him to understand the way the gauge works!

## ▄▄ Staffing Implications

To penetrate the Japanese domestic market, an optimal staffing pattern must be generated which would yield the desired sales capability. (Manufac-

E X H I B I T  1

*Projected Staffing Patterns, 1985–1987*

|  | APRIL 1985 | END 1985 | END 1986 | END 1987 |
|---|---|---|---|---|
| *Administration* | 5 | 5 | 5 | 5 |
| *Secretarial, clerical* | 5 | 5 | 5 | 5 |
| *Engineering* | | | | |
| *Sales and marketing 3* | | | | |
| *Engineering* | 8 | 11 | 13 | 15 |
| *Services group 3* | | | | |
| *Production 2* | | | | |
| *Production technicians* | 2 | 3 | 3 | 3 |
| | 20 | 24 | 26 | 28 |

turing takes place in the U.S., with the gauge being modified to the customer's needs in Japan by production engineers and technicians.) PM-J's president supplied a table of desired staffing patterns from the beginning of 1985 through 1987, which focuses on their probable staffing needs (Exhibit 1). Although PM-J found it very difficult to hire the eight engineers who presently represent the company, it is now faced with the need to engage seven more in just two and one-half years.

## ■ Engineering Labor Markets in Japan

The nature of Japanese labor markets, particularly for professionals and managers, directly affects attainability of the staffing patterns outlined by the company. Modern, large Japanese organizations generally hire people as they finish school for "lifetime employment." The employee then receives a traditional training, which consists of considerable job rotation, and general training, which develops broad skills; the employee, therefore, expects a pay system based primarily on length of service with the company rather than job-specific performance. Thus, PM-J's competitors would typically hire engineers on completion of university training and employ them until their early to mid-50s. Then, as is the practice with many managers, the senior employees are transferred to subsidiaries, client organizations, smaller plants, or less demanding jobs.

A small company, like PM-J, cannot easily compete in the labor market because it cannot guarantee its own survival for the career lifetime of the employees. Small organizations are more likely to go out of business and are, even if they survive, less likely to obtain a major share of the product market. This fact does little to instill confidence in the new graduate who expects lifetime employment as a condition of employment. The same weakness generally applies to foreign companies in Japan. They often do not share a commitment to lifetime employment, traditional pay systems, or a long business presence in Japan. This image formed by some foreign companies that came to Japan and then laid off many people or totally withdrew is widespread among Japanese professionals.

PM-J has generally been unable to recruit the immediate post-graduate because it is both small and foreign. This has necessitated acquiring its engineering force in various *ad hoc* ways, predominantly relying on recommendations from its joint venture partner, TEC. While not optimal, it has at least allowed the company to develop a skeleton staff.

The first two columns of Exhibit 2 show the name and recruiting source of engineers currently employed by PM-J. The third and fourth columns show the salaries of these people (millions of yen per year) as compared with the average pay of employees of the same age and education in large companies in Japan. The final column shows each employee's job performance evaluation as reported by company president Smith. Exhibit 2 clearly demonstrates that PM-J's hiring pattern has strongly deviated from the stereotypical post-university hire/lifetime employment pattern of Japanese industry in general.

## ▬ *Alternatives to the Current Situation*

Given the staffing and recruiting patterns of Japanese industries and the staffing dilemmas faced by PM-J, what alternative plans of action are available to a small, foreign company which will promote its stated objectives of expanded sales and increased market share? If PM-J is to predominate in the Japanese market, what alternatives to its current pattern of hiring mid-career engineers could move the company toward hiring newly graduated qualified engineers? Are there changes occurring in the Japanese labor culture which might benefit PM-J if the company recognizes and adapts the changes to fit its needs?

## ▬ *Attracting Younger Engineers*

How might PM-J increase its hiring ratio of younger engineers directly out of school? Will it be as difficult to hire new graduates in the future as previous experience suggests? The latter situation seems to be loosening a bit as professors' influence in directing students has declined. Indeed, some students are more willing to consider employers other than just the very largest and more traditional Japanese companies. Furthermore, the typical lifetime employment pattern seems to be eroding as some younger professionals with relatively recent dates of hire move to new companies after only three or four years of employment. Organizations like The Recruit Center (a

EXHIBIT 2

## Sales and Support Force, Spring 1985

| Name | Source | Annual Pay Including Bonuses (million yen) | Average Pay at Large Companies* (million yen) | Performance Evaluation |
|---|---|---|---|---|
| Sato | Small company experience, recommended by the general manager of PM-J | 9.5 | 9.7 | 55% effort rating; lower segment on performance |
| Suzuki | Formerly a representative for PM-J | 7.3 | 5.8 | 80% |
| Takahashi | TEC (age: late 40s) | 7.3 | 7.2 | 75–85% |
| Watanabe | Nihon Medical (age: early 50s), recommended by a classmate who is now a professor | 9.5 | 9.5 | Very high |
| Tanaka | Junior high school education plus 20 years in the instrumentation sales business; answered an ad in a trade journal | | | N/A |
| Ito | TEC (age: 32) | 5.8 | 5.8 | 90% |
| Kobayashi | New university graduate | 2.9 | 3.0 | N/A |
| Saito | TEC (age: about 40) | 6.3 | 6.3 | Very high |
| Yamamoto | TEC (age: mid-40s) | 8.4 | 7.8 | Very high |

*Equal to 18 months salary in the average large company, no housing or other allowances figured in. The extra six months' pay reflects the average level of bonuses in Japan. At present, large Japanese companies pay roughly two months' salary as a bonus three times a year (late spring, late summer, and at the Christmas–New Years season).
Source: Japan Institute of Labor Statistical Reports.

major recruiting and placement organization providing extensive published information on companies as prospective employers) and "headhunters" are supporting these changes in employment patterns by publicizing employment opportunities and company characteristics. Young professionals in engineering and other technical fields are beginning to rely on such data in making career decisions.

The advantages of this alternative, i.e., to employ personnel agencies, are straightforward. First, PM-J could more readily advertise the benefits and opportunities it is able to provide to career-minded professionals via the agencies and headhunters. Second, PM-J stands to gain credibility which the recruitment agencies and headhunters, as third parties, can confer as they present the company as a stable organization that demonstrates Japanese characteristics. Third, recruitment agents are financially motivated to match employers and employees; PM-J can capitalize on this by requesting younger, well-educated, technically qualified engineers who have a potentially longer career life with the company.

The principal disadvantages of personnel agencies are their high cost to the small organization, in terms of money and CEO time. Further caveats must be noted: Graduates of the best Japanese universities and engineering programs (University of Tokyo and Keio University) would probably not be interested in employment agencies because they would most likely be recruited by the large domestic companies via contacts with university professors. Likewise, headhunters would be less able to lure young new hires from large companies to work for a smaller foreign-based firm. Additionally, if PM-J accepted a large proportion of graduates from second- and third-tier universities, it would be unable to generate a level of credibility which a workforce of "better" educated employees from top-rated universities would confer.

## ■ Attracting Female Engineers

One intriguing labor market strategy might be to get women into PM-J's labor force as sales engineers. A growing number of women are enrolled in engineering programs at Japanese universities. Their employability, at least in principle, should be enhanced by equal opportunity legislation recently passed by the Diet (Japan's parliament). More distant observers, including some at the corporate offices of PMI, have occasionally brainstormed about job redesign and the use of women engineers; U.S.-based students may almost think this a natural option. Practical reaction at PM-J, however, stresses that the acceptability of women in many Japanese work roles is not immediately forthcoming, as the tale related in Exhibit 3 amply suggests. Moreover, it will be even longer in coming within the industrial setting where men are almost exclusively employed and where evening entertainment of customers is an expected job component.

E X H I B I T  3

*Prospects for Female Engineers*

The actual and potential roles of women in Japanese society and work life are undoubtedly changing. The increasing proportions of female students at universities is one index of this change and is directly related to PM-J's problems. Between 1970 and 1980, the female enrollment ratio more than doubled from 9.6 percent to 20.1 percent. In spite of this upsurge, the number of female engineering graduates in all fields remains very small; 1981 engineering graduates included 1,143 women as compared to 73,631 men.

Numbers alone fail to tell the full tale of how difficult it could be to employ women successfully in PM-J's sales engineering positions, where they would have to call on and entertain male customers. A recent event described in *Labor Trends in Japan*, 1983, may illuminate the employability of women in Japan today.

> A minor scandal erupted in 1983 with the publication of confidential employment guidelines of one of Japan's major bookselling chains employing 2,000 persons, over half of them women, in 28 outlets. The manual told office managers to guard against hiring certain types of women. Among these were women who wore glasses, short women (under 4 ft., 8 in.), ugly women and those with country bumpkin-like attributes. Educational criteria for exclusion included college drop-outs and graduates of four-year universities ("too headstrong"). Also to be avoided were potentially troublesome women including those who belong to political or religious organizations since they would not be able to easily change their way of thinking, those whose fathers are university professors or whose husbands are teachers or writers, and women who take an interest in legal affairs or who could otherwise be argumentative, such as those who belonged to school newspaper clubs. Another group which should not be hired, according to the manual, are women with complicated family situations or chronic illnesses. Lastly, presumably since their conduct might not be above suspicion, women who have changed jobs more than once, divorcées, single women renting their own apartments and women who respect "passionate artists" such as Van Gogh should be passed over. (*Labor Trends in Japan*, 1983)

## Engineers vs. Salespeople

A variant on the idea of increasing the number of engineers at PM-J is to reduce the company's reliance on engineers by employing non-technically trained salespeople; the sales component of the engineers' positions would be eliminated or substantially decreased. After all, engineers don't do all the selling in the United States; rather, they provide technical backup and design work after the salesperson has made the pitch.

Perhaps it is feasible to explore hiring graduates of technical high schools and vocational schools for sales, following the example set when Tanaka was hired (Exhibit 2). This could be accomplished by multiple testing (less restricted in Japan than in the United States), and increased training to identify and qualify strong sales candidates. In fact, PMI in the United States and other organizations in Japan succeeded in using a combination of both occupations in marketing products.

By using non-engineering salespeople, PM-J could easily expand its labor force with younger employees. Unfortunately, the company is small and foreign; in reducing the perceived qualifications of its salesforce, it will suffer a further loss of credibility conferred on employees holding an engineering degree from a respected university.

## Maintaining the Status Quo

Staying with the status quo is another strategy. PM-J could continue using mid-career people. Most of these employees have been recruited from the joint venture partner, TEC. This method is relatively inexpensive because the initial recruitment, selection, and training costs are absorbed by TEC since the engineers began employment there. An advantage of this method is that the engineers with 25 to 30 years' experience have far more business contacts than do fresh graduates. The principle disadvantage is that one cannot be certain that the TEC engineers are quality employees. After all, why should TEC give up its best people to PM-J and retain the marginal employees for its own use? It's quite conceivable that the joint venture could be receiving some of the less productive TEC personnel. This also perpetuates the current dilemma of a salesforce in its early to mid-50s, which does not assist the company's image, credibility, or ability to capture the difficult Japanese market.

A further complication in PM-J's reliance on TEC's transferred employees is that many mid-career professionals may be loyal to their previous employer; this will not result in a highly motivated salesforce which will be prepared to endeavor diligently to promote a new employer in the market.

## Supplementing the Status Quo

Another strategic option is to supplement the status quo (hiring mid-career professional engineers) with headhunters and/or employment agencies such as The Recruit Center. Headhunters are more prevalent in the Japanese labor market recently, and many Japanese companies report some successes in employing their services. Even though such agencies and headhunters are quite expensive and time consuming, they do represent one means in filling gaps created by internal rotations of employees or vacancies resulting from terminated employees. Perhaps the most likely recruit from headhunting would be in the 28 to 30 year old range who is making a career move. Although not fresh from school, these engineers would still be relatively recent university graduates with respectively longer career lives ahead of them. This would tend to stabilize PM-J's engineering and salesforce turnover while simultaneously conferring the credibility to be gained from the honored university degree.

## Toward an Appraisal of These Options

The likely success of these various strategies clearly depends on the prospective state of the Japanese engineer labor market. PM-J's hiring success will be *directly* enhanced by any developments which reduce the number of engineers absorbed by the rest of Japanese industry and by its ability to gain credibility as a stable "Japanese" company. *Indirect* effects are also possible.

For example, it's likely that any developments which loosen the supply of male engineers will make it even more difficult for female engineers to be accepted, especially in sales. Thus, a reliable forecast of engineering labor market conditions in Japan is central to any strategy recommendation to PM-J.

## Future Labor Market Developments

### Effects of an Aging Workforce

The Japanese labor force and population has aged in recent years, pressuring the social insurance and retirement systems, similar to the U.S. situation. This has led the government to explore postponing pension age from about 60 to about 65. The Japanese employment system for engineers (among other professions) initially moves employees in the 50 to 55 age range to secondary employment (within the firm) or to other employers.* Since the government has made early pension less likely, it seems that in coming years more men will seek longer second careers. As noted, this would dampen women's employability. It would also increase the availability of engineering resources to a company like PM-J.

### The Decline of New Workers

The declining number of young people entering the labor market and the declining pool of new engineering graduates implies that small companies like PM-J are more likely to be squeezed out of the market. Based on present hiring patterns, 80 percent of the graduates of the top 10 Japanese engineering schools would be recruited and absorbed by a select group of employers consisting of the largest domestic and foreign organizations. This tightening

---

*The age-related pay system (nenko), plus the common decline of productivity after a certain age implies that after that age older workers tend to become more and more expensive rapidly.

of the youth market decreases the viability of a strategy aimed at hiring fresh graduates into small, foreign companies.

### Foreign Product Competition and the Japanese Labor Market

One must consider the *labor market* effects of opening Japanese *product markets* to foreign competition. If Japan concedes to growing pressure from its allies to reduce import tariffs and trade barriers, who will be hit hardest? Which Japanese industries will be hurt by a policy of greater import penetration into Japan? First of all, it is not probable that agriculture will be hit heavily. Even though Japanese food prices are three to six times the world level, it's unlikely that the government would chance eroding its support base among small farmers. This is due to the fact that import restriction policies have supported the relatively large agricultural population who have in turn faithfully supported the incumbent government party, the Liberal Democrats, since the late 1940s.

Are import penetration liberalizations for non-agricultural products apt to affect big companies like Matsushita, Hitachi, or Asahi? These firms run the Japanese "economic miracle" and are closely tied to government policy through the coordinating activities of the Ministry of International Trade and Industry. Such an alliance between government and big business is likely to forestall serious import impacts on the key companies. Thus, won't any opening of Japanese markets to U.S. imports probably be designed to have the most impact on items produced by smaller businesses? As these smaller businesses cut back on employment; won't it have the effect of loosening the labor market exactly where PM-J is located (in terms of company size)?

Political considerations aside, it is also true that small-scale industry in Japan has much higher labor costs (relative to larger enterprises) than in the United States or Germany (another major trading country), as seen in Exhibit 4. Increased foreign product-market competition and a resulting loosening of the smaller-company labor market would increase a surviving small foreign company's ability to recruit and retain qualified employees.

To the extent that Japanese trade policy is liberalized, PM-J should be more successful on all fronts in trying to hire engineers in competition with Japanese firms. On the other hand, the staffing demands of other foreign firms which either expand or enter Japan as a result of this trade policy liberalization will have to be taken into account.

## ▬ Product Market Issues

Having considered some major human resource dynamics affecting PM-J's penetration into the Japanese market, it is necessary to review what product market considerations are relevant to the company's success of PM-J in the Japanese market.

Standards are more frequently mentioned as problems or barriers by

EXHIBIT 4

*Relative Labor Costs in Manufacturing by Size of Enterprise*

| NUMBER OF EMPLOYEES | JAPAN 1985 | USA (1977) | WEST GERMANY (1977) |
| --- | --- | --- | --- |
| 1–9 | 136 | | N/A |
| 10–49 | 129 | 102 | 97 |
| 50–99 | 124 | | 101 |
| 100–499 | 108 | 92 | 102 |
| 500–999 | 97 | | 99 |
| 1000 and more | 100 | 100 | 100 |

*Source: Toward a More Vital Society,* Japan Federation of Employers Assns., 1985.

would-be American importers of technical equipment. Japanese standards are simply not the same as the United States' and are very difficult to understand or change. With respect to the "cash cow gauge," PM-J spent six or seven years on the standards acceptance process.

The biggest issue regarding the product market is the prospect for increased penetration of imports into the Japanese market. Japanese government policy on this is evolving. During the spring of 1985, as PM-J grappled with the strategic issues, Prime Minister Nakasone undertook his famous shopping trip, urging all Japanese to spend 25,000 additional yen on foreign goods. Whether this will help sell PM-J's product is doubtful since its principal applications are industrial. But if it becomes easier for foreign firms to bid on government jobs (pursuant to GATT agreements), PM-J might see a direct sales payoff in major government projects.

## ■ Issues from This Case

There are at least two preliminary issues for the student to address in this case.

First, is TEC doing its job? Are they providing qualified people to the joint venture, PM-J, or are they "dumping" marginal employees who are past their peak performance and on the downslide?

The second preliminary issue that the student should address is whether PM-J's pay scale is appropriate. Data in Exhibit 2 provide comparisons with big companies' pay levels.

### The Longer-Run Labor Market Strategy Options

The student should identify the risks, benefits, and costs of various alternatives (including staffing options) against the backdrop of various "states of the world." Those states of the world will be dominated by the degree to which government policy changes so that PM-J (or more radically, a lot of foreign competition) is able to penetrate domestic markets in Japan. Some engineering labor market strategies will be higher risk and lower risk, with higher and lower costs and payoffs, depending on what one thinks will happen to the engineering labor market and PM-J's ability to penetrate the product market. Although Japanese government policies on foreign access to markets may dominate the scene, other things that will impinge upon the labor market should be considered:

- the aging population
- shortages of youth entering the labor force
- increased numbers of people (early to mid-50s) seeking longer second careers
- increased numbers of women seeking positions
- changing Japanese culture and labor markets

Considering the case as a whole, the basic issue can be starkly posed: How should PM-J attempt to recruit enough people to permit an effective penetration of the Japanese product market on which the survival not only of PM-J, but of its parent PMI, may depend?

# Recruiting a Manager for BRB, Israel

## WILLIAM ROOF
## BARBARA BAKHTARI

BRB Inc, a multinational electronics corporation, plans to establish a new subsidiary in Israel. The firm's base is in Los Angeles, California, with a second overseas headquarters in England. The U.S. office staffs and operates six North American divisions and three South American subsidiaries. The U.K. office is responsible for operations in Europe and Asia. The Israeli venture is the company's first business thrust in the turbulent Middle East.

During the past 10 years, BRB's phenomenal growth resulted largely from its ability to enter the market with new, technically advanced products ahead of the competition. The technology mainly responsible for BRB's recent growth is a special type of radar signal processing. With Fourier transforms, BRB's small, lightweight, and inexpensive radar systems outperform the competitions' larger systems in range, resolution, and price. It is this type of lightweight, portable radar technology that has enormous potential for Israel during conflicts with the Arab States.

BRB's human resource functions in the United States and Europe each boast a vice president. John Conners is the Vice President of Human Resources in the United States, and Francis O'Leary is the Vice President of Human Resources in the United Kingdom. Paul Lizfeld, the CEO of BRB, contacted the two vice presidents and told them to recruit a general manager for the Israeli operation. "I don't care who finds him, but he better be right for the job. I cannot afford to replace him in six months. Is that clear!" Lizfeld told them to look independently and then coordinate together to select the right person. They knew that their jobs could be in jeopardy with this task.

The two human resource operations were independent, and each was managed individually. Recruiting processes differed between U.S. and U.K. operations. Each had different organizational structures and corporate cultures. The only link between the two was Lizfeld's strong micromanagement style, which emphasized cost control.

Source: This article was written especially for this book.

# ▬ *U.S. Operations*

John Conners has worked for BRB for the past 20 years. He started with a degree in engineering and worked in the engineering department. After earning his M.B.A. in human resource management from UCLA, he transferred to the human resource department. Management felt that someone with an engineering background could hire the best technical employees for BRB. With BRB's high turnover rate, they felt that someone who could relate to the technical side of the business could better attract and screen the right people for the organization. BRB promoted Conners to vice president three years ago, after he hired the staffs for the subsidiaries in Peru and Brazil. Except for the general managers, they were all correct fits. Conners felt that the problem with the general managers was an inability to work with Lizfeld.

John Conners looked at many different strategies to determine how to begin recruiting for the Israeli position. He wanted to be sure he found the right person for the job. The first step in choosing the ideal candidate was to determine the selection criteria.

Conners defined the task in Israel to include control and management of BRB's Israeli operations. The GM must work with the Israeli government both directly and indirectly. The political unrest in Israel also requires the GM to conduct sensitive transactions with the Israeli government. This person would also work directly with Lizfeld, taking direction from him and reporting regularly to him.

As with many countries in the Middle East, Israel was in turmoil. Conners actually knew very little about the Israeli culture, but decided to ask different associates who had past dealings with Israel. He knew that the threat of war constantly hung over Israel. The country was also suffering from high inflation rates and troubled economics. Lately, he also learned that the country had become divided over certain political and cultural issues. The person accepting this job needed nerves of steel and extraordinary patience.

Conners decided the selection criteria that would be important for the candidate included technical skill, cultural empathy, a strong sense of politics, language ability, organizational abilities, and an adaptive and supportive family. He also felt that the GM would have to have the following characteristics: persuasiveness, ability to make decisions, resourcefulness, flexibility, and adaptability to new challenges. Now all he needed to do was find a person who had all these attributes.

He decided to begin his search for candidates within the organization. He knew this route had both advantages and disadvantages. Since BRB was still in the beginning stages of internationalization in Israel, a "home country" presence might prove to be very helpful. Lizfeld would appreciate this. The disadvantages would be many. It might be very difficult to find someone willing to relocate in Israel. The increased cost of living and the political unrest make it a tough package to sell. Conners knew of the "Israeli mentality." He also knew he would have to take care in sending someone who might either overpower the Israelis or break under their aggressive business style. Conners knew that Lizfeld wanted to have the home country atmosphere in Israel and planned to be very active in the management of Israeli operations.

The second option Conners had was to recruit from outside the company. The ideal candidate would have both domestic and international experience. Conners could recruit either by contacting an employment agency or by placing and ad in the *Wall Street Journal*. He thought he could find a person with the right qualifications, but he also knew it would be difficult to find someone Lizfeld liked outside the company. Conners had hired two managers for the South American offices, and Lizfeld had driven them over the edge within six months. Conners knew that he had to be extra careful. One more "unqualified" candidate might put his own job on the line.

Conners found three potential candidates for the Israeli position. One candidate, Joel Goldberg, was a recommendation from the headhunter Conners had commissioned. Goldberg had thirty-five years of electronics and radar experience. He had been CEO of Radar Developments Incorporated, a major electronics corporation in New York. Goldberg had taken control of Radar Developments Incorporated in 1981. By 1986, the company had tripled sales and increased profits fivefold. Goldberg had the technical knowledge to perform the job. He also had the necessary individual characteristics Conners felt would be important for this position. Goldberg had studied in Israel on a kibbutz for two years after college, spoke fluent Hebrew, and was a practicing Jew. He wanted to retire in Israel in a few years. Conners worried that Goldberg would not stay with the company long enough to establish a solid organization. Goldberg also liked running his own show, and that created a potential problem with Lizfeld.

The next candidate was Robert Kyle, Vice President of BRB's radar electronics department. Kyle had been with BRB for more than twenty years and headed two other international divisions for BRB in Japan and Canada. Kyle was familiar with the international process and the BRB corporate culture. Lizfeld had given him excellent reviews in the other two international positions. He had strong management skills and was highly respected both within the organization and in the industry. Kyle received his Ph.D. from MIT in electrical engineering and his M.B.A. from Dartmouth. He had the technical expertise and was familiar with the company and its procedures. Conners was afraid of Kyle's cultural acceptance in Israel since he did not speak the language and was not familiar with Israeli attitudes. He could require Kyle to participate in extensive cultural training, but Conners still had some reservations about sending a gentile to head operations in Israel.

The last candidate was Rochelle Cohen, an Israeli who relocated to the United States in 1982. She originally relocated to assist the head of the electronics division of Yassar Aircraft, an Israeli company that opened its first international office in 1978. Cohen did very well and brought Israeli thoroughness and assertiveness to the U.S. operations. She now wanted to move back to Israel to be with her family. Additionally, her fiancé recently relocated in Israel, and she wanted to return to marry and raise a family. Cohen had experience in the international circuit, having worked in the United States, United Kingdom, and Israel, but Conners was still worried about hiring her. Although she had the political knowledge and the proper connections in the Israeli government, the problems were her young age, lack of technical expertise, and sex.

Conners contacted O'Leary to see what progress he had made. Knowing the consequences that would come from this decision, Conners realized it was going to be a difficult one to make.

## ▬ U.K. Operations

Francis O'Leary reflected on his past eight years with BRB. His rise from the strife-torn east side of Belfast to BRB's corporate vice president for human resources was extraordinary. While most Irish business careers in large English firms peak at middle management, O'Leary's actually began at that point. He proved his capabilities through hard work, constant study, and an astute ability to judge the character and substance of people on first sight. His task of finding a suitable general manager for the new division in Israel offered a challenge he readily accepted.

O'Leary excelled at recruiting and hiring innovative employees who brought technical ideas with them to BRB. The management structure at BRB in England did not support internal growth of technology and innovation, so new ideas and technological advances were not rewarded with commensurate fiscal incentives. As such, turnover of experienced innovators forced O'Leary to recruit and hire innovation on a "rotating stock" basis. It was this success in hiring innovators that broke him from the shackles of middle management and thrust him to the top of the corporation. Four years ago, through a well-planned and well-executed recruiting program, O'Leary hired Rani Gilboa, a young Israeli engineer and former Israeli army officer. For Gilboa, the need for lightweight, inexpensive battlefield systems drove a desire to approach the problem from a new aspect: signal processing. After graduate study in this field, Gilboa sought and found a company that would support his concepts. That company was BRB. Gilboa's subsequent contributions to BRB's profits secured his and O'Leary's positions atop their respective disciplines within the firm.

Since that time, O'Leary had other successes hiring innovators from Israel. This stemmed largely from his tireless self-study of Israeli culture. With a feel for the Israeli people rivaling that of an "insider," O'Leary enjoyed success in pirating established innovators from Israeli firms. Now, he faced the task of recruiting and hiring a general manager for the newly established electronics division near Haifa.

Selecting the right manager would be more difficult than expected. With his knowledge of the Israeli culture, O'Leary knew intuitively that an Israeli should head the new division. Acceptance by the division's employees, ability to speak Hebrew, spousal support, and knowledge of Israeli government regulations and tax structures were vital to the success of the new division. Unfortunately, BRB's CEO preferred home country presence in the new division and directed O'Leary to recruit with that as the top priority. After O'Leary presented a strong case, however, the CEO agreed to review all candidates. Another potential problem arose when Lizfeld, the CEO, announced a hands-on management style with plans to participate actively in the management of the Israeli division. To O'Leary, this meant that Western values, along with the current innovative recruiting strategy practiced in England, would extend to Israel as well.

Until recently, O'Leary's recruiting for management positions concentrated on internal promotions. A known performer from within was a better bet than an outsider. When current employees could not meet the job requirements, O'Leary typically turned to newspapers as his primary source of candidates. The recent emergence of reputable executive placement services in England gave him an additional sourcing tool. At times, O'Leary had turned to social contacts, job centers, and the internal labor market as candidate sources, but the percentages of good leads from these were comparatively low.

After months of reading résumés, introductory letters, and job applications, three candidates emerged for the position in Israel. It was now up to O'Leary to decide the candidate he would recommend to Lizfeld.

Michael Flack worked for BRB for more than nineteen years. After graduating from Cambridge College with a degree in general engineering, Flack joined the company as a mechanical engineer. Initially, he worked in the mechanical design group of the radar division. After five years, BRB promoted Flack to engineering section manager. While in this position, he enjoyed various successes in radar miniaturization design. During his eleventh year, BRB again promoted Flack to department head in the manufacturing engineering group. Emphasis in this position shifted from design to production. During his seventeenth year, he became director of engineering design, where he was responsible for managing forty-three engineers' efforts in new-product design.

Flack had no international experience, and he was a reputed "tinkerer." He liked to spend time in the labs designing mechanical components along with his engineers. This generated tremendous esprit within his department but often resulted in inattention to his administrative responsibilities.

Rani Gilboa thought his friend Yair Shafrir was perfect for the position. Shafrir was currently vice-president of engineering at Elta Electronics in Israel. Elta is one of Israel's top radar firms, with several products proven in actual combat during the last Arab-Israeli conflict. Shafrir received his degree in electrical engineering from the University of Jerusalem. He had spent his professional career in Israel, usually changing companies to accept promotions. He had been with four companies since graduating from the university nineteen years ago. Shafrir was a strong-willed, organized individual who took pride in his record of technical management accomplishments. He had been able to complete projects on schedule and within budget over 70 percent of the time, a rare feat for an Israeli company. This record resulted mainly from the force of his personal leadership and strength of will. With his entire career spent in Israeli companies, O'Leary had little doubt that Shafrir could manage BRB's new electronics division. Culturally, he was perfect for the job. O'Leary had concerns, however, about Paul Lizfeld's injection of Western culture through his active management plan. The obstinate Shafrir, with no international business experience, might resent the interference.

A well-placed advertisement in the *London Times'* employment section drew a number of responses. One of the three final candidates responded to the ad about four weeks after it appeared in the *Times*.

Harold Michaelson was an English citizen of Jewish faith. Michaelson's family fled Poland in 1938 when Harold's father insisted that the "Nazi madman" would never attack England, especially after Prime Minister Chamberlain's successful visit to Munich. Harold was born to the newly naturalized couple in 1940. Later, he attended college in the United States, where he earned both bachelor's and master's degrees in electrical engineering at Georgia Tech. After graduating, Harold spent two years with General Electric until his father's illness forced him to return to England. He accepted an engineering position with Marconi, and he has remained with that company. Shortly after his return, his father died. Michaelson continued to take care of his mother for the next year. Mrs. Michaelson had always dreamed of living in the Jewish homeland—a dream not shared by her husband. One year after his death, she joined her sister's family in Haifa. Harold had readily accepted a position with Marconi in Israel to work on the new Israeli defense fighter LAVI. Unfortunately, cancellation of the LAVI program also canceled his chances to work in Israel for Marconi. At the time of the interview, Harold was vice president of engineering for Marconi's air radio division. He was also the youngest vice president in the corporation. His background in engineering and administrative functions, coupled with his ability to speak Hebrew, made Harold a strong candidate for the position. During the interview, he mentioned his mother's failing health and her refusal to leave Israel. He intended, if selected, to take care of her there. O'Leary wondered if that was Harold's main reason for wanting to live in Israel. Would he still want to live and work there if he lost his mother? O'Leary was anxious to discuss his candidates with John Conners.

# Cross-Cultural Training for Overseas Assignments

# A Practical but Theory-based Framework for Selecting Cross-Cultural Training Methods

## J. STEWART BLACK
## MARK MENDENHALL

Global citizenship is no longer just a nice phrase in the lexicon of rosy futurologists. It is every bit as real and concrete as measurable changes in GNP or trade flows" (Ohmae, 1989, p. 154).

There is little debate that for executives in large multinational corporations (MNCs) today globalization is a daily reality. But what exactly is unique about the international environment that MNCs face compared to non-MNCs, what skills do executives need to successfully lead firms in this emerging global village, and how can appropriate training be designed to facilitate the acquisition of these new skills? These are not trivial questions.

One of the first issues that MNCs face that non-MNCs do not is the fact that if a firm operates in multiple countries, it must deal with multiple sources of sovereign authority. This involves working with different laws and legal systems or, in some cases, the lack of systematic legal structures and processes. Executives in positions at headquarters or at foreign subsidiaries must have the skills to understand the impact of various laws, tariffs, taxes, enforcement practices, and overarching legal systems and be able to work with host government officials in enacting and maintaining reasonable legislation across a wide variety of countries and cultures.

Second, MNCs must also operate in different markets with different cultures, histories, values, social systems, and languages, which often require not only product diversification but intraproduct differentiation by country.

Source: J. Stewart Black and Mark Mendenhall. "A Practical but Theory-based Framework for Selecting Cross-Cultural Training Methods." This is an earlier version of a forthcoming article in Human Resource Management. Printed by permission.

This requires managers who have a "sensitivity to local conditions" (Doz and Prahalad, 1986) and who can understand, work with, and direct people from various cultures. Third, different "countries offer different strategic opportunities for MNCs. . . . Differences in size, resource endowment, economic development, political regime, national development and industrial policies . . . play roles in differentiating the opportunities offered to MNCs by individual countries" (Doz and Prahalad, 1986, p. 56).

Despite the need for cross-cultural skills and the shortage of managers who possess these skills, most human resource decision makers do nothing in terms of cross-cultural training (CCT) for employees in general or for selected employees embarking on international assignments (Baker and Ivancevich, 1971; Black, 1988; Runzheimer, 1984; Tung, 1981). For example, 70 percent of U.S. expatriates and 90 percent of their families are sent overseas without any cross-cultural training (Baker and Ivancevich, 1971; Black, 1988; Black and Stephens, 1989; Runzheimer, 1984; Tung, 1981).

This is significant given that studies have found between 16 and 40 percent of all expatriate managers sent on foreign assignments return before they are supposed to because of poor performance or the inability of the employee and/or the family to effectively adjust to the foreign environment (Baker and Ivancevich, 1971; Black, 1988; Dunbar and Ehrlich, 1986; Tung, 1981). Other studies have found that negotiations between businesspeople of different cultures often fail because of problems related to cross-cultural differences (Black, 1987; Graham, 1984; Tung, 1984). The costs of failed cross-cultural encounters are high; for example, studies have estimated the cost of a failed expatriate assignment to be $50,000 to $150,000 (Copeland and Griggs, 1985; Harris and Moran 1979; Misa and Fabricatore, 1979). For a firm with hundreds of expatriate employees worldwide, the costs can easily reach into the tens of millions of dollars per year. In fact, Copeland and Griggs (1985) have estimated that the direct costs of failed expatriate assignments for U.S. corporations is over $2 billion a year, and this does not include unmeasured losses such as damaged corporate reputations or lost business opportunities. In addition, Lanier (1979) estimates that up to 50 percent of American expatriates who do not return early are nonetheless ineffective in their overseas jobs, or what she terms "brownouts." Given that the average compensation package for a U.S. expatriate is between $200,000 and $250,000 (Black, 1988; Copeland and Griggs, 1985), the costs of brownouts are staggering.

Cross-cultural training has long been advocated as a means of facilitating effective cross-cultural interactions (Brislin, 1981; Landis and Brislin, 1983; Bochner, 1982; Harris and Moran, 1979; Mendenhall, Dunbar, and Oddou, 1987; Tung, 1981). However, its use in American business organizations is not widespread. Various reasons have been cited by business organizations for the low use of cross-cultural training; the most prevalent being that such training is not thought to be necessary or effective, and thus, top management sees no need for the training (Baker and Ivancevich, 1971; Mendenhall and Oddou, 1985; Runzheimer, 1984; Schwind, 1985; Tung, 1981; Zeira,

1975). However, the fundamental reason behind the lack of training seems to lie in the same assumption that causes American corporations to look only at domestic track records and to ignore cross-cultural-related skills when selecting expatriate candidates. The assumption is that good management is good management, and therefore, an effective manager in New York or Los Angeles will do fine in Hong Kong or Tokyo (Miller, 1973). Consequently, based on this assumption, it is logical for HR decision makers to conclude that CCT would not be needed or justified.

An extensive review of the cross-cultural training literature, however, suggests that HR managers are mistaken in their assumptions that good management is good management, that a firm can simply select employees who have been successful in the U.S. for overseas assignments, and that cross-cultural training is not necessary or effective. Harvey (1982) argued that domestic track record is not a good predictor of whether or not an expatriate will return early from an overseas assignment. A simple example can illustrate the reason for this finding. Generally in the U.S., setting clear, realistic, and difficult goals with specific time lines and then rewarding individuals who achieve the goals on time would be considered a good management practice (see Locke and Latham, 1984, for a detailed review). People will be motivated if they believe they know what is expected, believe they can achieve the goal, and believe they will be rewarded for their efforts. However, in Japan such goal specificity would be contrary to cultural norms, and the rewarding of an individual for personal achievement can often result in decreased motivation on the part of the rewarded individual because he or she would not want to stand out from or above the group (Mendenhall and Oddou, 1986a). This is a work-related norm that would be counterintuitive to an American expatriate manager with no training regarding Japanese culture or management practices.

A review of the CCT literature and its effectiveness also strongly indicates that American managers are mistaken in their belief that CCT is not necessary or effective. In a recent review of the empirical literature, Black and Mendenhall (1990) examined the effectiveness of CCT relative to three outcomes: (1) cross-cultural skill development, (2) cross-cultural adjustment, and (3) job performance. Of the ten studies that examined the relationship between CCT and self-confidence concerning one's ability to function effectively in cross-cultural situations, nine found a positive relationship. Nineteen out of nineteen studies found a positive relationship between CCT and increased cross-cultural relational skills. Sixteen out of sixteen studies found a positive relationship between CCT and more accurate cross-cultural perceptions. Nine out of nine studies found a positive relationship between CCT and cross-cultural adjustment. Finally, eleven out of fifteen studies found a positive relationship between CCT and job performance in the cross-cultural situation. However, the review also found that most of the empirical work was not founded on a theoretical framework per se and that the literature lacked a systematic approach to the study of CCT effectiveness. It is possible that the lack of a systematic stream of research has allowed the belief that CCT is not effective enough to persist. Additionally, the lack of a theoretical framework has left managers with little means of deciding who would benefit most from training, or what training method would be most effective, or how to best design such training programs. Perhaps until managers are presented with a systematic yet practical means of addressing these questions, they will continue to resist the prescriptions from academics (or consultants) that CCT is necessary and effective.

The purpose of this paper is to begin to shed some light on a framework for CCT that would be both theoretically sound and useful in practice. Recently, scholars have argued that social learning theory (SLT) provides a solid theoretical basis for understanding cross-cultural learning, training, and adjustment (Black and Mendenhall, 1990; Church, 1982; David, 1976). This paper explores the utility of SLT as a framework for systematically examining four important questions: (1) how can the level of training rigor of specific cross-cultural training methods be determined, (2) who would benefit most from cross-cultural training, (3) what CCT methods are most appropriate in specific situations, and (4) what level of CCT rigor is needed for maximum positive results? A brief review of past typologies and frameworks of CCT is followed by a discussion of the major components of SLT. Finally, a new framework of cross-cultural training based on SLT is delineated and practical implications are explored.

## ▰ *Review of Past Frameworks*

Most of the writing in the cross-cultural training literature has focused on the discussion of different methods of training and general classifications of these methodologies, while less attention has been focused on the development of frameworks that would determine which training methods to utilize or the important contingency factors to consider in such determinations. The first part of this section summarizes a generally accepted typology of CCT methods, and the second part of the section reviews two recent frameworks that try to help managers determine which cross-cultural training methods to use in organizations.

Landis and Brislin (1983) have proposed a typology of cross-cultural training methods that has largely been accepted as a broad and integrative classification scheme of cross-cultural training methods. They developed the typology based on a broad review of the cross-cultural training literature. Their classification scheme is summarized in Exhibit 1.

Given the fragmented state of the literature, the development of a classification scheme for various cross-cultural training methodologies was an important step in improving an understanding of the area. However, managers responsible for training within corporations were often left without a means of determining which of the methodologies were most appropriate for specific training situations or which methods were more or less rigorous and effec-

E X H I B I T 1

## Fundamental Cross-Cultural Training Methodologies

*Information or Fact-Oriented Training:* Trainees are presented with various facts about the country in which they are about to live via lectures, videotapes, and reading materials.

*Attribution Training:* The attribution approach focuses on explanations of behavior from the point of view of the native. The goal is to learn the cognitive standards by which the host-nationals process behavioral input so that the trainee can understand why the host-nationals behave as they do and adapt his or her own behavior to match the standards of behavior in the host country.

*Cultural Awareness Training:* The aim is to study the values, attitudes, and behaviors that are common in one's own culture so that the trainee better understands how culture impacts his or her own behavior. Once this is understood, it is assumed that he or she can better understand how culture affects human behavior in other countries.

*Cognitive-Behavior Modification:* The focus here is to assist trainees in linking what they find to be rewarding and punishing in their own subcultures (work, family, religion, etc.) and then to examine the reward and punishment structure in the host culture. Through an examination of the differences and similarities, strategies are developed to assist the trainee to obtain rewards—and avoid punishments—in the host culture.

*Experiential Learning:* The goal of this approach is to involve the trainees as active participants, to introduce the nature of life in another culture by actively experiencing that culture via field trips, complex role-plays, and cultural simulations.

*Interaction Training:* Here trainees interact with natives or returned expatriates in order to become more comfortable with host-nationals and to learn from the first-hand experience of the returned expatriates. The methods utilized can range from in-depth role plays to casual, informal discussions.

*Source:* Adapted from Landis and Brislin (1983).

tive. Recently, scholars have attempted to present means of making some of these determinations.

## Tung's Framework of Training Method Selection

Tung (1982) presented a contingency framework for choosing an appropriate CCT method and its level of rigor. She argued that the two determining factors were the degree of interaction required in the host culture and the similarity between the individual's native culture and the new culture. The related training elements involved the content of the training and the rigor of the training. Essentially, Tung argued that if the expected interaction between the individual and members of the target or host culture was low, and the degree of dissimilarity between the individual's native culture and the host culture was low, then the content of the training should focus on task- and job-related issues as opposed to culture-related issues, and the level of rigor necessary for effective training should be relatively low. If there was a high level of expected interaction with host nationals and a large dissimilarity between the cultures, then the content of the training should focus on the new culture and on cross-cultural skill development, as well as on the new task, and the level of rigor of such training should be moderate to high.

While this framework does specify some criteria (i.e., degree of expected interaction and cultural similarity) for choosing CCT methods, the conclusions that the framework allows the user to make are rather general. Essentially, the framework suggests that the user emphasize task issues by utilizing training methods with relatively low levels of rigor and to emphasize culture learning, skill development, and task issues by utilizing a relatively high level of rigor. However, the framework does not help the user determine which specific training methods to use. In addition, the framework does not define what training "rigor" is and, therefore, does not help the user determine which specific training methods are more or less rigorous.

### Mendenhall and Oddou's Framework for Selecting Training Methods

A more recent framework presented by Mendenhall and Oddou (1986b) moves beyond Tung's framework and provides more specificity. Like Tung, Mendenhall and Oddou acknowledge the importance of degree of expected interaction and similarity between the native and host cultures in determining the cross-cultural training method. In addition, Mendenhall and Oddou propose three key elements related to training. The first is the training method. Based on cross-cultural training typologies such as the one by Landis and Brislin (1983), Mendenhall and Oddou propose a three-part classification system and group specific training methods into low, medium, and high levels of rigor.

The framework presented by Mendenhall and Oddou is a significant improvement over the more general framework offered by Tung (1982). It provides a grouping of specific methods by level of rigor and also discusses the duration of training relative to the criteria of interaction and culture similarity. Despite these important improvements, the framework does not explain how the level of rigor of a specific CCT method or group of methods was determined and tells us little about the training and learning processes and, therefore, why the particular determinations are made. Also, the content of the training all seems to be "cultural" in nature and little integration of the individual's new job-related tasks and the new host culture is made. Finally, while both frameworks make intuitive sense, their theoretical grounding is never made explicit, and therefore, in the absence of empirical data to support the frameworks, it is difficult to evaluate their soundness for use and success in the real world.

## The Need for a Theoretical Framework

Despite the plethora of work advocating the use of cross-cultural training in organizations, the empirical research in this area and even the conceptual work have been almost totally devoid of a theoretical framework (Adler, 1986; Black and Mendenhall, 1990; Roberts and Boyacigiller, 1982; Schollhammer, 1975). Bochner states that cross-cultural "research cannot be said to have been conducted with a great deal of theoretical sophistication. The tendency has been to use lengthy and diffuse questionnaires and/or interviews that generate masses of unrelated information" (1982, p. 16). A previous review of the empirical literature in cross-cultural training indicates that, in general, cross-cultural training seems to have a positive impact on skill development, adjustment, and performance (Black and Mendenhall, 1990); however, the lack of a theoretical framework leaves questions like why cross-cultural training is effective and which situations are best served by which specific training methods essentially unanswered. The purpose of this next section is to examine social learning theory as a theoretical framework that would begin to shed light on these questions.

### Social Learning Theory

The potential of SLT to facilitate an understanding of the theoretical relationship between cross-cultural training and cross-cultural performance is significant (Church, 1982; David, 1976). Before discussing the particular relevance of SLT to cross-cultural training and its effectiveness, it is perhaps useful to briefly summarize the main points of the theory. SLT, as described by one of its leading authors (Bandura, 1977), argues that learning takes place both by the effect reinforcement has on behavior and by imitating or modeling the behavior of others and symbolically or vicariously making associations between behavior and consequence without direct, actual experience. As described by Bandura, SLT has four central elements: attention, retention, reproduction, and incentives (see Exhibit 2).

*Attention.* Before someone or something can be modeled, it must be noticed by the learner. Several factors have been found to influence the attention process of the subject or observer, including: (1) the status of the model, (2) the attractiveness of the model, (3) the similarity of the model, (4) the repeated availability of the model, and (5) past reinforcement for paying attention to the model (either actual or vicarious rewards).

E X H I B I T 2

## *Model of Social Learning Theory Process*

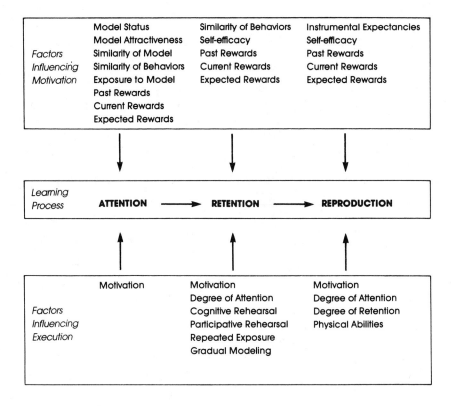

Retention. Retention is the process by which the modeled behavior becomes encoded as a memory by the observer. Two representational systems are involved. The imaginal system is utilized during exposure to the framework. During exposure, images are associated on the basis of physical contiguity. These images are stored as "cognitive maps" which can later guide the observer in imitation. The second system is the verbal system. It represents the coded information in abbreviated verbal systems and groups similar patterns of behavior into larger integrated units. It should be noted that both the repeated modeling of a behavior and the repeated cognitive rehearsal of the modeled behavior serve to solidify the retention process.

*Reproduction.* The third major component of the modeling process involves the translation of the symbolic representations of the modeled stimuli into overt actions. As individuals try to imitate the modeled behavior, they check their performance against their memory of what was modeled. Actual reproduction of the modeled behavior, of course, can be inhibited by physical differences between the model and the person imitating the model, how well the model is observed, and how well the modeled behavior is retained.

*Incentives and the Motivational Processes.* The fourth major component of SLT involves the influence of incentives on the motivational processes of modeling behavior. Incentives have three primary sources. Incentives can come from the direct external environment, from vicarious association, and from the individual him- or herself. In turn, each of these different sources of incentives can affect several aspects of the learning process. Incentives can affect which models are observed and how much attention is paid to observed models. Incentives can influence the degree to which the modeled behavior is retained and rehearsed. Also, incentives can influence which learned behaviors are emitted. It is important to note that Bandura (1977) argued on the basis of empirical work that incentives play a much larger role in influencing what behavior is emitted as opposed to what behavior is learned. He concluded that individuals learn numerous behaviors which are not usually emitted because they are not positively rewarded. However, if the reward structure is changed, the behaviors are performed.

*Expectancies.* In relation to the motivational processes of learning, Bandura (1977) distinguishes between two types of expectancies. The first type of expectations Bandura calls "efficacy expectations." The individual's self-efficacy is the degree to which the individual believes he or she can successfully execute a particular behavior. This expectation is similar to the "effort to performance" expectancy proposed by Vroom (1964). In his view of the literature, Bandura (1977) found that higher levels of self-efficacy led individuals to persist at imitating modeled behavior longer and to be more willing to try to imitate novel behavior. The sources for increasing self-efficacy, in order of importance, including past experience ("I've done it or something like it before"), vicarious experience ("other people have done it"), and verbal persuasion ("people say I can do it").

In addition to efficacy expectations, Bandura (1977) argues that outcome expectations influence the modeling process. Outcome expectations are people's beliefs that the execution of certain behaviors will lead to desired outcomes. These expectations are similar to the "expectancy-of-performance-to-outcome" (instrumentality expectancies) proposed by Vroom (1964). Bandura concluded that in addition to the modeling processes of attention, retention, and reproduction, incentives influence what people learn and incentives and efficacy and outcome expectancies influence what learned behaviors are emitted.

*Important Empirical Findings.* Although a number of empirical findings are reviewed by Bandura (1977), several are important to summarize because of the insight they provide about fundamental elements in the learning process. The first finding is that gradual modeling is more effective than "one-shot" modeling, especially if the modeled behaviors are novel to the observer. Gradual modeling involves providing successive approximations of the final behavior to be modeled. This modeling process is more effective than modeling only the final behavior for several reasons: (1) observers pay more attention to models and modeled behaviors which are more familiar, (2) observers can more easily retain models which are more similar to cognitive maps already possessed, (3) observers have higher expectations of efficacy and outcome of behaviors which are more familiar, and (4) observers are more likely to be able to reproduce more familiar behaviors.

Second, Bandura argues that individuals can learn completely through symbolic modeling, that is, just by watching and rehearsing mentally. This symbolic learning process can be facilitated by the other variables discussed (attractiveness of the model, similarity of the model, etc.) and by having multiple models. Also, Bandura found that participative modeling is generally more effective than symbolic processes alone. Participative reproduction simply means that the observer actually practices (as opposed to only cognitive rehearsals) the modeled behavior. The external, and especially the internal, feedback processes serve to refine the observer's ability to reproduce the modeled behavior at a later time in the appropriate situation.

## ▬ *Social Learning Theory and Cross-Cultural Training*

Social learning theory provides a theoretical framework for systematically examining the level of rigor that specific CCT methods generally contain and for determining the appropriate cross-cultural training approach for specific training cases and situations. Based on the central variable of "modeling process" in SLT, the first part of this section explores a means of ranking specific cross-cultural training methods by the degree of rigor generally contained in the methods and examining two other factors that are related to the total rigor a training program might have. The second part of this section examines how SLT processes can provide a heuristic framework for deciding which CCT methods would be appropriate in specific situations. Throughout the second part of this section, we examine the practical implications of the framework for Mel Stephen's dilemma.

### *SLT and CCT Rigor*

As was mentioned earlier, many of the past attempts to provide a means of choosing CCT methods have included the concept of training rigor but have not attempted to define what the term meant. Within the framework of SLT, rigor is essentially the degree of cognitive involvement of the learner or trainee. The modeling processes in SLT provide a useful means of not only defining rigor but also determining the relative degree of rigor that specific training methods generally have. Within SLT, there are basically two modeling processes—symbolic and participative. Symbolic modeling simply involves observing modeled behaviors. However, this observation can have two forms. The first form consists of the learner or trainee hearing about the behavior and then translating those verbal messages into imagined images. Thus, the learner or trainee observes the behaviors in his or her mind. Cross-cultural training methods that generally exhibit this type of modeling process include verbal factual briefings, lectures, and books. The second form of symbolic modeling involves the trainee actually seeing visually the behavior being modeled. In this case, the trainee both sees and retains a cognitive image of the behavior and is more cognitively involved than when the symbolic modeling process only involves translating verbal messages into cognitive images. Specific CCT methods that generally exhibit this type of modeling include films, role modeling, demonstrations, and nonparticipative language training.

The second basic form of modeling is termed participative modeling. Participative modeling essentially means that in addition to observing the modeled behavior, the trainee also participates in modeling the behavior. This participation can take two forms. The first form involves "verbal" participation. In other words, the trainee participates in modeling the behavior by describing verbally what he or she would do. Cross-cultural training methods that generally exhibit this type of participative modeling include case studies and culture assimilators. The second form of participative modeling involves more physical participation in modeling the behaviors being learned. Cross-cultural training methods that generally require this type of participative modeling include role plays, interactive language training, field trips, and interactive simulations. Trainees are more cognitively involved when they must physically, as opposed to only verbally, participate in modeling the behaviors being taught.

In addition, rehearsal increases the level of cognitive involvement during symbolic or participative modeling. Rehearsal also has two basic forms. Cognitive rehearsal involves the mental rehearsal or practice of the modeled behavior (e.g., practicing eating with chop sticks in one's mind). Behavioral rehearsal involves actual physical practice of the modeled behavior. Because behavioral rehearsal involves both mental and physical processes, it is more cognitively engaging than cognitive rehearsal alone and, therefore, is more rigorous. By definition, symbolic modeling can utilize only cognitive rehearsal, while participative modeling can utilize either cognitive or behavioral rehearsal or both. Thus, the rigor of any specific CCT method could be enhanced through cognitive or behavioral rehearsal. Thus, by examining the modeling and rehearsal processes involved, the relative rigor of a specific CCT method can be approximated. Exhibit 3 provides an illustration of the relative ranking in terms of rigor for a set of specific and common CCT methods.

In determining the rigor of a CCT program, one would need to consider the rigor of the specific CCT method(s) utilized and the duration and intensity of the total CCT program. The duration and intensity of a CCT program is a

EXHIBIT 3

*Modeling Processes, Rigor, & Training Methods*

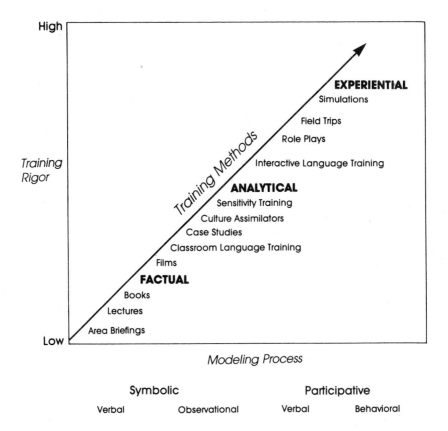

function of the total hours of training and the time frame within which the training is conducted. Thus, all other things being equal, a training program that involved a total of 25 training hours over five days would be less rigorous than a program that involved 100 total hours over three weeks.

In general, the SLT literature and the CCT literature provide evidence to strongly suggest that the more rigorous the training the more effective the training will be in terms of the trainee being able to actually and appropriately execute the learned behaviors (Bandura, 1977; Black and Mendenhall, 1990; Tung, 1981). The basic explanation for this relationship is that rigor (i.e., cognitive involvement) increases the level of attention and retention, which in turn increases reproduction proficiency. As an example, Gudykunst, Hammer, and Wiseman (1977) found that a more rigorous CCT training program involving the "Contrast American" role play, "BaFa BaFa" cross-cultural trading simulation, and field trips was significantly more effective for a sample of Navy personnel on overseas assignments in Japan than was CCT involving lectures on Japanese values and culture alone.

### Important Situational Factors

In addition to providing a means of determining the general level of rigor of specific CCT methods, SLT also provides a framework for identifying situational factors that are important to consider in choosing appropriate CCT methods in specific situations. Social learning theory argues that the more novel the behaviors are that must be learned, the more difficult it is to attend to, retain, and reproduce them. In addition, SLT argues that the more frequently or accurately the learned behaviors are required to be reproduced in actual situations (as opposed to training situations), the greater the importance of the attention and retention processes during training. Thus, the greater the novelty of the behaviors to be learned and the greater the required level of reproduction, the higher the requisite levels of attention and retention needed, and the higher the level of the rigor of the training needed. These specific situational factors that are relevant to CCT are briefly discussed below.

*Culture Novelty.* Based on SLT and the arguments just made, the more novel the host culture is, the more difficult it will be for the individual to attend to and retain the various models of appropriate behavior (in the training situation as well as in the actual host culture). Thus, the more novel the host culture, the more assistance through rigorous training the individual will need in order to be aware of, retain, and appropriately reproduce the new behaviors appropriate in the foreign culture.

An important practical question is "How does one determine the degree of novelty in the host culture?" Once this question is answered, then the HR decision maker can begin to determine what the appropriate levels of CCT rigor and corresponding specific CCT methods are. While definitive decision rules are perhaps impossible to create, past cross-cultural research presents some rough guidelines (Haire, Ghiselli, and Porter, 1966; England and Lee, 1974; Hofstede, 1980). Information provided in Hofstede (1980) presents perhaps the most comprehensive yet simple means of estimating cultural novelty. Hofstede (1980) examined native employees in a U.S. multinational firm in 48 countries along four different scales (power distance, uncertainty avoidance, individualism, masculinity). A rough estimate of culture novelty can be obtained by calculating the absolute difference in scores on each one of the four scales between the employees of the target country and the American employees and then summing these differences. The larger the final number, the greater the culture novelty relative to the American culture. The work of Torbiorn (1982) also gives insight into the degree of cultural novelty. Torbiorn (1982) found that for Scandinavians the most difficult regions of the world to live and work in were: (1) Africa, (2) Middle East, (3) Far East, (4) South

America, (5) Eastern Bloc, (6) Europe, (7) North America, and (8) Australia and New Zealand.

In addition to using Hofstede's (1980) results, one might estimate culture novelty by simply assessing whether the language of the host culture is different from that of the individual's home culture and whether learning the language will be a necessity for living and working in the host country. For example, even though Cantonese Chinese is the most common language of use in Hong Kong, English is still an official language and one can survive without Chinese language skills; however, survival would be more difficult without Spanish language skills in a country such as Chile (Kepler, Kepler, Gaither, and Gaither, 1983).

The next step in assessing the novelty of the target country and culture is to examine the previous experience of the specific individual candidate. Social learning theory would argue that the more experience the individual has had with a specific culture, even if that experience was in the distant past, the more the individual is able to recall and utilize those past experiences in coping with the present situation in the host culture. It should be mentioned that both the duration and intensity of the past experience serve to deepen what was retained from the experience and to facilitate later recall (Bandura, 1977). Thus, all things being equal, the Indonesian culture would be less novel for the candidate who lived there before than the candidate who had not. Likewise, all other things being equal, the candidate who had frequent and involved interactions with Indonesians during a three-year stay would find the culture less novel in a later visit than an individual who had infrequent and superficial interactions with Indonesians during a similar three-year stay. Thus, both the "quantity" and "quality" of an individual's previous experience must be examined. In addition, there is some empirical support that suggests that previous international experience, even if it is not in the host country's culture, reduces the novelty of the culture (Black, 1988). Based on SLT, one would expect that a candidate with previous experience in a country or region similar to the host country and culture would perceive less culture novelty, have an easier adjustment, and need less training than a candidate with previous experience in a totally different country or region, and that a candidate with frequent and involved previous interactions would need less training than a candidate with infrequent and superficial interactions. The following simple equation represents the basic assessment process: Net Culture Novelty = Objective Culture Novelty − (Quality + Quantity of an Individual's Previous Experience).

*Degree of Interaction.* The second situational factor in determining the degree of CCT rigor needed is the degree of expected interpersonal interaction between the individual and members of the host culture. The degree of interaction can be viewed in three ways. First, one can assess the degree of interaction through the relative frequency of interaction expected between the individual and members of the host culture. Also, one can assess the degree through the importance of the interactions. If one expects relatively few and mostly trivial interactions between the individual and members of the host culture, then the individual's ability to reproduce appropriate behaviors in the host culture is less important (and therefore, so would be the individual's attention and retention needs and the individual's need to get help to enhance attention, retention, and reproduction through rigorous training). If, on the other hand, one expects many and primarily important interactions between the individual and members of the host culture, then the individual's ability to reproduce appropriate behaviors is more important (and therefore, so would be the individual's need in getting help to enhance that ability).

In addition to the frequency and importance of the interactions, the nature of the interactions should also be assessed. Specific aspects of the nature of the interactions with host country nationals include the following:

1. how familiar or novel the interaction is;
2. the directionality of the interaction (one-way vs. two-way);
3. the type of the interaction (routine vs. unique);
4. the form of the interaction (face-to-face vs. other forms like mail);
5. the total duration of the cross-cultural interaction (e.g., one vs. five years); and
6. the format of the interaction (formal vs. informal).

Based on the communication literature (Jablin, Putnam, Roberts, and Porter, 1987), one would expect that novel, two-way, unique, face-to-face, long-term, and informal cross-cultural interactions would be more difficult than the opposite. The following equation represents the basic assessment of degree of interaction: Degree of Interaction = (Frequency of Interactions with Host Nationals) × (Importance of Interactions) × (Nature of Interactions).

*Job Novelty.* The third important situational factor involves the novelty of the new job and its related tasks. Based on precisely the same theoretical arguments that were presented concerning culture novelty, the more novel the tasks of the new job in the new culture, the more assistance the individual will need through rigorous training to produce the desired and necessary behaviors to be effective in the new job. Some scholars may reason that it is difficult to separate culture novelty from job novelty, arguing that if the culture is novel then to some degree the job will also be novel. Although culture novelty and job novelty are not independent of each other, there is both logical and empirical basis for separating the two issues. First, if there is little interaction between elements of the new culture and the job, and if the new job is very similar to the previous job, then it is quite possible to have a situation involving a novel culture but a nonnovel job. Likewise, it is possible to have a situation in which the new job is very different from the previous job but the host culture is similar to the individual's home culture. Recent empirical evidence suggests that individuals in international assignments adjust differentially to the culture and the job (Black, 1988; Black and Stephens, 1989), which suggests that while the novelty of the new job and culture can be linked they are not necessarily intertwined.

The question the HR decision maker must ask is "How novel is the new job and its tasks and responsibilities?" Although it is perhaps impossible to draw a definitive line between what would and would not be a novel job, Stewart's (1982) framework of job characteristics provides a useful means of determining where "job novelties" might occur. Based on Stewart's (1982) framework, the HR decision maker should first try to determine if the new *job demands* are similar to or different from those of previous jobs held by the candidate.

- Are performance standards the same?
- Is the degree of personal involvement required in the work unit the same?
- Are the types of tasks to be done similar?
- Are the bureaucratic procedures that must be followed similar?

Next the HR decision maker must determine how similar the new *job constraints* are.

- Are resource limitations the same?
- Are the legal restrictions similar?
- Are the technological limitations familiar?

Finally, the HR decision maker must determine the novelty of the new *job choices*.

- Is the freedom to decide how work gets done the same?
- Is the discretion about what work gets done similar?
- Is the freedom to decide who does which tasks the same?
- Are the choices about what work gets delegated similar?

If the HR decision maker examines the three job characteristics proposed by Stewart (1982), he or she should be able to make a rough estimate of the extent to which the new job is novel relative to a specific candidate. According to SLT, the more novel the new responsibilities and tasks, the more help the individual will need through rigorous training to learn and execute the desired and necessary behaviors.

### The Family and CCT

The previous discussion has been presented as though the only person the HR decision maker needed to consider was the employee; however, research provides strong evidence to suggest that the candidate's family, especially the spouse, is also important to consider (Black, 1988; Black and Stephens, 1989; Harvey, 1986; Tung, 1981).

*Culture Novelty.* The process of determining the extent of training the family needs also begins with an assessment of culture novelty. The process of assessing the novelty of the culture obtained in relation to the candidate can be used for the family with two important qualifications. First, the final assessment of the host country's culture novelty must be made relative to the family's previous experience. Second, children under the age of about thirteen may need much less preparation than older children because they seem to have less difficulty adjusting to foreign cultures (Tung, 1984), and spouses must be given nearly as much consideration as the candidate is given because their adjustment or lack of adjustment can be a critical determinant of the candidate's success or failure in the foreign culture (Black, 1988; Black and Stephens, 1989; Tung, 1981).

*Degree of Interaction.* The spouse should also be given considerable attention concerning the degree of expected interaction in determining the level of CCT rigor needed to prepare him or her for the living and functioning effectively in the foreign culture. The degree of expected interaction can be assessed in much the same manner as was suggested for the candidate (i.e., frequency and intensity). However, some important differences between candidates and spouses need to be considered. First, most spouses do not work in the host culture even if they worked before the foreign assignment (Stephens and Black, in press). Second, even if spouses are not required to interact with host country nationals, lack of the ability to interact can lead to feelings of isolation and loneliness, which in turn can be the primary cause of inadequate adjustment to the host culture and an early or premature return on the part of the entire family (Harvey, 1986; Tung, 1984; 1988). Consequently, even if the required degree of interaction between the spouse and host country nationals is low, the spouse will be better adjusted if he or she has the ability to interact effectively (Black and Stephens, 1989). Thus, it may be important to facilitate this ability through rigorous CCT even if the required degree of interaction does not seem to merit it.

### Integrating Culture Novelty, Interaction, Job Novelty, and CCT Rigor

The theoretical reasoning behind the integration of culture novelty, interaction, and job novelty is relatively straightforward. The greater the culture novelty, required interaction, and job novelty, the greater the need for rigorous CCT. However, each of these three conditions is not "created equally." Research shows that adjusting to the culture and interacting with host country nationals is more difficult than doing the job (Black, 1988; Black and Stephens, 1989). This can be represented pictorially by a three-dimensional cube with a line running through the cube diagonally from the front left corner to the back right corner (see Exhibit 4).

The vertical axis represents the dimension of job novelty, ranging from low to high novelty. The bottom horizontal axis represents the dimension of interaction, ranging from low to high required interaction. The top horizontal

E X H I B I T   4

*Integration of Cross-Cultural Training Rigor and Main Contingency Factors*

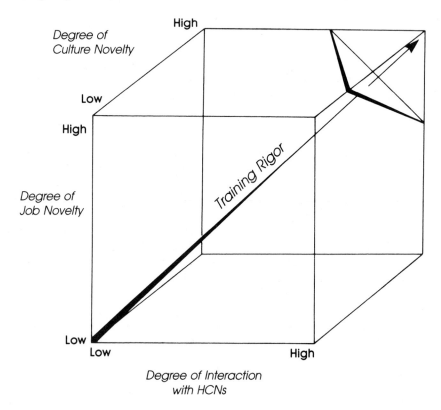

Degree of Interaction
with HCNs

axis represents relative culture novelty, ranging from low to high novelty. The diagonal line, which runs from the front left corner to the back right corner, represents training methods and rigor, ranging from low to high rigor. Thus, a point can be plotted in the three-dimensional space by estimating the culture novelty, degree of required interaction, and job novelty of a specific impending cross-cultural assignment. The intersection of the plotted point and the diagonal line, and therefore the determination of the requisite level of rigor, can be determined by imagining a plane at a right angle to, and traveling on the same diagonal as the CCT rigor line. When the plane intersects the point plotted based on estimates relative to each of the three dimensions, it also intersects with a point on the diagonal line representing CCT rigor. That intersection provides a rough estimation of the CCT rigor required.

The plane is placed at a right angle because research has demonstrated that adjusting to a novel job in the work situation of an overseas assignment is easier than adjusting to the general culture or interacting with host nationals (Black, 1988; Black and Stephens, 1989). Thus, even in the case of a highly novel job but low culture novelty and low required interaction with host nationals, the highest level of CCT rigor is not required. By contrast, even if the level of job novelty is moderate, a high level of culture novelty and required interaction necessitates a high level of CCT rigor.

The content of the training would, of course, be a direct function of the three dimensions discussed. If the assessment indicates that there will be a high level of job novelty, then the CCT program should include content relative to the new behaviors that need to be learned to effectively perform the job. If there is a high degree of interaction required, then the CCT program should include in its content such topics as cross-cultural communication, interpersonal skills, perception, and ethnocentricity. If there is a high degree of culture novelty, then topics such as the host country's values, religious systems, political systems, social customs, and business practices should be included. The relative emphasis of the content would be a direct reflection of the relative low or high scores on each of the three dimensions.

### Two Case Illustrations

Wave, one of the market leaders in the computer software industry, had just sealed a joint venture pact with one of Japan's largest designers and manufacturers of computers, Nippon Kankei. Wave, a Seattle-based company, agreed to send six Americans to work in Tokyo with fifteen of Nippon Kankei's best "high potential" software designers. The purpose of this effort was to train the Japanese designers in state-of-the-art software design while working on software applications for Nippon Kankei's products. Also, Nippon Kankei, through its distribution network, would market any products created by the joint venture research and development team to other computer manufacturers, distributers, and retailers as well. Wave would retain the copyright and share significantly in profits generated by the joint venture.

Wave retained complete managerial and creative control of the R & D team. The project manager was to be designated by Wave, and John Selby was selected and had agreed to go. John had vast experience in all aspects of the industry and had overseen four projects in the U.S. from the idea to the final product. The other five designers had limited managerial experience—they were pure designers. Nippon Kankei's management hoped that by rubbing shoulders and working jointly with these American designers their own staff would get "up to speed" in software design.

All of the designers agreed to relocate to Japan after feeling that their families' financial position and standard of living would not suffer because of the move. All of the designers were married. None of the designers indicated any reluctance on the part of their spouse concerning the three-year assignment; however, there were rumors that at least three of the wives were "less than thrilled" about disrupting their childrens' education and creating a new life in Japan.

What practical guidance concerning the cross-cultural training of this team of expatriates who are about to be sent to Japan can the framework we have discussed provide? The first step is to assess the culture novelty of the host country to which the team is being sent.

If Wave generalized Hofstede's (1980) research of Japanese who worked for an American multinational corporation to those Japanese who will be working with Wave's people in the joint venture, it would find the following: (1) Japanese have a much higher power distance (the degree workers accept power difference between managers and subordinates) of about 20 index points, (2) Americans are much more risk taking (53 index points on uncertainty avoidance), (3) Americans are much more individual and less group oriented than the Japanese (45 index points), and (4) Japanese accept traditional sex roles and have a higher work ethic than Americans (35 point differential). Hofstede's results suggest that not only does Japan have a culture quite different from American culture but it is one of the most different. The main language of Japan is also different. But to what degree will the expatriates from Wave need to speak Japanese? The ability of the Japanese assigned to the joint venture to read English is quite high, but their speaking and listening comprehension skills are marginal. Also, the American expatriates are likely to find it difficult to function effectively without Japanese language ability outside the workplace.

Next, Wave must assess the previous experience of the candidates. Unfortunately, though many had vacationed a time or two overseas, none of the candidates have lived or worked in Japan or have lived and worked outside the U.S. Thus, their previous experience would not reduce the culture novelty or the need for CCT. Based on all this information, it seems clear that the level of "culture novelty" that the Wave expatriates will experience will be quite high.

At first the degree of required interaction with Japanese workers for the American software designers would be fairly low, but would be much higher for John Selby, the project manager. However, the group-oriented nature of Japanese work organizations and the practice of consensus decision making increases the likelihood that all of Wave's expatriates will be interacting frequently with the Japanese. Additionally, the interactions are likely to be face-to-face, two-way, informal, and both routine and unique in nature over several years. Thus, while the degree of required interaction is likely to be higher for John Selby, it is still likely to be high for the other expatriates as well.

For Wave, on the surface it does not appear that the job novelty for the group of expatriates is very high. John Selby has managed four "start-up" projects before, and all the designers have had considerable experience in new product design. There are no new technical skills needed by the designers, and coming up with programs for new hardware systems is what they do for a living. Upon closer examination of the job demands, it seems that there is a high potential for performance standards, the tasks concerning training or working with Japanese, the way in which decisions get made, and the bureaucratic procedures that must be followed to all be different compared to their old jobs back in Seattle. Wave must also consider the novelty of job constraints. There is a high probability that resource limitations (e.g., communicating with colleagues and experts back at Wave), budgets, and legal restrictions are significantly different in Japan compared to Seattle. Finally, Wave needs to examine the novelty of job choices or discretion. Will the American designers be free to decide how to get work done (e.g., working hours) as they were in Seattle? Will John Selby be able to assign tasks and manage the team the same way he did back home? It is quite likely that all the members of the Wave team will need to make adjustments in order to work effectively with the Japanese. Wave's answers to these questions suggest that job choice novelty will be moderately high as well.

While there may be limits to Wave's budget, if it can, spouses should be included in the CCT program. This is because the novelty of the culture is high, and the ability to interact with shopkeepers, neighbors, banks, etc. greatly facilitates the spouse's ability to adjust to the new culture. As mentioned earlier, the spouse's adjustment is important because of the significance it has on expatriate adjustment (Black, 1988; Black and Stephens, 1989).

Thus, based on Figure 3, Wave needs to design or purchase a CCT program of fairly high rigor. The program should include some elements of symbolic modeling (both symbolic and observational) such as lectures, articles, books, and films on Japanese culture and business. But the CCT program should also include training methods that involve participative modeling as well. Specific methods might include case studies, culture assimilator exercises, interactive language study, role plays, and perhaps a premove visit to Japan. Additionally, the content of the training should include job, business, and general culture issues given the novelty of both task and culture. Obviously, a training program that includes all of these specific training methods will take time to execute. A reasonable estimate is that at least sixty hours of training will be needed. If time and scheduling constraints prevent all the training from occurring before departure to Japan, some follow-up training might be useful once the expatriates were settled in Japan.

A second case may provide further illustration of the practical implications of the framework presented. An academic association of management educators, primarily university and college business professors, was planning to hold a joint conference in Japan with Japanese business and business education leaders. The American professors were asked to submit professional papers on a wide range of business topics, and sixty were selected to participate in the international conference. The conference organizers decided to provide some type of CCT for the selected participants.

The designers of the training program had to first determine the culture novelty of Japan relative to the U.S. As has already been described, the work by Hofstede suggests that Japan is one of the most novel countries in relationship to America. However, the previous international experience of the selected participants in general or specifically in Japan were not known. Because participation in the training session could not be required, it was assumed that those who had the least amount of previous experience with Japan would be most likely to attend the training session. This, in fact, turned out to be the case. Thus, the degree of culture novelty was high.

Next the degree of interaction with host nationals had to be assessed. The design of the conference was such that there would be a mixture of formal, one-way interaction and informal, two-way interaction. The conference was scheduled to last only four days, so the duration of the interaction would be quite short but would involve frequent interactions during the four days. Although one of the purposes of the conference was to create better ties between the American and Japanese business scholars, the importance of the interactions was considered moderate. Also, the degree that the American scholars would need to know and utilize Japanese was small. It was expected that the Japanese participants would have a reasonable command of English since the entire program was to be conducted in English with very few sessions providing translators. Thus, the overall degree of interaction between the Americans and Japanese was expected to be low to moderate.

Finally, the job novelty for the American scholars had to be assessed. At first glance, the job novelty would seem quite low. In terms of presenting and listening to papers at an academic conference, this conference on paper looked quite similar to conferences held in the U.S. However, the demands of presenting research results to a culturally mixed audience (Japanese and Americans) were somewhat different from those of presenting to just an audience of American scholars. Overall, however, the job novelty for the American scholars was considered to be low to moderate.

Based on these assessments, Figure 3 would suggest the use of moderately rigorous training methods. Figure 2 indicates that moderate levels of training rigor consist of primarily symbolic modeling processes. Consequently, the training program was scheduled for a single day and included symbolic verbal modeling via (1) short lectures on specific aspects of Japan and Japanese culture that the American professors would likely encounter in their four-day stay, (2) a short video on the specific location of the conference, and (3) classroom language training focused on simple Japanese greetings and phrases. The training program also included some symbolic observational modeling via (1) demonstrations of such things as greetings and the exchanging of business cards and (2) role plays done for the training participants on presenting to a culturally mixed audience and on presenting using a translator.

# ▄▄ *Conclusion*

A variety of implications can be derived from an SLT-based approach to CCT. The first three implications are related specifically to international or expatriate assignments. The next two implications are related to broader issues of good global development practices.

## CCT Is a Necessity Not a Luxury

It is very clear from the research literature that the vast majority of senior executives do not support CCT programs for their employees who must work with foreign business people. The research literature is equally clear that American expatriates who work with foreigners without the benefit of CCT are less effective than those who have been trained. With so much at stake, from the success of business negotiations to the effective operation of overseas subsidiaries or joint ventures, there seems to be little reason not to invest time and money into training one's people who must work internationally. The training costs are small compared to the potential costs of early returns or business losses due to the lack of cross-cultural competency. As with any training intervention, unless top management support exists, the potential of a successful CCT program is low. HRM staff generally do not try to push through programs that are not sanctioned from on high; American senior executives need to start blessing the utilization of CCT programs—it's as simple as that.

## It's a Family Affair

Of the few firms in the U.S. that do offer CCT to their expatriates, few offer such training to their spouses or other family members, despite the fact that research has demonstrated the impact that spouse and family adjustment can have on premature expatriate returns. A simple way to counteract this problem is to simply send spouses to the training sessions and to give them the same CCT the employee receives. While large portions of the training may be business related, much of it will be applicable to the nonworking spouse because cultural values and norms that affect business behavior also affect social behavior outside of the workplace. Also, knowing the challenges the employee will face at work may assist the spouse in offering support to the employee during the assignment. A more substantial effort would be to tailor a program that deals with the specific daily and cultural challenges that the spouse will face overseas. In some aspects, the spouse faces more challenges than does the employee. While the employee has his or her job and people at work, the spouse often has an empty house, no friends, and isolation with which to contend. Although much of the focus of this paper has centered on the employee and determining appropriate CCT methods for the employee, we have argued that these same assessment processes could be used to determine when it would be more or less critical to provide CCT for the spouse as well.

## Avoid "Dog and Pony" Shows

Since many firms do not have the in-house expertise to design CCT programs, the use of external consultants and trainers is common. The lack of internal CCT expertise means that the ability of the HR staff to evaluate the quality and suitability of external CCT programs may be less than desired.

The framework presented in this paper provides HR decision makers with at least a rough template by which they can evaluate the quality, rigor, and appropriateness of training programs offered by consultants or universities. The decision maker could use the framework to evaluate consultants' bids or university programs in a more analytical fashion by comparing the training methodology to the various methods described in the paper. Next, by examining the various dimensions discussed, the decision maker could determine if he or she were buying more than was needed or whether the proposed training program would be inadequate and not sufficiently rigorous to meet the needs of the trainees in order to be more effective in their cross-cultural assignment.

## CCT Is Not Just for Expatriates

Throughout this paper, much of the focus has been on expatriate employees; however, CCT is necessary for repatriated employees, for employees who go on short-term assignments, for good succession planning, and for general managerial development.

Just as the framework can be a guide for selecting or designing CCT for expatriates being sent overseas, it can also be used for selecting or designing training programs for employees returning to their home country after an international assignment. Although many managers would think that "coming home" would be "no big deal," Adler (1986) found that most managers found returning to the U.S. more difficult than adjusting to the foreign country.

In addition to CCT for employees being sent on or returning from long-term international assignments, the framework and theory presented suggests that employees sent on short-term assignments need CCT as well. The content of the training may need to be more focused and topic specific than for those headed for two-to-four-year assignments, as illustrated in the case of the American professors going to Japan for a four-day conference, but it is still necessary. Companies often send managers overseas for important tasks that take a relatively shorter period of time, yet fail to train these individuals as well. Sending someone to Korea to "explore business opportunities" or "work through the details of a joint venture agreement" require cross-cultural knowledge and skills. For example, Graham (1985) has demonstrated that Americans who do not understand Japanese negotiation tactics and their underlying values often utilize negotiation tactics and strategies that are counterproductive. The framework outlined in this paper regarding CCT methodology provides a means of determining the level of CCT rigor that is needed and specific methods that are appropriate.

The lack of CCT for international assignments can have a rather significant impact on succession planning for American firms. Consider the following scenario. U.S.A. MNC, Inc. does not provide CCT before international assignments. As a consequence, many good employees fail in their international assignment because they were not adequately prepared. Also, the firm does not provide CCT for returning expatriates or managers sent on short-term assignments. Some of these employees also fail because of inadequate preparation. Other bright employees notice this. Not wanting the same fate to befall them, the best and the brightest decline to accept international assignments. These best and brightest, who lack any in-depth international experience, then continue to move to the top of the firm. Once they make it to the top, one has to wonder how capable they will be at dealing with foreign competitors, with global markets, with international suppliers, with multicultural workforces, and so on.

In the introduction, we cited scholars who argue that corporations need to develop managers with the new skills, such as global visioning skills, multicultural relation skills, and so on, to effectively lead firms in the 1990s and into the twenty-first century. Consequently, developing these skills is a critical element of succession planning. At a macro level, the framework presented suggests that if managers in the future must deal with cultures different from their own, must tackle tasks quite novel from those in which they currently engage, and must be proficient in interacting with people from other cultures, then they must receive over the course of their career and development quite rigorous cross-cultural training. Thus, the framework can provide guidance concerning the level of CCT rigor and specific training methods, such as culture assimilators, necessary for a specific international assignment, but it can also suggest the level of CCT rigor and training methods, such as international assignments, needed to prepare individuals for general positions and responsibilities in the future.

### Ethics and CCT

In addition to the "utilitarian" functions that CCT may serve, firms may want to consider the issue from a social responsibility or ethical perspective. The military trains its soldiers before sending them into battle, churches educate and train their missionaries before sending them out to proselytize, and governments train secret agents before they go under "deep" cover, but U.S. firms send employees overseas cold. Such a "sink-or-swim" approach would seem irresponsible and unreasonable to the military, clergy, or government, why then does it seem logical to the industrial sector? One must wonder if it is ethical to uproot an individual or a family, send them across the Pacific or Atlantic Oceans, and expect them to make their way skillfully through an alien business and social culture on their own. Perhaps American executives reason that the extraordinary compensation packages expatriates receive make the exchange a fair and ethical one. Living and working overseas involves adjustments and stress of a high magnitude. Placing individuals in such conditions without giving them the tools to manage these conditions seems not only economically costly to the firm, and personally costly to the individuals, but simply wrong. Ignorance is not held to be justifiable for failure domestically—why then should it be a justification for failure regarding international assignments? If U.S. firms are to successfully compete in what is becoming a global battleground, they must provide their soldiers with the weapons and ammunition necessary to wage effective and victorious campaigns.

# ▬ *References*

Adler, N. *International dimensions of organizational behavior.* Boston, Mass.: Kent, 1986.

Baker, J. C. and Ivancevich, J. M. "The assignment of American executives abroad: systematic, haphazard, or chaotic?" *California Management Review*, 1971, 13, 39–44.

Bandura, A. *Social learning theory.* Englewood Cliffs, N.J.: Prentice-Hall, 1977.

Black, J. S. "Japanese/American negotiations: The Japanese perspective." *Business and Economic Review*, 1987, 6 (1), 27–30.

Black, J. S. "Work role transitions: a study of American expatriate managers in Japan." *Journal of International Business Studies*, 1988, 19, 277–294.

Black, J. S. and Mendenhall, M. "Cross-culture training effectiveness: a review and theoretical framework for future research." *Academy of Management Review*, 1990, 15, 113–136.

Black, J. S. and Stephens, G. K. "The influence of the spouse on American expatriate adjustment and intent to stay in Pacific Rim assignments." *Journal of Management*, 1989, 15, 529–544.

Bouchner, S. *Culture in contact: Studies in cross-cultural interaction.* New York: Pergamon Press, 1982.

Brein, M. and David, K. H. "Intercultural communication and adjustment of the sojourner." *Psychology Bulletin*, 1971, 76, 215–230.

Brislin, R. W. *Cross-cultural encounters.* New York: Pergamon Press, 1981.

Church, A. T. "Sojourn adjustment." *Psychological Bulletin*, 1982, 91, 540–571.

Copeland, L. and Griggs, L. *Going international.* New York: Random House, 1985.

David, K. H. "The use of social learning theory in preventing intercultural adjustment problems." In Pedersen, P., Lonner, W. J., and Draguns, J. (eds.), *Counseling across cultures.* Honolulu, Hawaii: University of Hawaii Press, 1976.

Doz, Y. and Prahalad, C. K. "Controlled variety: a challenge for human resource management in the MNC." *Human Resource Management*, 1986, 25(1), 55–71.

Dunbar, E. and Ehrlich, M. "International practices, selection, training, and managing the international staff: a survey report." The Project on International Human Resource. Columbia University, Teachers College, 1986.

Early, P. C. "Intercultural training for managers: a comparison of documentary and interpersonal methods." *Academy of Management Journal*, 1987, 30, 685–698.

England, G. and Lee, R. "The relationship between managerial values and managerial success in the U.S., Japan, India, and Australia." *Journal of Applied Psychology,* 1974, 59, 411–419.

Graham, J. "The influence of culture on the process of business negotiations: an exploratory study." *Journal of International Business Studies,* Spring, 1985, 81–95.

Gudykunst, W. B., Hammer, M. R., and Wiseman, R. L. "An analysis of an integrated approach to cross-cultural training." *International Journal of Intercultural Relations,* 1977, 1, 99–110.

Haire, M., Ghiselli, E. E., and Porter, L. W. *Managerial thinking: An international study.* New York: Wiley, 1966.

Harris, P. and Morgan, R. T. *Managing cultural differences.* Houston, Tex.: Gulf, 1979.

Harvey, M. C. "The other side of the foreign assignment: dealing with repatriation problems." *Columbia Journal of World Business,* Spring 1982, 53–59.

Harvey, M. C. "The executive family: an overlooked variable in international assignments." *Columbia Journal of World Business,* Spring 1985, 84–92.

Hofstede, G. *Culture's consequences: International differences in work related values.* Beverly Hills, Calif.: Sage.

Jablin, F. M., Putnam, L. L., Roberts, K. H., and Porter, L. W. *Handbook of organizational communication.* Beverly Hills, Calif.: Sage, 1987.

Kepler, J. Z., Kepler, P. J., Gaither, O. D., and Gaither, M. C. *Americans abroad.* New York: Praeger, 1983.

Latham, G. "Human resource training and development." *Annual Review of Psychology,* 1988, 39, 545–582.

Landis D. and Brislin, R. *Handbook on intercultural training.* Vol. 1. New York: Pergamon Press, 1983.

Lanier, A. R. "Selection and preparation for overseas transfers." *Personnel Journal,* 1979, 58, 160–163.

Locke, E. and Latham, G. *Goal setting: A motivational technique that works.* Englewood Cliffs, N.J.: Prentice-Hall, 1984.

Mendenhall, M. and Oddou, G. "The cognitive, psychological, and social contexts of Japanese management." *Asia Pacific Journal of Management,* 1986a, 4(1),24–37.

Mendenhall, M. and Oddou, G. "Acculturation profiles of expatriate managers: implications for cross-cultural training programs." *Columbia Journal of World Business,* 1986b, 21, 73–79.

Mendenhall, M., Dunbar, E., and Oddou, G. "Expatriate selection, training, and career-pathing: a review and critique." *Human Resource Management,* 1987, 26, 331–345.

Mendenhall, M. and Oddou, G. "The dimensions of expatriate acculturation." *Academy of Management Review,* 1985, 10:39–47.

Miller, E. "The international selection decision: A study of managerial behavior in the selection decision process." *Academy of Management Journal*, 1973, 16, 234–252.

Misa, K. F. and Fabricatore, J. M. "Return on investment of overseas personnel." *Financial Executive*, April 1979, 42–46.

Ohmae, K. "Managing in a borderless world." *Harvard Business Review*, May–June, 1989, 152–161.

Roberts, K. H. and Boyacigiller, N "Issues in cross national management research: the state of the art." Paper presented at the National Meeting of the Academy of Management, New York, 1982.

Runzheimer Executive Report 1984. "Expatriation/repatriation survey." No. 31. Rochester, Wisconsin.

Schollhammer, H. "Current research on international and comparative management issues." *Management International Review*, 1975, 15, 29–45.

Schwind, H. F. "The state of the art in cross-cultural management training." In Doktor, Robert (ed.), *International Human Resource Development Annual* (Vol. 1), 7–15, Alexandria, Vir.: ASTD, 1985.

Stephens, G. K. and Black, J. S. "The impact of the spouse's career orientation on managers during international transfers." Forthcoming in *Journal of Management Studies*.

Stewart, R. *Choices for managers*. Englewood Cliffs, N.J.: Prentice-Hall, 1982.

Sundaram, A. "Unique aspects of MNCs: a top-down perspective." Working paper series. Amos Tuck School of Business Administration, Dartmouth College, 1990.

Torbion, I. *Living abroad*. New York: Wiley, 1982.

Tung, R. "Selecting and training of personnel for overseas assignments." *Columbia Journal of World Business*, 1981, 16:68–78.

Tung, R. *Key to japan's economic strength: Human power*. Lexington, Mass.: Lexington Books, 1984.

Vroom, V. *Work and motivation*. New York: Wiley, 1964.

Zeira, Y. "Overlooked personnel problems in multinational corporations." *Columbia Journal of World Business*, 1975, 10(2),96–103.

# Expatriate Assignments: Enhancing Success and Minimizing Failure

## ROSALIE L. TUNG

A major U.S. food manufacturer was seeking someone from corporate staff to head its Japanese marketing division. Mr. X was selected because he was clearly one of the company's bright young talents; he had also demonstrated superior marketing skills in the home office. Those making the appointment did not assess his ability to relate to and work with the Japanese because it was assumed that a good manager in the United States would be a good manager abroad. Prior to his 18-month assignment, Mr. X was given some literature pertaining to Japan's geography, climate, banking, and educational institutions and was asked to share this material with his family.

However, during the initial six months in Japan, Mr. X was unable to devote much time to company activities because he was preoccupied with problems he and his family were having in adapting to the new environmental setting. Similarly, in the last six months, he often worried about his upcoming job change. He heard that a peer and rival at home had just been promoted to a position for which both men had aspirations. What must he do to get back into the race? While he was trying to strategize about this new assignment, his wife continually questioned him about their new West Coast relocation. The result: In the course of Mr. X's 18-month assignment to Japan, his company lost 98% of its existing market share to a major European competitor.

What went wrong? Why was Mr. X, a person with a proven track record in corporate headquarters, such a dismal failure in his assignment to Japan?

Mr. X's experience is not unique. In a questionnaire survey of expatriate assignments within 80 U.S. multinationals, it was found that more than half of the companies had failure rates of 10–20%. Some 7% of the respondent

*Source:* Rosalie L. Tung. "Expatriate Assignments: Enhancing Success and Minimizing Failure." *Academy of Management Executive,* 1987, 1(2). 117–126. Reprinted by permission.

firms had recall rates of 30%.[1] ("Failure" in the survey was defined as the inability of an expatriate to perform effectively in a foreign country and, hence, the need for the employee to be fired or recalled home.) These statistics are consistent with the findings of others that approximately 30% of overseas assignments within U.S. multinationals are mistakes.

These "casualties" not only represent substantial costs to the companies, but also constitute a human resource waste since most of those who failed had a noteworthy track record in the home office prior to overseas assignment. Such failures often constitute a heavy personal blow to the expatriates' self-esteem and ego. Hence, even if they are accepted back by corporate headquarters, it may take some time before they regain confidence in their own abilities. The unsettling experience for the person's family, both emotionally and physically, represents yet another consequence.

## Problems of U.S. Expatriates

What are the causes of expatriate failure in U.S. multinationals?

In the survey, the respondents were asked to indicate the most important reasons for expatriate failure. The reasons given, in descending order of importance, were:

1. Inability of the manager's spouse to adjust to a different physical or cultural environment;
2. The manager's inability to adapt to a different physical or cultural environment;
3. Other family-related problems;
4. The manager's personality or emotional immaturity;
5. The manager's inability to cope with the responsibilities posed by overseas work;
6. The manager's lack of technical competence; and
7. The manager's lack of motivation to work overseas.

These findings are consistent with other studies that show that the "family situation" and "relational abilities" factors are usually responsible for failure or poor performance abroad. In the case of Mr. X, we see that the family situation and lack of cultural awareness were largely responsible for his poor performance in Japan. Mr. X's problems were compounded by four other factors: (1) the short duration of his overseas assignment; (2) the expatriate's concern with repatriation; (3) overemphasis on the technical competence criterion to the disregard of other attributes necessary for effective performance abroad; and (4) lack of training for overseas assignment. Each of these compounding factors is discussed briefly below.

Although most overseas assignments of U.S. multinationals are for two or three years, such short stints abroad are not conducive to high performance. The expatriate barely has time to adjust before transfer home or to another overseas location. In the case of Mr. X, there were only six months out of the 18 months in which he was contributing to the subsidiary's operation. Research has shown that when expatriates are exempted from active managerial responsibilities in the first several months of foreign assignment, particularly to countries with great cultural differences, "This will ease their acculturation and help prevent mistakes they tend to make during this period [which are] usually detrimental to both the expatriate and his organization."[2]

However, extending the overseas assignment can lead to the second factor, namely, concern by the employee about repatriation. Since the "plum" positions in U.S. multinationals are back home, expatriates are understandably reluctant to accept extended periods of overseas assignments because of their concerns about being forgotten and hence passed up for promotion. These fears are to a large extent justified, as a result of the revolving door policy at the top management level in U.S. corporations. An expatriate who has been away for a number of years may find himself or herself a stranger to members of the board. This was apparently Mr. X's principal concern—he learned that while he was away from center stage his rival had been promoted over him.

The third compounding factor is overemphasis on the technical competence criterion to the disregard of other important attributes. In the case of Mr. X, technical competence was used as the sole criterion for selection and no assessment was made of his ability to relate to and work with the Japanese. According to E. L. Miller, this practice is fairly common among U.S. multinationals and stems from two primary causes: the difficulty of identifying and measuring attitudes appropriate for cross-cultural interaction and the self-interest of the selectors. Since technical competence almost always prevents immediate failure on the job, particularly in high pressure situations, the selectors play safe by placing a heavy emphasis on technical qualifications and little on the individual's ability to adapt to a foreign environment.[3] There is abundant research to show that while technical competence is an important factor in the overall determination of success, relational abilities appear to increase the probability of successful performance considerably.[4] Lack of relational abilities, i.e., the inability of the individual to deal effectively with one's clients, business associates, superiors, peers, and subordinates was found to be a principal cause of failure. However, the relational skills criterion is seldom emphasized in the selection decision.[5]

The fourth factor that often compounds the problem is inadequate training for overseas assignments. In the case of Mr. X, he was presented with the most basic factual information about Japan. These are commonly referred to as environmental briefing programs. When used alone, the environmental briefing is inadequate in preparing trainees for assignments that require extensive contact with the local community, as was the case with Mr. X as head of marketing in Japan.

One apparent solution to the problem of high expatriate failure is the use of host country nationals, which is already an extensive practice. In the survey, it was found that U.S. multinationals used local nationals more extensively at all levels of management in industrialized countries than in the less developed regions. This is logical, as one would expect the more developed nations to have a larger pool of personnel who possess the necessary manpower and technical skills to staff management-level positions.

This practice of employing local nationals, however, does not resolve all the problems of international human resource management for at least three reasons. First, local nationals may have problems relating to organizational members in the head office because of nonfamiliarity with corporate culture. As such, many multinational companies perceive the need to use expatriates to serve as an interface between corporate head office and the local subsidiary. This was a reason behind IBM's decision in early 1985 to expatriate some 250 American families to Japan as part of their restructuring efforts in checking Fujitsu's growing market share in that country. Second, companies need to send expatriates (or other alternative sources of manpower) to the less developed nations because of the lack of talent in these countries. In most instances, these are the countries that pose the major problems of adjustment for expatriates. Third, given the increasing globalization of industries and business activities, international experience in strategic markets (Japan being one of them) should be considered an integral part of any high flyer's career development program. While Japan is a highly industrialized country, its widely divergent cultural norms and practices are a major source of adjustment problems for Westerners. According to Seward, nine out of ten expatriates were significantly less productive in Japan than they were back home. This was consistent with an earlier finding by Adams and Kobayashi.[6]

Given the continued need to use expatriate staff, what should companies do to redress the situation?

To shed light on the issue, let us examine how the European and Japanese multinationals are faring in this regard. European and Japanese multinationals represent interesting study and comparative analysis cases for several reasons. First, multinationals from these countries assign very high priority to their international market because of the smaller size of their domestic markets. Second, there is a significantly longer history of overseas operations and expatriation among European multinationals. Third, while the Japanese as a result of culture and history do not readily mix with *gaigins* (foreigners), they have performed extremely well in foreign markets within the short span of two or three decades. The Japanese who were sent abroad to establish foreign subsidiaries have succeeded in making Japan a formidable economic power.

A questionnaire survey similar to the one administered to U.S. multinationals was given to 29 West European and 35 Japanese multinationals. For both the Europeans and the Japanese, failure rates were lower than the Americans'. Fifty-nine percent of the West European firms had recall rates of under 5%, 38% had recall rates of 6–10%, and only 3% had failure rates of 11–15%. For the Japanese sample, 76% of the firms had failure rates of below 5%, 10% had recall rates of 6–10%, and 14% had failure rates of 11–19%.[7] A cursory review of these statistics would suggest one of two possible explanations for the lower failure rates among European and Japanese multinationals. West Europeans and Japanese expatriates are by nature, selection, and training more adept at living and working in a foreign environment. Also, European and Japanese multinationals use different criteria for judging whether a person could work effectively in a foreign country. In the case of Japan, this may arise from the more paternalistic role assumed by the firm and the practice of life-time employment among the career staff from which the expatriate population is drawn.

To gain a better understanding of the reasons for the lower expatriate failure rate among European and Japanese firms, in-depth interviews were conducted with another sample of 17 European and Japanese multinationals in diverse industries. On the average, two senior executives responsible for expatriate assignments were interviewed from each of these multinationals. The failure rates for the European and Japanese multinationals interviewed were under 6 and 5%, respectively. These studies provide insights into the human resource management programs in European and Japanese multinationals, particularly as they relate to overseas assignments. The highlights of this study follow.[8]

## Reasons for Lower Failure Rates Among European and Japanese Multinationals

Based on the interviews, there appear to be several common denominators to successful performance among European and Japanese multinationals. These are:

1. Their long-term orientation regarding overall planning and performance assessment;
2. Use of more rigorous training programs to prepare candidates for overseas assignments, particularly by Japanese multinationals;
3. Provision of a comprehensive expatriate support system;
4. Overall qualification of candidates for overseas assignments; and
5. Restricted job mobility.

In the European multinationals, there are three additional factors that may account for their greater successes with expatriation. These include their

- international orientation,
- longer history of overseas operations, and
- language capability.

In the case of Japanese multinationals, two factors may also account for low rates of expatriate failure: selection for overseas assignments and the role of the family. The common denominators to success in both European and Japanese multinationals will be examined first.

## Long-term Orientation with Regard to Overall Planning and Performance Evaluation

U.S. multinationals generally possess a short-term orientation with regard to planning and assessment of performance. In contrast, European and Japanese multinationals espouse a long-term orientation in their human resource management practices. This is shown in several ways. First, the rate of turnover among managerial personnel is very low. Mid-career changes are rare since most companies espouse a policy of promotion from within. This "cradle to grave" philosophy implies certain obligations and responsibilities on the part of the employer and the employee. In Europe and Japan, employers are generally more tolerant of circumstances that may temporarily affect a person's performance. Consequently, they tend to make allowances for performance that is less than average in the initial period of assignment abroad. Some of the European multinationals interviewed allowed an adjustment period of up to one year. In the case of Japanese multinationals, many indicated they did not expect the expatriate to perform to full capacity until the third year of assignment.

A second implication of this long-term orientation among European and Japanese multinationals is a greater willingness to invest large sums of money in career development programs, particularly in the case of Japanese multinationals. These will be discussed later.

A third way in which this long-term orientation affects international human resource management practices is the extended periods of overseas assignments. Except for overseas postings that are strictly for career development purposes, expatriate assignments in European multinationals average five years or more. Similarly in Japanese multinationals, the average duration of an overseas assignment is five years.[9] This is consistent with a 1982 survey by the *Japan Economic News* on 612 expatriates, which found that the average duration of an overseas assignment was 4.67 years. This longer duration of overseas assignment is possible because "plum" positions may be abroad rather than at domestic headquarters. Companies also provide a comprehensive support system to allay expatriate concerns about repatriation. The longer durations of overseas assignments allow the individual more time to adjust. In addition, these firms provide greater incentive for the expatriate to learn and adapt to local circumstances.

A fourth implication of the long-term orientation among European and Japanese multinationals is the tendency to place equal, if not heavier, emphasis on a person's potential (as opposed to actual performance) in assessing his or her overall contribution to the organization. Given the practice of lifetime employment among most managerial personnel, the company can afford to take such an approach.

## Training for Cross-Cultural Encounters

As noted earlier, a principal reason for expatriate failure in U.S. multinationals is a lack of relational abilities. Despite this recognition, most U.S. multinationals do not provide formal training to prepare expatriates for cross-cultural encounters. This reluctance to invest large sums of money in training stems from the fear that employees may leave the company. This fear is justified, to a large extent, because of the high mobility of the U.S. workforce.

In comparison, given the very low turnover rates among management personnel in European and Japanese multinationals, these companies feel safe investing in an employee's future by spending large sums of money to develop overall management skills. Since international experience is considered an integral part of one's overall career development, most European companies provide some programs to prepare candidates for assignments to locations outside Western Europe, North America, and Australasia. Similarly, 70% of the 267 largest companies in Japan offer some preparatory courses for their expatriates (1982 survey by *Japan Economic News*). While the programs differ in content and emphasis, they often consist of the following components:

- *Language training.* Most employees of European multinationals have studied a second or third language in school. Consequently, refresher courses like those conducted by Berlitz are often sufficient. While the majority of European multinationals studied did not offer training in exotic languages such as Japanese, Chinese, or Arabic, some did.

Almost all the Japanese companies interviewed sponsored intensive language training programs, ranging from three months to one year in duration. To promote fluency in a foreign language, many Japanese companies invite Caucasians to share the same dormitories to provide their trainees ample opportunity to practice their language skills and to gain a better understanding of the foreign country.

- *Cross-cultural training.* Many of the European multinationals studied used a training facility known as the Center for International Briefing at Farnham Castle in the United Kingdom. The Center offers two types of residential programs: a four-day regional program and a week-long cultural awareness program. These programs are generally attended by both husband and wife. The regional program, as its name suggests, focuses on the specific region or country to which the individual is sent. Over the course of the four-day program, the trainee is exposed to factual information about the historical, political, religious, and economic factors that shape the mentality of the people in a given region, and how these factors differ from those in Western Europe. The objective is "To help the individual adjust, in a very practical way, to the work environment and the personal situation," to quote the Center's director. For example, if the target region is the Middle East, the course will examine "What Islam means in the way that people actually behave, and in their attitudes toward each other, their families, age, education, women and, most important, expatriates or foreigners who come to live among them."

The information is conveyed through a mix of lectures, audiovisual presentations, and discussions with outside speakers. The latter includes returned expatriates and foreign nationals. The Center has recently begun to offer courses to fit the specific needs of a firm.

The second type of residential program, the cultural awareness program, does not focus on a specific region of the world per se. Rather, the purpose is to broaden an individual's understanding of and sensitivity to other countries through lectures and experiential exercises. The Center trains about 1,000 people every year, with slightly more than half the candidates coming from the United Kingdom and the remainder from continental Europe. Virtually all British multinationals interviewed for this study used the Center's facilities, and a number of Swiss and Italian firms currently enroll or propose to enroll their candidates.

Besides Farnham Castle, other cross-cultural training facilities used by the European multinationals studied include the Tropen Institute (the Netherlands), the Carl Duisberg Center, and Evangelische Akademie (both Federal Republic of Germany).

Most European multinationals, in addition, provide ample opportunities for outgoing families to discuss their overseas assignments with expatriates who have returned. Since most of the European multinationals included in the study have a longer history of overseas operations, there is usually a fairly large contingent of resident experts, either located in corporate headquarters or abroad, who can brief expatriates and their spouses about the overseas situation.

Japanese companies typically provide a more comprehensive and rigorous training program to prepare their expatriates for cross-cultural encounters. Besides language training, a typical program would include:

• *Field experience.* Many of the Japanese multinationals surveyed select members of their current staff to their overseas offices to serve as trainees for one year. As trainees, their primary mission is to observe closely and, hence, learn about the company's foreign operations.

• *Graduate programs abroad.* Every year, many of the Japanese multinationals surveyed send 10 to 20 career staff members to attend graduate business, law, and engineering programs overseas. The company will pay tuition and all expenses, in addition to the employee's regular salary. While attending graduate school, the Japanese employee is exposed to foreign principles of management, which will prepare him for eventual overseas assignment. Furthermore, during the two-year program, the Japanese employee gains a better understanding of the broad functioning of foreign societies.

• *In-house training programs.* Besides language training, the expatriates take courses in international finance and international economics, and are exposed to environmental briefings about the country of assignment.

Many Japanese companies now realize the importance of developing the management skills of expatriates to prepare them for the added responsibilities of overseas work. One study found that a principal reason for expatriate failure among Japanese multinationals was their inability to cope with the larger responsibilities of overseas work.[10] The situation arises because in a foreign assignment, the Japanese expatriate has to operate largely on his own, without the kind of close interaction he was accustomed to at home. To a Japanese who has been used to working in a group, this may pose a major problem of adjustment.

• *Outside agencies.* Besides in-house training programs, there are a number of institutes in Japan that prepare expatriates for overseas assignments. One such agency is the Institute for International Studies and Training, which was established under the auspices of the Ministry of International Trade and Industry. The Institute offers two types of residential programs: three-month and one-year. The Institute annually graduates 150–200 trainees, with the average attendee having six years of work experience in industry or government. The three-month program is designed for specialists and covers courses in English and international business transactions. The one-year program is designed to "foster generalists and internationally minded businessmen." Trainees enrolled in this program have to master English plus one other foreign language and receive intensive training in area studies. Classes are held from 9:00 a.m. to 4:00 p.m.. In the evening, there are seminars given by ambassadors, ministers, foreign businessmen, and overseas researchers living in Japan. Besides the use of visiting professors from foreign countries, there is an exchange program so that students from other nations can share dormitories with Japanese trainees, thus facilitating the acquisition of foreign language skills and knowledge of foreign ways of life. The Institute has formal exchange programs with INSEAD (France), American University and American Graduate School of Management (United States), and Euro-Japanese Exchange Foundation (United Kingdom).

### Support Systems in Corporate Headquarters

In general, both European and Japanese multinationals provide a more comprehensive support system to help allay expatriate concerns about problems of repatriation. One such mechanism is "parenting" or "mentoring," whereby an expatriate is paired to a superior in corporate headquarters who takes on the role of sponsor. The sponsor, who is usually a member of senior management, apprises the expatriate regularly about the situation at home, and has the responsibility of finding a position for the expatriate upon his return. Since the turnover rate at the senior management level in most European and Japanese firms is virtually nonexistent, the expatriate can feel secure that the sponsor will be there when he returns. In the words of a British petroleum executive, even though the sponsor may have taken up a new position elsewhere in the company, "The personal link is the vital thing, not the link by way of the role the general manager was at when the expatriates went out." This sentiment was echoed by a Japanese expatriate: "My boss will continue to be my boss for a long time. I know he will take care of me."

Where there is no sponsor–expatriate pairing, most companies have separate departments or divisions that are responsible for overseeing the material well-being and career path of expatriates. The expatriate is required to talk to personnel from these departments on his home leave, which is usually once a year. In addition, some companies have a senior manager in their overseas subsidiaries who has a "part time responsibility as a career manager or godfather." The expatriate community in foreign countries also plays a major role in reinforcing the support mechanisms provided by corporate headquarters. Given the longer history of overseas operations of European multinationals, their foreign subsidiaries are generally well established with a relatively large expatriate community. As such, the new arrivals are "fairly well looked after." In the case of Japanese multinationals, the "early settlers" will provide assistance to the new arrivals because of their commitment to a strong group orientation.

### Qualification of Candidates

Given the importance assigned to the international market, both European and Japanese multinationals tend to send abroad their best people. In the words of a British executive, "We won't have any hope of acceptance in the host country unless [the expatriate] is visibly and perceptibly better than the local people." This theme was echoed by numerous executives from the United Kingdom, Italy, Switzerland, and Japan.

### Restricted Job Mobility

Because of the smaller size of domestic markets in Europe, each country can generally support a limited number of firms in a given industry. This restricts job mobility, with the result that employees are generally more dedicated to organizational goals.

In Japan, this is reinforced by the traditional loyalty to one's company. According to many Japanese expatriates, one "has to endure" and do his best even if he does not like the overseas assignment. Under the system of lifetime employment, a Japanese career staff member knows he must not disrupt the foreign operation because it will hurt his future career in the company.

While the values of Japan's younger generation may be changing (reflected in the findings of a 1979 survey by the Public Opinion Research Institute, in which respondents voiced a greater need to distinguish between work and personal lives) many executives indicated these findings can be partly attributed to a greater willingness of the younger generation to vocalize opinions and comments. Another more compelling reason to believe this changing trend may not have a negative effect on future performance of Japanese organizations can be ascribed to the projections by the Japan Ministry of Labor. These projections indicate that senior management positions in Japanese companies will become more competitive in years ahead, particularly in light of the recent slowing down of the Japanese economy. Given the more limited chances of upward mobility and the overall competitiveness of the Japanese, it is unlikely this overall loyalty and commitment to their organizations will slacken as the younger generation matures.

# Factors Unique to European Multinationals

## International Orientation

Virtually all European executives interviewed for the study indicated that a primary reason for their success in expatriation is their employees' greater international orientation and outlook, compared with their U.S. counterparts. This accounts for the relative ease with which many European expatriates adapt to new cultural settings.

This spirit of internationalism can be ascribed to several factors. First, there is the smaller size of the European multinationals' domestic markets. In the United Kingdom, for example, one-third of the country's GNP is exported. This export mentality is best characterized by the British slogan, "Export or die." A company has to concentrate on overseas expansion to grow. For example, 98% of sales for a large Swiss chemical manufacturer are generated from abroad. This export mentality and heavy dependence on the international market stand in stark contrast to the situation in the United States, where multinationals typically derive a sizable portion of their sales and revenues from domestic operations. Second, because of the relatively small size of a European country and its physical proximity to others, most Europeans have greater exposure to foreigners and foreign ways of life. Third, executives from several European multinationals contend that the military and economic strength of the United States has led Americans to be too complacent about their own culture, which often is interpreted as arrogance and creates resentment among local people. Some British executives note that since World War II, the balance of economic and military powers has migrated westward across the Atlantic. This "humbling or sobering" experience, to quote one British executive, forced most Britons to make a more pragmatic assessment of their own limitations and adopt a "more realistic attitude overseas." In countries like Switzerland and Italy, where there is a history of emigration to improve one's fortunes, people have a more accepting attitude toward foreign lands. Fourth, there is the legacy of empire. In fact, many of the companies included in this study established their overseas operations during the height of European empire building. In the words of a British executive, "I suppose there is still a legacy of the empire on this side. It is a part of British culture to travel and work overseas. It is not unusual for many members of one's family to have been abroad or to know many people who have worked abroad." This theme was echoed by the executives in the German, Swiss, and Italian multinationals.

This spirit of internationalism has affected the human resource management practices of European multinationals in several ways. First, a greater value is placed on international experience and overseas assignments. In most of the companies studied, international experience is considered an important prerequisite for promotion to top management.

A second way in which this spirit of internationalism has affected human resource management practices in European firms is the recruitment of candidates for management level positions. Besides the criterion of technical competence, when recruiting candidates for management training programs many European companies seek "well traveled young graduates."

A third implication for human resource management practices is the heterogeneity or multinational composition of a management team to ensure an international perspective in all aspects of the company's operations. In a large British petroleum company, for example, there is a system of cross-country rotation of management personnel. Under this system, while most employees join a local operating company, they must have two to three years' experience in another overseas operating company before promotion to management level. Furthermore, each management team should normally have a foreign national who is on assignment from an overseas sister affiliate.

A fourth implication of the greater international orientation of Europeans is that spouses are typically more adaptive to foreign ways of life.

### Longer History of Overseas Operations

As noted previously, many European firms surveyed expanded overseas in the heyday of European imperialism. This longer history of overseas operations has facilitated international human resource management in two important ways: First, the company has accumulated a wealth of experience in dealing with foreign nationals. Many companies have resident experts who can provide valuable advice, whether on a formal or informal basis, to the younger generation of expatriates. Second, foreign operations are generally already well established. Hence, in most cases, the expatriate moves into a developed operation abroad, which facilitates adaptation to the local environment.

### Language Capability

Because of their close physical proximity to other European countries and the importance assigned to the international market, many Europeans are bilingual or even multilingual.

Knowledge of a foreign language may not always guarantee effective performance abroad, but it does facilitate adaptation by enabling the expatriate to develop a better rapport with co-workers, customers, and other members of the local community.

## ▬ Factors Unique to Japanese Multinationals

### Selection for Overseas Assignments

While a Japanese multinational may not administer specific tests to determine a candidate's adaptability prior to overseas assignment because of the unavailability of such tests in Japan, organization officials would carefully review every aspect of the employee's qualifications before making a final decision. This is possible because of the unique system of personnel management in Japan. The strong group orientation and the after-hours socializing among the male career staff enables the immediate supervisor in a Japanese company to become thoroughly familiar with an individual's family background, general preferences, and qualifications. Given such knowledge, the Japanese supervisor generally would not make unreasonable recommendations. Most Japanese companies also keep very detailed personal inventories on their career staff. These are compiled from the annual or semiannual performance evaluations completed by the individual, his immediate supervisor, and the chief of the division. In addition, candidates who are considered for an overseas assignment (excluding those who have been selected to study abroad) typically have been with the company for ten years. Hence, the company has ample time to assess capabilities and qualifications.

### Role of the Family

A principal reason for expatriate failures in U.S. and European multinationals is the family situation factor.[11] Japanese wives, however, are generally more "obedient and dependent" than their American or European counterparts. Given the greater emphasis on face saving, a Japanese woman would not want to "fail" in her role as a wife by complaining about the problems encountered living in a foreign country.

## ▬ Implications for U.S. Multinationals

Based on the foregoing analysis of expatriate assignments among a sample of European and Japanese multinationals, there appear to be common denominators to successful performance. Both European and Japanese multinationals benefit from the heavier emphasis placed on the international market and the adoption of long-term orientation with regard to overall planning in the area of international human resource management. These factors lead to a greater willingness to (1) sponsor rigorous programs preparing expatriates for cross-cultural encounters, (2) provide comprehensive support systems facilitating adaptation abroad, and (3) allay concern about problems of repatriation. In addition, Europeans enjoy an inherent advantage of having been abroad longer, thus providing them with greater experience and a larger pool of in-house talent and resources. To compensate for their relatively recent entry into the international economic arena, the Japanese multinationals have acquired advantage by embarking on meticulous programs to prepare their expatriates for the challenges of living and working abroad. U.S. multinationals, on the other hand, possess neither the inherent advantage of the Europeans nor the acquired advantage of the Japanese.

Can this situation among U.S. multinationals be rectified? If so, how?

Based on the foregoing analysis, at least three primary implications for U.S. firms can be drawn.

*First,* U.S. multinationals should develop a longer-term orientation with regard to expatriate assignments, overall planning, and assessment of performance. While U.S. companies have traditionally espoused a short-term orientation, this strategy is incompatible with the evolving trend toward the globalization of industries, which necessitates greater international outlook among top management. This international perspective can be engendered through one or two tours of duty abroad. The solution, however, does not lie in short stints abroad. Even if the overseas assignment were undertaken primarily for career development purposes, it is doubtful that it would serve a useful purpose if the dismal performance abroad erodes the expatriate's self-confidence. Short stints abroad are not conducive to high performance because the expatriate barely has time to adjust before transfer home or to another location. To allay expatriate concerns that prolonged absence from corporate headquarters may negatively affect their chances of promotion within the corporate hierarchy, the implementation of some support mechanisms (similar to those found in European and Japanese multinationals) will help alleviate these fears. While individual mentoring may not be possible given the rapid turnover of American management personnel, multinationals might consider setting up separate departments or divisions whose sole function is to oversee the career paths of expatriates.

A longer-term orientation among U.S. companies may also engender greater commitment and loyalty among employees and increased willingness to undergo temporary inconveniences to advance the company's overall goals. Furthermore, increased loyalty on the part of employees may lower the turnover rate, which should result in a greater willingness by the company to invest in training programs.

*Second,* U.S. multinationals and U.S. society at large must develop a more international orientation and outlook. Without a fundamental change of attitude in this regard, the international market will continue to be relegated to a secondary role in the company's overall planning. Under these circumstances, it is unrealistic to expect that the company will devote sufficient attention to the area of international human resource management. Because of the narrowing technological gap among the United States, Europe, and Japan, U.S. multinationals can no longer rely solely on technology to gain a competitive edge in international markets. The successful operation of a multinational is contingent on the availability of additional resources, such as capital, know-how, and manpower. It is argued that manpower is a key ingredient in the efficient operation of a multinational because other resources are not as effectively or efficiently allocated to subsidiaries by corporate headquarters in the absence of a highly developed pool of managerial talent with international orientation.

The international competitiveness of U.S. multinationals has to depend on the ingenuity of its workers and, more important, the workers sent overseas as representatives of corporate headquarters. There are encouraging signs that the United States has finally awakened to this need, evidenced by the burgeoning interest in international business and cross-cultural programs at academic institutions, particularly at the university level. This is just a beginning, however, and much needs to be done.

*Third*, U.S. multinationals must provide more comprehensive training programs to prepare expatriates for cross-cultural encounters. Studies have shown that technical competence alone is a necessary but insufficient condition for successful operations abroad. Because of the greater mobility of the U.S. workforce, American multinationals may be reluctant to sponsor more rigorous programs such as those found in the Japanse multinationals. However, programs along the lines of those offered by the Center for International Briefing at Farnham Castle in England should certainly be feasible. It is clearly impossible to prepare expatriates for all the contingencies of living and working abroad within the course of a program that lasts only a week. An executive with a large European transnational corporation suggests that a program like the one at Farnham can "at least dent people's over-confidence" in the superiority of their own ways of thinking and operating. Such programs emphasize that things are different in other countries and there is no way the expatriate can change that fact because it has been like that for centuries.

By examining and then implementing the aforementioned changes, the dismal record of U.S. expatriate performance can begin to improve.

## ▬ *Notes*

1. For a more detailed discussion of the questionnaire survey of U.S., European, and Japanese multinationals, see Tung, R. L. "Selection and Training Procedures of U.S., European, and Japanese Multinationals." *California Management Review,* 1982, 25(1), 57–71.

2. Details of this study can be found in Harrari, E. and Zeira, Y. "Training Expatriates for Managerial Assignments in Japan." *California Management Review,* 1978, 20(4), 56–62.

3. For an elaboration on this argument, see Miller, E. L. "The Selection Decision for an International Assignment: A Study of the Decision Maker's Behavior." *Journal of International Business Studies,* 1972, 3, 49–65.

4. Details of these findings can be found in Hays, R. D. "Ascribed Behavioral Determinants of Success-Failure Among U.S. Expatriate Managers." *Journal of International Business Studies,* 1971, 2, 40–46, and Howard, C. G. "Model for the Design of a Selection Program for Multinational Executives." *Public Personnel Management,* March–April 1974, 138–145.

5. For further information on this study, see Tung, R. L. "Selection and Training for Overseas Assignments." *Columbia Journal of World Business,* Spring 1981, 68–78.

6. Details of these findings can be found in Seward, J. "Speaking the Japanese Business Language." *European Business*, Winter 1975, 40–47, and Adams, T. E. M. and Kobayashi, N. *The World of Japanese Business*. Tokyo: Kodnsha International, 1969.

7. See Tung, 1982.

8. For a comprehensive description and analysis of the human resource management practices in Japanese and European multinationals, see Tung, R. L. *Key to Japan's Economic Strength: Human Power*. Lexington, Mass.: Lexington Books, 1984, and *Managing Human Resources in the International Context*. Cambridge, Mass.: Ballinger Publishers (in press).

9. See Tung, 1982.

10. Ibid.

11. Ibid.

# Fred Bailey: An Innocent Abroad— A Case Study in Cross-Cultural Management

## J. STEWART BLACK

$F$red gazed out the window of his twenty-fourth floor office at the tranquil beauty of the Imperial Palace amidst the hustle and bustle of downtown Tokyo. It had been only six months since Fred Bailey had arrived with his wife and two children for this three-year assignment as the director of Kline & Associates' Tokyo office. Kline & Associates was a large multinational consulting firm with offices in nineteen countries worldwide. Fred was now trying to decide if he should simply pack up and tell the home office that he was coming home or if he should try to somehow convince his wife and himself that they should stay and finish the assignment. Given how excited they all were about the assignment to begin with, it was a mystery to Fred how things had gotten to this point. As he watched the swans glide across the water in the moat that surrounds the Imperial Palace, Fred reflected on the past seven months.

Seven months ago, Dave Steiner, the managing partner of the main office in Boston, asked Fred to lunch to discuss business. To Fred's surprise, the business they discussed was not about the major project that he and his team had just finished, instead, it was about a very big promotion and career move. Fred was offered the position of managing director of the firm's relatively new Tokyo office, which had a staff of forty, including seven Americans. Most of the Americans in the Tokyo office were either associate consultants or research analysts. Fred would be in charge of the whole office and would report to a senior partner. Steiner implied to Fred that if this assignment went as well as his past projects, it would be the last step before becoming a partner in the firm.

*Source:* This case was written especially for this book.

When Fred told his wife about the unbelievable opportunity, he was shocked at her less than enthusiastic response. His wife Jennifer (or Jenny as Fred called her) thought that it would be rather difficult to have the children live and go to school in a foreign country for three years, especially when Christine, the oldest, would be starting middle school next year. Besides, now that the kids were in school, Jenny was thinking about going back to work, at least part time. Jenny had a degree in fashion merchandising from a well-known private university and had worked as an assistant buyer for a large women's clothing store before having the two girls.

Fred explained that the career opportunity was just too good to pass up and that the company's overseas package would make living overseas terrific. The company would pay all the expenses to move whatever the Bailey's wanted to take with them. The company had a very nice house in an expensive district of Tokyo that would be provided rent free, and the company would rent their house in Boston during their absence. Moreover, the firm would provide a car and driver, education expenses for the children to attend private schools, and a cost-of-living adjustment and overseas compensation that would nearly triple Fred's gross annual salary. After two days of consideration and discussion, Fred told Mr. Steiner he would accept the assignment.

The current Tokyo office managing director was a partner in the firm but had been in the new Tokyo office for less than a year when he was transferred to head up a long-established office in England. Because the transfer to England was taking place right away, Fred and his family had about three weeks to prepare for the move. Between transferring things at the office to Bob Newcome, who was being promoted to Fred's position, and getting furniture and the like ready to be moved, neither Fred nor his family had much time to really find out much about Japan, other than what was in the encyclopedia.

When the Baileys arrived in Japan, they were greeted at the airport by one of the young Japanese associate consultants and the senior American expatriate. Fred and his family were quite tired from the long trip, and the two-hour ride to Tokyo was a rather quiet one. After a few days of just settling in, Fred spent his first full day at the office.

Fred's first order of business was to have a general meeting with all the employees of associate consultant rank and higher. Although Fred didn't notice it at the time, all the Japanese staff sat together and all the Americans sat together. After Fred introduced himself and his general idea about the potential and future directions of the Tokyo office, he called on a few individuals to get their ideas about how the things for which they were responsible would likely fit into his overall plan. From the Americans, Fred got a mixture of opinions with specific reasons about why certain things might or might not fit well. From the Japanese, he got very vague answers. When Fred pushed to get more specific information, he was surprised to find that a couple of the Japanese simply made a sucking sound as they breathed and said that it was

"difficult to say." Fred sensed the meeting was not achieving his objec
so he thanked everyone for coming and said he looked forward to their all
working together to make the Tokyo office the fastest growing office in the
company.

After they had been in Japan about a month, Fred's wife complained to
him about the difficulty she had getting certain everyday products like maple
syrup, peanut butter, and good-quality beef. She said that when she could
get it at one of the specialty stores it cost three and four times what it would
cost in the States. She also complained that since the washer and dryer were
much too small, she had to spend extra money by sending things out to be
dry cleaned. On top of all that, unless she went to the American Club in
downtown Tokyo, she never had anyone to talk to. After all, Fred was gone
ten to 16 hours a day. Unfortunately, at the time Fred was preoccupied,
thinking about a big upcoming meeting between his firm and a significant
prospective client, a top 100 Japanese multinational company.

The next day, Fred, along with the lead American consultant for the
potential contract, Ralph Webster, and one of the Japanese associate consultants, Kenichi Kurokawa, who spoke perfect English, met with a team from
the Japanese firm. The Japanese team consisted of four members: the VP of
administration, the director of international personnel, and two staff specialists. After shaking hands and a few awkward bows, Fred said that he knew
the Japanese gentlemen were busy and he didn't want to waste their time so
he would get right to the point. Fred then had the other American lay out
their firm's proposal for the project and what the project would cost. After
the presentation, Fred asked the Japanese what their reaction to the proposal
was. The Japanese did not respond immediately, so Fred launched into his
summary version of the proposal thinking that the translation might have
been insufficient. But again the Japanese had only the vaguest of responses
to his direct questions.

The recollection of the frustration of that meeting was enough to shake
Fred back to reality. The reality was that in the five months since that first
meeting little progress had been made and the contract between the firms
was yet to be signed. "I can never seem to get a direct response from Japanese," he thought to himself. This feeling of frustration led him to remember
a related incident that happened about a month after this first meeting with
this client.

Fred had decided that the reason not much progress was being made
with the client was that Fred and his group just didn't know enough about
the client to package the proposal in a way that was appealing to the client.
Consequently, he called in the senior American associated with the proposal,
Ralph Webster, and asked him to develop a report on the client so that the
proposal could be reevaluated and changed where necessary. Jointly, they
decided that one of the more promising Japanese research associates, Tashiro
Watanabe, would be the best person to take the lead on this report. To im-
press upon Tashiro the importance of this task and the great potential they

saw in him, they decided to have the young Japanese associate meet with both Fred and Ralph. In the meeting, Fred had Ralph lay out the nature and importance of the task, at which point Fred leaned forward in his chair and said to Tashiro, "You can see that this is an important assignment and that we are placing a lot of confidence in you by giving it to you. We need the report by this time next week so that we can revise and represent our proposal. Can you do it?" After a somewhat pregnant pause, the Japanese responded hesitantly, "I'm not sure what to say." At that point, Fred smiled, got up from his chair and walked over to the young Japanese associate, extended his hand, and said, "Hey, there's nothing to say. We're just giving you the opportunity you deserve."

The day before the report was due, Fred asked Ralph how the report was coming. Ralph said that since he had heard nothing from Tashiro that everything was under control, but that he would double-check. Ralph later ran into one of the American research associates, John Maynard. Ralph knew that John was hired for Japan because of his language ability in Japanese and that, unlike any of the other Americans, John often went out after work with some of the Japanese research associates, including Tashiro. So, Ralph asked John if he knew how Tashiro was coming on the report. John then recounted that last night at the office Tashiro had asked if Americans sometimes fired employees for being late with reports. John had sensed that this was more than a hypothetical question and asked Tashiro why he wanted to know. Tashiro did not respond immediately, and since it was 8:30 in the evening, John suggested they go out for a drink. At first Tashiro resisted, but then John assured him that they would grab a drink at a nearby bar and come right back. At the bar, John got Tashiro to open up.

Tashiro explained the nature of the report that he had been requested to produce. Tashiro continued to explain that even though he had worked long into the night every night to complete the report it was just impossible and that he had doubted from the beginning whether he could complete the report in a week.

At this point, Ralph asked John, "Why didn't he say something in the first place?" Ralph didn't wait to hear whether or not John had an answer to his question. He headed straight to Tashiro's desk.

Ralph chewed Tashiro out and then went to Fred explaining that the report would not be ready and that Tashiro, from the start, didn't think it could be. "Then why didn't he say something?" Fred asked. No one had any answers, and the whole thing just left everyone more suspect and uncomfortable with one another.

There were other incidents, big and small, that had made especially the last two months frustrating, but Fred was too tired to remember them all. To Fred it seemed that working with Japanese both inside and outside the firm was like working with people from another planet. Fred felt he just couldn't communicate with them, and he could never figure out what they were thinking. It drove him crazy.

Then on top of all this, Jennifer laid a bombshell on him. She wanted to go home, and yesterday was not soon enough. Even though the kids seemed to be doing all right, Jennifer was tired of Japan—tired of being stared at, of not understanding anybody or being understood, of not being able to find what she wanted at the store, of not being able to drive and read the road signs, of not having anything to watch on television, of not being involved in anything. She wanted to go home and could not think of any reason why they shouldn't. After all, she reasoned they owed nothing to the company because the company had led them to believe this was just another assignment, like the two years they spent in San Francisco, and it was anything but that!

Fred looked out the window once more, wishing that somehow everything could be fixed, or turned back, or something. Down below the traffic was backed up. Though the traffic lights changed, the cars and trucks didn't seem to be moving. Fortunately, beneath the ground, one of the world's most advanced, efficient, and clean subway systems moved hundreds of thousands of people about the city and to their homes.

# Mel Stephen's Dilemma

## MARK MENDENHALL

$M$el Stephens had not found solace in his commute home from the office. Ordinarily, Mel found that ruminating over a problem during his commute, with a Mozart compact disc reverberating through his car's interior, allowed his mind to slowly bring even the most complicated problem into focus. "I guess I must be out of my league on this one," Mel thought as he pulled into his driveway. Mel had faced many challenges as the vice president of human resources since he arrived at Recor Engineering, but none had stumped him like this one.

Recor Engineering, one of the leaders in the U.S. domestic construction industry, had just sealed a joint venture pact with one of Japan's largest construction firms, Dentsu Hogen, K.K. Recor Engineering, a San Francisco-based company, agreed to send a large team of American experts to work in Osaka with a special group of Dentsu Hogen's best engineers. The purpose of the effort was to team up with their Japanese counterparts and collectively work on bidding for the runway project for the Osaka Airport expansion, as well as pursuing other related ventures. This would solve two problems: (1) for Dentsu Hogen, it buffers the pressure of the Japanese government to allow American construction firms into the bidding process for the airport expansion; and (2) it allows Recor to gain experience in the Japanese construction industry to see if they want to attempt to enter into that market in the future. Both sides would share significantly in profits generated by the joint venture.

The project manager was to be designated by Recor, and Larry Runolfsson was selected and had agreed to go. Larry had vast experience in all aspects of the industry and had overseen four projects in the United States from the idea stage to completion.

All the engineers (a total of twenty) agreed to relocate to Japan after being assured that their families' financial position and standard of living would not suffer because of the new assignment. Most of the designers were married. None of the designers indicated any reluctance from their spouses concerning the three-year assignment; however, Mel's secretary—his hidden

*Source:* This case was written especially for this book.

ears in the company—told him three weeks earlier that she knew that at least eight of the wives were "less than thrilled" about disrupting their children's education and creating a new life in Japan. Moreover, five of the wives had indicated that they were not pleased at having to quit their current jobs and follow their husbands to Japan—even though the pay was good.

Mel had put together a compensation package comparable to what most firms provided for expatriates in Japan—a task that was much easier than trying to decide what to do about any predeparture training for the group of expatriates. His phone calls to colleagues had yielded mixed responses. Some felt that no training was necessary, some felt a little "area briefing" was sufficient, and a few had heard of some consulting firms that offered comprehensive training packages for expatriates (but none knew if the programs were any good or cost effective).

"I don't have time to figure out all the particulars of this—they leave in three months. Go find out what kind of training these people need or if they need it at all," he had told his training and development manager. "I need it in about a week." A week later, his manager came back with her report. The prices quoted by consultants on the West Coast pushed the upper limits of the quarterly training budget, and she had talked with a variety of firms with expatriates in Japan, all of whom reported that they hadn't done any in-depth predeparture training for their expatriates. She concluded that Recor ought to follow the lead of others and offer a good financial package and leave it at that.

Mel ejected his Mozart disc and found a news station on his radio; he tried to relax as he listened absently to the news, but the nagging feeling that more should be done for the team of expatriates would not go away. "We're sending these guys into a strange country—at least to me the Japanese seem strange—and its seems as though we should do something to prepare them to go . . . other firms don't do much, if anything . . . if this joint venture melts down, I'll be in a tight spot . . . but the people being sent have all been successful here, especially Larry Runolfsson . . . they should do fine . . . besides if they're worth what we're going to be paying them, they should be able to work through whatever problems come up." Mel willed his thoughts on hold and turned his attention to the weather report.

# Management Development in a Global Context

# Management Development: An African Focus

## MERRICK L. JONES

Anyone interested in issues of Third World development is painfully aware of the complexities, contradictions, and cruel paradoxes involved. Recent events in Africa have thrown the issues into stark focus. Africa is a cockpit of turbulent change, where the transition from traditional societies to modern nation states confronts those involved with painful and complex puzzles. The myriad problems facing the continent are reflected daily in Western newspapers. Great human tragedies unfold as whole nations are devastated by droughts and other natural calamities. Famine, population growth, deforestation, the advancing deserts, civil wars, border disputes, military coups, political intrigues, one-party states, tribalism, guerrilla movements: the catalogue is reported with scant sympathy—indeed, it sometimes seems, with gleeful smugness. Meanwhile, the peoples of Africa struggle with the awful natural and man-made problems that confront them in building nation states within the arbitrary boundaries bequeathed to them by the departed colonial powers. No one can doubt that it will be a long and supremely difficult struggle. There have been, and will be, many failed experiments, many dead ends, many setbacks in the process. But one central reality seems inescapable: in coping with acute scarcity of resources and lack of developed infrastructure, great skills of management and organization will be imperative.

The question is: Will the importation of management concepts and practices from the industrialized West meet Africa's needs? Questions concerning the transferability across nations of management concepts and practices are complex and controversial. There is as yet no consensus about the nature of the arguments involved or about how empirical data can usefully be obtained and compared.

Onyemelukwe [1] considers the educational implications, asserting that "The belief is that whatever is not going well can always be rectified by train-

*Source:* Merrick L. Jones. "Management Development: An African Focus." *International Studies of Management and Organization,* 1989, 19(1), 74–90. Originally published in *Management Education and Development.* Reprinted by permission.

ing. The result is a staggering investment in foreign-orientated training schemes with little in the way of return in investment." And:

> Looking through courses and lectures on management organised in various parts of Africa by universities and institutes of management, one is faced with a galaxy of do-it-yourself kits and shorthand prescriptions. . . . it is the refusal of many authors and researchers in the field of management to give a significant place to social and cultural factors that limits the usefulness of their work.

In this paper I consider some of the issues in relation to an investigation of managerial thinking in one African country, Malawi. In particular, I focus on the data concerning the way Malawian managers think about their work, and implications for management education and training. Very briefly, the study involved 105 Malawian senior and middle-level managers from both the private and public sectors in a questionnaire survey designed to elicit their thinking on aspects of their work, especially their satisfactions and their relationships with subordinates. The questionnaire was based on an instrument used originally by Haire, Ghiselli, and Porter [2] in 14 countries, and subsequently in similar studies in many other parts of the world (including 3 African countries). In addition, 47 managers were involved in a semistructured interviewing survey, which was intended to focus on similar issues and to provide insights on the contextual fabric of the Malawian manager's world. The aims of the study were:

1. to investigate managerial thinking about a limited number of important issues in a national context (Malawi);
2. to compare data from this investigation in a practical way with those produced by similar studies in other countries;
3. to examine factors in the Malawian context that might account for similarities and differences between the thinking of the Malawian managers and that of other managers;
4. to relate these findings to the education and training of managers in Malawi, and to consider their appropriateness; and
5. to consider possible areas for further investigation.

In this paper my intention is to focus mainly on item 4 above. Before considering the data from the study and their implications for the education and training of Malawian managers, it might be useful to present *very briefly,* some relevant information about the country.

Malawi is located in southern central Africa, bordering Zambia to the west, Tanzania to the north east, and Mozambique. By African standards it is not a big country, its area totaling 118,500 square kilometers, of which about one-fifth comprises the great lake that dominates the country, Lake Malawi. However, Malawi's population density is about four times as high as the African average, at 47 persons per square kilometer overall. At the time of the last population census, in 1982, Malawi's population stood at a little over 6.5 million.

In common with other nations in this part of Africa, Malawi has a turbulent history, experiencing long periods of stability and at other times the eruptions of migratory peoples entering the region from other population centers. Although the details of these movements are still being elaborated, it is clear that the great lake, the third biggest in Africa, has been a focal point for centuries in this part of the continent. In more recent times, the territory that now constitutes Malawi was subjected to the depredations of slave traders operating from the Indian Ocean coast, and to the influx of Ngoni peoples from the south, driven to their northward odyssey by the turmoil, in what is now the Republic of South Africa, caused by the rise of the great Zulu empire. Another powerful influence was the coming of European missionaries and explorers in the latter half of the nineteenth century. As the scramble for Africa divided the continent into spheres of influence for the European powers at the turn of the century, the area of the lake eventually became the British colony of Nyasaland.

Unlike other British colonies in Africa, Nyasaland offered no exploitable natural resources and did not attract large numbers of European settlers. Evidence suggests that Britain's attitude toward its colony of the lake was at least ambivalent, and possibly at times downright unenthusiastic. An attempt in 1953 to form a federation in central Africa consisting of Northern Rhodesia (now Zambia), Southern Rhodesia (now Zimbabwe), and Nyasaland was doomed to failure. The independent nation of Malawi emerged after a long and complex struggle that had its roots early in the present century, but developed as a significant movement during the 1950s.

The "wind of change" was then gathering strength in southern Africa, and the British colonies there were experiencing a common, if individually manifested, movement toward self-government. For Malawi the crucial moment came when Dr. H. K. Banda returned to Nyasaland, in July 1958, after having lived and practiced medicine in the USA, Europe, and Ghana for many years. From that day, events were set in train that led, with historical inevitability, to independence from Britain in July 1964 and, in 1966, to the status of a republic within the Commonwealth. Dr. Banda became President (and in 1971 was made the Life President) of the new Republic of Malawi. The story of Dr. Banada's apparently historic destiny in liberating the country of his birth from its colonial masters is extraordinary, and his continued dominance as leader of Malawi is an overwhelming factor in the nation's development. Since this reality forms a part of the national context in which Malawian organizations function and Malawian managers work, it may be useful to explore briefly the nature of Malawi's political milieu.

Since the 1960s we have observed the achievement of independence by most of Africa's former colonial territories. The dominant picture we in the West receive of Africa through our media is one of a continent in a turbulent transition, with national regimes apparently changing, sometimes violently, with bewildering frequency. Some states seem to have tried almost every conceivable form of government, from multiparty democracy to military dictatorship, in search of a suitable system. Malawi has been notably absent in reports of such developments. The overwhelmingly powerful and pervasive influence of the Life President on all facets of Malawian life is important, because we could expect that the consequences of such a situation would inevitably include the ways in which organizations operate and managers behave.

Turning to Malawi's economic position, the country is, in terms of per capita income, one of the world's poorest nations. At independence the country had a small industrial sector and a rudimentary economic infrastructure. Few exploitable mineral resources have been located in any quantity. The policies of the government since independence therefore have emphasized the development of agricultural, transport, and communications infrastructure. As a landlocked country, Malawi faces problems, sometimes acute, in routing its crucial agricultural exports and its imports. Problems of transporting goods great distances across difficult terrain are frequently aggravated by climatic conditions and guerrilla activity. Since Malawi's independence, the protracted war in Rhodesia (now Zimbabwe) and the continuing civil insurrection in Mozambique have presented intractable difficulties for Malawian administrators and businessmen.

Malawi, by African standards, enjoys a good climate for a variety of agricultural activities and is blessed with relatively productive soils. There has been impressive development in the production of a number of cash crops, including tobacco, tea, coffee, and sugar, which form the bulk of the country's exports. In addition, greater yields of subsistence crops, importantly maize, have been consistently achieved. Malawi is one of the few African countries that are largely self-sufficient in staple foodstuffs.

Although the industrial base remains modest in size, development in this sector also has been impressive. The following figures relating to paid employment in Malawi (1980) are relevant:

> Total in paid employment—294,707
> In professional, technical, and related posts—21,716 (7.4%)
> In managerial/administrative occupations—4,127 (1.5%).

These figures, supplied by the Manpower Planning Unit, Office of the President and Cabinet, relate to December 1980 and are the most recent available in this form. By 1983 (the latest figures available), the number of individuals in paid employment was approximately 387,000, over fifty percent of whom were engaged in agriculture.

## ▬ *Malawian Managers*

It would be neither possible nor relevant to report in this paper the details of findings from the interviewing and questionnaire surveys. My intention is to put forward some fairly direct statements about Malawian managers and the organizations in which they work, and to consider their implications for management development. These statements appear to reflect as directly as possible the data produced by the investigation.

In general terms, management education and training have attracted some rather critical comments, and it may be useful to look very briefly at this wider context before we focus on the Malawian situation.

Safavi [3], reporting on a project involving the 57 countries and territories of Africa during a 4-year study of management education and development programs, paints a "gloomy picture" of "a number of areas of conflict between classroom and culture, between Western theory and African reality." A number of observers have similar concerns. Nyerere (cited by Onyemelukwe [1]) has observed that the training of African managers appears to have been designed to divorce them from the societies it is supposed to equip them to serve. Hofstede [4] claims that Western management theories, although widely taught, are not practiced by non-Western managers. Successful managers "perform a cultural transposition of ideas . . . there is no single formula for management development to be used in different cultures" (P. 380); there is a need to ascertain what constitutes "success" in a particular culture. Hyden [5] comments on the absurdity of what he calls "technique peddling" by Western management consultants in Africa, exemplified by bizarre attempts to undertake Organization Development (OD) consultancies (with their accompanying American individualistic, humanistic values) in African organizations: "The African personality is full and wholesome in a sense that does not tally with the demands of systematic rationality." Yet African managers "have been moulded in a type of management thinking that makes them strangers in their own environment" (P. 159).

It is difficult to dispute the view that strategies and methods used to educate and train African managers have generally been based on Western theories and practices, with little, if any, consideration of the environments in which African organizations function. What can be done to change the situation? Simply asserting, as so many observers do, that management education and training must take cognizance of the environmental realities of Africa does not get us very far. Do the data from this study of Malawian senior and middle managers provide any pointers? It is perhaps appropriate to preface the discussion of the issues with two notes of caution.

First, it is important to avoid the common assumption that education and training can be relied upon to accomplish changes in human behavior and thinking. There is a line of reasoning (or rather, assumption) that:

TRAINING
(usually equated with classroom-based courses)
↓
INDIVIDUAL LEARNING
↓
IMPROVED INDIVIDUAL JOB PERFORMANCE
↓
IMPROVED ORGANIZATIONAL PERFORMANCE

At each level the assumption can be challenged, and experience indicates that, without positive managerial action, the training of individuals rarely leads to improved organizational performance. I am therefore conscious of the need to exercise caution in advancing ideas about the education and training of Malawian managers, especially since I believe that the causes of important aspects of their thinking are to be found in fundamental national sociocultural and political elements.

Second, there is at present no way of judging with any degree of accuracy the extent to which Malawian organizations and management have developed distinctive features. Malawi was a British colony, and is now a member of the Commonwealth. Its systems (for example, in education, communications, industry, commerce, technology, health care, public utility provision, and government organization) would be familiar to British expatriates and visitors. The major language of business and government is English. Most Malawian administrators and executives will have been trained on the Western model, many of them in Britain; and, as the data confirm, most have worked with expatriate (predominantly British) managers, often taking over from an expatriate boss. The study has shown that traditional modes of social and family organization still inhere in contemporary Malawi as fundamental aspects of the life of individuals, even those, such as managers, who have moved out of the rural subsistence economy to paid employment in the expanding urban sector. To ask the question "How Westernized are Malawian organizations and managers?" is not to anticipate a precise answer, but to realize that more research will be necessary before we can even begin to make useful judgments about this important issue.

Using the data from this study, supplemented by those from other relevant studies, I propose the following general statements about Malawian managers and the organizations in which they work, which may serve as a useful base for a discussion of relevant strategies for management education and training:

1. Malawian organizations function in an environment of acute resource scarcity, economic uncertainty, and highly centralized political power.

2. These organizations tend to retain the major characteristics of structures developed in the colonial era, namely, rather rigid bureaucratic, rule-bound hierarchies.

3. Organizations tend to be viewed by society as a whole as having a wider mission than is generally understood in the West, being expected to provide socially desirable benefits such as employment, housing, transport, and assistance with important social rituals and ceremonies; considerations of profit maximization and efficiency may be viewed as secondary or incidental.

4. There is among Malawian workers a generally instrumental orientation toward work, involving high expectations of the benefits, to the worker and his extended family, that employment brings, but less in the way of loyalty and commitment to the organization (or profession) that is said to typify the employer–employee relationship in the West.

5. There is in Malawian society an emphasis on prestige and status differences, creating relationships of dependency, which in organizations finds expression in wide differentials between organizational levels, particularly between managers and workers, extreme deference to and dependence upon one's boss, and a paternal, concerned, but strict style of management.

6. The collectivist values of Malawian society are reflected in organizations in the high regard managers have for their subordinates as people; in a view of workers as a network of people rather than as human resources; in an emphasis on maintaining relationships rather than on providing opportunities for individual development; in an emphasis on "highly ritualised interpersonal interactions which often place greater value on the observance of protocol than the accomplishment of work-related tasks" [6. P. 159]; in a desire by workers for a close relationship with the boss; and in a reluctance by managers either to accept individual blame for mistakes or to criticize individual subordinates in a direct manner.

7. Malawian managers tend to view their authority, professional competence, and information as personal possessions, rather than impersonal concomitants of their organizational role, and as a source of status and prestige.

8. This, coupled with the emphasis on the wide differential—in status, power, education, experience, and perceived ability—between managers and workers makes Malawian managers very reluctant to delegate authority, to share information, and to involve subordinates (who may be perceived as a potential source of threat) in decision-making processes.

9. Malawian managers regard security as an important factor in their work, to be reinforced by unchanging structures, detailed procedures, and close supervision of subordinates.

10. Malawian managers desire a good relationship with their boss, whom they perceive as a key figure, but frequently find this to be a problematic relationship because the boss manages them in a manner similar to that they employ with their own subordinates; this may find expression in dissatisfaction with their perceived opportunities for autonomy and self-actualization.

11. Individualistic (as opposed to universalistic) criteria tend to influence organizational behavior; hence, insecurity is increased because decisions cannot be consistently predicted, and blame for mistakes tends to be assigned on a personalized basis.

12. Malawian managers have constantly to be sensitive to political pressures and aware of developments that might affect them as power coalitions change.

13. Malawian managers tend to recognize their role in achieving organizational performance (this, on the basis of our limited data, does not seem to apply to civil servants to the same degree), and to emphasize their individual professional or technical expertise rather than their "managerial" functions.

14. Malawian managers have a keen awareness of the necessity to acknowledge and manage their wider social obligations to extended family and

kinship systems, and of the possible conflicts that may thereby exist in relation to their formal organizational roles.

15. Malawian managers often find their relationships with expatriate bosses and colleagues problematic and tend to view expatriate executives as lacking in the sensitivity they view as essential, especially in their dealings with workers.

The data from the study appear to confirm that the demands of formal organizations create tensions and conflicts for Malawian managers. It is well understood that the processes of industrialization on the Western model demand the utilization of technical and scientific knowledge, but it is perhaps less clearly recognized that the use of such knowledge depends somewhat on the acceptance of the values and "world view" that are its sociocultural foundation.

The data from this study provide several examples of the tensions and problems that can occur when Western management ideas and practices are transplanted into a non-Western environment. There is, for instance, the apparent contradiction that Malawi is a newly independent nation in the process of rapid change, a characteristic shared by all African states to a greater or lesser degree and likely to continue. Yet the organizations that are to be instrumental in bringing about and managing change are, as a number of commentators have observed, generally bureaucratic, rigid, and rule-bound. On the level of managerial motivation, there is another apparent contradiction: Malawian managers reflect in many aspects of their thinking African traditional, communalistic values, yet they stress the importance of their needs for autonomy and self-actualization at work (the individualistic focus more characteristic of Western societies).

Jenkins[1] and Rutherford,[2] in studies of Malawian managers, remark on the strong, expressed need for structure, guidelines, and clear direction (reflecting a preoccupation with security). This apparent acceptance of "universalistic" criteria for behavior in organizations is contrasted with the evidence that managers regularly bypass organizational structures and make decisions on the basis of "particularistic" (i.e., what the managers in the study referred to as "personalized") criteria.

## Education and Training of Malawian Managers

Organizational behavior is influenced by a complex set of interrelated factors. The Western notion of "rational" behavior is itself the product of such factors, but it is not automatically applicable in other contexts. What appears to a Western observer of African organizations to be "irrational," on closer examination can be seen to reflect a set of values that are different from, but no less valid than, those of the West. For this reason I take the view, in considering the education and training of Malawian managers, that it would be unrealistic and inappropriate to advance prescriptive proposals for changing the existing realities of Malawian organizational life.

The following propositions are intended rather to accept the sociocultural, economic, and political realities and to suggest how Malawian managers might be assisted to be effective and, if they so desire, to change existing systems and practices:

1. Because the Malawian environment is less stable and predictable than is the case in the industrialized nations, "the probability of planned actions going wrong is high . . . margins of error are likely to be particularly large" [5. P. 157]. It is therefore important to recognize that the use of Western planning techniques cannot be assumed to guarantee any anticipated outcome. Malawian managers will need to reflect on experiences, since independence, of planning and its effectiveness, and to identify the particular factors that have influenced success or failure.

2. There is a need to acknowledge the collectivist values that inhere in contemporary Malawian society and to consider which Western management practices and techniques might tend to contradict them. For example, it is not difficult to understand why Western performance appraisal and Management by Objectives schemes may find intellectual acceptance by Malawian managers, yet fail in practice. Seddon [7] has observed that in many African societies it is a sign of weakness to admit incompetence or ignorance. Mistakes are believed to be beyond the control of individuals, and the maintenance of "face" is of crucial importance. There is a highly developed sensitivity to individual criticism, "the most powerful contingencies determining behavior (informally) are 'social evaluations'—pride and shame." In my study there was considerable evidence of a reluctance by managers to criticize individuals.

In such circumstances, the use of Western practices for assessing individual performance appears to be inappropriate. For Malawian managers to have to learn such practices without a comprehensive analysis of their chances of success and their consequences in terms of Malawian values seems both impractical and wasteful.

3. Similar considerations apply to teaching Malawian managers about the benefits claimed, in the Western context, for delegation of authority, sharing of information, and a generally more participative management style. In the situation I have described, such practices can be seen to contradict many Malawian social values, and have little chance at present of successful adoption. It is important, however, that Malawian managers clearly understand the consequences of their current management style, which (1) tends to push decisions upward in the organizational hierarchy; (2) involves managers in routine, trivial activities; (3) hinders the sharing of information within the organization, thus possibly reducing its capacity to anticipate and cope with change; (4) encourages highly dependent subordinate behavior; (5) reduces opportunities for subordinates to engage in more interesting work; and (6) on the evidence of my interview survey, appears to be a source of dissatisfaction for managers in terms of relationships with their bosses.

4. Malawian managers require highly developed political skills, both in monitoring developments that may affect them, as "particularistic" criteria

influence decision makers inside and outside their employing organizations, and in their relationships with organizational superiors, colleagues, and subordinates. Such skills are not necessarily a major focus in Western management development strategies.

5. Malawian managers require well-developed diplomatic skills, particularly in two contexts. First, their bosses expect them to behave in a deferential manner, far more than is the case in Western views of such a relationship. It seems important that the implications of this type of relationship should be examined in relation to organizational performance. If managers are to be able to cope with change and to provide solutions to emerging problems, will their extreme deference to, and dependence on, more senior executives not inhibit them? Malawian managers expressed dissatisfaction with this relationship and wanted more opportunities (clearly delineated, nevertheless) for autonomy. They also wanted their bosses to behave in a more predictable (i.e., "universalistic") manner and to give them recognition for good performance. In such circumstances of dependency and unfulfilled expectations, Malawian managers need diplomatic and influencing abilities of a high order. Secondly, as we have seen, Malawian managers are often faced with demands from outside the organization, from extended family and kinship groups and (less frequently) from the Party. Such demands may well conflict with the manager's organizational role, and he will need to be skilled in explaining the demands and limitations under which he operates in the organization.

6. When Malawian managers are taught the paramount Western organizational values of effective and efficient use of scarce resources, it is important that they consciously consider and understand the implications of implementing these values in Malawian society, where there is a greater concern for social relationships than for performance, where there are social expectations about the role of organizations that are greater than is customary in the West, and where the notion of considering the individual as a "resource" is strange.

7. Malawian workers tend to have higher expectations about the organization's ability and willingness to accept a degree of responsibility for their welfare and development than is the case in the industrialized West. At the same time, there is a more instrumental attitude toward work, involving fewer considerations of loyalty to the organization. In these circumstances, managers could well consider the implications in terms of employee motivation. Western assumptions about the desirability of self-expression and fulfillment appear to be inappropriate, and uncritical teaching of Western motivation theories to Malawian managers needs to be challenged.

8. The managers in this study indicated that they derived considerable satisfaction from the use of their professional or technical competence, and were generally concerned about performance (this was decidedly less so in the case of the Malawian civil servants in the study). These strengths might be used in developing managers' understanding of their more directly managerial functions if it can be shown that job satisfaction can be enhanced when

management work is viewed as requiring equally prestigious, admirable skills, and that effective performance is more likely when professional and technical expertise is reinforced by managerial capabilities.

9. Although the presence of expatriate managers will lessen in significance, it is at present an area of concern for many Malawian managers. Since it is not realistic to expect that expatriate executives will be selected primarily on the basis of their cultural sensitivity, it might be useful if Malawian managers were helped to understand more about the backgrounds, perspectives, and values of the expatriates. This may go some way in enabling Malawian managers to handle their relationships with expatriates effectively.

## ▆ Strategies and Methods

Turning to considerations of appropriate methods for education and training of Malawian managers, I suggest that the foregoing discussion indicates that the following *outcomes* are priorities:

- In an environment of turbulent change, learning should become a conscious and continuous process for Malawian managers.
- Malawian managers should develop a profound awareness of, and sensitivity to, the sociocultural context in which they operate.
- They should also have a clear understanding of the implicit demands of Western management ideas and practices, and of the facets of Malawian society that might be congruent and incongruent with such demands (for example, deference and dependent relationships).
- There should be a deliberate and reasoned rejection of the uncritical adoption of Western (or other alien) organization and management theories.
- Managers and educators should acknowledge, analyze, and reflect upon the experience of Malawian organizations and develop from it indigenous explanatory concepts.
- Malawian managers should develop more confidence in the validity of their own experiences and their views on management (rather than deferring to outsiders).

When we consider how such outcomes might be achieved through education and training, several factors have to be borne in mind. First, just as Western management ideas must be critically examined in the light of Malawian sociocultural realities, Western notions concerning the education and training of managers have to be understood in terms of the assumptions they make about people and the values that influence them. Many current Western ideas about management development can be seen clearly to reflect values such as individual responsibility for self-actualization; learning as problem solving, involving puzzlement, perturbation, even discomfort for the learner; the value of self-discovered knowledge as opposed to prescribed knowledge; a view of the teacher–earner relationship as involving interdependence and assumed equality; development as involving risk and change for learners; a view of the professional as an individual of independent judgment, self-confident in his relationship with his employing organization; and an increasing degree of openness in relationships. Contrasted to this I have detailed Malawian values that might be expected to influence management education and training, including the collectivist (as opposed to Western individualist) nature of social relationships; greater awareness of hierarchical levels and deference to authority, which, according to Clarke[3], is expressed in the teacher–learner relationship by "a greater need (by the learner) for clear and unequivocal direction . . . and regular face-to-face contact"; education seen as a way to enhance status rather than for personal growth; learning viewed as a way of avoiding risk by acquiring additional information, to be hoarded and protected as a source of power; and training viewed as a threat rather than an opportunity for self-actualization if it involves an admission of ignorance or shortcomings.

In addition, managers indicated in the questionnaire survey that the most effective ways in which they had learned their managerial abilities were: by doing, by discussing real problems with colleagues, through training by the boss, by observing effective managers, and by analyzing their successes and failures.

This seems to suggest that approaches to management education and training in Malawi should include the following general criteria:

1. As Hyden [5] has noted: "For a manager to be effective he needs to be sensitive to and work in response to his proximate environment. Many African managers lack a grasp of how they can combine good management with effective response to their environment" (P. 59). People are intuitively and experientially aware of their environment, but it is suggested that managers need to be helped to develop a fuller understanding of and sensitivity to the sociocultural facets of their environment that affect their roles. This will involve teaching strategies that draw upon the experiences of managers and encourage them to reflect on the implications for future action.

2. It must be made clear in organizational policies that the organization accepts a substantial share of responsibility for the development of individuals, and that further education and training do not imply that a manager is incompetent or lacking in some area. It must be understood that management development does not involve a risk for the individual and that the learning environment will be supportive.

3. Learning strategies and methods should reflect the collectivist nature of Malawian society. This would imply that methods should be avoided that focus on individual performance (especially shortcomings). Small-group methods and other supportive techniques seem to be appropriate.

4. There needs to be an explicit focus on continuous learning from experience. Learning opportunities in the organization (such as deputizing for an absent boss, introduction of structural or technological change, launching of a new product, coping with unanticipated difficulties) should be identified

and utilized. This will demand that attention be given to developing skills in analyzing successes and failures in a conscious, structured way.

5. Management education and training should help managers understand the processes of organizational change. As noted earlier, the structures of Malawian organizations tend predominantly to be rigidly bureaucratic (embodying security and stability in an environment of accelerating change). Managers need to understand the implications of such organizational patterns for the effective performance of the roles Malawian society expects organizations to undertake.

6. Managers should be trained in coaching skills, in order to be fully effective in developing subordinates. Organizations need to ensure that the job descriptions of managers include the coaching of subordinates as a priority function.

7. Management development strategies should include structured, on-the-job, developmental activities.

8. The group-oriented methods and problem-solving focus of Action Learning suggest that it might be worthwhile to experiment with this approach to management development. Revan's [8] notion of "comrades in adversity" may address the needs of Malawian managers for security and social interaction while enabling them to identify real problems and to use their shared experience to develop solutions.

## Conclusion

In the literature about the transfer of Western management concepts and practices, one can detect a developing dichotomy. Some writers assert that the imperatives of organizational life are so powerful, so pervasive, that the "culture of production" will sweep aside local variations in culture, values, and behavior. Others would claim, on the contrary, that in some countries the culture is so distinctive and so enduring that imported notions about organizations and their management will be radically modified or even rejected. The findings from the study of Malawian managers upon which this paper is based provide evidence that both tendencies are present. The "convergence–divergence" debate will continue as cross-cultural research adds to the stock of data for comparison.

For management educators this is inconvenient. It demands that strategies for management development should recognize the complex and distinctive realities of the contexts in which managers perform. The search for relevance will, I suspect, be a crucial task.

## Notes

1. Jenkins, C. "Management Problems and Management Education in Developing Economies: A Case Study of Malawi." Working paper. University of Aston, Management Centre, 1982.

2. Rutherford, P. "Attitudes of Malawian Managers: Some Recent Research." Unpublished paper. University of Malawi, 1981.

3. Clarke, R. "Independent Learning in an African Country, with Special Reference to the Certificate of Adult Studies in the University of Malawi." Ph.D. thesis. University of Manchester, Department of Adult and Higher Education, 1981, 240.

## References

Onyemelukwe, C. *Man and Management in Contemporary Africa.* London: Longmans, 1973.

Haire, M., Ghiselli, E., and Porter, L. *Managerial Thinking: An International Study.* New York: Wiley, 1966.

Safavi, F. "A Model of Management Education in Africa." *Academy of Management Review,* 1981, 6(2), 319–331.

Hofstede, G. *Culture's Consequences: International Differences in Work-related Values.* London: Sage, 1980.

Hyden, G. *No Shortcuts to Progress: African Development Management in Perspective.* London: Heinemann, 1983.

Blunt, P., and Popoola, O. *Personnel Management in Africa.* London: Longmans, 1985.

Seddon, J. "The Development and Indigenisation of Third World Business: African Values in the Workplace." In Hammond, V. (ed.), *Current Research in Management.* London: Frances Pinter/ATM, 1985.

Revans, R. *The Origins and Growth of Action Learning.* Bromley: Chartwell-Bratt, 1982.

# Managing High Potentials in Europe: Some Cross-Cultural Findings*

## C. BROOKLYN DERR

### The Issues in High-Potential Management

Assessing, selecting, and developing high potentials (HIPOs) or possible future leaders of the firm is an important process for any company. Every successful firm must identify what qualities it values, what norms and standards it wishes to maintain, what characteristics its future leaders should possess, and where on the scale of conformity/diversity valued employees should be. Any organization will logically select for its next generation of leaders those who reflect its objectives and values. A firm's high potentials are examples for the rest of the employees of the qualities the company rewards and wishes to maintain.

Three human resource issues make the management of high potentials an important topic.

1. Top-level executives must assure the future prosperity of the firm. In fact, according to Dalton and Thompson (1) establishing future leaders is one of four important leadership functions which corporate statesmen must accomplish. (The other three are providing vision or a sense of direction for the firm, exercising power responsibly on behalf of the enterprise, and representing the organization both externally and internally.) As one senior vice president in a financial institution put it during an interview, "I've invested a lot of my life in this company. The most important thing I can do before I retire is assure myself that the next few generations of leaders are in place—the kinds of leaders who will make the company better in the future."

2. Managing high potentials is a strategic planning issue. A high-level

*The research on which this paper is based was supported by the Raoul de Vitry d'Avancourt Chair in International Human Resource Management at the European Institute of Business Administration (INSEAD) from January to August 1985.

Source: C. Brooklyn Derr. "Managing High Potentials in Europe: Some Cross-Cultural Findings." European Management Journal, 1987. 5(2), 72–80. Reprinted by permission.

executive in a multinational oil company told me, "We've got the technology and the capital but we don't have the right people to make the move." Ensuring that the right people will be in place to manoeuver the company flexibly within today's changing international business environment is an important part of successful business planning.

3. Effective human resource management depends on understanding how to reward and motivate the most valued employees (not just general managers but also individuals with good ideas, essential specialists and individuals loyal to the company) by offering them long-term career opportunities which correspond to the company's needs and values. Recent best-selling books such as *In Search of Excellence* (2) and *Theory Z* (3) state the extent to which managing valuable human resources has become a priority for all managers, not just for human resource specialists. Effective HIPO management involves deciding on future organizational needs, discovering what mix of people is needed for success, knowing how to select candidates, and knowing what to offer them to ensure and motivate service to the company throughout their career.

This paper investigates HIPO selection and development in European firms. The pattern in Europe shows that there are national cultural influences at work, and not just random borrowing from the American way of doing things.

Between March and June 1985, I contacted human resource managers in about 70 European companies and, in the course of many interviews, they gave me access to information about how they developed future leaders. The sample includes major companies in Germany, Switzerland, France, Great Britain and Sweden. The organizations ranged in size from 2,000 to 350,000 employees, with an average of around 40,000 employees. In each country, at least one representative of the following industries was interviewed: airlines, cars, banking, chemicals and pharmaceuticals, computers, consumer products, high technology (but not computers), manufacturing, and retailing. The various organizations were chosen because of their reputation for being progressive in human resource practices, their willingness to cooperate with researchers, and their importance in each industrial group. The sample does not necessarily include all or even the best organizations in terms of career development practices. It is, however, representative.

The interviews involved questions about: how the company viewed high-potentials: HIPO selection, development and management; problems and issues in the management of high-potential employees.

The interviews were conducted either in person or by telephone. The respondents were all knowledgeable about the career and high-potential management practices of their companies. Where necessary, research assistants who were fluent native speakers conducted the interview. Although many of the companies did employ female managers, the masculine pronoun is used throughout for convenience.

This article reports the findings of the study which asked five major questions:

1. How do European firms define a high-potential employee?
2. How do European firms identify and select HIPOs?
3. How do European firms develop their HIPOs?
4. What are the major problems companies experience in HIPO management?
5. What impact does national culture have on high-potential management practices?

## Defining High Potentials

A high-potential is someone singled out—often literally—on a select, secret, and exclusive list. A HIPO is considered a possible future leader of the firm, who will receive special scrutiny and get special opportunities to develop. If he is successful, he will be given a top-level post.

Most organizations evaluate a HIPO candidate on ability and achievement: most often he is a general manager who has the possibility of moving up two or three levels on the management hierarchy by a certain time. Many companies are quite specific about which positions a HIPO must be ready to fulfill at three- or four-year intervals. Most agree that a HIPO must eventually be able to head a division or major function by the age of forty.

During one interview, for example, an executive in a department-store chain said, "The high potentials are the ones on a short list in the chief executive's vault." In another case, an executive in a large car company said, "HIPOs are those scheduled to fill certain important positions over the next five years—all general manager posts." Only in the instance of a national airline was a significant distinction made between performance and potential. As an airline executive stated in an interview, "We are not so much interested in past history as we are in future potential. How to assess the future without examining the past is another problem."

## Identifying High-Potentials

Several generalisations can be made about identification and selection of HIPOs in Europe. First, many U.S. companies use assessment centres and other systematic programmes for appraising performance to help identify HIPOs, including taking an inventory of future human-resources (*Management Review*, 1984). In contrast, only three European firms I studied (four per cent) reported using assessment centres, either their own or those run by external consultants, to identify HIPOs.

A more popular European system—used by about 50 per cent of the companies I interviewed—is a nomination process. Managers, or regional managers, proposed potential HIPOs to top managers who formed a corporation-wide Management Review Committee (MRC). The MRC, made up of a few human resource specialists and top-level line managers, made the final selection based on subjective judgment and personal acquaintanceships.

Some of the companies who use this nomination system have pre-selected sets of formal criteria. For example, one French company favoured candidates who had graduated from a certain *grand école,* although good performance and results were also important. In one bank, it was an advantage to have come from a commercial or lending background, while in another it was an advantage to have been in marketing. In many cases international experience was considered important.

The complexities of corporate politics also play a part. Even where a well-defined system for appraising performance exists, top management nearly always controls the final selection. These managers are often defending and enlarging their own spheres of influence and at the same time selecting their own successors. About half of the executives interviewed described the process as "horse trading" among high-level influentials.

A majority of the seventy-three firms in the study evaluated candidates on recruitment and provided early-career training as part of the process of identifying and selecting HIPOs. Many also took into consideration their recruits' future potential. The most common practice is to recruit from specific universities (usually elite institutions) which produce graduates with the talents and values the firm is looking for. Another common practice is to "steal" experienced managers from other companies which have already successfully recruited and trained the HIPOs. A third strategy is to give extensive psychological tests and attitude tests before recruiting, in order to identify potential. Some firms even employ industrial psychologists to screen potential recruits.

The early-career period is also a time for the company to evaluate a new recruit's performance. Executives confirmed that they looked for exceptional competence, the ability to learn quickly, sensitivity to and harmony with the company, hard work, loyalty, and the skillful advancement of company interest—in short, "paying dues." The most common and most important method of evaluating a recruit's success in meeting these criteria is his boss's informal recommendation.

A notable exception to early performance evaluation is the "fast track" option of some companies, usually those experiencing rapid growth. They need new managers and future leaders quickly. Some label the employee as a HIPO early on, even at entry. He then moves much more rapidly than his colleagues up the management hierarchy. His HIPO status is "assumed" and must be continually confirmed rather than earned from the beginning. Some of the companies interviewed had established "fast-lane" options within the last ten years but expressed some doubts. Human resource specialists and managers wondered if these HIPOs were staying in positions long enough to acquire skills and be properly evaluated. The natural resentment of other employees gave further cause for doubt.

## Developing HIPOs

More and more top managers in Europe view international expertise as essential for a high-potential candidate. About 50 per cent of the companies interviewed (and 75 per cent of the large multinational firms) specified this criterion.

Most of the companies interviewed which had specific HIPO-management programmes also sent their HIPOs to executive development programmes (such as those at the European Institute of Business Administration, INSEAD, at the IMEDE Management Development Institute, at the International Management Institute (IMI), or at the London Business School) appropriate to their level of responsibility and range of experience. Others held in-house seminars, sometimes lasting as much as a week, where a combination of outside experts and senior executives would provide the formal training. This in-house option, they observed, has three advantages: It gives HIPOs the chance to meet their peers and senior executives; it trains them; and it focuses on the specific needs and requirements of their own organization. Sending HIPOs away to be trained has the advantage of broadening their view and encouraging cross-fertilisation.

Some companies systematically assigned their HIPOs to work with certain key people—either excellent mentors who could provide good training or influential executives with whom it was essential to be acquainted. However, few of the European firms investigated reported using systematic and formal "assigned mentor" programmes.

The most common and, according to most, the best development option for HIPOs is to rotate them through a number of important job assignments (job rotation) and provide them with the background and on-the-job experience needed to assume future leadership positions. Most companies had informal job rotation programmes, which included working in key functions and key areas, with key people, and on important problems. Some corporations had very systematic career planning programmes which sent their HIPOs through a carefully designed portfolio of prescribed assignments on the way to the top. As in a tournament (where winning allows the candidate to remain in the game and losing eliminates the candidate forever or puts him into a less prestigious game), this portfolio process of elimination theoretically identifies "the best of the best." Executives in these companies conceded, however, that winning is often an issue of endurance, mobility, willingness to subordinate one's private life to the job, and political skill, as much as outstanding performance or inherent ability.

## Problems in HIPO Management

Twenty-three firms (32 per cent) reported that identifying and selecting high potentials is often sabotaged by "boss deception." Many supervisors "hide" their best people in order to retain the services of highly productive people who will continue to make them look good by producing high-quality results. Some managers also try to advance their less able subordinates to HIPO status in order to move them out. To solve this problem of "manager deception," some firms have offered career rewards to bosses who identify and develop future leaders. Other firms promise a boss a comparable replacement if his HIPO is transferred or promoted. Some companies ask both the new employee's boss and his boss's boss to provide evaluations so they can have more than one opinion. Some companies identify and label HIPOs only after their second or third assignment so that the evaluations of several supervisors can be compared.

One large French multinational company in the chemical/pharmaceutical industry cross-checked supervisor evaluations using a team of human resource specialists whose single function was to tour the branches, and meet the HIPOs (thus, forming their own opinions), peers, and supervisors to discuss the HIPO's performance and potential. They then made separate evaluations and recommendations to the Management Review Committee.

Some of the executives interviewed complained that their HIPOs were reluctant to be geographically mobile. Scandinavian employees had strong geographical attachments. Many of them had spouses with established careers, children and family commitments which they did not want to disrupt. In France, many high potentials would not leave the country after their children reached a certain age because the rigid French educational system makes it difficult for children to reenter France and gain access to a *grand école*, on which future success depends.

A third problem was how to deal with faltering senior executives so that the positions would be open for up-and-coming high potentials. Many of them, quite predictably, are very influential and therefore difficult to remove. Organizations must adopt more creative ways of removing faltering senior executives by, for example, offering them consultancy positions, part-time work, special project assignments, and even lateral or downward moves in order to make room for the next generation of leaders.

This option might help solve a related problem: how to manage temporary "burn outs" of the high potentials themselves. The high-potential tournament is so emotionally and psychologically demanding that up-and-coming HIPOs often pay a great price in their private lives. Family problems are common, as are fatigue, ill-health and over-absorption in work. One Swedish HIPO working in France confessed that if his company's expectations did not level off to give him more time for himself, he might voluntarily plateau for two or three years just to get his personal life back in balance. He realized that such a decision might jeopardise his career but he felt that other important aspects of his life were in jeopardy from his work commitments. It would seem beneficial for those who manage high potentials to take a long-term perspective. The best talents and energies of future leaders somehow need to be reserved for the future and not totally used up in the present.

A person who makes unusual personal sacrifices to follow a HIPO career route often becomes depressed, and causes problems during plateaus or periods of waiting for the right position to open up. As one executive commented, "Edward was a real pain, asking what was next and complaining of boredom every day. Finally, he left the company and joined another." At least one career development expert has suggested that top management deal with slow-growth or no-growth by setting up a "slow burn" route to the top, offering high potentials more lateral moves and rest periods along the way (4).

Another issue mentioned by a dozen interviewees in the study was the need to expand the definition of high potential so that valuable specialists, functional generalists, and people with new ideas, all of whom are very much needed in senior roles for the future well-being of a company, are more explicitly rewarded, and moved into positions of influence. While most of the interviewed executives felt that their companies would always need more general managers than anything else, they all believed that these other kinds of HIPOs were of equal value in some smaller proportion and that the career paths and reward systems should reflect this corporate reality.

A related issue that came up repeatedly in interviews was that good human resource managers must provide viable career alternatives for its non-HIPOs. Those I interviewed repeatedly expressed concern that the ordinary hard workers in the firm, cut off from glamorous HIPO status and rewards, became non-productive through neglect. Various career-oriented individuals have different definitions of career success. Only one type is attracted to getting-ahead throughout an entire career. It is inefficient to ignore the other career-oriented individuals and fail to provide appropriate opportunities for developing their productivity (5).

## The Impact of National Cultures on HIPO Management

### Germany

German firms appear to be the most bureaucratic. Deviating from the rule and even individual innovation disrupts the chain of command and established practices within the organization. German interviewees thus reported fewer HIPO programmes and fewer alternative career paths to meet the diverse career needs of the employees.

Accompanying a clear bureaucracy, however, there seemed to be an equally clear emphasis on making sure that it works and that individuals are accountable. After dealing with French and British organizations, I was surprised to learn that when dealing with German organizations, I could simply pick up the phone, without the help of a contact who "knew the right person," and ask for a high-level official in a German or Swiss company, such as the director of personnel. In nine out of sixteen cases, the call simply went from the switchboard to his office and the next voice I heard was that of the director himself or his secretary when he was out. In the other seven cases, I talked first to an executive assistant. In short, I found that if I could say exactly who I needed, few intermediaries were necessary.

### France

In general, French companies view high-potential management as a systems problem and regard procedures for selecting such employees and placing them in specific career paths as being of great importance. They also place importance on planning for successors and they clearly value general managers from technical (usually engineering) backgrounds and from certain *grands écoles*. The French also seem to have the least flexibility in their various career options. If a HIPO somehow loses his status, he is essentially removed from consideration for further career progress.

At the same time, it was surprising in this research to discover how many large French companies have redefined the HIPO-concept within the last few years and are experimenting with variations on the traditional concept. They still recruit from the *grands écoles* but most of them use well-defined processes for quickly assessing the managerial capabilities of their recruited elite, placing the top candidates on carefully prescribed career paths which will lead to top managerial positions. They rely strongly on performance reviews, succession planning, and career pathing as part of a complex system for managing their high potentials.

The French give the impression that they value external executive education least among the national groups and that they view HIPO management as a systems issue. Many of the firms I contacted are developing sophisticated computer programs to aid in this succession planning, paying detailed attention to the logic of various movement options. French personnel specialists are intensively involved in helping top management select HIPOs. This systems approach, rather than the informal personal-recommendation approach, is also consistent with advancement through merit which has operated for nearly all of the candidates since early education.

### Great Britain

The unique British style HIPO management, which has traditionally matched future leaders against a profile of appropriate behaviours, attitudes, and skills, is clearly in a period of reappraisal and transition. Far from trusting and rewarding technical experts, British firms have traditionally valued classical generalists as best suited for high-level management positions. In a traditional British firm, a HIPO would usually emerge from an elite public school or university (perhaps from a known military unit), be a "gentleman," converse knowledgeably about the classics, philosophy, and history, and approach business problems with a broadly humanist perspective. Several interviewees reported the current debate among top-level directors about whether to continue all or parts of that model or whether to place more reliance on

HIPOs with a more technical business education—for example, MBAs. The debate has been fueled by the intense world competition in most international markets and a sense that Britain's managerial/business understanding of those markets is not always as good as it should be.

Interviews with British managers also revealed a dual system of identifying and developing HIPOs. A fully defined and formal merit system coexists with a highly informal set of practical assessments to discover if the candidate fits in with the organization's image. Fascinating stories are often told about "knife and fork" tests—dinners where executives carefully appraised candidates' table manners, speech accents and conversational skills. Many of the interviewees went out of their way to deny that anything but a formal merit system exists, even while jokingly reporting incidents that indicate the importance of personal appearance, dress, personality, speech habits, and fitting in with the organization's image.

### Sweden

Swedish companies had fewer specific HIPO programmes than did the other national groups. Seventy per cent of the Swedish companies were among those that complained about the difficulty of sending their employees abroad, even for training in international posts. This is due to the large number of two-career families in Sweden, where the spouse's career would be disrupted by frequently moving from one place to another, and to the reluctance of many Scandinavians to leave their roots in Scandinavia. This must have a serious effect on careers, since 79 per cent of the companies surveyed in this study reported that geographical mobility is an important factor in career advancement.

In terms of training, Swedish businesses, like American firms, seem to value those with a business education, even though the MBA degree is much less common in Europe than in the United States. Swedish companies provide extensive development and training opportunities for managers who are valued; but many Swedish firms make these training opportunities available to a greater number of people—to some extent self-selected by their willingness to participate—rather than reserve them for a small select group. Thus, in this and other ways, social democracy influences much of the managerial thinking in Swedish companies.

I interviewed a manager in one of the two major car companies in Sweden who was newly appointed to run part of the French company. He tried to learn the business by doing a bit of everyone's job in the best social democracy tradition, including bringing coffee for his secretary and cleaning up his own dishes after a break. He genuinely did not see himself as being in a position of authority, but his French subordinates were extremely confused by him and labeled him as a weak supervisor. In the Swedish tradition, social equality is extremely important. Few people want to be boss because there are few rewards for it; the job often comes with little authority—in fact, having more authority than others is often considered undesirable. Part of this car executive's eventual success as a manager depended on his ability to adopt the French style of management, even though it was not compatible with his own style.

### Switzerland

The Swiss companies, while scoring slightly more than the U.S., French, and British companies in how they value HIPO general managers, seem unique in their attitude about keeping career separate from personal life. The survey showed that Switzerland has the lowest score in valuing an employee who balances his professional career against his private life. It also showed that Swiss companies scored highest in not taking into account an employee's personal circumstances when making career decisions about him.

## ▬ Results of a Survey on HIPO Practices

I also surveyed some 120 high-potential executives in comparable large multinational companies home based in these various countries. Many of these respondents were participating in executive development programmes for HIPOs only at INSEAD. These subjects, including about 50 per cent of those interviewed above, were asked to complete a twenty-item questionnaire about the HIPO management practices in their various firms. Included in the questionnaire were items asking them about their perception of high-potential individuals and qualities in their companies.

All of the respondents from the five countries report that their companies value HIPO general managers. I tested various other concepts from career theory and the literature. A broad concern of the study was to deal with diverse career opportunities for different kinds of high potentials and the management of career diversity (5). I postulated, for example, that some firms might regard specialists and technical/functional gurus as high potentials.

Exhibit 1 summarises the responses to a question designed to test this idea. While no statistically significant differences (at the .05 level of confidence) were uncovered in analysing their various responses, we see that the French and British have a lower regard for technical/specialist HIPOs than do the other countries. The interviews help explain these findings.

In France, interviewees clearly stated that while it was important to have a technical education (for example in engineering), it was equally important to develop quickly and adopt a general-manager perspective. The French are likely to give experts the negative status of "technicians."

The British seem to remain sceptical about the value of a technical background and education (including one in business). They favour a more general approach and a more classical education. For many years the British have rejected the narrow "technician" approach to leadership and management. Many would argue, for example, that there is less status attached to being an engineer in the U.K. than in many other European countries.

EXHIBIT 1

## *Firms Regard Specialists and Technical/Functional Gurus as HIPOs*

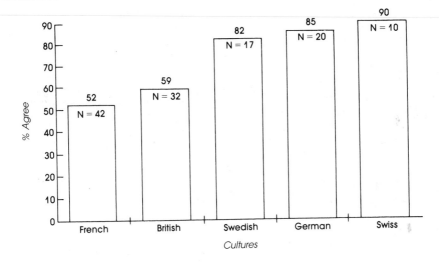

In contrast, one of the most striking aspects of HIPO management revealed from the interviews in Germany and Switzerland was the importance assigned to expertise. In a majority of the German companies studied, for example, it was possible for a functional generalist to achieve remarkably high positions. One leading company, for example, distinguishes between functional and general senior managers. It also seems more important for a HIPO to demonstrate his technical competence more convincingly and over a longer period of time in German organizations than in other countries. As a result, German companies give experts and specialists great respect. This is similar to Laurent's finding that a "creative mind" was seen as vital for career success within German companies (6).

While this position has undeniable strengths for the German companies, at least half of the German interviewees warned that those who chose to become technicians were most likely to plateau in their careers because they would be unable or unwilling to broaden their horizons and become functional generalists or high-level specialists in the future. German management makes a crucial distinction between becoming a functional generalist and remaining a narrow specialist.

A second characteristic which reveals the German reliance on expertise, is that German companies more consistently sought the services of industrial psychologists and various experts to identify and select their HIPOs than did other national companies. They also reported a stricter merit system for advancement. There are no elite German universities at which attendance is considered essential as there are in the U.K., the US, or in France. However, advanced degrees such as the PhD or certificates of merit *are* essential for high potential selection.

Another concept that I wished to test in Europe was the extent to which companies valued innovators or internal entrepreneurs as high potentials. *In Search of Excellence* by Peters and Waterman (2) makes the point that creating the conditions for internal entrepreneurs to develop occurred in almost every successful U.S. firm they studied.

Exhibit 2 illustrates some statistically significant differences on the item used to gather this data. Here we see the French and Swedish executives reporting that their companies value HIPO entrapreneurs less than do the others. These results are also a little surprising because the Germans and Swiss reported in the interviews that they were generally uncomfortable about separating out an elite group because such a practice disrupted the smooth operation of a bureaucratic organization. The Germans and the Swedes in the interviews attached greater value to hard working, loyal, life-long employees than to HIPOs, probably because of the norms of social democracy in Sweden and the strict adherence to bureaucratic systems in Germany. Perhaps German companies see entrapreneurship as important in the world of competition regardless of their past practices, norms, and values.

The strict French position planning approach to organization, where HIPOs are systematically moved along a complex succession map, would not seem to value or trust parallel subsystems of internal entrepreneurs. This data corresponds to Crozier's findings (7) that the central issue in French organizations is ensuring both rational collective action and individual autonomy. This

E X H I B I T   2

## Companies Value Innovators and Internal Entrepreneurs as HIPOs

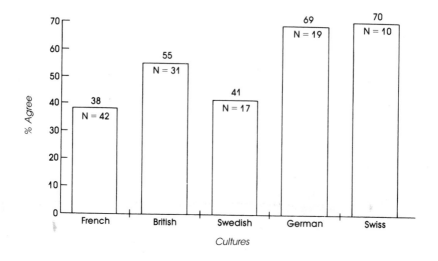

is done by using a very formal Weberian bureaucratic structure in which individuality is protected as long as members obey the formal rules, private life is strictly separate from organizational life and there is discretion within the rules and structure.

An analysis of the questionnaires also reveals that size of the organization and the nature of its business account for some significant variation. In general, the larger the company the more developed the HIPO management programme and the more varied the possibilities for various kinds of HIPO careerists. The following industries have more high-potential management programmes: banking, computers, consumer conglomerates and chemical/pharmaceuticals, whereas airlines, the car industry and retailing firms have fewer and less varied HIPO programmes for their employees. Further research is necessary to find out why the size of the organization and the nature of the business produce different HIPO management programmes.

## Conclusion

All of the companies studied in Europe were interested in the high-potential concept. They all saw managing of high potentials as an important strategic and human resource issue. Most of them defined a HIPO as a future high-level general manager with the potential of moving up to a top management position. Consequently, most of the firms have formal and informal programmes for identifying, selecting, and developing HIPOs.

However, these general patterns and practices are culturally influenced. Viewed according to the national origin of the firm, interesting variations in the HIPO concept and management practices emerge. It is probably not stating the case too strongly to say that in Europe, HIPO management seems to depend on national culture and its effect on an organization's culture.

German firms are the most bureaucratic and attach the most value to specialists and functional generalists. The Germans value qualifications, demonstrated competence, and a creative technical mind. Their bureaucratic structures tend to work efficiently and effectively.

In general, French companies view high-potential management as a systems problem and emphasise procedures for selecting such employees and placing them in specific career paths. They also emphasise systems which plan for succession and clearly value general managers from technical (usually engineering) backgrounds and from certain *grands écoles*. The French also seem to have the least flexibility in their various career options. If a HIPO somehow loses that coveted status, he is essentially removed from consideration.

The British still seem to put much emphasis on fitting in with the corporate culture, either by success in certain institutions (public schools, certain universities, certain military units) or by conformity with the norms and values of the culture. Should corporations continue to emphasise a classical education and a broad general approach to business problems or should they change to newer business education methods? This question, currently at the centre of a widespread debate in the U.K., is stimulated by the need to be more competitive in world markets.

Swedish firms have many norms of social democracy which restrain the development of elites. There are, as in U.S. companies, many viable options for those who do not choose (or are not chosen for) the high-potential path. It is sometimes difficult to get well-qualified persons with the preferred engineering and business educations to adopt HIPO status, especially because of the large number of dual-career families in Sweden and the reluctance of many Scandinavians to be geographically mobile. Once they choose such a path, however, it appears that they work hard, are geographically mobile, usually receive international experiences of various kinds, and otherwise conform to the more typical definition of high-potential general manager.

The Swiss are an unusual cultural mix. In some ways, they are bureaucratic and similar to the Germans. They attach great importance to functional expertise but also value steady workers and company loyalists instead of reserving high status only for HIPOs. They very much value hard work.

The study of national culture and its impact on corporate culture is just beginning; but if, for example, we look at trends in international management, attempts to achieve Japanese productivity by adopting Japanese management styles, and the crucial need to understand how to improve worker motivation in multinational corporations, more systematic research is obviously required.

## ■■■ *References*

Dalton, G. W., and Thompson, P. H. *Novations: Strategies for Career Management.* Glenville, Ill.: Scott, Foresman, 1986.

Peters, T., and Waterman, R. H., Jr. *In Search of Excellence.* New York: Warner, 1982.

Ouchi, W. G. *Theory Z: How American Business Can Meet The Japanese Challenge.* Reading, Mass.: Addison-Wesley, 1981.

Bailyn, L. "The Slow-Burn Way To The Top: Some Thoughts On The Early Years of Organizational Careers." In Derr, C. B. (ed.), *Work, Family and the Career.* New York: Praeger, 1980, 94–105.

Derr, C. B. *Managing the New Careerists.* San Francisco and London: Jossey-Bass, 1986.

Laurent, A. "Perceived Determinants of Career Success." In Trebesch, K. (ed.), *Organizational Development in Europe.* Bern, Switzerland: Houpt, 1980.

Crozier, M. *The Bureaucratic Phenomenon.* Chicago: University of Chicago Press, 1964.

# The Overseas Assignment: A Practical Look

## MARK E. MENDENHALL
## GARY ODDOU

John McNally, aged 38, is assistant to the vice president of marketing in a medium-sized firm in the electronics industry. He was recently approached by his boss about heading up the company's Far East operations. This position would offer John greater responsibility, decision-making authority, job autonomy, and a substantial increase in salary and perks. In many ways it would allow John the opportunity to do what he has always wanted to do—manage a sector of the firm that is unequivocally "his" from top to bottom. John's boss made it clear that this would be a great opportunity for him, and that it was his job to take or turn down because of his strong track record in the company.

How would John's wife, Nancy, and their two kids react to moving from the Bay Area to Tokyo? Like John, Nancy has never lived overseas. As John reached for the phone to call his wife, the initial excitement of the offer was tempered by a nagging doubt. It seemed so appealing on the surface, but he wondered what the down sides were to this move. Even knowing the down sides, could he really afford to turn it down? He began to dial, wondering if he could sort all of this out in the two weeks he was given to make the decision.

John McNally's experience is not different from that of most managers who have been approached about relocating overseas. Since most managers do not like to take leaps of faith in their careers, they sometimes feel as though they are stepping into the unknown in their family life, social life, and career path, when they accept overseas assignments. What does John need to learn in the next two weeks about the reality of international assignments before making his decision? More generally, what should every executive know before agreeing to an overseas assignment?

*Source:* Mark E. Mendenhall and Gary Oddou. "The Overseas Assignment: A Practical Look." *Business Horizons.* September–October 1988, 78–84. Reprinted by permission.

## The Potential Failure of Expatriates

It has been estimated that approximately 20 percent of personnel sent abroad return prematurely from an overseas assignment, so John has reason to be concerned.[1] Many others endure to the end of their assignments but find themselves ineffective in their jobs, unhappy in their social lives, and often close to a broken marriage. Why does this occur?

The main reason is called culture shock. This term covers anxieties about customs and security that appear when one must deal with a foreign culture. It manifests itself among expatriates in many ways: change in sexual drive, eating binges, bouts of depression, idiosyncratic nervous habits, manifestations of anger and aggression, substance abuse, alienation from others, homesickness, insomnia or oversleeping, lack of motivation at work, and impatience with family members.

The problems of expatriation are not limited to the overseas stay. Many expatriates report experiencing culture shock upon returning to the U.S. Culture shock can occur in many ways, but probably the most difficult for the expatriate is the shock of his or her new position. Returning managers nearly always experience less decision-making power, autonomy, and salary, and fewer perks upon return. No one seems to care that the expatriate spent three intriguing, eye-opening years in Venezuela, Japan, or wherever.

Even worse, however, is the estimate that about one-quarter of all American expatriates do not even gain a position in the firm upon return from a foreign assignment. One executive was told he had six months to find a place in the company or he would have to start looking elsewhere. He found a job in another firm. Some executives launch an informal in-house search and find positions within the firm. Some look elsewhere immediately. Others take demotions or find they must relocate or accept other constraints they had not expected to face.

Such consequences are traceable to the failure of organizations to anticipate problems and create policies to deal with them. With so much at risk, how can an executive know whether to accept the overseas assignment? Two areas must be considered: his or her personal cross-cultural adaptation skills; and his or her organization's philosophy and orientation toward an international assignment.

## Cross-Cultural Adaptation Skills

Research in expatriate adaptation clearly indicates that success in an overseas work assignment depends upon the possession of specific skills. These skills can be fit into one of three categories: personal skills, people skills, and perception skills.[2]

### Personal Skills

Those techniques and attributes that facilitate the expatriate's mental and emotional well-being are personal skills. They can include meditation, prayer or other means of finding solitude, and physical exercise routines, all of which tend to decrease the executive's stress level. One's abilities to manage time, delegate, and manage his or her responsibilities are also personal skills.

### People Skills

Effective interaction with others, particularly with foreigners, is another necessity for successful adaptation. The executive who desires or needs to communicate with others, is willing to try to speak the foreign language (even when not necessary), and doesn't worry about making linguistic mistakes is much more likely to be successful than the executive who is introverted, self-conscious, or otherwise not comfortable when interacting with foreigners.

### Perception Skills

These skills deal with the cognitive processes that help the executive understand why foreigners behave the way they do. The willingness to make tentative conclusions from the first observation of different actions or attitudes is an important cognitive dimension. Managers have been taught to size things up quickly to make an equally quick decision. Perception skills also relate to one's consciousness of social cues and behaviors, one's attentiveness to them, and one's ability to imitate what he or she perceives.

## ▬ The Firm's Philosophy About International Assignments

Each firm looks at international assignments in a different way. The executive can understand this philosophy by looking at five elements, each of which will be discussed below.

### The Strategic Importance of the International Assignment

Some overseas assignments are springboards to career growth within the firm. These positions usually are in overseas operations viewed by top management as keys to the firm's future performance. For example, a vice president of marketing for the Caribbean region does not carry the same clout as the vice president of marketing for the expanding markets in the Far East. The more strategic the overseas position, the greater the executive's visibility.

Being key to a firm's future growth is not the only sign that an area is strategic, however. If the subsidiary is the cash cow of the European region, for example, there is a higher status level than if the position is in a dog or question-mark subsidiary in the same region.

If career advancement is your primary goal, you should not accept any overseas assignment unless you will get high visibility. If you have been with the firm for a relatively short time and don't know how valuable the various operations are, ask to look at the financial statements and talk to some of the old-timers. Don't be shy. It's *your* career.

### The Degree of Integration of Human Resources Into Strategic Planning

Human-resource directors are not involved in strategic planning of MNCs, at least at the corporate level. At the strategic business unit (SBU) level some tying of human-resource issues with SBU international strategy exists, but the degree varies with each firm.[3] In the firms with the most integration, management training, selection, support, development, and other human-resource concerns are covered by formal policies created especially for the international needs of the SBU and based on valid information from the SBU's other functional areas.

An executive can get an indication of how formalized the worldwide human-resource-planning function is by the amount of lead time given before the expected departure. If lead times range from a few days to a couple of months, there is probably little to no international human-resource strategic planning. This lack of planning is a warning that the firm places relatively little value on international assignments in general. If the firm typically projects its worldwide needs several months to a year ahead of time, but only gives the executive a short amount of time to decide and leave, a forest-fire situation may exist. Either the previous expatriate failed and is returning home prematurely, or a sudden turn of events in an overseas operation requires immediate attention. In either case, the executive should be very cautious.

If very short lead times are typical of your firm, upper management probably places little real significance on overseas operations. It is doubtful that performing well overseas will enhance your career. Because chances for failure are great and the "out of sight, out of mind" syndrome must be considered, you should probably turn the offer down if you plan to advance in your present firm.

If another expatriate is returning home early, find out why. Is the work situation or the family situation the cause? If the work situation has been particularly difficult, what exactly is the problem and will you be able to solve it? Is the difficulty a perennial problem, typical of that assignment, or is it an emergency—open rebellion by the foreign employees, a political overthrow leading to a hostile government? Talk to the returning expatriate and get his or her perception of the problem. If it's the family situation, how different is your family from the one returning? Is yours more likely to adapt well?

## The Amount of International Experience in Senior Management

A firm reveals how much value it places on overseas assignments by the amount of overseas experience its senior managers have. Some firms, such as AlCan of Canada, require their senior managers to have had overseas experience. But over two-thirds of senior managers in U.S. firms have had no real overseas experience.[4] Very little overseas experience at the senior level probably indicates that very little value is placed on such assignments.

However, one must be attentive to the trends within the firm. The expanding global market has many firms scrambling to take advantage of some of the opportunities abroad. If a firm is headed in such a direction, it probably will be looking for some of its best personnel to head up overseas operations.

Find out what the backgrounds of your senior managers are. Determine how much overseas experience they have, in which countries and in which assignments. It may be that value is placed on specific functional or geographical areas. If most of them have had European assignments, for example, then an assignment to South America might not be the plum you anticipated. But if senior managers have little overseas experience, beware. Executives who have not worked abroad do not really understand the difficulties involved or the growth that results from working abroad. With the added responsibility and independence usually experienced abroad, the executive typically develops more quickly than in the U.S. Unfortunately, the expatriate usually returns unappreciated and underutilized in the domestic operation.

## The Validity of the Performance Evaluation Instrument and System

Valid performance evaluation is difficult enough to achieve in the U.S. Overseas assignments simply make a complex problem nearly impossible. What normally works in one culture might not in another. While delegating is generally considered a good management practice in the U.S., in some countries it is considered a management weakness. A motivational scheme based on job rotation might work in the U.S. but have disastrous consequences in countries where job specialization is mandated by law.

The distance from the corporate office to the overseas post can also create problems. The corporate office is almost always involved in the evaluation of the expatriate's performance. But how does someone in New York evaluate performance of someone in Peru? In such situations, the corporate personnel are forced to rely on global types of performance indicators: return on investment, cash flow, market share, and so forth. Situational factors that are outside the executive's control are usually not considered. Such factors can include devaluation of the domestic currency, runaway inflation, government-controlled work forces, political instability, and so on. These factors will have a definite effect on the overseas operation's performance.

Even if the executive overseas is not normally considered responsible for the total operation, performance evaluation problems can exist. For example, the comptroller of one of the largest electronic firms in the world once complained that in reality he, not the host national chief operating officer, was held responsible for maintaining the profit line of the overseas division he worked in. (He was the only U.S. citizen working in upper management in that division.) The ambiguity of the performance criteria can also cause problems. Expatriates are not always told how their performance will be evaluated, so they do not know where to expend their energy.

The more the evaluation is done by foreigners, the less control the expatriate has, since the evaluation can be culturally defined to a large extent. Similarly, the more the criteria are of the global type, the less control the expatriate has, particularly in countries where economic, social, political, and material resources are unstable.

Know before you leave what the performance evaluation system will consist of. Who will be evaluating you, and with how much validity can these individuals appraise your performance? If one or more of the evaluators will be from the foreign country, how much exposure have they had to Americans? Find out what their attitudes are through the grapevine. What will the criteria be, and are they ones over which you have a large degree of control? The more the criteria are of the global type (market share, profit status, ROI), the more likely it is that the corporate office's evaluation will count the most.

The less control you would have over the evaluation process and the results, the more suspicious you should be about the assignment.

### The Degree of Formalization and Rigor of the Selection, Training, and Overseas Support Systems

*Selection.* The vast majority of MNCs in the U.S. select their expatriates based on managerial or technical excellence. They assume that managing well in the U.S. takes the same characteristics as managing well in Amman, Jordan. This assumption is as false as the belief that managing one division in a firm is the same as managing another, and very different, division. Or they assume that the ability to solve a technical problem will lead to success in any environment. Technical competence has nothing to do with one's ability to adapt to a new environment, deal effectively with foreign coworkers, or perceive and if necessary imitate the foreign behavioral norms.

Furthermore, since the reason most often cited for early expatriate return is the spouse's inability to adapt, the selection procedure should include an appraisal of the spouse's likelihood to succeed overseas. The issue is further complicated when both spouses work. One of the two generally has to put a career on hold. In addition, families who have children in their middle and late teens often have more problems than those with younger children.

You should probably be flattered if you have been selected above others for an overseas assignment. It usually means you are admired for your technical or managerial competence. So the real assessment lies with you. Do you have the cross-cultural skills (personal, people, and perception skills) to adapt? How appealing is the assignment to your family? How likely are they to succeed? Are there support systems for them overseas?

Don't be afraid to turn the assignment down if you don't think you or your family will adapt. It is generally better to say "no thanks" up front rather than to return early from overseas with frayed nerves, an upset marriage, and a failure mark on your record.

*Training.* Firms vary in the type of training they offer executives. A few firms have an intensive, month-long training session, while others hand the executive a few brochures just before he or she boards the plane.

The content also differs widely. Those firms who understand that working abroad is more than solving a technical problem cover a much wider range of topics: foreign customs, thinking patterns, societal values, language, the organizational culture, environmental factors, support systems, and so forth. Other firms simply rely on the brochures they hand the executive to cover the necessary material. While brochures are sometimes quite informative, they do not treat factors that will directly facilitate adaptation.

When an executive is sent to a culture that closely resembles his or her own, information is probably sufficient. However, for the executive (and family) going to Malaysia or Japan, where the cultures differ significantly from the U.S., information might not be enough. Training should include role playing, culture confrontation, and behavioral situations. Only in behavioral situations is an individual forced to deal with the emotions that result from misunderstandings, frustration, and differences in customs and courtesies. The executive will confront these same emotions overseas. It is far better to try to understand and deal with them before leaving to reduce the amount of culture shock.

Finally, since the top reason for early returns is the spouse's inability to adapt, the wise firm will include the spouse and any other family members in their teens and older in the training. In fact, such training is actually more important for the spouse than it is for the executive. Although the executive changes job locations, often the exact nature of the job itself may not change drastically. It is the spouse who experiences extreme changes: a postponed career, a different language, different stores and shopping habits, a lack of friends and family upon which to rely, and so on.

An extensive cross-cultural training program reflects a firm's commitment to you and your success overseas. Chances are that such a firm also forecasts its worldwide human-resource needs months in advance and strategically values its overseas operations. If the training also includes your spouse and older family members, your probability of success abroad is much higher. If the assignment fits into your personal career plans, you should probably accept it.

On the other hand, if you are headed to Japan and are handed brochures as you are boarding the plane, you should probably hope there is one domestic stop before reaching the foreign country. If so, deplane and tell your firm you changed your mind.

*Overseas Support Systems.* Just as firms vary in their commitment to selection and training, they vary in their support of the executive and his or her family overseas. One executive of a large office-equipment multinational reported that his firm had a very organized support system overseas. The highest-ranking expatriate, as part of his job, was responsible for helping the other expatriates adjust. His duties included informal counseling, the sponsorship of monthly social gatherings to discuss problems and successes as expatriates, and the function of his spouse as a mentor to newly arrived spouses.

An organized effort such as this really helps. However, what if the executive and his or her family are the only ones at the foreign site? How do firms support them? The better ones encourage the executive to call corporate or division headquarters as often as needed. He or she must be able to ask questions for guidance, receive suggestions from other expatriates about difficulties the family is experiencing, or just have someone who will listen. This takes a great deal of pressure off the spouse.

A committed firm also informs the executive of any local support systems. For example, if the family is active in a religion, the firm should tell them about the nearest congregation of their faith. If the executive is a member of a club such as Rotary or Lion's, the firm can inform the executive of the nearest chapter. If another U.S.-owned firm or subsidiary in the area has expatriates, the two firms might have an understanding that encourages them to share information and otherwise help each other.

A firm can do many things to support its employees overseas. But some firms practice the "out of sight, out of mind" philosophy. One executive, for example, complained that calls to the home office were rarely returned. There were no organized social systems, no mentors to give advice, and no information about any local groups that might help ease his adjustment to the foreign country. The total experience put an extreme strain on his marriage and several times he vowed to return home. He finally sent his wife home with the children and remained overseas for the rest of the year.

If you are going to a distinctly different culture, don't leave without knowing what types of support you will find in the home office and overseas. Has your firm identified other expatriates that have recently been to your site, and encouraged you to call them as the need arises? Do you know what to expect once you arrive overseas? Are there other Americans? Has your firm identified support sources for you if there isn't an organized support system in your division? Is the system especially strong for spousal support, rather than being focused around your needs?

The stronger the support system, and the more it is directed toward spousal/family needs, the more likely you are to succeed overseas. If your firm cannot identify support resources and has no organized system overseas, think seriously about refusing the assignment if your location contrasts starkly with your home situation and your family is accompanying you. Don't build in failure.

## What If I Am Stuck?

It may be that for political or other career reasons an overseas assignment just cannot be turned down. The organizational system may be full of red flags, but you are told that you must go anyway; you feel you have no choice. What can you do?

### Prepare Yourself

There is no reason for anyone who will be living overseas to be ill-prepared for the experience. A list of books, articles, and other sources of information for the neophyte expatriate are given in the Reference section. In addition, various foreign-language packages can help prepare the expatriate linguistically for the overseas stay. If your firm has no language materials, talk to the foreign-language department of your local university.

In most cases, self-education will likely match the program most companies provide for their expatriates. The key is the executive's level of determination to be prepared for his or her overseas stay.

### Keep Yourself in Touch

If your company has no program to keep you abreast of changes in the home office while you are away, create one. Consistent correspondence and phone calls to peers, superiors, and other significant players in the U.S. will inform them of your successes and progress, as well. Never assume that the corporate or division managers will try to watch your work by reading your reports. Realize that you will have to keep the communication lines open yourself.

### Build Options Overseas

By the end of your stay you will have gained skills that most others in your profession do not have—how to operate, negotiate, and manage in one or more foreign countries. Despite your best efforts to stay in stay in touch with the home office, you may sense six months before your return that the home office will not have a suitable position for you upon your return. Begin your job search, both in-house and with other firms, at least a year before you are scheduled to return.

If you are willing to stay overseas, many companies who may be newcomers in the region might value your business skills. If you desire to return home, seek out firms who are either in the early stages of joint-venture development or trying to determine whether to export or set up operations in your country of expertise. They will likely view you as an important resource in their strategic planning efforts.

Never assume that you will have a position suitable to your experience guaranteed to you upon return. Use your overseas assignment to expand your skills and enhance your marketability, both domestically and internationally. Get involved in the activities of the expatriate community—they are one of the best sources of career opportunities.

### Enjoy the Benefits of Personal Growth

Expatriates almost always say they would advise others to accept an overseas assignment. Their rationale is not that it really helped their careers, but that it expanded their minds. There is something about having to live in, adapt to, attempt to understand, and accept different behaviors and ways of thinking that broadens one's horizon.

A new culture can give you new lenses that highlight new dimensions of the human experience. Cultures tend to focus on certain aspects of life, and when you live and work in a culture that focuses on dimensions of life largely downplayed in the U.S., you can come to understand and value experiences and traditions previously unknown.

### Revel in the Adventure

The overseas assignment can be a wonderful adventure if it is viewed as one. Modern conveniences and other artifacts of our society have taken much of the adventure out of life and made our existence much more predictable. Living overseas is perhaps one of the last great adventures for individuals and families. Taking this view makes the inevitable setbacks and barriers a little easier to deal with, creating a positive context for daily existence.

Living overseas is not easy. It takes much cognitive and emotional effort to learn the new culture, and some soul-searching at times when accepted behaviors abroad violate ethical or moral norms of one's value system. An executive must depend on others to accomplish things that were second nature in his or her own culture. These can be seen as negative aspects of living overseas or as positive challenges leading to the enrichment and refinement of one's personality. The choice really is up to the expatriate.

## ▬ *Notes*

1. See Copeland, L. and Griggs, L. *Going International.* New York: Random House, 1985; Misa, K. F. and Fabricatore, J. M. "Return on Investment of Overseas Personnel." *Financial Executive,* 47(4), 42–46; Torbiorn, I. *Living Abroad: Personal Adjustment and Personnel Policy in the Overseas Setting.* New York: Wiley, 1982; Tung, R. L. Selection and Training of Personnel for Overseas Assignments." *Columbia Journal of World Business,* 16(1), 68–78.

2. Mendenhall, M. and Oddou, G. "The Dimensions of Expatriate Acculturation: A Review." *Academy of Management Review,* 1985; 10, 39–47.

3. Miller, E, Beechler, S, Bhatt B, and Nath, R. "The Relationship Between the Global Strategic Planning Process and the Human Resource Management Function." *Human Resource Planning,* 9(1), 9–23.

4. Adler, N. *The International Dimensions of Organizational Behavior.* Boston: PWS Kent, 1986.

## ▬ Reference

Adler, N. *The International Dimensions of Organizational Behavior.* Boston: PWS Kent, 1986.

Copeland, L. and Griggs, L. *Going International.* New York: Random House, 1985.

Gaylord, M. "Relocation and the Corporate Family." *Social Work,* May 1979, 186–191.

Hall, E. *The Silent Language.* Garden City, N.Y.: Doubleday, 1959.

Harris P. R. and Moran, R. T. *Managing Cultural Differences.* Houston, Tex.: Gulf, 1979.

Harvey, M. G. "The Executive Family: An Overlooked Variable in International Assignments." *Columbia Journal of World Business,* Spring 1985, 84–93.

Mendenhall, M. and Oddou, G. "The Dimensions of Expatriate Acculturation: A Review." *Academy of Management Review,* 1985, 10, 39–47.

Torbiorn, I. *Living Abroad: Personal Adjustment and Personnel Policy in the Overseas Setting.* New York: Wiley, 1982.

Tung, R. L. "Selection and Training of Personnel for Overseas Assignments." *Columbia Journal of World Business,* 16(1), 68–78.

Walker, E. J. "Til Business us do Part?" *Harvard Business Review,* January–February 1976, 94–101.

# Ciba-Geigy—
# Management
# Development

## YVES DOZ

On December 18, 1981, Arnold Delage, soon to become Managing Director of Ciba-Geigy's French subsidiary, was looking forward to his dinner meeting in Basel, Switzerland (headquarters to Ciba-Geigy), with the top management of the parent company's Pharma Division. Together they were going to review candidates for the position of Sales and Marketing Manager for the French subsidiary's pharmaceutical business, an important position since this division accounted for nearly a quarter of total French sales and had shown rapid growth in recent years.

Until recently, Delage had been general manager of Ciba-Geigy's French Pharma Division and President of "Laboratories Ciba-Geigy," the pharmaceutical subsidiary of Ciba-Geigy in France, with sales of about Fr700 million. René Lamont, the current Managing Director of Ciba-Geigy France, was scheduled to retire effective at the end of the year, and Delage had been chosen by Ciba-Geigy's top management to succeed him, a selection announced in early December.

Delage had had a successful career with Ciba-Geigy. A Frenchman, he joined Esso-Africa upon graduation from INSEAD in 1965 and worked in Switzerland (Geneva) and in Madagascar, in sales and marketing positions. He was subsequently recruited by Ciba-Geigy and, after a year at Pharma Division's headquarters in Basel, was sent to Hong Kong in a sales and marketing management position. After four years in the Far East he was appointed Marketing Manager in Belgium, where he successfully launched a number of new pharmaceutical products. In 1973, he was promoted to Pharma Division Manager in Belgium, a position he held for three years. Delage was recalled to France in 1976 as Marketing Manager, where he successfully

Source: This case was prepared by Yves Doz with the assistance of Ms. Martine van den Poel. (c) INSEAD, 1983. This case was adapted by Mark Mendenhall for this book in 1990 by permission from the author. Reprinted by permission.

launched a new antirheumatic formulation (Voltarene) and, in 1979, was promoted to Pharma Division Manager. During the last two years he had considerably strengthened the management of the French Pharma division.

Delage's promotion to Managing Director of Ciba-Geigy France had opened the position of Pharma Division Manager within the French subsidiary. Jules Breton, an experienced manager recently hired from Sanofi (a major French pharmaceutical company where he had held the position of President and General Manager of one of its subsidiaries), was promoted to the post. The position of Pharma Marketing Manager therefore became vacant. Delage and Breton presented the candidacy of Pierre Dumont, a Frenchman who had recently been recruited from Specia (another French competitor) to head marketing and sales for the Geigy product line in France. Pharma Division headquarters in Basel had suggested several other candidates. Among them, their preference fell on Michel Malterre, a Swiss national from Montreux, currently heading Pharma marketing in West Africa and based in Abidjan, Ivory Coast.

Such decisions as the appointment of key executives in subsidiary companies were usually the result of joint agreement by divisional management in Basel and the local managing directors and were often debated at the highest levels within the company. A long-standing corporate commitment to human resource and management development ensured that such choices received considerable attention and that all relevant aspects were carefully weighed before a decision was reached.

## ■ *The Company and Its Organization*

Ciba-Geigy resulted from the 1970 merger between two long-standing Basel chemical companies: Ciba (created in 1884) and Geigy (created in 1758). Both companies were active competitors in certain business areas, e.g., dyestuffs, pharmaceuticals, industrial chemicals, and agrochemicals. In other areas, their activities were complementary. Both were strong internationally, although Geigy had a stronger worldwide presence in agro-chemicals and Ciba a wider experience in pharmaceuticals.

The management styles and structures of the two companies, however, differed widely. Ciba was centrally managed by one person, Dr. Kappeli, its chairman. He relied on strong and entrepreneurial division managers to control Ciba's widely diversified activities. In contrast, Geigy had been reorganized in 1968 into a three-dimensional organizational structure where businesses, national subsidiaries, and corporate functions were managed by an Executive Committee regrouping Geigy's top management.

Following the merger, the Geigy structure was retained. By 1980–1981 the structure comprised the following units:

1. Divisional structure covering the seven main product areas: dyestuffs and chemicals, pharmaceuticals, agro-chemicals, plastics and addi-

tives, the Airwick consumer products group, the Ilford photographic products group, and the recently constituted electronic equipment products group

2. Geographic structure with 80 group companies organized in a loose administrative way into six main regions: North America, Western Europe, Latin America, Africa/Middle East, Eastern Europe, and Asia/Australia

3. Ten central corporate functions (legal, finance, technology, etc.) at group headquarters in Basel, Switzerland

In general, Ciba-Geigy had a policy of 100 percent ownership of group companies. As a rule, these group companies were responsible for all Ciba-Geigy activities in a given country, for making use of available opportunities for the local development of Ciba-Geigy's business, and for the overall financial results within their territories. The various product divisions and the Executive Committee *(Konzernleitung)* coordinated and integrated the group companies' activities.

*Product divisions* were responsible to the Executive Committee for the worldwide management of their businesses and their overall results. Research and development, production, and marketing of products were specific responsibilities of the divisions. Divisional plans and budgets for the group companies were discussed with headquarters' divisions in Basel and coordinated with group companies' managing directors. Major investment projects in the group companies were reviewed by the product divisions, which were also responsible for business development on a worldwide basis.

Divisional management also participated in establishing the organizational structure of, and in nominating candidates for top positions in, their corresponding divisions within group companies. Product divisions were managed through divisional management committees reflecting the main functions of a division.

*Group companies* combined all Ciba-Geigy's divisions and functions into one managerial entity in each country. The company believed that this structure allowed Ciba-Geigy to operate locally as a homogeneous unit, consolidate financial results across divisions, and optimize local financial resource utilization. In addition, central administrative functions could serve several local units more economically than if each division had to do so independently. Finally, relations with local government, industry and trade associations, and other national entities could be made more effective.

The group company Managing Director was responsible for the total activity of local units as well as for overall local financial results, but had to operate within the framework of policies and guidelines set from the center and harmonize plans between the various central units (divisions and central functions) and local requirements. The divisional heads within the group companies were administratively responsible to the Managing Director but were also functionally responsible to the corresponding division in Basel.

The *Executive Committee,* in Basel, had 10 members and was responsible for:

- Formulation and implementation of the group policy
- Approval of long-term objectives and strategies, and resource allocation decisions
- Approval of organizational structures and appointment of key managers within the product divisions, central functions, and group companies
- Creation of corporatewide uniform management systems and guidelines (especially for planning, resource allocation, and management information)
- Review of major integrated plans, budgets, and investment projects and decisions on their approval
- Control of the performance of the individual units and evaluation of the business and its results from a corporatewide perspective

Each member of the Executive Committee was overseeing, as a "patron," a number of countries and one or two divisions or central functions, so that all major units were covered. For example, the Executive Committee member responsible for the Pharma Division also was responsible for the plastics and additives division and the Southeast Asian and Chinese region. Another patron was responsible for the Airwick division, the finance function, Eastern Europe, and Latin America. The Executive Committee met as a group frequently, usually once a week.

The preparation and negotiation of decisions involving several divisions, group companies and/or central functions could be delegates to the Executive Committee to regional staffs. These provided an intermediate level between the group companies and the Executive Committee, since all 80 or so group companies could not effectively be supervised directly by the individual Executive Committee members.

*Central services* fell into two categories: Executive Committee staffs and corporate functions. They formulated, for the approval of the Executive Committee, opinions, guidelines, and procedures specific to their field, commented on functional plans and budgets to the heads of group companies, and participated in the nomination of group companies' functional executives. Central functions and staffs also placed their specific expertise at the service of group companies.

Two key Executive Committee staff functions were corporate planning and management development (the latter is described below in detail). Recently, planning had acquired more prominence with the redefinition of Ciba-Geigy's businesses into about 30 "corporate segments," and the establishment of a corporate strategic plan drawn from a bottom-up planning process at segment level rather than only at divisional level. The corporate planning staff at Ciba-Geigy employed only four people and was directly responsible to the Chair of the Executive Committee. Franz Hartmann, its Director, ex-

plained the changes in corporate strategy and in the way resources were allocated that had transpired over the past few years:

> During the 1960s and early 1970s the resource allocation process in Ciba-
> Geigy was not very sophisticated. It was rather informal since there were
> no financial constraints. The real beginning of strategic planning occurred
> in 1974, in the sense of it being more than simple operational planning
> with a longer-term horizon. The 1974–1975 economic crisis was quite help-
> ful to us, because it forced us to put more emphasis on actual strategic
> thinking and less on number pushing. We introduced a long-term strate-
> gic plan and conceded more flexibility in the process, emphasizing key
> issues and implementation through strategic projects and action plans.
> The strategic projects involved business entries and exits, new plant con-
> struction in foreign countries, etc. . . . In recent years, it became quite
> clear that the chemical industry was maturing. Some of our businesses
> were plagued by slow innovation and very intense competition and, there-
> fore, needed different strategies and different managers from those re-
> quired by businesses that were still growing rapidly.

> In 1980 we started to introduce portfolio approaches for the first time. We
> also faced a trend toward lower profitability and started a "turnaround"
> program. The program was not only designed to reduce inventories, cut
> personnel and cut costs but also to strengthen strategic planning and to
> allocate proper strategic roles and resources to each segment. This re-
> flected the growing differentiation among our businesses and the need to
> account for different success factors in how and by whom they were man-
> aged. For example, the divisions are now moving from worldwide seg-
> ment strategies to local portfolios. After the merger in 1970, we had
> needed to integrate operations centrally. Now there is growing delegation
> in operational matters by the Executive Committee to divisions and group
> companies.

> This segment approach questions the divisional structure. We will need
> to implement substructural changes to fit the segments and reallocate
> functional responsibilities within divisions. We are also going to need bet-
> ter managers and more general managers. We are now recruiting MBAs
> and putting a lot of emphasis on young people and training, sending them
> abroad early in their careers to take up responsibility. In fact, we have
> been forced to look outside to find general managers for some of our new
> activities.

> One implication of all this is that there is going to be a lot more internal
> competition within the firm. Changes are being made in the role of group
> company managers. Originally, they were mainly administrators and care-
> takers. The turn-around project has given them more control as they had
> to play a key role in cost cutting measures and had to make difficult trade-
> offs among divisions within their companies on issues of employment,
> investment, plant location, and so on. They are increasingly being asked
> to contribute to the planning dialogue between local and headquarter divi-
> sion management.

# ▬ *The Origins of Management Development at Ciba-Geigy*

Leopold Luthi, a lawyer who joined Geigy in 1951, worked in line management positions in the Agchem division for over 15 years, and later became head of management development for Ciba-Geigy. He explained the early development of the management development (MD) function in the company as follows:

> After the 1968 reorganization which gave Geigy its three-dimensional structure a separate staff unit was created called "Executive Development" whose role was to assure a supply of qualified managers for top and line management positions. The unit was to report directly to the Executive Committee, and I was given responsibility for it. The idea was to make management development planning an automatic component of the yearly divisional and regional plans. At the beginning we overestimated the possibility of developing precise instruments of measurement and evaluation from which to derive the development potential. In fact, a formal system would not work. Line managers might comment quite differently on their people according to whether they evaluated current performance or future development potential. Then, in 1969, the merger with Ciba was announced and everything slowed down for a while.

From 1971 onward, the management development unit took shape and developed rapidly. According to Dr. Luthi:

> The units in Basel and abroad started to work on MD plans, we discussed these plans with them, and we started to present them to the chairman of the Executive Committee and to the unit's patron. One of the early issues was to get comparability of people and profiles on a lateral basis among the units. While in the late 1960s at Geigy, we dealt with only 400 people (200 executives and 200 potential executives); after the merger we had about 1,000 executives included in our MD program. At the beginning, the system we developed worked mainly with the executive group within each company where the immediate preoccupation with succession was the highest. We later expanded the process to reach those young men and women of high potential in the organization, and to increase the supply of them over time.

# ▬ *Management Development: Purposes and Functions in 1980–1981*

By 1980, the management development staff unit at corporate headquarters employed 14 people, roughly half of them working in management education, running and organizing in-house and external training courses, and the other half dealing with succession planning, recruitment, job rotations, MD plans, etc. (see Exhibit 1).

The Central Management Development program focused on some 2,100 employees (2 percent of total employment) of the company, the so-called ex-

EXHIBIT 1

## *Management Development Staff Unit*

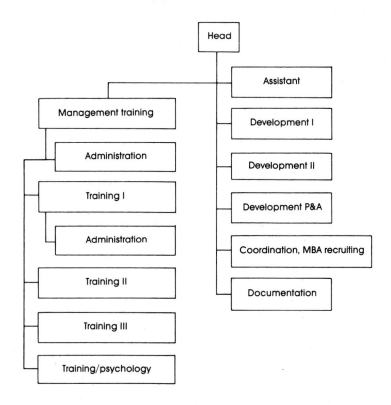

ecutives and potential executives. In addition to slightly over 100 senior executives in top management positions, the executives occupied the 1,000 or so most senior management positions in Ciba-Geigy worldwide (400 in Basel and 600 abroad) including Directors, Deputy Directors, and Vice Directors of the parent company, and the top management positions within the group companies. The potential executives, numbering about 1,000, were employees at lower-and middle-management levels who in the opinion of their supervisors were likely to advance some day to an executive position. The final responsibility for appointments and selection to the list was with line management: the Executive Committee for executive appointments, and with the various group company, divisional, and central functional heads in the case of potential executives.

This corporate-wide management development program had several objectives:

1. Planning executive successions for the whole group on the basis of corporate, divisional, and group company MD planning reports.

2. Identification of potential executives and planning their next development steps
3. Monitoring the quality and age structure of each unit's executive and potential executive population
4. Setting up career moves and job rotation for both executives and potential executives [During 1980, for example, 281 job rotations took place, mostly local, with a smaller number of international rotations between headquarters and group companies, as shown in Exhibit 2.]
5. Coordination of the moves of obsolete executives into new positions to give them new incentives and added motivation
6. The educational development of all executives and potential executives through internal (in-house) and external (business schools) management courses

As such the role of the MD unit was *conceptual* (policy and system development): *pedagogical* (assignment and coordination of management training activities): and *advisory* (to the Executive Committee). It follows that the three mainstays of Ciba-Geigy's MD program were the MD plans, its training programs, and its role in executive appointments.

### The MD Plans

Drawn up every two years by the heads of every group company and every division and function of the parent company, each MD plan showed the current executive positions in the organization, indicated future moves and candidates for job rotations, proposed internal successors and offered

E X H I B I T  2

## Total Job Rotations, 1979–1980, and International Job Rotations, 1980

|  | TOTAL | | | | | |
|  | 1980 | | | 1979 | | |
|  | Total | Local | Int'l | Total | Local | Int'l |
|---|---|---|---|---|---|---|
| *Executives* | 96 | 76 | 20 | 66 | 51 | 15 |
| *Potential executives* | 185 | 154 | 31 | 181 | 156 | 25 |
| *Total* | 281 | 230 | 51 | 247 | 207 | 40 |

|  | INTERNATIONAL | | |
|  | Total | Headquarters to group company | Group company to headquarters | Group company to group company |
|---|---|---|---|---|
| *Executives* | 20 | 3 | 8 | 9 |
| *Potential executives* | 31 | 14 | 5 | 12 |
| *Total* | 51 | 17 | 13 | 21 |

positions for outside candidates, showed potential executives, and defined action programs (see Exhibit 3 for examples). Upon receipt of an MD plan, the MD staff at headquarters would first discuss it with the unit head who wrote it, and then present it to the Chair of the Executive Committee and to the appropriate patrons. In the case of an MD plan for a group company, it would also be discussed with each corporate division or function as far as its corresponding local subunit was concerned. Dr. Luthi added:

> The way in which the various group companies are handling this question varies a great deal. In the United States and Italy, for example, the local group company's Executive Committee discusses the plan and then holds additional discussions with the various divisional management commit-tees. The whole system permeates the group company. In Mexico they are now going to do a two-day human resource planning meeting in Cuer-navaca. One day is going to deal with the strategic plan, and another day with implications in terms of the MD plan. That is good because they can couple the two systems very closely.

> Other countries do it with a lot more secrecy. They do not discuss this as a group, only face to face with the relevant managers. It is very important for us in Basel to have the confidence of line management. Therefore, we have to assure them that each unit's MD plan will be treated with appro-priate confidentiality. . . .

> A critical element in the successful implementation of our objectives is the full commitment and backing of the Chair of the Executive Committee and its members. The general managers of large group companies come personally to Basel to discuss the management development plan with the Chairman of the Executive Committee, the patrons, and our staff. . . .

> Putting full responsibility for MD plans with line managers made the plan adaptive. Rather than try to forecast centrally what managerial profiles would be required, when and in what numbers, the process was designed to develop, cultivate and track a large inventory of diverse people, from which could be extracted those with the skills required for a particular position at any point in time.

## Management Development in the Pharma Division

While some divisions were facing a slowdown in profitability and low growth prospects, the Pharma division was growing rapidly. Divisional man-agement was concerned that there would be a shortage of executives and potential executives to fill future positions. Alfred Steiner had been head of management development for the Pharma division for the past three years, and prior to that a member of the corporate MD staff for seven years. He explained the situation:

> Five years ago a new Pharma division head developed a strategy to branch out more broadly into the health care market, rather than stay exclusively

E X H I B I T   3

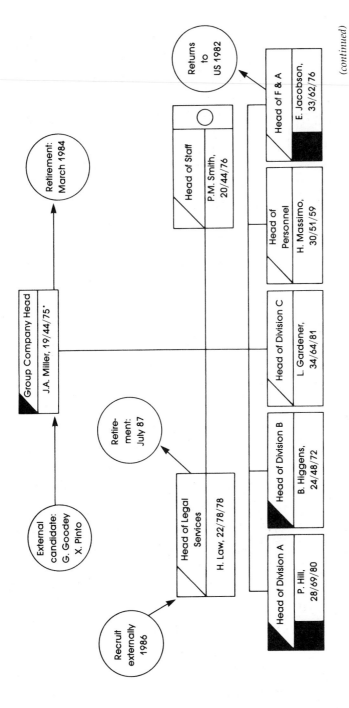

(*continued*)

*Note:* It is suggested that this chart show the top management organization and the succession situation for the company head and for any other key management positions not shown on the divisional/functional charts. The successor situation for the heads of divisions and functions is usually best shown on their respective charts.

*X/Y/Z figures, below names, mean: X, year of birth; Y, year when joined Ciba-Geigy (or the pre-merger companies), and Z, year when appointed to current position. Therefore, Mr. J. A. Miller was born in 1919, joined Ciba-Geigy in 1944, and has been head of the group company since 1975 (in the example given above).

EXHIBIT 3
*(Continued)*

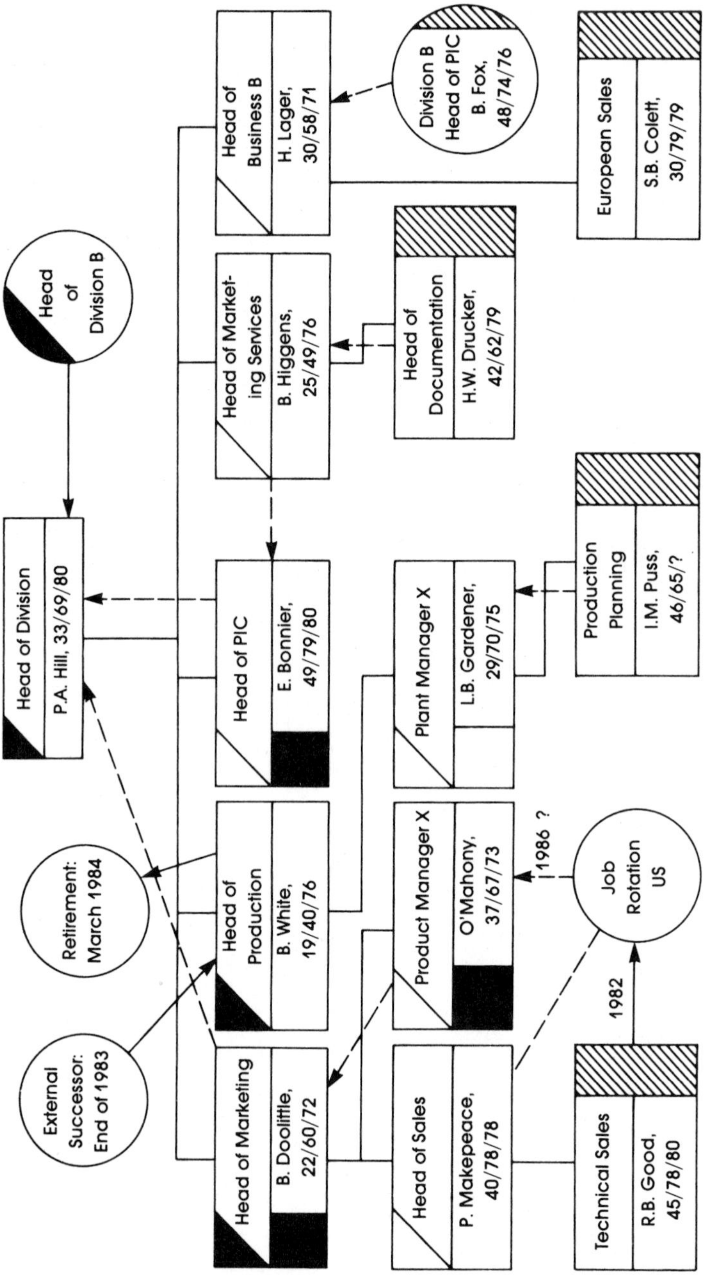

Head of Division B

Head of Division
P.A. Hill, 33/69/80

Head of Business B
H. Lager, 30/58/71

Division B
Head of PIC
B. Fox, 48/74/76

European Sales
S.B. Colett, 30/79/79

Head of Marketing Services
B. Higgens, 25/49/76

Head of Documentation
H.W. Drucker, 42/62/79

Head of PIC
E. Bonnier, 49/79/80

Plant Manager X
L.B. Gardener, 29/70/75

Production Planning
I.M. Puss, 46/65/?

Retirement: March 1984

Head of Production
B. White, 19/40/76

Product Manager X
O'Mahony, 37/67/73

1986 ?

Job Rotation US

External Successor: End of 1983

Head of Marketing
B. Doolittle, 22/60/72

Head of Sales
P. Makepeace, 40/78/78

Technical Sales
R.B. Good, 45/78/80

1982

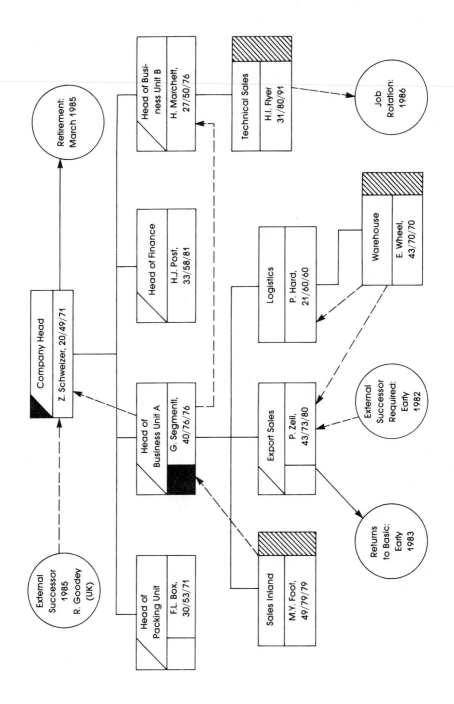

in ethical pharmaceuticals. This diversification led divisional management to become overburdened and to the realization that what the division had as available potential executives was in no way sufficient to staff our needs for the next 5 to 10 years given the new growth targets. In fact, the division realized that it had too few potential executives even for current replacement alone.

Part of the problem was that management development had not been taken seriously and that after the merger we had found ourselves with a top-heavy organization and no new people were recruited. The new division head realized that he couldn't cope with that problem and saw a need for an MD function within the Pharma division. Discussions took place with Dr. Luthi, since this was the first attempt at decentralizing a corporate function.

When I first came to the Pharma division I soon realized that the secretary of the division's management committee had sat down over a weekend to get the MD plan done. The forms were filled in, but not taken very seriously. The official MD planning system was conceived as a corporate instrument with too-restrictive definitions for actual development purposes in critical stages. Potential executives were 35 to 40 years old, but by that age a career is almost over in development potential!

Another problem is that the MD plan reflects today's organizational structure and does not project requirements into the future. The organization is changing constantly, you can't do tomorrow's succession planning based on an interpretation of today's structure. Therefore, it isn't a real plan: it remains a mere inventory, not an action program. But at least it shows us who are the potential executives and what they may become.

Steiner set out in 1978 with an action plan for management development in the Pharma division. Several goals were formulated such as achieving an even ratio between executives and potential executives, since currently the former far outnumbered the latter who would eventually be needed to fill an ever-increasing number of executive positions. He also initiated a program to recruit 40 young people each year, mainly MBAs, and put them on a fast-track development. This was a major change from Ciba-Geigy's traditional recruitment policy. A study of the age structure in the Pharma division had revealed that only 24 percent of the potential executives were below age 35. Finally, systematic MD planning was instituted that would account for different profiles of executives needed for the traditional drug business, new business sectors, and acquisitions (see Exhibit 4).

In total the MD unit in Pharma dealt with nearly 600 people, 330 executives and 250 potential executives on a worldwide basis, covering operations in over 60 countries. The MD action plan was specifically tailored to the needs of the Pharma division as Steiner remarked:

Obviously, what we developed here would not apply to Ciba-Geigy as a whole since other divisions face different management development problems. But we were also in a Catch 22 situation because while the corporate

E X H I B I T   4

## Pharma Division—Business, Structure, and Executive Assumptions

| TYPE OF BUSINESS | FUTURE BUSINESS STRUCTURE | TYPES OF EXECUTIVES REQUIRED |
| --- | --- | --- |
| Traditional drug business (3 pillars) | Same basic structure but trend toward more independent profit center units | Fewer functional managers, more entrepreneurs than in the past |
| New business sectors (e.g., antibiotics, OTC, generics) | Creation of self-contained business units | All-around managers, entrepreneurs |
| Acquisitions | Normally will remain independent units | All-around managers, entrepreneurs |

**283**

turn-around rationalization plans placed an almost complete ban on recruitment, we were told to go ahead with our strategic recruitment program.

The Pharma division is growing fast but competing head-on with other companies like Hoechst or MSD. If we want to compete successfully for executives, we have to offer salary levels comparable to those offered by our main competitors. Clearly we have a conflict between the salaries our division has to pay and those other divisions want to pay. Also, as a rule, the most profitable divisions believe that they should have a higher standard of living.

## ▄ *The Pharma Division in France*

Pharma division operations in France had always been rather autonomous. In the old days, the French Pharma Division had been headed by Dr. Henri d' Encausses, a pharmacist and the Mayor of Gaillardon, a village in Southern France. He gladly entertained visiting executives from headquarters but carefully protected his autonomy. In this he had the implicit support of the company's Managing Director, Antoine Roux, who ran the French subsidiary quite successfully and kept headquarters at bay. Middle managers were caused to think that Basel was trying to influence the group company unduly. Since his thinking was often ahead of that in Basel, Roux maintained his advantage and kept the management of the French company close to his chest.

With the divisional reorganization which followed the merger, tensions grew between Roux and divisional and corporate management in Basel. He was replaced in 1977 by R. Lamont, a French-speaking Swiss national of English origin, who had been head of the French Pharma division since 1974. Lamont was succeeded in this role by Maitre Guillaume, a French lawyer, who was appointed at age 65, and retired in September 30, 1979, upon his replacement by Delage. Lamont was a skillful negotiator who did much to improve communications between headquarters and the French company.

Neither Lamont nor Guillaume had a strong feeling for management development. They did not have the necessary potential executives to fill new positions and let an enduring weakness develop in their supply of managers. At headquarters the situation was made difficult by a hiring freeze in the early 1970s that led to a scarcity 10 years later of promotable managers age 35 to 40. Following the merger, Ciba-Geigy had found itself with too many managers and with a commitment to its employees that no layoffs would result from it. Furthermore, some divisions, such as dyestuffs, faced shrinking markets and increasing competition. Pharma, alone, was growing rapidly in France from Fr250 million in sales in 1975, to over Fr700 million by 1981. When Delage came back to France in 1976, for instance, he was the only manager with a marketing background and a good knowledge of English. Lamont and Guillaume had satisfied corporate MD formal requirement by drawing up MD plans when requested, but concrete implementation actions rarely followed these plans, and little was done to recruit and develop potential managers.

Between 1976 and 1981, Delage strengthened the French Pharma Division considerably. First, he spent much time in the field improving the quality of the medical representatives' force by training, selection, and replacement. He then created two positions of product line managers—one for Ciba products, the other for Geigy's—to provide additional sales and marketing management competence and support. He also replaced several of the weaker product managers. By 1981, the Pharma organization in France (see Exhibit 5) was in much better shape.

## ■ *The Choice of a New Marketing Manager*

When Lamont retired, Delage was chosen to replace him in competition with a Swiss expatriate. Among many factors in the decision it was felt that national feelings in France would favor a Frenchman to head the local group company. According to the manager of the European region in the Pharma division:

> Delage is a prototype of a successful career within Ciba-Geigy Pharma. He has been successful wherever he was. Delage is the type of person we really like. Among possible candidates he was closest to the ideal profile: a Frenchman to head the French group company, but with good experience of headquarters, several successful assignments abroad and a clear perspective on relationships with Basel. We want that type of person in key positions abroad. He already was an ideal division manager who understood the Ciba-Geigy philosophy well. There is nothing worse than having key people in group companies who know nobody in Basel, are not known to headquarters, and lack the company culture.

The major issue with Delage's appointment was that he had been division head in France for less than two years and, in reviewing the French MD plan, the Executive Committee had put a hold on him as recently as October 1981. Yet, since no other candidate came close to his profile, he was selected.

Finding a new Pharma division head to replace Delage was more difficult. In 1979, Delage proposed to hire Charles Mortier as Marketing Manager for Pharma-France. Nobody from the French Pharma division was well-qualified for the job, and the only candidate suggested by the corporate MD unit was a Swiss manager from Canada, Paul Aubert. Unfortunately, he came from another division and was not well-known to the Basel Pharma division management. Mortier had a good track record with a U.S. pharmaceutical company in France, where his career progression had been stifled, and he was a seasoned marketing and sales manager. After much discussion, his appointment was agreed to by all parties.

Yet, after a year with Ciba-Geigy, Mortier went back to his former employer. The unexpected dismissal of their marketing manager and a financially attractive offer had hired him back. Soon thereafter, the U.S. company

EXHIBIT 5

*French Pharma Division—Sales and Marketing Structure, 1981*

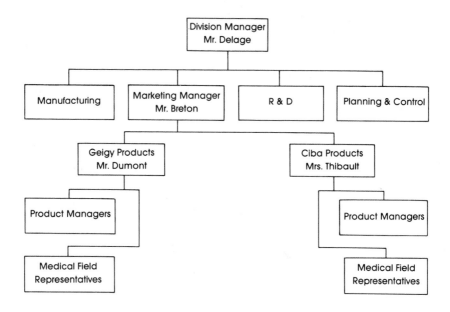

introduced a product in direct competition to Ciba-Geigy's very successful Voltarene.

In the spring of 1980, Delage hired Jules Breton from Sanofi to become the new marketing manager.[1] Breton joined Ciba-Geigy by the late summer of 1980 and was more a general manager than a marketing specialist. Over a year later, with Delage's appointment as Managing Director, the opportunity to promote him as division head came. According to Mr. Steiner: "Breton was promoted; there was no better candidate. We are reluctant to go out on the market for division heads. Breton knew the French market and his people." The major difficulty was that Breton had only been with the company a very short time. He did not know headquarters or the Ciba-Geigy culture and was not well-known to headquarters' managers.

Breton and Delage then suggested Dumont as a replacement for Breton as marketing manager. Dumont had been recruited in March 1980 from Specia (a French competitor) to take responsibility for the marketing of the Geigy line of pharmaceutical products. He was a pharmacist (graduated in 1972) with an additional degree in political science (from "Science-Po" in Paris, 1974). In 1975, following military service, he had joined Boehringer-Ingelheim in Reims as product manager for over-the-counter (OTC) drugs. A

---

[1]In the meantime. Delage had stepped back into the vacant marketing manager's role, spending about 60 percent of his time as division head on marketing and sales issues.

year later, he joined a Specia subsidiary, overseeing two products which between them accounted for over 50 percent of the subsidiary's sales. In 1977 he became responsible for all product managers at Specia and was very successful. In 1979 he was offered to head a newly acquired market research subsidiary and to create, for the whole of Specia, a marketing "methodology" unit to advise and assist line managers. Seeing himself more as a line manager, he was not very pleased with the new position when he was approached by an executive placement firm on behalf of Ciba-Geigy in November 1979. Following interviews and discussions with Mortier and Delage, he decided to join Ciba-Geigy.

By the time Dumont came on board, in March 1980, Mortier had left the company, and for the next six months (until Breton actually arrived) the French Pharma Division had no marketing manager. Delage, in addition to his divisional management duties, concentrated most of his attention on the Ciba products, where rapid product line management turnover had created problems. Dumont was immediately given full responsibility for the Geigy product line with very little supervision. This included a marketing and sales force of about 120 people, supported by a service staff of more than 20 people. He handled them successfully, continuing the 20 percent per annum real rate of growth started under Delage. According to Dumont, the quality of the products, the commitment of management, and the financial means of Ciba-Geigy explained that continued success.

In less than one year, Dumont had created a good impression at headquarters. According to the Pharma European regional manager, Dr. Grunwald, "he attended meetings in Basel and left good impressions everywhere; he elicited positive feelings and was known within headquarters."

In spite of this positive view about Dumont among Pharma division management in Basel, headquarters routinely initiated a wider search for candidates. According to Mr. Steiner: "We were suggested 'why not go with Dumont?' by Delage and Breton. Our initial reaction was 'we do not really know Mr. Dumont, he has been in the company only a few months. Let us look at him. At first sight he is very young—he was born in 1948—but maybe we are getting old?' We then looked into who else we had. Delage knew all of them anyway."

Dumont had been very successful in France and knew both the techniques of marketing and the specific character of the French pharmaceutical markets extremely well. The French pharmaceutical market was considered to be one of the most difficult for foreign competitors, among European markets. France had some strong national competitors, such as Specia, with extensive positions on their domestic market but little international presence. Furthermore, prices were tightly controlled, and complex administrative and political procedures governed the registration of new drugs. In a price inelastic market, margins were slim. In 1981, the new Socialist government in France was about to initiate discussions with foreign pharmaceutical companies with the objective of granting price increases only to those which agreed to increase their local investment and employment levels.

Despite these difficulties the French market was important to Ciba-Geigy and one of the largest national markets for its pharmaceutical products. Among the group companies, France had had the most success with Voltarene, and this product now accounted for a substantial proportion of Ciba-Geigy's sales in France. Steiner and Grunwald drew up a profile of an ideal candidate. According to them, international exposure and headquarters experience were desirable characteristics that Dumont lacked. Together, they drew a more formalized profile to assess candidates. This blank profile would be sent to each senior manager within Ciba-Geigy who knew the candidate.

Steiner started to go through files of possible candidates from outside the French group company. On November 23, 1981, a first list of about 40 candidates was drawn from Steiner's files on 600 Pharma managers, worldwide. He then started to go through these, one by one. The three main criteria used to pare the list were: suitability for the position, availability, and career development considerations. The requirement for full "perfect" fluency in French quickly eliminated all but 6 candidates. Only 3 of these could be considered as "genuine" candidates by Steiner and Grunwald. They were submitted to Delage.

Delage quickly brushed aside one candidate who looked perfect on paper but that he knew personally from his previous positions in the Pharma division and whom he did not consider suitable for the position. Another candidate turned out not to be available, having been in his current position only nine months and not being easily replaceable there. This left one possible candidate: Michel Malterre. Malterre, however, had been slotted to go to Greece in 1982 and was not, therefore, technically available.

Malterre, a French-speaking Swiss, born in 1944, was Marketing Manager for Pharma in West Africa. He had started with Ciba in 1970, two months before the merger, as a lawyer working on legal problems resulting from the merger. For the next two years he was legal assistant to the Pharma division's Manager for Planning, Information, and Control in Basel.

During the uprising of Bangladesh against Pakistan in 1971, the International Committee of the Red Cross (Geneva) asked Ciba-Geigy for Malterre's detachment on leave to Bangladesh, where he had worked with the Red Cross prior to his joining Ciba-Geigy. After four months spent organizing medical relief programs there, often flying in helicopters through combat zones, he returned to his job in Basel. The company's Executive Committee was interested in the value of lending executives to nonprofit organizations for humanitarian purposes and asked Malterre to make a detailed presentation of his experience upon his return.

In 1972–1973 Malterre was named product manager for anesthetics in Switzerland, after which he was appointed to the secretariat of the Chair of the Executive Committee. In 1978, he applied for a line job and was sent to the Ivory Coast to market Pharma products. By 1981 he had been quite successful in developing sales in Africa and had developed good relationships with local health officials and ministers. His MD plan called for his transfer to Greece at the end of 1982.

Headquarters executives were sensitive to various aspects of Malterre's career. According to Grunwald: "Malterre has worked in Pharma at corporate level and abroad. His big disadvantage is not to be French, but his mother tongue is French. He is well-experienced in the Ciba-Geigy organization and knows the French group company, since most products sold in French West Africa are made in France."

# Suji-INS K.K.

## WILLIAM H. DAVIDSON

Mike Flynn, president of the International Division of Information Network Services Corporation, was undecided as to how he could best approach several delicate issues with his Japanese joint venture partner. He needed to develop an agenda for his trip to Japan, scheduled for the following day. In many ways, he considered this trip of vital importance. For one thing, the problems to be discussed were likely to affect the long-term relationship between his company and the Japanese partner in the management of their joint venture. Moreover, this was his first trip to Japan in the capacity of president of the International Division, and he was anxious to make a good impression and to begin to build a personal relationship with senior executives of the Japanese firm.

Flynn had assumed the position of president several months previously in May of 1988. He was 40 years old and was considered to be one of the most promising executives in the company. After 2 years of military service followed by business school, he had joined a consulting company for several years prior to accepting a position with Information Network Services Corporation (INS). Prior to his promotion to the presidency of the International Division, he had served as managing director of INS's wholly owned subsidiary in Canada.

INS was a major provider of value added network (VAN) services in the United States. Its principal products included high-speed data communications (packet switching), data base management, transaction processing services, and a variety of industry-specific information services. The company's total sales for 1988 were roughly $250 million, and it had recently established successful presences in the United Kingdom and other European countries. International operations accounted for roughly 25 percent of the company's total sales, and the company's top management felt that international markets represented a major field for future growth.

The company's management recognized that in order to capitalize on the rapidly growing Japanese market, a direct presence was needed. By the

*Source:* This case was written by Professor William H. Davidson on the basis of original research by Professor Michael Yoshiuo at the Harvard Business School. Copyright © 1988 by the University of Southern California. Reprinted by permission.

mid-1980s, the company began to receive a number of inquiries from major Japanese corporations concerning licensing possibilities. INS was particularly interested in the possibility of establishing a joint venture to provide VAN services.

The company, after 2 years of demanding negotiations, was successful in establishing a joint venture in Japan with Suji Company, a leading Japanese telecommunications equipment manufacturer. The arrangement was formalized in the summer of 1987.

Suji was one of the companies that approached INS initially to arrange a licensing agreement involving VAN technology and expertise. It appeared to be an attractive potential partner. Suji was a medium-sized telecommunication equipment vendor that was directly tied to one of the major Japanese industrial groups. The company had only limited sales to Nippon Telegraph and Telephone (NTT), the national telephone company. About half of its sales were exported, and the remainder went largely to other Japanese firms within the same industrial group. Suji had established a reputation for high quality, and its brands were well established.

In the mid-1980s, as the Japanese telecommunications market was deregulated, Suji began to explore opportunities in the telecommunication services market, particularly in paging and mobile phone services. Prior to deregulation, telephone and related services were monopoly markets served only by NTT. Under the terms of the 1984 New Telecommunications Law, other Japanese firms were permitted to offer these services to the general public. VAN services in particular could be initiated simply by notifying the Ministry of Posts and Telecommunications. The Ministry of International Trade and Industry had established several programs to provide incentives for new VAN services, including tax breaks and low-cost loans. Suji's management felt that VAN services would be a major growth area. Suji's management, after some investigation, concluded that the quickest and most efficient way to achieve entry into these markets was through either licensing or a joint venture with a leading U.S. company. Suji's management felt that timing was of particular importance, since its major competitors were also considering expansion into these markets. Suji's expression of interest to INS was timely, as INS had become increasingly interested in Japan. Suji was at first interested in a licensing arrangement, but INS, anxious to establish a permanent presence in Japan, wished to establish a joint venture.

The negotiations concerning this joint venture were difficult in part because it was the first experience of the kind for both companies. INS had virtually no prior experience in Japan, and for Suji this was the first joint venture with a foreign company, although it had engaged in licensing agreements with several U.S. and European firms.

The ownership of the joint venture was divided between the two companies, such that Suji owned two-thirds and INS one-third of its equity. Japanese law limited foreign ownership in telecom services vendors to one-third equity participation. In addition to a predetermined cash contribution, the agreement stipulated that INS was to provide network technology and the

Japanese partner was to contribute facilities and network equipment. The joint venture was first to market data communication services and later was to introduce transaction processing services. The services were to be marketed under the joint brands of INS and Suji. The agreement also stipulated that both companies would have equal representation on the board of directors, with four people each, and that Suji would provide the entire personnel for the joint venture from top management down to production workers. Such a practice was quite common among foreign joint ventures in Japan, since given limited mobility among personnel in large corporations, recruiting would represent a major problem for foreign companies. The companies also agreed that the Japanese partner would nominate the president of the joint venture, subject to approval of the board, and the U.S. company would nominate a person for the position of executive vice president. INS also agreed to supply, for the time being, a technical director on a full-time basis.

INS had four members on the board: Flynn, Jack Rose (INS's nominee for executive vice president of the joint venture), and the chair and the president of INS. Representing the Japanese company were the president and executive vice president of Suji, and two senior executives of the joint venture, the president and vice president for finance.

By the fall of 1988, the venture had initiated tests of its data communication services, and a small sales organization had been built. Although the venture was progressing reasonably well, Flynn had become quite concerned over several issues that had come to his attention during the previous 2 months. The first and perhaps the most urgent of these was the selection of a new president for the joint venture.

The first president had died suddenly about 3 months before at the age of 68. He had been a managing director of the parent company and had been the chief representative in Suji's negotiations with INS. When the joint venture was established, it appeared only natural for him to assume the presidency; INS management had no objection.

About a month after his death, Suji, in accordance with the agreement, nominated Kenzo Satoh as the new president. Flynn, when he heard Satoh's qualifications, concluded that he was not suitable for the presidency of the joint venture. He became even more disturbed when he received further information about how he was selected from Jack Rose, the executive vice president of the joint venture.

Satoh had joined Suji 40 years previously upon graduating from Tokyo University. He had held a variety of positions in the Suji company, but during the previous 15 years, he had served almost exclusively in staff functions. He had been manager of Administrative Services at the company's major plant, manager of the General Affairs Department at the corporate headquarters, and personnel director. When he was promoted to that position, he was admitted to the company's board of directors. His responsibility was then expanded to include overseeing several service-oriented staff departments, including personnel, industrial relations, administrative services, and the legal department.

Flynn was concerned that Satoh had virtually no line experience and could not understand why Suji would propose such a person for the presidency of the joint venture, particularly when it was at a critical stage of development.

Even more disturbing to Mr. Flynn was the manner in which Satoh was selected. This first came to Mr. Flynn's attention when he received a letter from Rose, which included the following description:

By now you have undoubtedly examined the background information forwarded to you regarding Mr. Satoh, nominated by our Japanese partner for the presidency of the joint venture.

I have subsequently learned the manner in which Mr. Satoh was chosen for the position, which I am sure would be of great interest to you. I must point out at the outset that what I am going to describe, though shocking by our standards, is quite commonplace among Japanese corporations: in fact, it is well-accepted.

Before describing the specific practice, I must give you a brief background of the Japanese personnel system. As you know, the major companies follow the so-called lifetime employment where all managerial personnel are recruited directly from universities, and they remain with the company until they reach their compulsory retirement age, which is typically around 57. Career advancement in the Japanese system comes slowly, primarily by seniority. Advancement to middle management is well-paced, highly predictable, and virtually assured for every college graduate. Competence and performance become important as they reach upper middle management and top management. Obviously, not everyone will be promoted automatically beyond middle management, but whatever the degree to which competence and qualifications are considered in career advancement, chronological age is the single most important factor.

A select few within the ranks of upper-middle management will be promoted to top management positions, that is, they will be given memberships in the board of directors. In large Japanese companies, the board typically consists exclusively of full-time operating executives. Suji's board is no exception. Moreover, there is a clear-cut hierarchy among the members. The Suji board consists of the chair of the board, president, executive vice president, three managing directors, five ordinary directors, and two statutory auditors.

Typically, ordinary directors have specific operating responsibilities such as head of a staff department, a plant, or a division. Managing directors are comparable to our group vice presidents. Each will have two or three functional or staff groups or product divisions reporting to them. Japanese commercial law stipulates that the members are to be elected by stockholders for a 2-year term. Obviously, under the system described, the members are designated by the chair of the board or the president and serve at their pleasure. Stockholders have very little voice in the actual selection of the board members. Thus, in some cases, it is quite conceivable that board membership is considered as a reward for many years of faithful and loyal service.

As you are well aware, a Japanese corporation is well known for its paternalistic practices in return for lifetime service, and they do assume obligations, particularly for those in middle management or above, even after they reach their compulsory retirement age, not just during their working careers. Appropriate positions are generally found for them in the company's subsidiaries, related firms, or major suppliers where they can occupy positions commensurate to their last position in the parent corporation for several more years.

A similar practice applies to the board members. Though there is no compulsory retirement age for board members, the average tenure for board membership is usually around 6 years. This is particularly true for those who are ordinary or managing directors. Directorships being highly coveted positions, there must be regular turnover to allow others to be promoted to board membership. As a result, all but a fortunate few who are earmarked as heir apparent to the chair, presidency, or executive vice presidency must be "retired." Since most of these executives are in their late fifties or early sixties, they do not yet wish to retire. Moreover, even among major Japanese corporations, the compensation for top management positions is quite low compared with the U.S. standard, and pension plans being still quite inadequate, they will need respectable positions with a reasonable income upon leaving the company. Thus, it is common practice among Japanese corporations to transfer senior executives of the parent company to the chair or presidency of the company's subsidiaries or affiliated companies. Typically, these people will serve in these positions for several years before they retire. Suji had a dozen subsidiaries, and you might be interested in knowing that every top management position is held by those who have retired from the parent corporation. Such a system is well routinized.

Our friend, Mr. Satoh is clearly not the caliber that would qualify for further advancement in the parent company, and his position must be vacated for another person. Suji's top management must have decided that the presidency of the joint venture was the appropriate position for him to "retire" into. These are the circumstances under which Mr. Satoh has been nominated for our consideration.

When he read this letter, Flynn instructed Rose to indicate to the Suji management that Satoh was not acceptable. Not only did Flynn feel that Satoh lacked the qualifications and experience for the presidency, but he resented the fact that Suji was using the joint venture as a home to accommodate a retired executive. It would be justifiable for Suji to use one of its wholly owned subsidiaries for that purpose, but there was no reason why the joint venture should take him on. On the contrary, the joint venture needed dynamic leadership to establish a viable market position.

In his response to Rose, Flynn suggested as president another person, Takao Toray, marketing manager of the joint venture. Toray was 50 years old and had been transferred to the joint venture from Suji, where he had held a number of key marketing positions, including regional sales manager and assistant marketing director. Shortly after he was appointed to the latter position, Toray was sent to INS headquarters to become acquainted with the company's marketing operations. He spent roughly 3 months in the United States, during which time Flynn met him. Though he had not gone beyond a casual acquaintance, Flynn was much impressed by Toray. He appeared to be dynamic, highly motivated, and pragmatic. Moreover, Toray had a reasonable command of English. While communication was not easy, at least it was possible to have conversations on substantive matters. From what Flynn was able to gather, Toray impressed everyone he saw favorably and gained the confidence of not only the International Division staff but those in the corporate marketing group as well as sales executives in the field.

Flynn was aware that Toray was a little too young to be acceptable to Suji, but he felt that it was critical to press for his appointment for two reasons. First, he was far from convinced of the wisdom of adopting Japanese managerial practices blindly in the joint venture. Some of the Japanese executives he met in New York had told him of the pitfalls and weaknesses of Japanese management practices. He was disturbed over the fact that, as he was becoming familiar with the joint venture, he was finding that in every critical aspect such as organization structure, personnel practices, and decision making, the company was managed as though it were a Japanese company. Rose had had little success in introducing U.S. practices. Flynn had noticed in the past that the joint venture had been consistently slow in making decisions because it engaged in a typical Japanese group-oriented and consensus-based process. He also learned that control and reporting systems were virtually nonexistent. Flynn felt that INS's sophisticated planning and control system should be introduced. It had proved successful in the company's wholly owned European subsidiaries, and there seemed to be no reason why such a system could not improve the operating efficiency of the joint venture. He recalled from his Canadian experience that U.S. management practices, if judiciously applied, could give U.S. subsidiaries abroad a significant competitive advantage over local firms.

Second, Flynn felt that the rejection of Satoh and appointment of Toray might be important as a demonstration to the Japanese partner that Suji-INS was indeed a joint venture and not a subsidiary of the Japanese parent company. He was also concerned that INS had lost the initiative in the management of the joint venture. This move would help INS gain stronger influence over the management of the joint venture.

Rose conveyed an informal proposal along these lines to Suji management. Suji's reaction to Flynn's proposal was swift; they rejected it totally. Suji management was polite, but made it clear that they considered Flynn unfair in judging Mr. Satoh's suitability for the presidency without even having met him. They requested Rose to assure Flynn that their company, as majority owner, indeed had an important stake in the joint venture and certainly would not have recommended Satoh unless it had been convinced of his qualifications. Suji management also told Flynn, through Rose, that the selection of Toray was totally unacceptable because in the Japanese corporate system such a promotion was unheard of and would be detrimental not only to the joint venture but to Toray himself, who was believed to have a promising future in the company.

Flynn was surprised at the tone of Suji's response. He wondered whether it would be possible to establish an effective relationship with the Japanese company. Suji seemed determined to run the venture on their own terms.

Another related issue which concerned Flynn was the effectiveness of Rose as executive vice president. Flynn appreciated the difficulties he faced but began to question Rose's qualifications for his position and his ability to work with Japanese top management. During the last visit, for example, Rose had complained of his inability to integrate himself with the Japanese top management team. He indicated that he felt he was still very much an outsider to the company, not only because he was a foreigner but also because the Japanese executives, having come from the parent company, had known each other and in many cases had worked together for at least 20 years. He also indicated that none of the executives spoke English well enough to achieve effective communication beyond the most rudimentary level and that his Japanese was too limited to be of practical use. In fact, his secretary, hired specifically for him, was the only one with whom he could communicate easily. He also expressed frustration over the fact that his functions were very ill-defined and his experience and competence were not really being well utilized by the Japanese.

Flynn discovered after he assumed the presidency that Mr. Rose had been chosen for this assignment for his knowledge of Japan. Rose graduated from a midwestern university in 1973, and after enlisting in the Army was posted to Japan for 4 years. Upon returning home, he joined INS as a management trainee. In 1984, he became assistant district sales manager in California, Oregon, and Washington. When the company began to search for a candidate for executive vice president for the new joint venture, Rose's name came up as someone who was qualified and available for posting to Japan. Rose, although somewhat ambivalent about the new opportunity at first, soon became persuaded that this would represent a major challenge and opportunity.

Flynn was determined to get a first-hand view of the joint venture during his visit. He had many questions, and he wondered whether he had inherited a problem. He was scheduled to meet with Mr. Ohtomo, executive vice president of Suji Corporation, on the day following his arrival. Ohtomo, who had been with Suji for over 40 years, was the senior executive responsible for overseeing the joint venture. Flynn had not met Ohtomo, but he knew that Ohtomo had visited the United States and spoke English reasonably well. He wondered how best to approach and organize his meetings and discussions with Mr. Ohtomo. He also wondered if his planned stay of 1 week would be adequate to achieve his objectives. While practicing with chopsticks, he returned to reading *Theory Z,* a popular book on Japanese management, in the hope of gaining insight for the days ahead.

# PART 7

# Cross-Cultural Issues in Motivation and Productivity

# The Transfer of Human Resource Management Technology in Sino–U.S. Cooperative Ventures: Problems and Solutions

## MARY ANN VON GLINOW
## MARY B. TEAGARDEN

By most assessments, China will not join the ranks of the industrial mighty by the year 2000,[1] the ambitious goal of the "Four Modernizations," modernization of agriculture, industry, science and technology, and defense. Although not making progress as quickly as planned toward accomplishment of this herculean modernization effort, China has experienced impressive growth in agriculture and both light and heavy industry. Far reaching economic reforms which support this modernization effort, have been the basis for China's much heralded Open Door Policy. These economic reforms are occurring within China, and between China and various trading partners. Internally, China has modified its centrally planned economy by placing a greater emphasis on enterprise profitability and by allowing enterprise managers greater decision-making autonomy.

To compete effectively in the international marketplace and to enhance internal development, China has aggressively sought importation of modern industrial technology and the management and marketing technologies that support industrialization. There are now numerous examples of the successful transfer of technology from industrialized countries to China. For example, U.S. firms such as AMC and Cummins Engine have successfully transferred automotive and deisel engine technology, Westinghouse and G.E. have transferred power generation technology successfully, and Boeing and McDonnell Douglas have transferred aircraft technology successfully. Japa-

Source: Mary Ann Von Glinow and Mary B. Teagarden. "The Transfer of Human Resource Management Technology in Sino-U.S. Cooperative Ventures: Problems and Solutions." *Human Resource Management*, 1988, 27(2), 201–229. Reprinted by permission.

nese firms, such as Hitachi and Mitsubishi have also successfully transferred power generation technology to China. EEC country firms have led the way in the transfer of nuclear power generation technology to China. In many of the above cited cases, the overall pattern of technology transfer that seems to be emerging is one in which the industrial technology transfers with relative success, while management and marketing technologies do not transfer nearly as well.

Those technologies are herewith referred to as soft technologies, and it has been noted that soft technologies transfer with much greater difficulty than do the harder technologies.[2]

Management expertise is consistently cited by foreign and Chinese researchers and business people, as problematic in Sino-foreign business relations, and particularly in Sino-foreign cooperative ventures. These cooperative ventures, equity and contractual joint ventures combined, accounted for about 80 percent of the almost $9 billion U.S. foreign investment in China at the end of 1984.[3] Cooperative ventures are said to provide not only an infusion of foreign capital, but of equal importance, they are currently the primary medium through which technology is transferred to China. A lag in the absorption of management technology in these cooperative ventures creates enterprises where the task structure (technological subsystem) is out of synchronization with the management structure (social subsystem). This is particularly true in those cooperative ventures where the technology transferred is of medium technological intensity, that is, technologies that require a high level of interaction between workers and hardware. The end result is that these cooperative ventures perform short of their potential efficiency and effectiveness.[4]

Within the array of modern management technologies, the hard or more easily quantifiable technologies, such as accounting, finance, production, and management information systems, have met with more success in the transfer process than have the soft, behavioral-based technologies, such as marketing, organizational development, and human resource management (Schnepp, 1987). Human resource management (HRM) stands out as an area where China's practices are far behind those encountered in most industrialized countries (Simon, 1986; McLaughlin, 1987). China's absorption of modern HRM technology in these cooperative ventures has been minimal, thereby impeding the overall technology assimilation process (Teagarden and Von Glinow, 1988). This is despite the recent enterprise reforms that call for management modernization as the "Fifth Modernization" (Simon, 1986; Fischer, 1986, 1987).

In this article, we will compare Chinese and U.S. HRM systems followed by a prescription for introducing "state-of-the-art" HRM technology into Sino–U.S. cooperative ventures. First, however, we begin our analysis with an examination of the historical antecedents of current HRM practices in China, and then we examine the current context in which China's HRM systems exist. We then explore assumptions underlying these systems and compare them to the U.S. HRM systems context and underlying assumptions. This comparative analysis helps identify critical similarities and differences between the Chinese and the U.S. HRM systems. In conclusion, we offer some suggestions on how modern HRM practices may be more effectively introduced into Sino–U.S. cooperative ventures. These suggestions must be tempered with the knowledge that the HRM practices and technologies considered "good" in one context may suffer in the transfer process.

## Historical Antecedents of Current HRM Practices in China

There are a number of historical factors that have influenced current organizational or enterprise activities in China, including HRM practices. These factors include a very long recorded history of more than 6000 years, cultural and ideological factors, political–economic factors, social welfare factors, and the role of administrative bureaucracy.

Most analysts of Chinese enterprise activities begin with the founding of the People's Republic in 1949; however, many current practices and beliefs predate this period. The current form and structure of the Chinese enterprises may be traced in part to the Confucian Civil Services. It has been noted that the heavy emphasis on testing in China emanates from the Tang Dynasty (circa 700 AD), when centrally administered examinations were employed to choose officials. These Confucian beliefs have shaped the Chinese culture and dictated norms of behavior that are appropriate for government officials and cadres alike. The strong drive for individual enterprise self-sufficiency, which results in hoarding of production inputs, personnel, and technological know-how, is rooted in a long history of scarcity that has persisted into the present, albeit to a lesser degree. Regionalism and industry level factionalism are partly derived from a history of scarcity, partly from prerevolutionary military-realted factionalism, and partly from Confucius' "five relations," specifically loyalty between sovereign and ministry (Castaldi and Soerjanto, 1988).

Political–economic factors have also strongly influenced the functioning of the Chinese enterprise. The Chinese concept of the planned economy was an outgrowth of the Soviet model, which China embraced during the early years after 1949. Rural communes became a way of life, with virtually all aspects of the economy controlled by the Central Planning Committee. Over the years, these communes have given way to other economic entities; however, some have argued that the economy has benefitted from tight political and economic controls. After all, China has managed to feed and employ a population in excess of one billion people (McLaughlin, 1987). The 1950s and 1960s brought tremendous economic upheaval with the devastations wrought by the Great Leap Forward, where Mao's dream caused the starvation of 25–30 million people, and the Cultural Revolution, where wealth, education, science and technology were considered the enemies of the people. In consideration of those difficult periods, it is not hard to imagine a system whereby jobs are guaranteed, and people were able to receive equitable entitlements from the state. Such are the concepts of the iron rice bowl and the *danwei*, where workers were guaranteed most of their material needs (Tung, 1982).

Since 1979, when Deng XiaoPing became the head of the Chinese Government, China has gradually shifted from the Soviet model of the centrally planned economy. Since that time, market-style economic reforms have almost doubled Chinese incomes[5] and during this time, the economy has grown at 8 percent annually, surpassing U.S. and European growth rates. Deng's concept of a planned economy was one in which the economy allowed some economic entrepreneurism with tight political controls. China has chosen to decentralize economically, and the most recent National People's Congress, March 1988, called for the reduction of the state's role in the economy from planner to indirect market regulator. Government leaders Zhao Ziyang and Li Peng (the new Premier) have recently announced that increased productivity must be their chief criterion. The economic ramifications of these words are yet to be determined; however, Zhao has noted that development must take precedence over political ideology if China is to end its chronic poverty. It has also been observed that prices in China, long distorted by state subsidies, will continue to be gradually decontrolled through market mechanisms. Li Peng has further noted that within the next five years, that grain production must be increased, and scientific development must be encouraged. The bureaucracy should be further "revitalized" and the enterprises should have reduced state controls.

The role of the enterprise historically has been ubiquitous in worker lives. In many enterprises, the workers live in apartments or complexes owned by the enterprise. Therefore, work and family life become highly intertwined. The concept of HR management might include resolving family disputes, arranging hospitalization for workers, counselling young people on family planning, as well as getting the work done. Historically, the enterprises have had little discretion in hiring, firing, and wage setting. These have been set by the state or the government's planning committee. There are some pay differentials according to job and family, and wages are generally divided into eight steps, whereby workers progress according to tenure and "proficiency." Managers also have steps, and promotions do not necessarily mean greater wages. The wage ratio of senior-level, factory director to the lowest worker is approximately 4:1. Before Deng took over, "spiritual" incentives prevailed over "material" incentives, thus contributing to this low ratio in pay differentials. When we consider that the standard work week is six days, and that extensive employee benefits are provided to all workers and cadres, we come to understand the important role that the enterprise has played in the lives of all Chinese workers.

Party leaders and political analysts have noted that enterprise reform is critical if China is to improve its industrial productivity levels. Many of the state-owned enterprises operate at a loss, with others receiving marginal marks (McLaughlin, 1987). Qualified managers are difficult to find, recruitment of workers is rarely done, job mobility is infrequent, financial incentives are quite new and only slowly are beginning to influence work behavior. The concept of the iron rice bowl was said to have occurred after the worker passed the probationary period ranging from six months to two years. To forego this meant giving up the stability of the state-owned enterprise for private sector work that has been viewed as risky at best, given the newness of the Party policy under Deng's leadership.

All of these political, economic, and organizational factors are the backdrop for the current reform movement in China in the 1980s. The factors have heavily influenced current enterprise practices. The next section examines the socio-structural characteristics of Chinese enterprises, to help frame the current HRM practices more precisely.

## Chinese Enterprises

Before delving into how the Chinese system of HRM differs from the U.S. system of HRM, we examine the contexts in which these HRM systems operate. Therefore, we begin with the identification of key differences among Chinese enterprises and other differences that subsequently dictate Chinese HRM practices. Currently, there are over 400,000 enterprises in China, ranging from a small scale, fairly autonomous, "private sector" enterprises which include, for example, mom-and-pop noodle stands, to centrally controlled, sophisticated manufacturers of high technology products. Following is a brief discussion of four contextual issues that surround these different enterprises: degree of external control; enterprise characteristics; enterprise structure; and the role of "Management Modernization." These four issues are highlighted now because of the recent trends toward decentralizing enterprises and modernizing the management of those enterprises. The new enterprise law is a significant reform, and worthy of some discussion at this point.

### Degree of External Control

In China's centrally planned economy, the degree of external control largely dictates how enterprises operate. An enterprise is controlled at one of four levels, ranging from highly centralized, extensive external control to highly decentralized, limited external control. Enterprises can be Ministry-controlled, an external, highly centralized and extensive, national level of control. Secondly, they may also be locally controlled by the local province or municipality, which is analogous to state or city level control. This is also a form of external control, but is less centralized, and usually less extensive, than Ministry control. An estimated 20 percent of the state-owned enterprises operate at a loss, with the remainder barely meeting their output quotas.[6]

The third type of control is dual control, a hybrid incorporating both

Ministerial and local control. The fourth type of control, collective ownership enterprises, has a highly decentralized level of control that enables a relatively high level of autonomy similar to private ownership in the United States. In enterprises with more decentralized external control, the collective ownership enterprises and some locally and dual controlled enterprises, day-to-day control is theoretically reduced over the operations of the enterprise. However, key areas, like procurement of supplies, distribution of products, and hiring and firing require external approval. Additionally, managers in the more decentralized enterprises have greater responsibility for the profitability of the enterprise.

It is clear that with industrial productivity lagging, that greater emphasis will be placed upon enterprise performance in the future. The recent National People's Congress has called for further reduction of controls on enterprises. Thus, we would expect that the fourth category of control would be applied to a growing number of enterprises in the years ahead, if China continues its policy of economic decentralization.

### Enterprise Categories

Chinese enterprises can be classified into one of four categories based on the degree to which they embrace or resist the economic reforms underway in China (Simon, 1986).

*Iron Rice Bowlers.* Twenty to twenty-five percent of the enterprises fall into this category, comprised mostly of heavy industry. These enterprises, which operate similar to the pre-reforms Soviet model, are not concerned with quality or efficiency, but rather with meeting externally set output quotas. They have not felt the impact of the new reforms.

*Bandwagoners.* Constituting an additional 30 percent, these enterprises pay lip service to the reforms, but operate in a manner similar to the Iron Rice Bowlers. The Bandwagoners go through the motions of reform, but cling to pre-reform values and behaviors. Within these enterprises, status and power are given to technical experts.

*Incrementalists.* These are the enterprises which, although threatened by the reforms, attempt to minimally incorporate these reforms into their practices. For them, change is incorporated at a very slow, steady, and cautious rate. Incrementalists also comprise about 30 percent of the Chinese enterprises, and feel the impact of the new reforms. However, they do not stick their necks out to initiate change—they are followers.

*Entrepreneurs.* For these enterprises the reforms present opportunities of which they can take advantage. They embrace the economic reforms and are moving ahead at full speed to incorporate change. The remaining 10 to 15 percent of the enterprises can be considered entrepreneurs.

Most technology transfer takes place between foreign firms and Bandwagoners or Incrementalists although the Entrepreneurs are seeking technology at a quickly growing pace. Although enterprise managers in these two categories see the introduction of new technology as a risk and inconvenience, they reluctantly adapt, since most industries in China are driven by technology, or at least by the desire to acquire industrial technology to upgrade productivity. The concept of the market-driven economy is slowly emerging with the emphasis on economic decentralization and reforms. However, like their Iron Rice Bowler counterparts, Bandwagoners and Incrementalists are averse to risk and not likely to welcome or embrace the introduction of western HRM technology. They have been observed as resisting many of the current economic reforms.

### Structure

Most Chinese enterprises are structured similar to the organization chart in Exhibit 1. This figure depicts the strong emphasis placed on the enterprise's technical subsystem with elements of strong vertical integration and self-sufficiency within ministries. Within the enterprise, the chief engineer reports directly to the factory director and is the hub through whom other deputies report. This structure reinforces the importance of technology and engineering, by channeling communication through the chief engineer. The structure is also self-reinforcing, since the ability to control enterprise communication confers power and status on the chief engineer. The enterprise is also part of a vertically integrated system in which the factory director relies on the local bureau or a Ministry for inputs, such as raw materials and human resources, and for the distribution of outputs. Little direct horizontal communication occurs between enterprises whether they are in the same or related industries or unrelated industries: any that occurs is channeled through local provincial bureaux or Ministries.

### Management Modernization

After the acquisition of technology and foreign exchange, management modernization is at the crux of current economic debates on enterprise reform. As mentioned earlier, management modernization has been referred to as the "Fifth Modernization." Political conservatives favor scientific management, in the tradition of Fredrick Taylor, as the appropriate approach to management modernization (Battat, 1986). Liberals see management modernization as much further reaching, requiring fundamental changes in industrial organization, such as linking pay to performance, implementing bonus incentive systems, developing performance management and appraisal systems, and permitting enterprises to hire and fire (Battat, 1986). While there is consensus by the heads of government that management modernization is essential, there is little consensus about the form it should take.

This brief overview of the contextual issues that surround Chinese HRM systems allows three observations. First, Chinese HRM systems exist in a highly centralized economy which, in the late 1980s, is undergoing radical reform. Second, there is a very strong emphasis on hard technology within enterprises, especially technologies related to industries designated critical

EXHIBIT 1

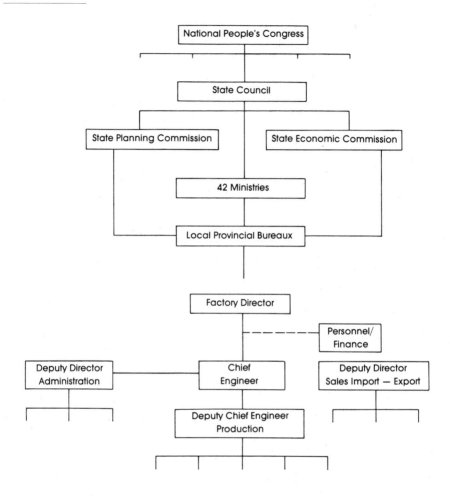

by the Four Modernizations, such as electronics and energy. Third, while management modernization is desired by the government, there is no clear consensus which management technologies this should include. With this as background, the following discussion will elaborate differences and differing assumptions that underly Chinese and U.S. HRM systems.

## ■ *Differences in Chinese and U.S. HRM Systems*

China prefers and aggressively seeks to acquire "state of the art" technology. Therefore, we discuss comparisons of HRM differences between the U.S. and China, by anchoring organizational and work-related assumptions in the practices of U.S. firms that the Chinese view as "state of the art" technology-providers, for example IBM or G.E.[7] While not all firms seen by the Chinese as "leading-edge" companies have the same views on HRM practices, we present a typology used by Leskin[8] which discussed organizational and work-related assumptions—assumptions about people and performance, assumptions about reward systems, training, and development. In addition, we examine differences in the educational backgrounds of HR practitioners in both countries. This typology was deemed useful in highlighting different assumptions held by progressive U.S. firms and Chinese enterprises. The typology is not meant to compare unfavorably a developing country's practices with the Western view of HRM. Rather, it attempts to delve into the different assumptional frameworks that both possess, to develop a normative framework to assist in the transfer of HRM technology, keeping in mind the enterprise's political, economic and social realities.

After identifying different assumptions that govern HRM practices in both countries, we then identify the major differences that present impediments to the modernization of HRM practices in Sino–U.S. cooperative ventures. Having identified key impediments, we offer a normative framework for the introduction of modern HRM practices into these ventures. We conclude with suggestions for future research.

### Organizational Assumptions

*U.S.* In the United States, HR managers believe that the organization's principle constituency is the employees of the firm (Leskin, 1986). There are, of course, other stakeholders that the firm must consider, and other important criteria for organizational success; however, the HR function has generally focused on the internal organizational processes, systems, and people, rather than on external factors. As such, these professionals are highly concerned about improving internal organizational functioning. That of course may mean interfacing with customers and other relevant stakeholders; however, it is generally accepted that people are the firm's greatest asset (Leskin, 1986; Von Glinow and Chung, 1987). Further, they believe that there is no best organization structure or job design, and these factors are frequently changed to take advantage of new technologies, people, or processes.[9] Reorganization has frequently been the result of these changes. HR managers believe the ability to change, in response to internal or external factors is fundamental to human growth and development (Leskin, 1986). These managers believe, however, that change requires the proper conditions, which rests on senior management support and with such support, revolutionary change is possible. Without this support, U.S. HR managers would most likely agree that the requisite conditions that facilitate change are missing, thus decreasing the likelihood that the change will produce the desired outcomes.

*China.* In China, the enterprise's principle constituency is the Central and/or local provincial government. Historically, many enterprises have been vertically integrated, and the primary goal, as articulated by the Party Congress and State Planning Commission, has been self-sufficiency particularly in energy development and use, and industrial productivity (Schnepp, Bhambri, and Von Glinow, 1987). Today, most enterprises are highly self-sufficient, and do not rely on those outside their own vertical chain for local content or human talent. Although an argument may be advanced that in some industrial activities the Chinese enterprise must rely heavily on others outside the vertical chain for sourcing of raw materials, energy acquisition, and the like, the recent trend is toward greater self-sufficiency through greater productivity.[10]

In general, organizational change is tied to political and ideological values. These values include a Marxist sensitivity to the exploitation of labor and secrecy regarding "internal" matters. Consequently, there is a failure to see HRM as a legitimate part of modern management. When there is a unit head labelled Personnel, this individual is almost always a top party official who deals with people through "rule enforcement," similar to a coercive Employee Relations function.

### Work Environment

*U.S.* In the United States, managers and employees alike enjoy employment-at-will. It is quite likely that most HR managers have had a variety of work experiences in a variety of firms. Employees are selected to fit jobs, and are then expected to achieve high levels of performance in those jobs. Beyond that, employees are encouraged to excel or outperform previous standards in those jobs.[11] Salaries are highly differentiated within organizations based on equity and merit: generally, the more complex the job, the more pay, and the better the performance, the more pay. Regarding their colleagues, HR managers' assumptions include that they work with competent professionals who have comparable values and skills, including beliefs in due process and self-development.[12] Therefore, decision making is generally pushed downward in organizations. HR managers are rewarded for being good team players, and for recommending innovative changes. In general, the work of the firm is conducted within a fixed annual budget, and most HR managers have limited salary, bonuses, and perks to distribute for excellent performance.

*China.* One critical difference in Chinese and U.S. work environments is that Chinese enterprises are assigned workers by the central government, which continues to govern employment contracts. There is very little concept of employment-at-will. Students[13] who graduate from college may have some choice—generally from among three to five alternatives—as to which enterprises they will join. Until recently, once workers were hired by a particular enterprise, they enjoyed lifetime employment. There is some evidence now that technical professionals and a few managers have participated in interunit mobility; however, this is not widely practiced (Bai et al., 1986). Labor contracts are newly emerging as experimental devices allowing a few enterprises to hire on an as-needed basis, and fire workers who repeatedly violate work rules. Similarly, the Joint Venture Law of 1979 allows enterprises engaged in cooperative ventures with foreign firms to hire and fire workers.

In China, unlike the U.S., the Marxist–Leninist doctrine has influenced performance, and except for meeting output quotas, workers have not been under pressure to perform. While current policy discussions at the state level are attempting to confront this problem of industrial productivity, some sectors remain low producers.

Poor performers have rarely been terminated, despite highly variable levels of performance. Perhaps because of the wide variability in performance, individuals have virtually no authority to make decisions without clearance from those in higher authority, and individual decision making is actively hampered by bureaucratic interference. All decisions that are made go through hierarchical channels and recommendations for change and innovation are rarely seen. It should be noted that, in addition to meeting output quotas, the criterion for successful performance, other social welfare goals must be met as well. Toward that end, the "extended enterprise" or *danwei* may have attached to it a school, a hospital, or other social structures, for example, housing which is generally provided by the enterprise. This all relates to the fact that all workers receive government subsidized living,[14] including rent, health care, transportation, and utilities, which compared to the U.S., represents a widely broadened benefit package.

In China, managers do not have collegial relationships with co-workers. They manage individuals with widely varying abilities, skill levels, and experience, who may also have dissimilar political or ideological values. Further, they manage downward, one-on-many. The "many" function together as a team, unit or group of which the manager is not a member until it comes to the distribution of material incentives. In general, managers distribute salary, bonuses, and perks according to level in the enterprise; however, there is very little pay differential across all levels. Finally, managers are not responsible for financial planning. This function is handled primarily by the State Planning Commission or the local finance bureau.

### Assumptions About People

*U.S.* In the United States, HR professionals make the assumption that people must be "motivated to perform." To motivate employees, the HR manager has an arsenal of tools which include compensation; situational change, for example, through reward systems or job design; selection; and training. Particularly in the 1980s, it is believed that employee participation and involvement can eventually lead to increased organizational performance, as well as enhanced employee satisfaction (Leskin, 1986; Lawler, 1986). Participation frequently manifests itself in teamwork and organizational commitment, which progressive HR managers view as essential. A further assumption is that managerial influence is, and should be, based on consensus and participation. HR managers assume that an overly controlling manager inhibits individual growth and employee development. Many HR professionals embrace change and innovation, tending to believe that line managers resent innovation and are unable to see the "big picture."

*China.* The Chinese believe that people should be treated equally; egalitarianism is the rule. If workers are not performing properly, they must be "educated" to ensure performance. "Correct thought," they believe, leads to correct behavior. Historically, there has been a strong linkage between employee education and ideological training. A manager's tools for employee "education" include training workers to improve their skills, reassignment, and placing each person in the right job. Change and innovation are almost universally resented and resisted. A manager's influence stems from rule compliance and strong control ensures compliance with objectives. In general, the cooperation that occurs is within a department or unit, and rarely across units. Extreme departmentalism inhibits cooperation between individuals and between units, and people hoard information within their departments. Finally, the work unit retains ultimate control over its employees, and bears ultimate responsibility for their welfare.

### Assumption About Performance

*U.S.* HR professionals in the United States believe that the effective management of human resources improves "bottom line" productivity, at least in the long term. HR professionals do not believe that short-term results are the only measure of performance. Long-term measures and the creation of a "learning organization" are also important (Leskin, 1986). Senior-level managers who stress short-term results at the expense of long-term development are seen as mortgaging the firm's future. Thus, regardless of productivity, or how the "numbers" look, managers are viewed suspiciously by HR managers if they fail to emphasize development, delegation, and participation (Leskin, 1986).

*China.* The need to increase productivity, and improve quality in management and labor was first enunciated in 1984. Historically, the Chinese have equated performance with meeting output quotas. There was no incentive to surpass designated quotas, nor to improve output quality under the concept of the iron-rice bowl. Recently, with increasing frequency, performance has been discussed and sweeping enterprise reforms have been enacted, including an Enterprise Law, which gives new power and discretion to the enterprise. Lagging productivity has increasingly been the center of discussions at the state level. The ability to obtain sophisticated technology through association with a foreign firm in a cooperative venture has been one index of productivity. Once an enterprise has acquired this technology, even though the technology may not have been assimilated, the enterprise is viewed as having performed successfully. This is not to suggest that the Chinese are not interested in utilizing the technology. However, local absorptive capacity has often impeded the successful utilization of acquired technology.[15] Since neither the meeting of output quotas, nor acquiring new technology in and of itself encourages or contributes to the development of a "learning organization," while necessary to growth, neither is sufficient if China is to meet its modernization goals.

### Perspectives on Training and Development

*U.S.* Human resource development professionals in the United States see training and development as tightly linked to bottom line performance. Within highly integrated HR systems, training and development are linked to the performance appraisal and reward system. The key to performance is in developing human potential: HR managers believe that they "win the war" based on how well developed their employees are (Leskin, 1986). Here, the assumption is that if a person is not performing well, then most likely he or she has not been properly developed by higher management. Facilitation is requisite to proper development and with the proper amount of development and training, people can be made to change reasonably quickly, especially if the change includes humanistically expressed work values. Again, U.S. HR managers tend to believe that the release of human potential by management represents the ultimate untapped organizational resource (Leskin, 1986).

*China.* In general, Chinese managers have resisted rapid change. Mao believed in "Red versus Expert," which means that all challenges could be overcome by political will, not expertise. Deng Xiaoping believes in expertise, and training is seen as the key to acquiring this expertise. The Chinese currently believe that training is the primary vehicle for creating productive Chinese enterprises, and it is seen as very prestigious to be allowed to train outside China. Acquiring expertise through training accords a certain amount of power to the person who has been trained, and two likely scenarios result. The individual is asked to train others, similar to U.S.-based train-the-trainer programs. Recently, these programs have gained in popularity, but generally occur only within the individual's own enterprise. Inter-enterprise training rarely occurs because of the enterprise's strong vertical linkages (Schnepp, Bhambri, and Von Glinow, 1987). An equally likely outcome of training is that the individual will be placed into a managerial position elsewhere, to apply that training. This frequently results in engineers trained abroad returning to a managerial, not a technical, position (Von Glinow, Schnepp, and Bhambri, 1988).

For the most part, training revolves around technical training, and behavioral training is virtually nonexistent and exceedingly difficult to implement, even in joint ventures. Nevertheless, training is considered one of the most important tools to reinforce the expertise side of the "Red versus Expert" slogan.

### Assumptions About Rewards

*U.S.* There is a phrase that has become popular within the past decade in the U.S.: "You get what you reward." If you want performance, you must be able to reward it; if you do not reward it, chances are you will not see performance (Kerr, 1975). Organizational reward systems have become exquisitely varied and highly elaborated in the U.S., and the concept of pay for performance, the most visible criterion of a good reward system, is but one aspect of these systems. Broadly, reward systems include financial incentives, social status incentives, which are the organizational equivalent of "keeping up with the Jones's," and job-content incentives. The job-content aspects of reward systems include challenge, responsibility, feedback, and career-based rewards. Most HR professionals would favor a reward system that employs a broad spectrum of these types of rewards in order to encourage performance. In addition, the organizational climate, supportive supervision, participative decision making, and self-development opportunities for individuals are seen as important contextual components of the organization's reward system.

*China.* In post-1949 China, equality has traditionally been the best policy. Egalitarianism, however, is conceding somewhat to *duo lao, duo de,* an equity-based "more work, more pay" scheme. There has been a belief that higher wages in one enterprise will set disruptive precedents for workers and cadres (managers) in other enterprises. Thus, the concept of pay for performance is in the "experimental" stages at present.

While some cash bonuses for good performance are possible, and widely publicized when they occur, there is no equation for distributing these material incentives. Generally, when a unit within an enterprise performs meritoriously and a cash incentive is distributed, that incentive is distributed equally among all individuals, however remotely involved: the work group, the department, the division, and so on up the vertical chain, using egalitarian logic. Thus, while cash incentives are theoretically possible, in practice they are egalitarian-based, not equity-based. Prior to 1980, "spiritual incentives were preferred to material incentives, and high performers were given titles such as "Model Worker," suggesting a strong reliance on non-financial incentives" (McLaughlin, 1987).

As previously mentioned, Chinese workers are provided housing, medical coverage, and an extensive range of other benefits. While these would commonly be seen as part of the reward system in the U.S., in China these benefits are deeply interwoven in the enterprise and social structure. The concept of the "iron rice bowl" signifies a form of cradle-to-grave reward/entitlement system that is not related to work performance, and in some cases, has an intergenerational aspect. Sons will sometimes inherit the father's position, thus going beyond lifetime to intergenerational employment and entitlement.

### HR Practitioner Background

*U.S.* In the United States, most HR practitioners have fairly similar educational training. They generally hail from psychology or social psychology, and occasionally, education or organization behavior. They have had considerable experience throughout their college careers with classroom training. Much of this college training is targeted toward HRM, since this specific functional area is common to most U.S. organizations. The future HR practitioner takes classes in compensation, human resource planning, career planning, organizational change, organizational development, and consulting, among others. A Ph.D. is becoming more commonly required by many firms.

*China*. Those cadres who practice HR or "Personnel Management" have had very little training or education that would be typical of or considered appropriate to the HR function, by Western standards. In part, the Cultural Revolution wreaked havoc on many educational endeavors, and many managers between the ages of 30 and 45 will not have had more than rudimentary training. These educationally disenfranchised managers may elect to receive remedial training, however, this mostly occurs at the individual's own expense. Generally, it is those under 30 or over 45 who have received an education or speak a foreign language. The implication is that those engaged in "Personnel Management" have had little education and little background experience in that function; the "Personnel Manager" is a political appointee.

## Impediments to HRM Modernization

From an analysis of the preceding comparison, we have identified four major impediments to HRM modernization in Sino–U.S. cooperative ventures: (1) a closed versus an open society, (2) the HRM legitimacy issue, (3) the technology acquisition versus absorption issue, and (4) the need for management infrastructure creation.

### A Closed Versus an Open Society

Modern HRM practices that support industrial technology presuppose the existence of an open society with a concomitant availability and sharing of information. China is still, by and large, a closed society with political ideologies that run counter to many of the goals that Western HRM advocates. Information is frequently unavailable, and when it is available, as mentioned, it is hoarded rather than shared. The gap between the Chinese closed society and the more open U.S. society is significant, and the change required to close the gap, monumental. Suggestions on closing the gap must incorporate consideration of technoeconomic, social structural, ideological, and political differences between the two cultures (Pennings and Gresov, 1986).

### HRM Legitimacy

Western HRM practices are rooted in behavioral science. The introduction of a specific HRM technique, for example, high involvement work settings, in a new context does not have the immediate, clearcut, predictable results that the introduction of an inventory control system, for example, might have. One may even ask, "Are modern HRM practices relevant to the Chinese context"? and "Can modern HRM practices be applied in the China context"? The introduction of modern HRM techniques would require the risk-adverse Chinese to take a large risk based on research that is virtually nonexistent in their culture, nor which they find legitimate. In fact, in 1957 psychology was branded a "bogus bourgeois science" and abolished by the government. This attitude has relaxed since Mao's death (Butterfield, 1982).

The current Chinese personnel system has many flaws that the Party policy officials quickly admit (McLaughlin, 1987). These flaws include a tremendous shortage of management talent, as well as the political interference in enterprise activities. Although steps are currently underway to ameliorate those flaws, change of this magnitude will take a considerable amount of time. The acquisition of management talent has caused the party to implement policies to affect the "brain drain." Students educated abroad must now return to China to work. To guarantee their return, someone "back home" serves as guarantor; if the student fails to return, that person will be punished. In addition, the Chinese government is limiting the number of students that can study in any particular country.

Similarly, steps have been taken to reduce the party's role in the operation of enterprises. These so-called enterprise reforms serve to separate the political and management processes, and further increase productivity by implementing greater Western-based performance appraisal and evaluation systems, as well as adding greater material incentives into the enterprise (McLaughlin, 1987).

The focus of modern HRM practices in the West has been, by and large, within the organization, with the goal of optimizing human and organizational outcomes. HRM systems of a given firm in the U.S. are frequently judged on the extent to which they introduce a source of competitive advantage relative to the firm's strategic challenges.

For the Chinese, these strategic challenges have yet to be operationalized at the enterprise level. At the government policy-making level, the enterprise challenges are to increase productivity and acquire management know-how, while simultaneously lifting tight enterprise controls that have historically been in place. These challenges for the enterprise must, however, be discussed within the Chinese context of economic, political, and social/welfare goals for the country as a whole. In a sense, there are two levels of abstraction implicit in these goals: goals attainable at the country-level, and those that are set for the enterprise. While both sets are equally important and should be considered in any analysis of enterprise changes, it is the challenges which affect the enterprise that concern us here. For enterprises to acquire and maintain efficiency of production, performance must be accurately defined and monitored at the enterprise level. That suggests performance management, evaluation, appraisal, control, as well as reward systems diagnosis—all hallmarks of modern Western HRM systems. We believe that for enterprise reform to occur, HRM systems must have legitimation within the Chinese context.

### Technology Acquisition Versus Absorption

Knowledge, in and of itself, is not always useful. Usefulness lies, instead, in the ability to apply that knowledge. Thus, another stumbling block to the modernization of HRM practices is the Chinese perception that acquisition of a technology, for example, management know-how rather than the absorptive capability to apply that know-how constitutes performance. This technology acquisition versus absorption issue is not germane only for HRM, but for all hard and soft technologies. The Chinese government has historically controlled the enterprise activities. They simultaneously have designated which enterprise should receive new technology, via technology transfer, as well as controlling the paper flow during the transfer process (Von Glinow, Schnepp, and Bhambri, 1988). The Chinese government has, therefore, been able to keep its finger on the pulse of technology acquisition activities and thus has contributed to the acquisition versus absorption dilemma. It is believed that with deregulation of enterprise activities, greater assimilation will occur. However, as previously mentioned, absorptive capacity is a function of many different criteria, all of which must be addressed for success to occur.

### Management Infrastructure Creation

Management modernization sounds appealing; however, the issue may not be modernization of Chinese management practices as much as it is the need for creation of a management infrastructure within the enterprise. The management infrastructure in most enterprises predates 1950, if it exists at all. Thus, management information and control systems are not widely used, nor are any of the major Western management practices and techniques to increase individual and organizational productivity in place. Thus, the lack of a coherently developed management infrastructure, in and of itself, may preclude speedy attention to upgrading the HR function.

Modernization of the Chinese HRM system, recasting the iron rice bowl, is fraught with significant stumbling blocks. However, if Sino–U.S. cooperative ventures are to achieve world class performance, an outcome highly desired by both sides, development and/or modernization of Chinese HRM systems is necessary. To facilitate this modernization, we offer the following framework.

## ▄▄▄ Recasting the Iron Rice Bowl: A Normative Framework

Incorporation of modern HRM techniques within the Chinese enterprise should represent a significant component of any technology transfer. Gee (1981) notes that the effectiveness of a given technology transfer depends upon the ability of the technology recipient to learn and acquire sophisticated know-how. And this includes considerable person-to-person contact, education, training—ultimately communication. But Gee further argues that while effective communications are necessary, they are not sufficient to assure success in technology transfer. There are many other technical, economic, and social factors that bear on the success of any given technology transfer. Von

Glinow, Schnepp, and Bhambri (1988) examine success criteria from the perspective of U.S.–Sino cooperative ventures and focus on a number of different criteria, depending upon the perspectives of the different stakeholders. Given the relatively sparse empirical data currently available on successful U.S.–Sino technology transfers, it is difficult to generate specific prescriptions for the successful incorporation of modern HRM techniques into cooperative ventures. We do, however, offer general prescriptions that have had some consensual appeal to scholars and practitioners involved in U.S.–Sino cooperative ventures in the decade of the eighties. These general prescriptions focus on the integrity of the information that both sides have about modern HRM technologies, the decision-making process and difficulties surrounding this process, and finally, the costs associated with implementation.

### Information

Gee (1981) and others have noted that the transfer of information is a necessary prerequisite for the effective transfer of technology. The Chinese expend considerable effort ascertaining that they are receiving current, state-of-the-art industrial technology. Historically, their concerns have centered around the transfer of hardware—the equipment, components, and raw materials. It is an established fact, however, that it is the software and management know-how that transfers far less easily in U.S.–Sino technology transfers. The transfer of software typically includes training and consulting follow-up, whereas management know-how includes systems for getting the work done, i.e., accounting control, inventory control, distribution, performance planning, management, evaluation, and control. While somewhat greater attention is given to the software transfer, very little attention is currently paid to transferring management skills, including HRM skills, in negotiating cooperative ventures.

Most current assessments of existing U.S.–Sino cooperative ventures indicate that the major dilemma concerns the management of the cooperative venture's human resources.[16] Thus, we take a somewhat radical departure from the "traditional" model of knowledge acquisition, and suggest that the U.S. partner begin early on in the cooperative venture to educate the Chinese partner about the value of modern HRM technology as a subset of the much-desired management know-how. The U.S. partner is well advised to discuss the critical role that modern HRM technology plays in supporting the absorption of industrial technology.

Because these cooperative ventures are still fairly new, and in many cases "experimental," the U.S. partner should stress that they present a comparatively "safe" place to introduce HRM innovations. However, the Chinese look for bargains, and seek to pay as little foreign exchange as possible for technology; therefore, evaluating the cost or value of HRM innovations will undoubtedly be problematic.

A further dilemma exists with respect to acquiring information. Negotiators on behalf of the Chinese enterprise may resist the HRM technology, on grounds that the hardware is more important than the management software technology. The problem may be exacerbated by U.S. negotiators who may be unfamiliar with modern HRM technology, and its usefulness as supporting technology. We acknowledge such claims but suggest that new U.S.–Sino cooperative ventures will parallel the progress of other U.S.–foreign joint ventures that have suffered start-up and subsequent productivity problems due to lack of management know-how. We strongly believe that the U.S. firm that can persuade their Chinese colleagues that management support systems are critical in achieving joint venture performance, will have a distinct competitive advantage over firms that do not take the time to advocate these technologies.

Our strong belief, garnered by anecdotal data as well as case findings, suggests that discussions of this nature must occur if China is ultimately going to reform its cooperative venture enterprise management. The U.S. partner should ideally be willing and prepared to appeal directly to "higher ups," if the discussion regarding HRM innovation stalemates during the negotiation process.

### Decision Making and Its Problems

As discussed earlier, decision making in the Chinese system is time consuming, and the U.S. partner will not be privy to the multiple layers of consensus-seeking that will occur behind the scenes. Top down change implementation is the norm within the U.S. In China, it is the only way, and like any other change in China, approval must come from the top. At this stage, the U.S. partner must exercise patience to determine if the adoption of HRM innovation receives approval. If the U.S. partner receives a negative response at this stage, we strongly advocate that a decision must be made on the part of the senior negotiators to reopen this discussion. Since this is a common negotiating tactic of the Chinese, the U.S. side should be prepared as well to reopen discussions. It might behoove the U.S. side to have the senior HR officer discuss the importance of this type of technology directly with the Chinese negotiators, and answer questions with respect to usefulness of these Western technologies. The U.S. side should ultimately be prepared to terminate the negotiation process if the key negotiators conclude that inclusion of modern HRM techniques and management know-how are *essential* to the success of the joint venture and the Chinese appear *unwilling* to incorporate these technologies into the contract. Admittedly, this is a strong step to take; however, preliminary data now indicate that many joint ventures fail to reach a return on their investment, due to lack of management and HR infrastructure attention. Thus, we feel this conclusion is warranted at this stage, particularly to persuade the Chinese side of the importance the U.S. side places on modern HRM technologies.

## Implementation

The cooperative venture negotiation process is usually lengthy, and HRM innovation transfer should be a critical component of the overall technology transfer package (Teagarden and Von Glinow, 1988). HRM technology will have to be modified to accommodate many of the Chinese system constraints outlined earlier—U.S. HRM technology is not culture-free. We urge that both partners work together to define the specific form that HRM innovation should take in their venture. In the process of implementing these HRM technologies, we believe problem solving and ultimately learning occurs on both sides of the cooperative venture. When both sides participate in what is an ongoing process, both sides learn of impediments and how to deal with those impediments. We believe that education is a critical component at this stage, for all managers. Subsequently, that education will trickle down via training to shop floor personnel. Educating Chinese joint-venture personnel about relevant HRM technologies is not, however, a "one-shot" experience. We advocate an educational process that is repeated for all personnel, so that all recognize the importance of managerial and HR infrastructures. For example, if performance management is desirable to the joint venture, steps must be taken so that all personnel are evaluated according to relevant and recognized performance criteria. This means sensitizing the Chinese to performance indicators and encouraging measurement of those indicators at relevant time periods.

It has been noted that as local personnel become more and more familiar with the HRM processes and norms, it will be important to leverage their knowledge and skills by involving them in discussions of important issues facing the venture. This ensures that their involvement is more than superficial (Bartlett and Yoshihara, 1988).

Equally important is the issue relating to the U.S. expatriate managers. Managers who are on-site participants should be properly briefed by predecessors as to which systems are working properly, and which need improvement. Care must be taken by these expatriate managers to continue with the educational process; venture productivity may suffer otherwise.

Ultimately, for the joint venture to succeed, the HRM systems that have been implemented must be able to support the hardware in the way in which it was designed. Within the Chinese context, this requires frequent reiteration of the interdependence between hard and soft technology and the integral role that soft technology plays in management modernization and ultimately enterprise success. Of course, the ultimate reinforcement is a demonstrable increase in enterprise productivity. However, the ease with which the technology is ultimately diffused is an important criterion as well.

Recasting the iron rice bowl is a tremendous undertaking. It implies changing the existing work environment, and recognizing the Chinese social structural underpinnings. However, if China is to attain world class manufacturing status, it is necessary to implement world class technology, both hard and soft. A framework for the introduction of HRM innovation into Sino–U.S.

cooperative ventures only scratches the surface—there are many unanswered questions.[17]

## Suggestions and Conclusions

In progressive U.S. firms and in academia, discussions frequently focus on the integrated aspects of HR systems—namely the ability to chart essential information flows concerning the management of human resources throughout the organization in response to strategic challenges of the firm. An integrated HR system is one where "HR activities are holistically interdependent and connected, each of which informs the design and implementation of particular activities . . . individual and organizational parts are actively involved with one another."[18] If China is to vault itself into the 21st century, it too must begin to think in terms of integrating individual and enterprise parts, in addition to integrating the enterprise with economic goals of modernization. We believe that this internal alignment holds the most promise for increased organizational effectiveness and efficiency. Such integrated thinking requires a greater leap forward than current enterprise reforms suggest.

We believe the area of Chinese HRM systems is ripe for both research and practice. Researchers attempting to extend current thinking in the area should begin with two basic questions:

1. Will a knowledge of modern HRM theory and practice significantly add to an understanding of Chinese difficulties in absorbing transferred technology?
2. Will more attention to effective HRM systems and subsystems lead to greater individual and enterprise productivity?

The answers to these research questions can serve as a preliminary basis on which to begin testing hypotheses related to effective HRM in Chinese enterprises.

The result of inquiry into these research questions will additionally inform practice. For example, HRM diagnosis can be used to track enterprise change over time, which would allow practitioners to establish *a priori* conditions suitable for individual and/or enterprise change to occur. For example, the Chinese HRM system should be closely linked to the joint venture's business strategy. Once the business strategy is identified, then the strategic needs of the enterprise can be matched with other individual or enterprise factors, such as recruiting, and training processes. Absent these articulated linkages, changes introduced will be difficult to monitor; therefore, their likelihood for successful implementation will be diminished. HRM diagnosis further allows practitioners to design HRM systems that are uniquely appropriate to the Chinese setting and are maximally sensitive to internal and external demands, such as government control, enterprise efficiency or individual performance. It further allows specific HRM subsystems to be developed that will fit within the overall HRM system. This customization will further ensure successful implementation of HRM innovation.

In conclusion, we strongly believe that HRM technology is an integral part, *not an adjunct*, of the industrial technologies that China is importing. The success of these industrial technologies does not occur in a managerial void. Thus, given the differences between many HRM assumptions, the Chinese and U.S. partner will ultimately have to work together to develop a state-of-the-art HRM system that incorporates strengths from both sides. Currently, the Chinese refer to these cooperative ventures as "Sleeping in the same bed, dreaming different dreams." The Chinese dream is industrialization and the U.S. dream is long-term profit: these goals are interdependent and attainable. Our hope is that eventually through the introduction of soft technologies like HRM, Chinese and U.S. partners will be "Sleeping in the same bed, dreaming the same dreams."

## ▬ *Notes*

1. See Campbell (1986) for an in depth discussion of the problems reported by U.S., E.E.C., and Japanese firms engaged in business relationships in China. See also, the Suttmeier and Schnepp articles, at the Symposium on U.S. China Technology Transfer, Woodrow Wilson Center, Smithsonian Institution, Washington, D.C., 1987. Area experts at this conference, and the Philippines Conference, August, 1987 agree that industrial sector development is falling behind planned goals.

2. For considerable discussion, see Schnepp, Bhambri, and Von Glinow (1987), and Von Glinow, Schnepp, and Bhambri (1988).

3. c.f. *China Business Review*, 1986.

4. See Nigel Campbell's (1986) excellent discussion about shortcomings of cooperative ventures in China. (op cit.)

5. Speech by Li Peng, at the National People's Congress, March 25, 1988.

6. Source is Nicholas Lardy, Professor of Economics at University of Washington, 1987.

7. The Chinese Ministries have identified certain firms as leaders in their industry, and prefer to do business with the leaders, not the subsequent developers of the technology. See Schnepp, Bhambri, and Von Glinow (1987) for a discussion of this.

8. Leskin (1986) identified a typology of assumptions about a firm's human resources, employing a stakeholder analysis to uncover assumptional differences regarding HRM practices.

9. See Galbraith (1977).

10. Li Peng, op. cit.

11. Leskin, op. cit.

12. Leskin, op. cit.

13. Current figure estimate that 300,000 students enroll annually in Chinese Universities; Simon (1986).

14. Government compensation is broken down into two categories—direct worker compensation which accounts for 40% of total compensation, and indirect, or other, which accounts for 60% of total compensation.

15. See Von Glinow, Schnepp, and Bhambri (1988) and Schnepp, Bhambri, and Von Glinow (1987) for a discussion of the problems inherent in technology assimilation. In general, technology assimilation is a function of many different factors: the recipient enterprise's ability to manage the "paper flow" or documentation, the ability to change specifications and standards to the Chinese system, the ability of the "trained" workers to perform their new tasks, and the ability of the recipient enterprise to work carefully with the technology-provider. Finally, the receiver must be able to manage the transfer of the "hardware" and trouble-shoot through consulting, the inevitable problems associated with technology assimilation, over a period of time.

16. This conclusion was supported by consensual agreement at the Pacific Rim Management Program, "Doing Business in China," held at USC, June, 1987. In addition, more recent conferences, including the Philippines Conference: August, 1987, "China in a New Era of Science and Technology," and the "Dialectics of Technology Transfer Conference," USC, April, 1988 conclude the same.

17. Excellent references that discuss many of these questions follow. They have been useful in the development of our discussion of Chinese industrial management.
Helburn, I.B. and Shearer, J.C. "Human resources and industrial relations in China: A time of ferment." *Industrial and Labour Relations Review*, 1984, 38, 3–15.
Horsley, J.P. "Chinese labor." *China Business Review*, May–June 1984, 16–25.
Keck, B. "China's managers look West." *China Business Review*, May–June 1985, 36–39.
Laaksonen, O. "The management and power structure of Chinese enterprises during and after the Cultural Revolution: With empirical data comparing Chinese and European enterprises." *Organization Studies*, 5(1), 1–23.
Lee, R.W.H. "Training ground for a new breed of professionals." *China Business Review*, May–June 1985, 39–42.
Lockett, M. and Littler, C.R. "Trends in Chinese enterprise management." *World Development*, 1983, 11, 683–704.
Nelson, J.A. and Reeder, J.A. "Labor relations in China." *California Management Review*, Summer 1985, 27(4), 13–32.
Tung, R.L. *Chinese industrial society after Mao*. Lexington, Mass.: Lexington Books, 1982.
Tung, R.L. "Corporate executives and their families in China: The need for cross-cultural understanding in business." *Columbia Journal of World Business*, Spring 1986, 21(1), 21–26.
Warner, M. "Managing human resources in China: An empirical study." *Organization Studies*, 1986, 7(4), 353–366.
Zamet, J.M. and Bovarnick, M.E. "Employee relations for multinational companies in China." *Columbia Journal of World Business*, Spring 1986, 21(1), 13–19.

18. Von Glinow, Driver, Brousseau, and Prince (1983), p. 25.

# ▬ *References*

Bai Yiyan et al. "Evaluation index system (JXP system) for technological acquisition, digestion and assimilation." Working paper, Research Center for Promotion and Development of Chinese Science and Technology, October 13, 1985.

Bartlett, C. A. and Yoshihara, H. "New challenges for Japanese multinationals: Is organization adaptation their Achilles heel." *Human Resource Management,* Spring 1988, 27(1), 19–44.

Battat, J. Y. *Management in post-Mao China: An insider's view.* Ann Arbor, Mich.: UMI Research Press, 1986.

Butterfield, F. *China: Alive in the bitter sea.* New York: Bantam, 1982.

Campbell, N. *China strategies.* Manchester, England: University of Manchester Press, 1986.

Castaldi, R. M. and Soerjanto, T. "Post-Confucianism management practices and behaviors: A comparison of Japan versus China and South Korea." Paper presented at the Western Academy of Management, March 1988.

Fischer, W. A. *Chinese industrial management: Outlook for the eighties.* Washington, D.C.: U.S. Government Printing Office, 1986.

Fischer, W. A. "Update on enterprise reforms, a presentation at the Pacific Rim Management Seminars on Doing Business With China." USC, Los Angeles, Calif.: May 5–6, 1987.

Galbraith, J. R. *Organization design.* Reading, Mass.: Addison-Wesley, 1977.

Gee, S. *Technology transfer, innovation and international competitiveness.* New York: Wiley, 1981.

Kerr, S. "On the folly of rewarding 'A' while hoping for 'B'." *Academy of Management Journal,* 1975, 18, 769–783.

Lawler, E. E. *High involvement management.* San Francisco, Calif.: Jossey-Bass, 1986.

Leskin, B. "Two different worlds." *New Management,* 1986, 4(1), 22–23.

McLaughlin, D. J. "Personnel management for a billion people." Working paper, December 1987.

Pennings, J. M. and Gresov, C. G. "Technoeconomic and structural correlates of organizational culture: An integrative framework." *Organizational Studies,* 1986, 7(4), 317–334.

Rogers, E. M., *Diffusion of innovations,* 3rd ed. New York: Free Press, 1983.

Schnepp, O., Bhambri, A., and Von Glinow, M. A. "U.S.–China technology transfer: Problems and solutions." Paper presented at the U.S.–China Technology Transfer Symposium, Woodrow Wilson Center, Smithsonian Institution, Washington, D.C., April 12, 1987.

Simon, D. F. Presentation given at the University of Southern California, September 25, 1986.

Teagarden, M. B. and Von Glinow, M. A. "International joint venturing: The Sino–U.S. case." Working paper, Graduate School of Business Administration, University of Southern California, August 1988.

Tung, R. *Industrial society after Mao.* Lexington Mass.: Lexington Books, 1982.

Von Glinow, M. A. and Chung, B. J. "Human resource management: Comparative practices in the U.S., Japan, Korea, and mainland China." *Proceedings: Pan-Pacific Conference IV*, 1987, 69–72.

Von Glinow, M. A., Driver, M., Brousseau, K., and Prince, B. "The design of a career-oriented human resource system." *Academy of Management Review*, 1983, 8(1), 23–32.

Von Glinow, M. A., Schnepp, O., and Bhambri, A. "Assessing success in U.S.–China technology transfer." In Agmon, T. and Von Glinow, M. A. (eds.), *The dialectics of technology transfer.* New York: Oxford University Press, 1988.

# Managing from Below

## WARNER P. WOODWORTH

This article provides a brief overview of the trend toward a bottom-up approach and then focuses in depth on a system of managerial democracy in Spain. Finally, the implications of such an approach for researchers and American managers are evaluated by discussing the problems and prospects of contemporary worker-managed enterprises.

## Toward a System of Worker Participation in Management

The traditional form of labor-management relations in the United States has been the collective bargaining approach. Essentially an adversarial system growing out of earlier decades in this century, it has primarily consisted of fighting for bread-and-butter issues. More recently, new concerns have arisen which have broadened the agenda from wages to health and safety, job security, and so on. The latest thrust has been to institute a bargaining process which also emphasizes joint decision making and the social rights of workers.

Many firms have moved in the direction of work-place democracy, regardless of collective bargaining arrangements or unionization. Socio-technical strategies (Davis and Taylor, 1979; Hackman and Oldham, 1980) have attempted to give workers a voice in the redesign of their jobs. Autonomous work teams at Volvo (Gyllenhammar, 1977) and General Motors (Guest, 1979) have functioned to alter the traditionally exclusive domain of management to make production decisions. Especially since the late 1970s, mainstream U.S. industry has begun to experiment with a variety of innovations to involve workers, at least partially, in the managing of conventional firms (Lawler, 1978).

A more dramatic shift toward worker participation is occurring in some 6,000 American firms with a degree of employee ownership. In the past several years, a number of major airlines and trucking companies have given workers formal representation at the board-of-directors level in exchange for

Source: Warner P. Woodworth. "Managing from Below." Journal of Management, 1986, 12(3), 391–402. Reprinted by permission.

wage concessions. Although not state-mandated, as are the extensive systems of codetermination in Europe, the seeds of a broader, more fundamental change in power are being sown (Woodworth, 1984).

In the minds of most managers and organizational researchers, efforts to involve employee-owners are probably viewed as still somewhat experimental (Bernstein, 1980; Whyte and McCall, 1980). The bulk of worker participation efforts are clearly controlled and usually initiated by management (Conte and Tannenbaum, 1978; Hammer and Stern, 1980). The question of whether or not workers could actually run industry is debatable.

Internationally, some evidence is beginning to emerge that answers such a question affirmatively, or at least addresses its possibilities. The Mondragon system of nearly 90 worker-owned cooperatives sheds light on the possibility of a worker-managed economics. Drawing upon scant reports by other researchers and limited data of my own, a case is made for the potential of a bottom-up strategy for managing organizations.

## ▄▄▄ *The Mondragon Model*

The Mondragon system consists of 89 small- to medium-sized industrial cooperatives in the Basque region of northern Spain. After several decades of severe unemployment in the town of Mondragon, the first small worker cooperative was established in 1956. Subsequently, other co-ops were created, all based on the practical need for jobs and on the democratic ideals of a labor-managed economy.

The cooperatives worked together in forming a support organization, Caja Laboral Popular (CLP) (The People's Savings Bank). It began to operate as a source of funding and expertise services in 1960. The CLP and the associations of cooperatives continued to grow and expand. By 1984, the CLP had over 300,000 individual depositors and assets of $1 billion. During the past decade, Mondragon has produced about 5% of the entire national output in certain consumer goods and comprises 14% of the total industrial output of the province of Guipuzcoa, where the Basque community is located (Bradley and Gelb, 1981).

### *General Structure*

The cooperatives of Mondragon are all internally organized in basically the same way. The members of each cooperative are the ultimate authority. The general assembly of all members meets at least annually and is empowered to examine and approve the balance sheet and vote on organizational procedures. The assembly also elects those workers who are to serve on the supervisory board, which is a type of board of directors (Aranzadi, 1976).

The supervisory board appoints the managers who, in turn, are responsible to the board and through it to the general assembly. This indirect accountability of management has proved to be one of the strengths of the Mondragon cooperatives. It is important to note that managers can never be on the supervisory board. Management is directly responsible for administrative tasks.

The management council is an advisory and consultive body. The members of the council are usually managers, top executives, and outsiders with special expertise and skills.

The members of the cooperative also elect the social council, a body having wide prescriptive and advisory powers regarding all aspects of personnel management—work safety, social security, and wage levels. The watchdog council is the ultimate safeguard in ensuring the democratic running of the cooperatives' affairs. The general assembly elects three members to watch over the supervisory board and the two advisory councils and to inform cooperative members of any irregularities.

Exhibit 1 illustrates the organizational structure of the cooperative.

### Membership

The Contract of Association states that "membership in the Associated Cooperative shall be voluntary and open to all persons who can render the services for which it was established, provided they agree to assume the responsibilities membership entails." This open-door policy ensures that all those who desire and qualify for membership can apply for it. Members who do decide to join and who have the needed skills or training pay an initial contribution in cash of approximately $3,000. This initial investment and the allocation of funds to the individuals' capital accounts make the workers owners of the cooperative.

EXHIBIT 1

### Organizational Structure of the Mondragon Cooperatives

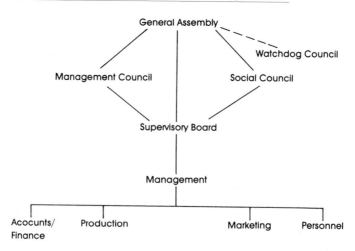

## Decision Making

The major decisions of each cooperative are determined in annual meetings of the general assembly. Simple majority vote is sufficient in determining any policy, approval of a budget, admission of new members, or disciplining violators. Decisions are not determined by the number of shares a person has in the company, but rather on the basis of one person/one vote. This bottom-up structure of workers' control provides a network of participation channels and ensures the democratic sharing of organizational power. Power is not concentrated in an elite group of decision makers at the top, but remains with the membership as a whole.

## Distribution of Wealth

The Mondragon system is unique in that money does not stay strictly within the cooperative. Under the Cooperative Law of Spain, it is permissible to form "second degree cooperatives," organizations that are not entirely worker-owned and controlled but which have associated cooperatives as institutional members. The Caja Laboral Popular is the primary second degree cooperative of the Mondragon system. It is designed to attract the savings of the local community and invest the money in the associated cooperatives. The bank provides computer services, conducts feasibility studies for new cooperatives, and loans up to 50% of the capital needed to launch a new business. Other bank support efforts include securing land for construction, designing new plants, and training workers as they launch their own businesses.

The initial capital contribution made by all new cooperators represents their capital share in the new enterprise. Thus, each new cooperative is financed in part by the capital contribution of its members and augmented by loans from the CLP. The employees' earning structure, being governed by solid principles and ideals of solidarity and equality, is different from that of a traditional firm. The maximum range of earnings is set at a 3 : 1 ratio. In other words, the gross earnings of the highest paid managers cannot be more than three times that of the lowest paid worker-members.

## Work Structures

Because the emphasis of Mondragon is on job creation and democratic control, work structures center on training and job security. For example, in the past the cooperatives' policy has been to send workers back to school to develop further expertise rather than lay them off during slow or bad times. Sometimes workers are temporarily sent to other cooperatives.

Nevertheless, cooperative factories that compete in markets have to organize their work efficiently. This has led to the division and diversification of work and the implementation of new technologies. Jobs center on teamwork rather than on assembly-line labor. The goal is to build a participatory organization by objectives rather than the traditional management by objectives. For instance, in a new furniture factory, all the work is planned by worker teams. A performance index is allocated to the entire team, which then decides how these gains should be distributed among members.

In 1977, several industrial cooperatives jointly established a research and development (R&D) center called Ikerlan in order to compete more efficiently with new technologies and products made elsewhere. Much time and money are devoted to the design of new components for existing products, to the study of competitors' products, and to keeping abreast of international developments.

### Social Organization

Because Mondragon is not a communal system, work and social life are somewhat segregated. However, Mondragon is a complex of organizations, and its cooperative structure and ideals have had an important spillover effect on such social structures as education.

Education has been an important part of the Mondragon model from the beginning. The first cooperative firm was preceded by 13 years of education. Jose Maria Arizmendi, the visionary priest whose ideals significantly shaped the Mondragon system, continually repeated the words, "Knowledge is power; socializing knowledge implies the democratization of power."

The League for Education and Culture was organized years ago as a full-fledged cooperative with a general assembly and supervisory board designed to support the socio-economic system of Mondragon through education. There is great coordination between the educational system and the cooperatives. Students are trained in the skills needed by the cooperatives, and the students' training and research help shape the future. Students are not only trained technically but are also socialized regarding the ideals and functions of Mondragon.

## ■ The Results of Bottom-Up Management

In response to the query, "Can workers run industry?" the Mondragon experience suggests an affirmative answer. Out of the rubble of war and economic stagnation, over 25,000 jobs have been created. Starting with one co-op in 1956, there were eight by 1960, 60 by 1970, and today a total of 89 cooperative firms. Some of the worker-owned firms are fairly large, such as Ulgor, which has 3,400 members and six factories. It is the leading manufacturer of appliances in Spain, producing 300,000 refrigerators and 250,000 stoves a year. Some 25% of its products are marketed internationally. Other firms are smaller, ranging from agricultural equipment to steel construction, graphic arts, plastics, and robotics.

The worker cooperatives are supported by second-degree institutions such as the peoples' bank, a localized system of social security called Lagun Aro which provides welfare benefits and cooperative medical care, an R &

D center, a technical school, and a college of engineering. An elementary cooperative educational system of 44 schools, day-care centers, 14 housing co-ops, some fifty cooperative supermarkets, and 7 agricultural co-ops round out the community structure for building an egalitarian society.

The track record of these cooperative businesses is impressive. Of 89 business start-ups thus far, there has not been a single failure, in contrast to the typical U.S. experience which suffers from a 50% failure rate in the first several years (Greene, 1985). Nor has the Mondragon system suffered massive layoffs during economic downturns. For instance, when the OPEC oil crisis hit in 1974, instead of losing their jobs as did their counterparts in traditional firms worldwide, Mondragon workers in hard-hit firms were simply transferred to the technical school for a few months to obtain new skills. Then they moved into other firms in the cooperative system which were experiencing growth, without losing a single day's pay in the process. In sharp contrast to most industries during that period, Mondragon increased employment by 7.5% while profits grew 26% and exports shot up 56% (Johnson and Whyte, 1977). Over the past decade, total cooperative sales have increased at a rate exceeding 25% annually, while industrial investment has grown 15% each year. Mondragon has a philosophy premised on Schumacher's *Small is Beautiful* (1973) logic, keeping the size of most firms well under 500 members. Such a scale seems to foster healthy interpersonal relationships and strong identification with the enterprise. An important result of this is that there has been only a one-day strike in the past 25 years of cooperative existence, and that was over job classifications in a large co-op. A labor relations climate such as this seems rather enviable when compared with the problems of distrust, alienation, and conflict which characterize all too many conventional firms.

## References

Aranzadi, D. *Cooperativismo industrial como sistema.* Bilbao, Spain: Editorial Elexpuru Hnos., S.A. 1976.

Argyris, C. *Intervention theory and method: A behavioral science view.* Reading, Mass.: Addison-Wesley, 1970.

Argyris, C. and Schon, D. *Organizational learning.* Reading, Mass.: Addison-Wesley, 1978.

Beckard, R. *Organization development: Strategies and models.* Reading, Mass.: Addison-Wesley, 1969.

Bernstein, P. *Workplace democratization: Its internal dynamics.* New Brunswick, N.J.: Transaction Book, 1980.

Bradley, K. and Gelb, A. *Obstacles to a cooperative economy: Lessons from Mondragon.* London: London School of Economics and Political Science, 1981.

Braverman, H. *Labor and monopoly capitalism.* New York: Monthly Review Press, 1974.

Conte, M. and Tannenbaum, A.S. "Employee-owned companies: Is the difference measureable?" *Monthly Labor Review*, 1978 101, 23–28.

Dahl, R.A. "Procedural democracy." In Laslett, P. and Fishkin, J. (eds.), *Philosophy, politics and society* (5th series, pp. 97–133). New Haven, Conn.; Yale University Press, 1979.

Davis, L.E. and Taylor, J.C. *Design of jobs.* Santa Monica, Calif.: Goodyear, 1979.

Drucker, P. *Managing for results.* London: Pan Books, Ltd., 1964.

Edwards, R. *Contested terrain.* New York: Basic Books, 1979.

French, J.R.P., Jr. and Raven, B.H. "The bases of social power." In Cartwright, D. (ed.), *Studies in social power* (pp. 150–167). Ann Arbor: The University of Michigan, 1959.

Gorrono, I. *Experiencia co-operativa en el pais vasco.* Bilbao, Spain, 1975.

Greene, R. "Do you really want to be your own boss?" *Forbes,* October 21, 1985, 86–96.

Guest, R.H. "Quality of work life—Learning from Tarrytown." *Harvard Business Review,* 1979, 57, 76–87.

Gurdon, M.A. "Is employee ownership the answer to our economic woes?" *Management Review,"* 1982, 71, 8–14.

Gyllenhammar, P.G. *People at work.* Reading, Mass.: Addison-Wesley, 1977.

Hackman, J.R. and Oldham, G.R. *Work redesign.* Reading, Mass.: Addison-Wesley, 1980.

Hammer, T. and Stern, R. "Employee ownership: Implications for the organizational distribution of power." *Academy of Management Journal,* 1980, 23, 78–100.

Harris, P.R. and Moran, R.T. *Managing cultural differences.* Houston, Tex.: Gulf, 1979.

Hirschhorn, C. and Associates. *Cutting back: Retrenchment and redevelopment in human and community services.* San Francisco: Jossey-Bass, 1983.

Jackson, S.E. "Participation in decision-making as a strategy for reducing job related strain." *Journal of Applied Psychology,* 1983, 68, 3–19.

Johnson, A.G. and Whyte, W.F. "The Mondragon system of worker production cooperatives." *Industrial and Labor Relations Review,* 1977, 31(1), 18–30.

Kimberly, J.R. and Miles, R.H. (eds.). *The organizational life cycle.* San Francisco: Jossey-Bass, 1980.

Lawler, E.E., III. "The new plant revolution." *Organizational Dynamics,* 1978, 6(3) 3–12.

Likert, R. *The human organization.* New York: McGraw-Hill, 1967.

Locke, E. B. and Schweiger, D.M. "Participation in decision-making: One more look." In Staw, B. and Cummings, L.L. (eds.), *Research in organizational behavior* (Vol. 1, pp. 265–340). Greenwich, Conn.: JAL Press, 1979.

Long, R.J. "The effects of employee ownership in organizational identification, employee job attitudes, and organizational performance: A tentative framework and empirical findings." *Human Relations*, 1978, 31(1), 29–48.

Macy, B.A., Ledford, G.E., and Lawler, E.E., III. *The Bolivar quality of work experiment: 1972–1979.* New York: Wiley-Interscience, 1981.

McGregor, D. *The human side of enterprise.* New York: McGraw-Hill, 1960.

Meek, C. and Woodworth, W. "Employee ownership and industrial relations: The Rath case." *National Productivity Review*, 1982, 1(2), 151–163.

Olson, D.G. "Union experiences with worker ownership. "*Wisconsin Law Review*, 1982, 5, 729–823.

Ouchi, W.G. *Theory Z.* New York: Avon, 1981.

Peters, T.J. and Waterman, R.H., Jr. *In search of excellence.* New York: Harper & Row, 1982.

Schaaf, M. *Cooperatives at the crossroads.* Washington. D.C.: Exploratory Project for Economic Alternatives, 1977.

Schumacher, E.F. *Small is beautiful: Economics as if people mattered.* New York: Harper & Row, 1973.

Steiner, G. *Top management planning.* New York: MacMillan, 1969.

Strauss, G. "Workers' participation in management: An international perspective." In Staw, B. and Cummings, L.L. (eds.), *Research in organizational behavior* (Vol. 4, pp. 173–265). Greenwich, Conn.: JAI Press, 1982.

Tannenbaum, A.S., Kavcic, B., Rosner, M., Vianello, M., and Wieser, G. *Hierarchy in organizations.* San Francisco: Jossey-Bass, 1977.

Taylor, F.W. *The principles of scientific management.* New York: Norton, 1967. (Original work published 1911.)

Thomas, H. *The dynamics of social ownership.* Paper presented at the Third International Conference of the International Association for the Economics of Self-Management, Mexico City, August 1982.

Thomas, H. and Logan, C. *Mondragon: An economic analysis.* London: George Allen and Unwin, 1982.

Watzlawick, P., Weakland, J., and Fisch, R. *Change: Principles of problem formation and problem resolution.* New York: Norton, 1974.

Whetton, D.A. "Organizational decline: A neglected topic in organizational behavior." *Academy of Management Review*, 1980, 5, 577–588.

Whyte, W.F. and McCall, D. "Self-help economics." *Society*, 1980, 17(4), 22–28.

Woodworth, W. "Hard hats in the boardroom: New trends in workers' participation." In Ritchie, J.B. and Thompson, P. (eds.), *Organization and people* (pp. 403–413). St. Paul, Minn.: West, 1984.

# *Cashbuild*

## ALAN BERNSTEIN
## SUSAN SCHNEIDER

Albert Koopman, managing director of Cashbuild, left the company's April 1983 conference deeply concerned. Despite a booming South African economy and a year in which sales revenue had grown by over 60 percent, earnings growth had slowed to a mere 6 percent. Of far deeper concern to Koopman, however, was that signs of severe organizational and motivational strain had begun to emerge. Results of the company's corporate culture survey showed a slip in procompany feeling among managers, from 89 percent in 1982 to 74 percent in 1983. More fundamentally, staff turnover had risen to 120 percent a year on average, and stock shrinkage had reached record levels.

## ■ Origins

Cashbuild started operations in July 1978 as a wholly owned subsidiary of Metro Cash & Carry, South Africa's largest wholesaler of consumer goods. Metro Cash & Carry, as its name implies, provides a wholesale service to retailers through vast warehouses countrywide. Cashbuild's formation resulted from Metro's need to diversify into new avenues of business, one of which was building materials.

Koopman and a colleague at Metro, Gerald Haumant, were given $500,000 and six months in which to start the new business. Their intention was to provide a wholesale cash and carry service, stocking primarily a range of heavy building materials, door frames, steel windows, corrugated iron, and cement. Cashbuild's initial target market was the small builder and shopkeeper, not the man in the street. The specific focus was on black housing—builders and shopkeepers in rural, underdeveloped areas.

The initial idea was to set up many stores in rural areas, but the com-

*Source:* This case was prepared by Alan Bernstein and Susan Schneider as a basis for class discussion rather than to illustrate either effective or ineffective handling of an administrative situation. (c) INSEAD, 1988. This case was adapted by Mark Mendenhall for this book in 1990 by permission from INSEAD. Reprinted by permission.

pany's choice of start-up locations was limited by the parent company. According to Haumant, "Where we could enter at the lowest cost, for example, where Metro had a vacant piece of land, we put up stores." This may, however, have been an advantage in that it allowed the market to be tested nationally.

*3 more locations next year*

The first branch was opened in King Williams Town (200 km inland from Port Elizabeth) in December 1978, followed in 1979 by branches in Vryburg (300 km inland from Durban), Louis Trichardt, and Pietersburg (400 km and 300 km north of Johannesburg, respectively).

In South Africa, country towns like these are typical of the extremely conservative, nationalistic character of white Afrikaaner politics. They form the core electoral base of South Africa's ruling National Party on the one hand, but also reflect a striking contrast between white (First World Culture) and black (Third World Culture).

*Profits #20K to #350K*

By the 1979 financial year end, the first stores were already operating on a profitable basis, and another four were under construction. Pretax profits rose from $20,000 in 1979 to $350,000 in 1981, and the number of stores had increased to twelve, with another five under construction. *# Stores 5 to 12*

Wholesaling is a low-margin, high-volume business, and Cashbuild's initial strategy had paid off. The company's limited range of about 2,000 line items had helped achieve the required stockturns. Emphasis had been placed on developing stringent control procedures and focusing carefully on merchandise mix. According to Haumant,

> We were very disciplined from the word go, in terms of positioning. We wanted to prove that the cash and carry market for building materials was big enough to support a multistore operation and that it could switch a portion of the credit market over to cash and carry. Traditionally, the building industry is undercapitalized and the nature of the materials, their weight and bulk, were not thought to lend themselves to cash and carry selling.

*culture*

*Corporate set in*

One consequence of Cashbuild's business strategy was that a traditional organizational structure and corporate culture had emerged. Staff members were assigned line functions on a strictly hierarchical basis. Job descriptions were rigidly defined in terms of this hierarchy, and an individual's ability to advance through the organization was almost entirely determined by the level at which he entered. This, in turn, was a function of his level of skills, qualifications, and experience at the time of joining the company.

*problems for less educated blacks*

This created problems for black employees. Generations of inferior education and racial prejudice meant that the majority of black workers entered the company at a very low level (general laborers, floor sweepers, goods-receiving clerks, etc.). Their limited prospects for promotion and their rigidly defined areas of responsibility served to demotivate these employees.

Koopman and his executive team had developed the company's original philosophy from their First World perspective. They had thought that they would build a successful organization if they concentrated on just three aspects of their business:

- Give value to the customer
- Innovation and adaptability
- Total commitment to the business and to efficient organizational structures and procedure

As Koopman explains it:

> The way it worked was simple and straightforward. Point number one was easy: In the early days of any business, the one and only thing you understand is that the customer is king. The person who knows all there is to know about the customer is the boss. Point number two is just as easy: The boss knows the market, determines the merchandise mix, refines and implements control systems, even if he doesn't work in them himself. Commitment, of course, is beyond debate. If the boss is 100 percent committed, why shouldn't everyone else be. After all, if business is successful, there will be pay increases, bonuses, better conditions—surely all employees would be committed. As for organizational matters, what would the average worker know about such things?

Cashbuild's management began to understand that the company's traditional organizational structure and autocratic management style had resulted in "corporate rigor mortis." The organization had lost the single-mindedness of its early days. The consequence of management's adherence to a hierarchical organizational chart (prominently displayed at Cashbuild's head office) was that individual goals and values were no longer congruent with management's goals and values, and neither of the two was in keeping with the company's philosophy.

## ■ Organizational Crisis

Koopman and his team had been monitoring Cashbuild's slipping performance for almost a year. With margins down, profits falling, and an unmotivated staff, Cashbuild had lost direction. Koopman, a restless and inquisitive character with an eclectic appetite for inspiration from sources as diverse as Marx and Sartre to Alvin Tofler's *Future Shock* and Schumacher's *Small is Beautiful*, set out to question his white managers about the company's poor state. "I went round all the branches and asked a thousand questions," says Koopman. "I found that most of my managers blamed their black force for being indolent, not interested, and unmotivated." When he probed further into their perceptions of his own management style, the response was that they found him to be "pompous, egocentric, dictatorial, and authoritarian."

Koopman recognized that these were precisely the kind of attributes inculcated by the system under which most whites are educated and brought up in South Africa. But what most concerned Koopman after this sobering

experience was the thought that if his white lieutenants had these perceptions, what were black workers' attitudes?

One of the questions he asked black workers on his systematic tour of
Cashbuild's then eighteen branches, was "How does Cashbuild make its
money? How do you make yours?" The standard reply went something like
this, "My wages come from the boss. He gets the money from the tin boxes
delivered by a green van (Fidelity Guards) which comes round on Fridays.
He buys stocks, and these get rung up on the till. Every night he takes the
money home, works out what he owes us, and pays our wages." For Koopman, this represented a perfect description of how it happened but revealed
total ignorance of how money was earned at Cashbuild.

Koopman became increasingly aware that the company's organizational
and motivational crisis was rooted in South Africa's complex social and economic structures, which were then so intrinsically part of Cashbuild's corporate culture. Black workers viewed their jobs from a perspective of generations of educational disadvantage and racial prejudice. As a result of being
denied the rewards of "free enterprise" in terms of land and business ownership, black workers' expectations were restricted to short-term needs. All too
often, a job became simply a means to earn enough money to survive on
a day-to-day basis. White workers, by contrast, viewed their jobs from the
perspective of long-term career planning. With the advantage of superior education and access to the rewards of the capitalist system, their expectations
tended to relate to the accumulation of wealth and personal status.

## Cashbuild's Transformation

Koopman embarked on a process of organizational change by conducting three regional workshops with managers, regional managers, and head
office teams. Each workshop dealt with questions such as:

- What do you think of the CEO as a leader?
- How do you rate your regional manager?
- How effective are our marketing strategies?
- What about black advancement?
- How do we cope with environmental change?
- Is our internal communication effective?
- How do you view union activities?
- How are we going to break across cultural lines?

According to the managers taking part in the workshops, black employees
were just not motivated. With disturbing consistency, managers responded
that blacks "don't care for the company," "are badly educated and don't understand the business," or "won't talk or open up."

Koopman concluded that employee demotivation could stem only from
inappropriate management practices. The Cashbuild culture with its boxed

hierarchy was meaningless to them. Workers could not see the connection between their worth and the company's efforts. With this conclusion came the general realization that, in South Africa, managers have separated the social man from the productive man who is paid for his capacity as a productive unit rather than for his pride in his labor. Further, most South African managers judge and reward their labor force by means of rank and status—something the Cashbuild workers said they despised. An individual had to "earn the right" to be a leader before he could step out ahead of the team, and the workers preferred the security of the team to individual treatment.

Finally, Koopman's perceptions of the cause of Cashbuild's organizational crises led to his understanding that any successful restructuring had to deal with two central issues:

1. Black workers would not relate to the business and its functions until they obtain full participation, with an accompanying right to benefit both materially and spiritually.
2. A hopelessly inadequate educational system leaves black job entrants at a considerable disadvantage to their counterparts, not only in knowledge and skills but in overall perception of business.

The three regional workshops served as precursors to many more formal and informal sessions that cut across every level of the company's structure. Koopman understood the level of risk that he was taking in search of appropriate management solutions. He nevertheless recognized that having decided to ensure survival by implementing a philosophy of worker participation, he had to be seen as taking action. Cashbuild called the process MBFA, Management By Fumbling Around. Koopman was convinced the process of discussion and "value-trading" at every level of the company was the key to the successful redirection of Cashbuild.

Throughout the process, Cashbuild's management attempted to categorize the issues that were raised, and five key elements came up repeatedly: the customer, the employee, the company, the competitor/supplier, and motivation.

> We realized that these five elements could give us our starting point. I started to see that our five key elements were interdependent, and at the same time, our marketing, sales—in fact, our whole business—revolved around each employee. The importance of the team started to mean something tangible to me—there could be no distinction in color, sex, class, or job classification. When you've heard a man's heartbeat, you can never think him into a rigid hierarchical box.

Cashbuild's first step in implementing participative management was to create a new "holistic" organizational structure, which redefined corporate objectives.

# ▬ *Participative Management: The Care Philosophy*

Koopman's views on participative management developed from the notion that Cashbuild's managers could no longer be seen as an extension of capitalist ownership. Since capital and land are out of reach for most black people in South Africa, either through lack of resources or simply through legislation, their only access to direct control is through the enterprise itself (policy and decision making) and through labor. By giving every employee a say in the policy and decision-making process, a sense of vested interest could be created. As a matter of necessity rather than ideology, participative management meant a move to communal ownership of Cashbuild's means of production. In late 1983, five years was envisioned to build a workable system.

Says Koopman:

> It's difficult now to reconstruct how the philosophy evolved. By no means was it a tidy sequence of events! We went into the whole process of change without any prerequisites or preconceptions. It was an article of faith that it should be an open-ended process. There was constant discussion. Management would come up with ideas, and we'd talk to workers about them—and they would respond with more ideals, suggestions, demands. So it went.

One of the enormous problems to be overcome was the immense communication gap that existed between black and white employees. Koopman was made especially aware of this gap when a puzzled black employee asked "Why are you angry with me, Mr. Koopman?" When this was met with an equally puzzled expression from Koopman, the employee went on to say "You must shake hands like this," serving him a limp handshake. To the employee, a firm handshake signaled anger.

Since 1983, Cashbuild had been developing a company philosophy and organizational environment that aimed at ensuring total commitment by all employees. A system of CARE groups had been embarked on in 1984 in an attempt to build team cohesion. Modeled on deeply rooted feelings of team, family, and nation cohesion in black African culture, the CARE group philosophy was based on the idea that "the company cares about its people, and the people must care about the company."

The CARE group concept evolved as a means of bridging this cultural gap. The groups were intended to provide a platform for participation in company affairs by all staff members. They were also intended to start the formation of an internal power base for staff. Cashbuild's employees were broken down into five main groups:

CARE group 1: Caddies, sweepers, and general laborers
CARE group 2: Goods-receiving clerks, cashiers, receptionists, and
other semiskilled tasks

CARE group 3: Managers, trainers, and long-term advancement trainees

CARE group 4: Administrators, bookkeepers, and regional managers

CARE group 5: CEO, operations manager, buyer, finance manager, and personnel manager

A president was elected for each group by a majority vote. The president's function was to interface with management on issues of common concern. Meetings were to be held each month with members of the next level of CARE group present so that issues between the different levels could be confronted. One of the first tasks of the CARE groups was to design a "statement of company policy." The resulting booklet was translated into nine languages, and all staff members—from CEO to tea person—could be reprimanded by anyone else for violation of the company philosophy.

*Formal policies into effect*

# *Computex Corporation*

## MARTIN HILB

Mr. Peter Jones
Vice President—Europe
Computex Corporation
San Francisco / USA

---

Goteborg, May 30, 1985

The writers of this letter are the headcount of the Sales Department of Computex Sweden, A.S., except for the Sales Manager.

We have decided to bring to your attention a problem which unsolved probably will lead to a situation where the majority among us will leave the company within a rather short period of time. None of us want to be in this situation, and we are approaching you purely as an attempt to save the team the benefit of ourselves as well as Computex Corporation.

We consider ourselves an experienced, professional, and sales-oriented group of people. Computex Corporation is a company which we are proud to work for. The majority among us have been employed for several years. Consequently, a great number of key customers in different areas of Sweden see us as representatives of Computex Corporation. It is correct to say that the many excellent contacts we have made have been established over years; many of them are friends of ours.

These traits give a very short background because we have never met you. What kind of problem forces us to such a serious step as to contact you?

Problems arise as a result of character traits and behavior of our General Manager, Mr. Miller.

Firstly, we are more and more convinced that we are tools that he is utilizing in order to "climb the ladder." In meetings with us individually, or as a group, he gives visions about the future, how he values us, how he wants to delegate and involve us in business, the importance of cooperation and communication, etc. When it comes to the point, these phrases turn out to be only words.

Mr. Miller loses his temper almost daily, and his outbursts and reactions are not equivalent to the possible error. His mood and views can

*Source:* Reprinted by permission of the author.

change almost from hour to hour. This fact causes a situation where we feel uncertain when facing him and consequently are reluctant to do so. Regarding human relationships, his behavior is not acceptable, especially for a manager.

The extent of the experience of this varies within the group due to our location. Some of us are seldom in the office.

Secondly, we have experienced clearly that he has various means of suppressing and discouraging people within the organization.

The new "victim" now is our Sales Manager, Mr. Johansson. Because he is our boss, it is obvious that we regret such a situation, which to a considerable extent influences our working conditions.

There are also other victims among us. It is indeed very difficult to carry through what is stated in our job descriptions.

We feel terribly sorry and wonder how it can be possible for one person almost to ruin a whole organization.

If this group consisted of people less mature, many of us would have left Computex Corporation already. So far only one has left the company due to the above reasons.

From September 1, two new Sales Representatives are joining the company. We regret very much that new employees get their first contact with the company under the present circumstances. An immediate action is therefore required.

It is not our objective to get rid of Mr. Miller as General Manager. Without going into details, we are thankful for what he has done to the company from a business point of view. If he could control his mood, show some respect for his colleagues, keep words, and stick to plans, we believe that we can succeed under his leadership.

We are fully aware of the seriousness of contacting you, and we have been in doubt whether or not to contact you directly before talking to Mr. Miller.

After serious discussions and considerations, we have reached the conclusion that a problem of this nature unfortunately cannot be solved without some sort of action from the superior. If possible, direct confrontation must be avoided. It can only make things worse.

We are hoping for a positive solution.

Six of your Sales Representatives in Sweden

Peter Jones let out a long sigh as he gazed over the letter from Sweden. "What do I do now?" he thought, and began to reflect on the problem. He wondered who was right and who was wrong in this squabble, and he questioned whether he would ever get all the information necessary to make a wise decision. He didn't know much about the Swedes, and was unsure whether this was strictly a work problem or a "cross-cultural" problem. "How can I tease those two issues apart?" he asked himself, as he locked his office and made his way down the hallway to the elevator.

As Peter pulled out of the parking garage and onto the street, he began to devise a plan to deal with the problem. "This will be a test of my conflict management skills," he thought, "no doubt about it!" As he merged into the freeway traffic from the on-ramp and began his commute home, he began to wish that he had never sent Miller to Sweden in the first place. "But would Gonzalez or Harris have done any better? Would I have done any better?" Few answers seemed to come to him as he plodded along in the bumper-to-bumper traffic on Interstate 440.

# *Performance Appraisal and Compensation*

# Continuity and Change in Japanese Management

## TOMASZ MROCZKOWSKI
## MASAO HANAOKA

The relationship between tradition and change in Japan has always been complicated by the fact that change itself is a tradition.

*—Edward Seidensticker*

For Japan, the era of competing on the basis of being the low-cost imitator of the West and of using exports to stimulate its domestic economy came to a dramatic end with the rise of the yen. Japanese companies reacted by shifting the competitive battleground to a different plane. They have moved up-market to compete on the basis of quality, innovation, and product leadership while defending their cost structures against NICs and Western competitors by rapid automation. They have also sped up the process of multinationalization, moving lower value-added production offshore and locating production facilities close to consumer markets in Europe and the U.S.

This strategy has required accelerated restructuring of the Japanese economy, including dramatic shifts in employment. It has also required that the Japanese management system be modified to make it more efficient. One of the most important changes is that the "new" management system will have to encroach upon the traditional practices of lifetime employment and seniority-based wages.

Recent economic results indicate that after the shock of the high yen the Japanese economy has pulled off another "miracle"; and those in the West who saw an end to Japanese competitiveness have been proven wrong again. In 1987, Japanese industrial output was 4% higher than in the previous year. The profits of Japanese manufacturers grew by 25–30% in fiscal 1987 (after falling by 29% in 1986) and investment in new plants and machinery grew by a total of 33% in real terms in 1984–86.

Remarkably, Japanese manufacturing wage costs have been kept in

*Source:* Tomasz Mroczkowski and Masao Hanaoka. "Continuity and Change in Japanese Management." *California Management Review*, Winter 1989, 39–52. Reprinted by permission.

check. After adding in productivity growth, Japanese firms now have lower unit wage costs than they did a year ago (while West Germany's have leapt by almost 5%). Japan has achieved all this while adjusting the size of its workforce, shifting manpower out of sunset industries and into new industries and the service sector, and also moving production offshore. This remarkable achievement could not have been possible without major changes in Japanese companies' employment and reward systems—changes that many Western observers believed would be so disruptive and difficult that they would take a much longer time to implement.

This article assesses the magnitude and direction of the changes in the employment and promotion systems inside Japanese companies. An evaluation of these changes is crucial to understanding Japan's competitive strategy for the 1990s.

## The Romantic Myth of Japanese Management

Almost all of the many books and articles on Japanese management published in the West have been written by non-Japanese observers. Frequently, these analyses have been used for the purpose of criticizing the shortcomings and failures of Western management. This practice has contributed to the creation of the myth of Japanese management. Until recently, this myth has gone largely unchallenged, especially in the United States.

The system of manpower management developed in the sixties and seventies that has served Japan so well is currently undergoing a gradual transformation. Even before economic and demographic conditions made it obvious, perceptive Japanese observers pointed out the inherent weaknesses of "Japanese management":

- The system of lifetime commitment and groupism encouraged employee dependency and suppressed individual creativity.
- The employment system discriminated against non-lifelong employees (temporary employees, women, part-timers, seasonal laborers and employees hired midway through their careers) and prevented the formation of a free horizontal labor market.
- The seniority-based system of rewards created a promotion gridlock for middle management and especially for the younger outstanding employee.[1]

Japanese executives have long been aware of the disadvantages of their system but believed these were outweighted by its strengths. However, by the mid-1980s many companies found themselves unable to fully maintain the "old system." The search for a new Japanese management system was assumed with a great deal of urgency.

# ▰ *Continuous Evolution and the Crisis of Japanese Management*

In order to understand how it was possible to effect major changes in Japanese manpower management relatively smoothly and effectively, it is important to realize that Japanese management practices have never been static but rather have evolved through continual adjustments to new economic, social, and competitive priorities.

Prior to World War II, Japanese industry used a rigid form of status promotion *(shikaku-seido)*. Employees were divided into *shokuin* (white collar) and *koīn* (blue collar) workers, with simple seniority promotion ladders within each category and no possibility of upward mobility for *koīn* workers into the *shokuin* category. After the end of World War II, during the American occupation, a number of important changes occurred. A labor standards law was introduced and labor union growth occurred. The U.S. Army introduced management training programs, and wage systems were changed as the old employee status classification system collapsed. An attempt was made to introduce an American-style job classification system. While this attempt largely failed, companies, to varying degrees, began using ability and skills instead of seniority alone as a basis for job grade assignment.

During the 1950s and 1960s, Japan experienced labor shortages due to very rapid industrial expansion. Many of the familiar features of "Japanese management" were broadly introduced at that time: by the mid-sixties more than 70% of companies used employee suggestion schemes and almost a third used regular employee morale surveys. Companies used core groups of lifetime employees who were promoted using systems of grade ladders within integrated functions. Because of the labor shortages, part-time employment of women outside the lifetime system became widespread. The actual number of hours worked was reduced while efforts were made to prolong the retirement age from 55 to 60.

Japanese management scholars regard the seventies as marking a "peak" in the development of the practices which the world learned to regard as "Japanese management." However, in the seventies there were also a number of factors that demanded modifications in Japanese personnel management practices. Economic growth rates were, on average, only half that of the previous decade. With broad introduction of automation, Japanese companies began hiring significantly fewer recruits into entry-level positions. Over the years, this caused the average age of employees moving up the seniority ladder to increase, putting pressure on average wage costs. Real opportunities for advancement became increasingly limited, and attempts to boost sagging morale brought a proliferation of new titles empty of substance.

Japanese management reacted to these problems by increasing flexibility in the employment and reward systems. Temporary transfers of surplus employees and flex-time systems were introduced. Systems of "specialist" or "expert" posts with grades similar to those for managers were created to provide ways of promoting staff workers who had already reached the highest grade and for whom managerial positions were unavailable. Efforts were made to decrease the importance of seniority as the major condition for pay raises and introduce merit components into wage and bonus systems.[2]

The early eighties saw the sharp rise in the value of the dollar, making Japanese goods very competitive in the U.S. The Japanese experienced an export boom which allowed them to postpone some of the inevitable changes in their economic policies.[3] The sharp rise of the yen in 1985 suddenly put enormous pressures on many Japanese companies. To remain competitive they had to control costs, innovate, restructure, and often move offshore. In 1986, Japan's exports declined by 15.9% and the profits of Japanese companies also declined dramatically. Because of the strong yen, the number of bankruptcies shot up (since May 1986, more than 60 companies have gone bankrupt every month) and unemployment increased.[4] Capital productivity has been decreasing in Japan in the past few years. While total factor productivity in Japan grew more rapidly than in other countries in the 1960s and 1970s, in the 1980s the growth rate leveled off. Japanese productivity specialists forecast that under these conditions it will be very difficult to continue to make the kind of productivity improvements that Japanese companies made in the past.[5] The Japanese have reached a watershed in their economic policies.

By the mid-1980s, the entire system of Japanese management faced three major challenges:

- Japanese companies have mainly relied on the variable bonus and flexible benefits to control their wage costs. After dramatic rise in the value of the yen, the problem of cost containment became much more difficult. Average wages in Korea and Taiwan are now respectively 8 times and 6 times lower than in Japan. The challenge many Japanese companies face is how to reduce labor costs, cut capacity, and restructure without resorting to massive layoffs.
- The second major challenge Japanese management faces is how to continue to *motivate* employees and managers in a new environment in which the system of evaluation and rewards, as well as employee attitudes and expectations, is changing.
- The third challenge for Japanese management is how to redesign employment relationships in a way that would blend the advantages of the older system of dependence on the company with the necessity to promote employee self-reliance, initiative, and creativity.

## The Emergence of a New Management Paradigm

### Restructuring: Methods of Employment and Wage Control

For many Japanese companies, especially those in mature industries, the most immediate problem is how to achieve significant reductions in employment levels as they reduce capacity and modernize. For example, over the next three years the three biggest Japanese steel companies plan to shed 40,000 jobs without hiring anyone.

This process is being carefully monitored by the Japanese Labor Ministry as well as by the Japanese Confederation of Labor, which compiled a survey of how Japanese companies carried out employment cuts and what methods they intended to use for future reductions (see Exhibits 1 and 2). The tables reveal the lengths to which Japanese companies will go to avoid lay-offs. All companies rely on hiring freezes and to a lesser extent on elimination of overtime. Both of these approaches are also commonly used in the West. What is peculiarly Japanese is the extensive use of job rotation and employee reassignments. In the case of larger companies (over 1,000 employees), almost half report using this as a major method of employment restructuring. Although part-time workers are indeed often laid off, firings and lay-offs of full-time employees are reported by less than 10% of the companies surveyed (with the exception of the very small companies). Interestingly, in their plans for the future, the companies intend to continue the same policies by putting even greater emphasis on job-rotation. Lay-offs of full-time employees will continue to be rare.

Some of the methods used by Japanese management to control wage and salary costs differ even more from Western practices. Wage, salary, and bonus reductions are shared by all groups in the enterprise: directors and managers as well as employees. Even when temporary or permanent lay-offs *are* used, they do not have the same implications for employees as similar practices in the West. Japanese companies widely use inter-company manpower leasing and transfer. The system is run by company groups called *igyōshu kōryu*[6] and is organized on a territorial basis with local government and Chamber of Commerce support. According to a 1987 survey by the NHK (*Nippon Hosō Kyokai*, Japan Broadcasting Corporation), there are 471 local centers in which 17,000 Japanese companies participate. These centers exchange information on manpower surpluses and shortages and arrange for temporary or permanent transfers between the participating companies. They may also engage in joint new business/new product development. In effect this system extends the lifetime employment principles while maintaining flexibility and economic rationality.

According to some Japanese manpower policy experts, Japanese companies will be moving towards more flexibility in their employment and wage policies. International and domestic competition may ultimately force companies to begin treating a larger portion of labor costs as variable costs rather than as fixed costs.[7]

## The New Motivational System: Performance-Based Evaluation and Rewards

### The Changing Importance of Seniority

It is broadly believed that the principle of seniority governs the Japanese system of motivating employees, rewarding loyalty, and maintaining group

EXHIBIT 1

## 1986 Employee Reduction (in number of companies and % of total responses)

| Methods of employment control | SIZE OF COMPANY (BY NUMBER OF EMPLOYEES) | | | | | All companies |
|---|---|---|---|---|---|---|
| | 1–99 | 100–299 | 300–999 | 1,000–2,999 | 3,000 + | |
| Hiring freeze | 54 | 48 | 57 | 23 | 21 | 203 |
| | 36.5% | 30.8% | 42.5% | 54.8% | 51.2% | 39.0% |
| Part-time workers terminated | 36 | 24 | 22 | 10 | 14 | 106 |
| | 24.3% | 15.4% | 16.4% | 23.8% | 34.1% | 20.3% |
| No overtime | 23 | 19 | 21 | 8 | 6 | 77 |
| | 15.5% | 12.2% | 15.7% | 19.0% | 14.6% | 14.8% |
| Shortening of working day | 11 | 12 | 7 | 2 | | 32 |
| | 7.4% | 7.7% | 5.2% | 4.8% | | 6.1% |
| Job rotation | 29 | 34 | 30 | 17 | 19 | 129 |
| | 19.6% | 21.8% | 22.4% | 40.5% | 46.3% | 24.8% |
| Temporary lay-offs | 2 | 2 | | 1 | 2 | 7 |
| | 1.4% | 1.3% | | 2.4% | 4.9% | 1.3% |
| Planned employee reductions | 9 | 3 | 5 | 2 | 3 | 22 |
| | 6.1% | 1.9% | 3.7% | 4.8% | 7.3% | 4.2% |

| | | | | | | |
|---|---|---|---|---|---|---|
| *Employees fired* | 23 15.5% | 12 7.7% | 8 6.0% | 23 7.1% | 3 7.3% | 49 9.4% |
| *Other* | 8 5.4% | 12 7.7% | 4 3.0% | 3 7.1% | 4 9.8% | 31 6.0% |
| **Methods of Wage Control** | | | | | | |
| *Overtime pay eliminated* | 46 31.1% | 66 42.3% | 64 47.8% | 23 54.8% | 22 53.7% | 221 42.4% |
| *Directors/managers pay reduced* | 45 30.4% | 32 20.5% | 31 23.1% | 6 14.3% | 9 22.0% | 123 23.6% |
| *Postpone increases or reduce basic pay* | 55 37.2% | 44 28.2% | 38 28.4% | 12 28.6% | 13 31.7% | 162 31.1% |
| *Director's bonus reduced* | 62 41.9% | 44 28.2% | 45 33.6% | 9 21.4% | 10 24.4% | 170 32.6% |
| *General bonus reduced* | 56 37.8% | 45 28.8% | 39 29.1% | 11 26.2% | 9 22.0% | 160 30.7% |
| *Other* | 6 4.1% | 3 1.9% | 8 6.0% | 2 4.8% | 3 7.3% | 22 4.2% |
| **Total number of companies** | 148 | 156 | 134 | 42 | 41 | 521 |

*Source:* Susumu KoyōChousei. Ministry of Labor Employment Rationalization Survey, 1986.

EXHIBIT 2

*Future Reduction Forecast (in number of companies and % of total responses)*

| *Methods of employment control* | SIZE OF COMPANY (BY NUMBER OF EMPLOYEES) | | | | | All companies |
|---|---|---|---|---|---|---|
| | 1–99 | 100–299 | 300–999 | 1,000–2,999 | 3,000+ | |
| Hiring freeze | 57<br>34.8% | 60<br>36.8% | 57<br>40.4% | 22<br>51.2% | 15<br>34.1% | 211<br>38.0% |
| Part-time workers terminated | 46<br>28.0% | 37<br>22.7% | 25<br>17.7% | 8<br>18.6% | 12<br>27.3% | 128<br>23.1% |
| No overtime | 42<br>25.6% | 28<br>17.2% | 26<br>18.4% | 7<br>16.3% | 7<br>15.9% | 110<br>19.8% |
| Shortening of working day | 23<br>14.0% | 12<br>7.4% | 12<br>8.5% | 4<br>9.3% | 1<br>2.3% | 52<br>9.4% |
| Job rotation | 38<br>23.2% | 37<br>22.7% | 40<br>8.4% | 17<br>39.5% | 27<br>61.4% | 159<br>28.6% |
| Temporary lay-offs | 7<br>4.3% | 4<br>2.5% | 4<br>2.8% | 1<br>2.3% | 3<br>6.8% | 19<br>3.4% |
| Planned employee reductions | 10<br>6.1% | 7<br>4.3% | 6<br>4.3% | 4<br>9.3% | 2<br>4.5% | 29<br>5.2% |

| | | | | | | Total |
|---|---|---|---|---|---|---|
| Employees fired | 20 12.1% | 8 4.9% | 9 6.4% | 2 4.7% | 2 4.5% | 41 7.4% |
| Other | 6 3.7% | 9 5.5% | 5 3.5% | 4 9.3% | 7 15.9% | 31 5.6% |
| **Methods of wage control** | | | | | | |
| Overtime pay eliminated | 69 42.1% | 77 47.2% | 72 51.1% | 23 53.5% | 21 47.7% | 262 47.2% |
| Directors/managers pay reduced | 45 27.4% | 28 17.2% | 29 20.6% | 8 18.6% | 10 22.7% | 120 21.6% |
| Postpone increases or reduce basic pay | 70 42.7% | 55 33.7% | 28 19.9% | 6 14.0% | 13 29.5% | 172 31.0% |
| Director's bonus reduced | 74 45.1% | 49 30.1% | 43 30.5% | 8 18.6% | 8 18.2% | 182 32.8% |
| General bonus reduced | 85 51.8% | 70 42.9% | 56 39.7% | 12 27.9% | 15 34.1% | 238 42.9% |
| Other | 7 4.3% | 5 3.1% | 3 2.1% | 2 4.7% | 3 6.8% | 20 3.6% |
| **Total number of companies:** | 164 | 163 | 141 | 43 | 44 | 555 |

Source: Susumu KoyōChousei. Ministry of Labor Employment Rationalization Survey, 1986.

harmony. In fact, the pure seniority principle has been systematically eroding in Japan, as evidenced by results of surveys carried out in Japanese companies by the *Romu Gyosei Kenkyujo* (a private research foundation). In the decade between 1978 and 1987, according to the personnel departments of the surveyed companies, the contribution of the seniority factor to pay raises systematically declined from an average of 57.9% to 46% while the contribution of the performance factor increased from 42.1% to 54% (see Exhibit 3).

Low economic growth rates, which result in fewer recruits being hired, have made it uneconomical for companies to continue to pay ever higher wages to an increasing proportion of their senior employees. Japanese companies have reacted to this situation by remodeling the motivational system. While the retirement age in Japan has been extended, many companies are using various forms of early retirement incentives. Often, employees are finding their wage increases capped at age 40–45. In fact, in many companies average pay may drop by as much as 20% after age 50.

In order to gauge the magnitude of change taking place in the motivation systems employed by Japanese companies, it is necessary to understand the relationships between seniority and the other factors that affect employee promotion. However important, seniority has never been the only factor determining a wage or salary in a Japanese company. Assignment of an individual to a wage/salary grade depended largely on education and job-related skills. In inter-grade promotions, both of these factors also played an important part. In the process of annual within-grade raises and bonus awards, however, it is general company performance which is the important factor in the increment negotiations. Under the traditional system the final outcome in terms of a wage increment would typically incorporate a combination of the negotiated raise and seniority. The raise formula would thus look like this:

| individual base wage/salary within grade | × | negotiated % raise ("up rate") | − | distribution by length of service years (expressed in yen not as a %) | = raise |
|---|---|---|---|---|---|

Loyalty to the company and peer pressure were judged to be sufficiently strong to motivate employees. The outstanding employee was not singled out for immediate large rewards but was kept motivated by interesting assignments, training opportunities, and eventual promotion to a higher grade or managerial position ahead of his peers.

According to a study performed by the authors at the Institute of Business Research at Daito Bunka University, this system has been undergoing substantial modifications. The personnel managers from thirty large and medium-sized companies representing a cross-section of Japanese manufacturing and service sectors were surveyed and they felt without exception that the old seniority system could not be maintained without substantial change. On the other hand, only a handful of the managers wanted to abolish it com-

EXHIBIT 3

## Relative Contributions of Seniority and Merit Factors to Pay Raises

|      | Seniority | Ability (Merit) |
| ---- | --------- | --------------- |
| 1978 | 57.9%     | 42.1            |
| 1983 | 54.4      | 45.6            |
| 1984 | 49.0      | 51.0            |
| 1987 | 46.0      | 54.0            |

Source: Rōmu Gyōsei Kenkyūjo. July 8–September 11, 1987. (1,900 Japanese companies surveyed).

pletely. The majority of companies were planning and implementing gradual modification of the system allowing them to keep some of its most useful features. Modifications usually started with the introduction of merit evaluation into the promotion/reward process.

### Performance Appraisal Japanese Style

The *Shikaku* (position title) classification system is used to form the basis of grading, promotion, wage, and bonus decisions in Japanese companies. This gradually has been giving way to performance appraisal and merit rating systems. Rather than replacing the old system with a new one, Japanese companies grafted performance evaluation onto the old system by incorporating it as a factor in the formulas used for pay increment calculation. In companies which have embraced the individual merit rating system, the formula would typically look as follows:

$$
\begin{array}{l}
\text{individual} \;\times\; \text{average} \;\;\;\;\times\; \text{individual} \;\;\times\; \text{seniority} \;\;= \text{raise} \\
\text{base salary} \;\;\;\;\; \text{"up rate"} \;\;\;\;\;\;\; \text{merit rating} \;\;\; \text{coefficient} \\
\text{wage} \;\;\;\;\;\;\;\;\;\;\;\; \text{within each} \\
\;\;\;\;\;\;\;\;\;\;\;\;\;\;\;\;\;\;\; \text{grade (\%)}
\end{array}
$$

The actual impact of performance evaluations on pay varies from company to company and also depends on the position and grade of the employee. According to a 1985 study by the Japan Personnel Policy Research Institute, 35% of managerial bonus awards depended on the performance appraisal component, while for clerks this rate was only 22%.[8] Individual performance appraisal results can account for anywhere from 20% to 50% of the pay increment. The higher percentage is found in those companies that have pursued change most aggressively, including companies under Western management and joint-venture operations.

The Japanese concepts of performance and achievement are not the same as in the West and the relative importance of different components and ways of measuring and weighting them are different. The concept of personnel evaluation most widely used in Japan is the merit rating (*jinji kōka*). This concept is based on educational attainment and job ability factors such as communication skills, cooperativeness, and sense of responsibility. *Jinji koka* is being gradually replaced by performance evaluation based on work results. The Japanese concept of performance (*gyō seki*) is distinct from the Western concept and includes not only the achievement of actual results, but the expenditure of good faith effort. New performance evaluation systems are currently being introduced in 75% of Japanese companies.[9]

Individual achievement based rewards are likely to continue to grow in importance in the motivational systems in Japanese companies. One of the factors contributing to the problems of motivating Japanese employees is the erosion of labor unions. At one time, 56% of the labor force belonged to unions. As the Japanese economy matured, labor union membership declined and union participation rates have now fallen below 28%.[10] As Japan moves out of the smokestack industries and becomes a "service" economy, further declines in union membership are expected to occur. Company and work-group loyalties are being replaced by individualism.

The trend away from seniority and towards individual performance-based pay has been documented in a survey carried out by the Social and Economic Congress of Japan which asked management and labor unions about changes in the factors that will determine Japanese wages by the year 2000 (see Exhibit 4).

### Redesigning the Employment Relationships

While maintaining considerable continuity with past practices, the system of lifetime employment is undergoing change. A 1984 survey conducted by the prime minister's office found that nearly half of all Japanese between the ages of twenty and twenty-nine expressed a preference for an "employment changing" job environment to the assurance of lifetime employment. In another survey conducted by a large job placement firm, a quarter of the college graduates interviewed had already changed jobs at least once.[11]

Most Japanese employers feel that it is advantageous to maintain the lifetime employment principle even if only in a modified form. Only a minority feel that the idea has outlived its usefulness. Most employers feel they must maintain lifetime employment for core employees in order to attract recruits of sufficient calibre. However, the group of "core" employees who enjoy lifetime employment can be quite small (it is only 10% in the fast-food industry).

While most companies have postponed the retirement age (as noted earlier), employees are now obliged to consider whether they will continue to stay with the company after the age of 40 or 45 or face the possibility of being transferred to affiliated companies. Companies are also using "specialist" positions for senior employees who are either being retired from managerial posts or are not considered promotable to managerial ranks.

The lifetime employment system is also being modified through increased use of diversified hiring methods. The routine hiring of school gradu-

E X H I B I T   4

## Emphasized Factors of Wage System Around in 2000 (in %)

| | MANAGEMENT | | | LABOR UNION | | | NEUTRAL | | | TOTAL | | |
|---|---|---|---|---|---|---|---|---|---|---|---|---|
| | Will increase | Not change | Will decrease | Increase | Not change | Decrease | Increase | Not change | Decrease | Increase | Not change | Decrease |
| Age | 6.7 | 21.0 | 69.0 | 15.5 | 26.1 | 57.1 | 5.5 | 21.9 | 71.6 | 8.8 | 22.7 | 66.4 |
| Service years | 6.7 | 28.6 | 61.9 | 11.2 | 33.5 | 55.3 | 3.3 | 32.8 | 62.3 | 6.9 | 31.4 | 60.1 |
| Educational background | 5.7 | 17.6 | 73.8 | 10.6 | 18.6 | 70.2 | 4.4 | 19.7 | 76.0 | 6.7 | 18.6 | 73.5 |
| Experience years | 25.7 | 49.5 | 21.4 | 33.5 | 44.7 | 22.4 | 23.5 | 51.9 | 20.8 | 27.3 | 46.9 | 21.5 |
| Job, occupational category | 80.0 | 15.7 | 0.5 | 82.6 | 13.7 | 1.9 | 77.0 | 19.1 | 2.7 | 79.8 | 16.2 | 1.6 |
| Ability for achievement | 91.0 | 4.8 | 1.0 | 84.5 | 9.3 | 5.0 | 86.9 | 10.9 | 0.5 | 87.7 | 6.1 | 2.0 |
| Amount of work done | 50.0 | 35.7 | 11.0 | 34.2 | 42.2 | 21.1 | 38.3 | 48.1 | 13.1 | 41.5 | 41.7 | 14.6 |
| Family size | 2.4 | 45.7 | 47.1 | 7.5 | 47.8 | 44.1 | 7.7 | 49.7 | 40.4 | 5.6 | 47.7 | 44.0 |

Source: Takoa Watanabe. Demystifying Japanese Management. Tokyo: Gakuseisha Publishing, 1987, 195.

ates is being more and more frequently supplemented by the hiring of contract employees and part-timers.[12] Hiring on the basis of skills for a specific,
narrowly defined job opening is growing. For example, in 1988 Niko Shoken
(Nikko Security, Co. Ltd.) started recruiting foreign exchange traders at high
salaries on a contract basis. These employees in principle cannot transfer to
the lifetime employment track and if their performance is below expectations
their salaries may be cut or they may be fired. Similarly, Sumitomo Trust
bank has been hiring security traders and economic analysts on a contract
basis. As Mr. Osamu Sakurai, President of the Bank, put it: "Under the lifetime employment system we could not offer appropriately high salaries to
obtain top talent. Nor could we hire on a short-term basis."[13] With these new
hiring practices, labor mobility is rising and is expected to continue to increase gradually in the future (see Exhibit 5). Mobility among Japanese managers and professionals is also increasing. According to a study performed by
Nippon Manpower, a Japanese human resource development company, 75%
of those surveyed declared that they would entertain a lucrative offer from a
headhunter.[14]

While Japanese management clearly wants to continue to tap the advantages of lifetime employment for selected employee groups, there is growing
evidence that a partial horizontal labor market is emerging rapidly. For years,
Japanese employees demonstrated a preference for security over risk and opportunity. This attitude began to change after the oil shocks. Japanese employees realized that they could not place all their reliance on their companies
and that they would have to start relying on themselves. Today, the latest
catch word among personnel specialists in Japan is "employee self-reliance."
It is not only that the attitudes and expectations of employees—especially
younger employees—are changing, but the companies themselves are creating programs designed to promote new attitudes of self-reliance. Career development programs have been among the most popular new personnel systems adopted by Japanese companies in the past few years.[15] Today,
companies like Toshiba and Yamaha use extensive career counseling to help
employees develop new skills and attitudes that would enable them to survive in a horizontal labor market.

## ▬ *The Multi-Track Employment System*

As they gradually redesign the employment and reward system in their
companies. Japanese managers are trying to maintain the advantages of
group harmony, employee loyalty, and cooperation (based on the lifetime
employment principle) while both eliminating the burdens of employment
hypertrophy and enhancing flexibility by shifting more of the risk on a greater
proportion of employees. At the same time, for many companies which base
their strategies on product leadership and innovations, stimulating employee
initiative and creativity is a high priority.

The way Japanese management hopes to reconcile these conflicting

EXHIBIT 5

## The Prospect of Worker's Mobility in Future Japanese Society

|  | MANAGEMENT | LABOR | NEUTRAL | TOTAL POLLED |
|---|---|---|---|---|
| *It will increase remarkably* | 3.2% | 2.2% | 3.3% | 2.9% |
| *It will increase a bit more or less* | 69.4 | 59.0 | 66.9 | 65.4 |
| *Unchanged* | 17.2 | 19.4 | 9.9 | 15.4 |
| *It will decrease a bit* | 0.6 | 1.5 | 0.6 | 0.9 |
| *It will decrease remarkably* | 0.6 | — | — | 0.2 |
| *No answer* | 8.9 | 17.9 | 19.2 | 15.2 |

*Source:* Takao Watanabe. *Demystifying Japanase Management.* Tokyo: Gakuseisha Publishing, 1987, 185.

goals is through the creation of a multi-track employment system. Employees hired for "life" enter the general track and can be moved horizontally (job rotation) as well as vertically (grade promotion). In the past, vertical promotion was often restricted by rules governing the minimum and standard "staying years" within one grade—effectively ensuring promotion by seniority. As companies relax those rules, more rapid promotion becomes possible. As job rotation and the hiring of specialists becomes more common, it becomes possible for a relatively junior employee to achieve a high grade. As companies choose to limit the percentage of lifetime employees, they expand hiring into the restricted tracks—which may include hiring more women, part-timers, and specialists.

As specific expertise becomes increasingly more important and seniority increasingly less, promotion grades become defined more precisely in terms of specific tasks rather than experience, general educational attainment, and general skills. Expanded flexibility can then also be applied at the higher (managerial) levels. However, promotion into these higher grades does not have to mean a managerial post. A variety of specialist positions offering high pay can be made available, which would allow for moving less able managers into specialist positions and more able specialists into management positions. A separate "subtrack" can be created for the failed or nonpromotable. This is the well known *taigu shoku* or "without job" track.

Compared with the grade systems that were used in the sixties and seventies, the systems emerging today offer more flexibility and more options to personnel management. Hiring methods have diversified. Today, Japanese personnel departments use headhunters to fill managerial and specialist technical positions, they lease groups of needed employees from manpower agencies, they entertain "walk in" offers from candidates, and they write a variety of contracts with employees on restricted tracks—including, to a greater extent, foreigners.[16] This is indeed a far cry from the standard practices in the past of relying primarily on school and university graduates. The flexibility of the system is being continually expanded. Many high-tech companies are diversifying grade denominations and promotion rules within particular tracks—especially research and development—to stimulate employee initiative and creativity.

# ■ Conclusion

Many of the critical practices on which the Japanese company bases its functioning depend on the principles of lifetime employment, company loyalty, and employee commitment. The Japanese will make every effort to maintain these principles in the foreseeable future. The changes going on in employment practices and employee motivation are not designed to destroy the old system but to increase its flexibility. This is very much in keeping with the traditional Japanese approach to change: however fast and deep it is, continuity with the uniquely Japanese "essence" must be maintained. The new Japanese management paradigm will certainly be different, yet like the modern Japanese home which usually retains a Japanese style room among Western style rooms and furniture, the Japanese company will retain a core of Japanese practices.

Western assessments of Japanese capabilities tend to oscillate between total awe and serious underestimation. The difficulties in changing to a new management system should not be underestimated. Japanese company presidents find that responsibility for decisions that have to be made rapidly is being transferred to them, that they have to act boldly and quickly, and that often there is no time for gradual consensus building. Popular Japanese magazines have noted a large number of company presidents who have died in office during the past 18 months or so, blaming their untimely deaths on the pressures of diversifying, building offshore plans, cutting costs, and laying off employees.[17]

The Japanese have handled profound change in the past very well (during the Meiji era and after World War II). This suggests that they are in a good position to overcome the obstacles and difficulties. Research on the introduction of robotics and flexible manufacturing systems in Japanese and Western companies show the Japanese to have superior capabilities in effective implementation of new manufacturing technology.[18] The Japanese appear very well positioned for the age in which competitive survival will depend on the ability of human groups to manage very rapid change. After the strains and difficulties of the current transformation. Japanese companies are likely to emerge in the 1990s as even more formidable competitors than ever before.

# ▰ *References*

1. Odaka, Kunio. "Japanese Management: A Forward Looking Analysis." *Asian Productivity Organization*. Tokyo, 1986.

2. Hanaoka, Masao. *Nihon no Romukanri (Personnel Management in Japan)*, 2nd ed. Tokyo: Hakuto Shobo, 1987.

3. Drucker, Peter F. "Japan's Choices." *Foreign Affairs,* 1987.

4. Ministry of Foreign Affairs. "Background Statistics on the Japanese Economy." Japan. May 1987.

5. Watanabe, Takao. *Demystifying Japanese Management*. Tokyo: Gakuseisha Publishing, 1987.

6. *Igyōshu Kōryu* are groups or networks of small and medium-sized enterprises organized to exchange technical information, promote management development, and engage in manpower exchange.

7. Hanaoka. op. cit.

8. *Nippon Jinji Gyōsei Kenkyujo* (Japan Personnel Policy Research Institute) survey, February 8, 1985.

9. *Nihonteki Koyokanko no Henka to Tenbo* (Ministry of Labor Research Center), Tokyo, 1987.

10. "All That's Left." *The Economist,* November 28, 1987.

11. Christopher, Robert C. *Second to None: American Companies in Japan*. New York: Crown 1986.

12. *Nikkei High Tech Report*. "Japanese Research Organizations Tap Foreign Technical Talent," April 13, 1987.

13. *Nihon Ketzat Shinbun*. February 15, 1988.

14. Mroczkowski, Tomasz and Hanaoka, Masao. "Japan's Managers Merit More Attention." *Asian Wall Street Journal*, October 29, 1987.

15. Hanaoka, Masao. "Setting Up a Hypothesis of the Characteristics of Personnel Management." Institute of Business Research, Daito Bunka University, 1986.

16. *Nikkei High Tech Report*. op. cit.

17. Wysocki, Bernard. "In Japan, Breaking Step Is Hard to Do." *Wall Street Journal*, December 14, 1987.

18. Jaikumar, Ramchandran. "Postindustrial Manufacturing." *Harvard Business Review*, November–December 1986.

# Expatriate Performance Appraisal: Problems and Solutions

## GARY ODDOU
## MARK MENDENHALL

For more and more companies, gaining a competitive edge increasingly means making decisions that reflect an acute understanding of the global marketplace—how other countries utilize and view marketing strategies, accounting and financial systems, labor laws, leadership, communication, negotiation and decision-making styles. Gaining a knowledge of these components is most directly accomplished by sending managers to work in an overseas subsidiary and utilizing them on reentry.

Our research shows clearly that expatriates develop valuable managerial skills abroad that can be extremely useful to their development as effective senior managers. Based on current research on expatriates, including our own surveying and interviewing of more than 150 of them, probably the most significant skills expatriates develop as a result of their overseas assignments include the following:

- Being able to manage a workforce with cultural and subcultural differences
- Being able to plan for, and conceptualize, the dynamics of a complex, multinational environment
- Being more open-minded about alternative methods for solving problems
- Being more flexible in dealing with people and systems
- Understanding the interdependencies among the firm's domestic and foreign operations

These skills are the natural outgrowth of the increased autonomy and potential impact expatriates experience in their international assignment. In fact, in our study, 67 percent reported having more independence, and they

Source: This article was written especially for this book.

also indicated they had more potential impact on the operation's performance than in their domestic position. With increased decision-making responsibilities in a foreign environment, expatriates are subjected to a fairly intense working environment in which they must learn the ropes quickly.

The skills expatriate managers gain are obviously crucial to effectively managing any business operation, particularly at the international and multinational level. Nightmares abound in the business press (see, for example, *Big Business Blunders*) of the inept decisions sometimes made by top management due to ignorance of cross-cultural differences in business practices. The ability to plan and conceptualize based on the complex interdependencies of a global market environment with significant cultural differences is required of top management in MNCs.

In short, expatriates can become a very valuable human resource for firms with international or multinational operations. However, one of the most serious stumbling blocks to expatriates' career paths is the lack of recognition of the value of expatriation and the informality with which firms accurately evaluate their expatriates' overseas performance. Although the attributes expatriates gain overseas can and do translate into concrete advantages for their firms, a quick glance at the skills previously listed indicates intangibles that are often difficult to measure and usually are not measured—or are measured inaccurately—by present performance evaluation methods. Hence, it is critical to more closely examine this potential stumbling block to expatriates' careers and to make specific recommendations to improve the process and accuracy of such reviews.

## ■ Appraising the Expatriate's Performance

Several problems are inherent to appraising an expatriate's performance. First, an examination of those who evaluate an expatriate's job performance is relevant. Those evaluators include the host national management and often the home office management.

### Host National Management's Perceptions of Actual Job Performance

That local management evaluates the expatriate is probably necessary; however, such a process sometimes is problematic. Local management typically evaluates the expatriate's performance from its own cultural frame of reference and set of expectations. For example, one American expatriate manager we talked to used participative decision making in India but was thought of by local workers as rather incompetent because of the Indian notion that managers, partly owing to their social class level, are seen as the experts. Therefore, a manager should not have to ask subordinates for ideas. Being seen as incompetent negatively affected local management's review of this expatriate's performance, and he was denied a promotion on return to the

United States. Local management's appraisal is not the only potential problem, however. In fact, based on our research with expatriates, local management's evaluation is usually perceived as being more accurate than that of the home office.

### Home Office Management's Perceptions of Actual Job Performance

Because the home office management is geographically distanced from the expatriate, it is often not fully aware of what is happening overseas. As a result, for middle and upper management, home office management will often use a different set of variables than those used by local management. Typically, more visible performance criteria are used to measure the expatriate's success (for example, profits, market share, productivity levels). Such measures ignore other, less visible variables that in reality drastically affect the company's performance. Local events such as strikes, devaluation of the currency, political instability, and runaway inflation are examples of phenomena that are beyond the control of the expatriate and are sometimes "invisible" to the home office.

One expatriate executive told us that in Chile he had almost single-handedly stopped a strike that would have shut down their factory completely for months and worsened relations between the Chileans and the parent company in the United States. In a land where strikes are commonplace, such an accomplishment was quite a coup, especially for an American. The numerous meetings and talks with labor representatives, government officials, and local management required an acute understanding of their culture and a sensitivity beyond the ability of most people. However, because of exchange rate fluctuations with its primary trading partners in South America, the demand for their ore temporarily decreased by 30 percent during the expatriate's tenure. Rather than applauding the efforts this expatriate executive made to avert a strike and recognizing the superb negotiation skills he demonstrated, the home office saw the expatriate as being only somewhat better than a mediocre performer. In other words, because for home office management the most visible criterion of the expatriate's performance was somewhat negative (sales figures), it was assumed that he had not performed adequately. And though the expatriate's boss knew a strike had been averted, the bottom-line concern for sales dollars overshadowed any other significant accomplishments.

The expatriate manager must walk a tightrope. He must deal with a new cultural work group, learn the ins and outs of the new business environment, possibly determine how to work with a foreign boss, find out what foreign management expects of him, and so on. He must also understand the rules of the game on the home front. It is difficult, and sometimes impossible, to please both. Attempting to please both can result in a temporarily, or permanently, railroaded career. So it was with an individual who was considered a high potential in a semiconductor firm. He was sent to an overseas operation without the proper product knowledge preparation and barely kept his head above water because of the difficulties of cracking a nearly impossible market. On returning to the United States, he was physically and mentally exhausted from the battle. He sought a much less challenging position and got it because top management then believed they had overestimated his potential. In fact, top management never did understand what the expatriate was up against in the foreign market.

In fact, expatriates frequently indicate that headquarters does not really understand their experience—neither the difficulty of it nor the value of it. One study found that one-third of the expatriates felt that corporate head-quarters did not understand the expatriate's experience at all. In a 1981 Korn/ Ferry survey, 69 percent of the managers reported they felt isolated from do-mestic operations and their U.S. managers. It is clear from others' and our own research that most U.S. senior management does not understand the value of an international assignment or try to utilize the expatriate's skills gained abroad when they return to the home office. The underlying problem seems to be top management's ethnocentricity.

### Management Ethnocentricity

Two of the most significant aspects of management's inability to under-stand the expatriate's experience, value it, and thereby more accurately mea-sure his or her performance are (1) the communication gap between the expa-triate and the home office and (2) the lack of domestic management's international experience.

*The Communication Gap.* Being physically separated by thousands of miles and in different time zones poses distinct problems of communication. Not only does the expatriate have difficulty talking directly with his manager, but usually both the U.S. manager and the expatriate executive have plenty of other responsibilities to attend to. Fixing the day-to-day problems tends to take precedence over other concerns, such as maintaining contact with one's boss (or subordinate) in order to be kept up to date on organizational changes or simply to inform him or her of what one is doing. Most of the expatriates in our research indicated they had very irregular contact with their home office and that often it was not with their immediate superior. Rarely did the boss initiate direct contact with the expatriate more than once or twice a year.

*The Lack of International Experience.* The old Indian expression "To walk a mile in another man's moccassins" has direct meaning here. How can one understand what another person's overseas managerial experience is like— its difficulties, challenges, stresses, and the like—without having lived and worked overseas oneself? According to one study, more than two-thirds of upper management in corporations today have never had an international assignment. If they have not lived or worked overseas, and if the expatriate and U.S. manager are not communicating regularly about the assignment, the U.S. manager cannot evaluate the expatriate's performance appropriately.

Of course, how the U.S. manager and foreign manager perceive the expatriate's performance will depend partly on the expatriate's actual performance and partly on the managers' perceptions of the expatriate's performance. Up to now, we have discussed the managers' *perceptions* of the expatriate's performance. Let's now turn our attention to what usually composes the expatriate's *actual* performance to better understand why evaluating it is problematic.

### Actual Job Performance

As repeatedly mentioned by the expatriates in our study and in other research, the primary factors relating to the expatriate's actual job performance include his or her technical job know-how, personal adjustment to the culture, and various environmental factors.

*Technical Job Know-How.* As with all jobs, one's success overseas partly depends on one's expertise in the technical area of the job. Our research indicates that approximately 95 percent of the expatriates believe that technical competency is crucial to successful job performance. Although common sense supports this notion, research shows that technical competence is not sufficient in itself for successful job performance. For example, an engineer who is an expert in his or her field and who tends to ignore cultural variables that are important to job performance will likely be ineffective. He or she might be less flexible with local personnel, policies, and practices because of his or her reliance on technical know-how or because of differences in cultural views. As a result, the host nationals might become alienated by the expatriate's style and become quite resistant to his or her objectives and strategies. A less experienced engineer, with less technical competence, might be more willing to defer to the host country's employees and their procedures and customs. A shade of humility is always more likely to breed flexibility, and in the long run, the less experienced engineer might develop the trust of the foreign employees and might well be more effective than the experienced engineer.

We have been given numerous examples by expatriates, in fact, where this has been the case. One expatriate who represented a large construction firm was sent to a worksite in India. The expatriate was an expert in his field and operated in the same fashion as he did in the United States. He unintentionally ignored local work customs and became an object of hatred and distrust. The project was delayed for more than six months because of his behavior.

*Adjustment to a New Culture.* Just as important as the expatriate's technical expertise is his or her ability to adapt to the foreign environment, enabling him or her to deal with the indigenous people. Nearly every expatriate in our survey felt understanding the foreign culture, having an ability to communicate with the foreign nationals, and being able to reduce stress were as—if not more—important to successful job performance than was technical competence. Regardless of how much an expatriate knows, if he or she is unable to communicate with and understand the host nationals, the work will not get done.

An expatriate's adjustment overseas is also related to at least two personal variables: (1) one's marital and family status (that is, whether accompanied by a spouse and children) and (2) the executive's own personal and the family's predisposition to acculturation. Research clearly indicates that expatriates who have their family abroad are often less successful because of the stress on the family of being in a foreign environment. The stress on the spouse negatively affects the employee's concentration and job performance. With an increasing number of dual-career couples being affected by expatriation, the problems are even keener. A number of expatriates reported that their formerly career-positioned spouse suffered from depression most of the time they were overseas. Moving from experiencing the dynamics of a challenging career to having no business-world activity and being unable to communicate the most basic needs is a grueling transition for many career-oriented spouses.

Company variables affecting cultural and work adjustment also come into play. The thoroughness of the company's expatriate selection method and the type and degree of cross-cultural training will affect expatriate adjustment and performance. In other words, if the firm is not selective about the personality of the expatriate or does not appropriately prepare the employee and dependents, the firm may be building in failure before the manager ever leaves the United States.

All these factors influence the expatriate's learning curve in a foreign business environment. More time is thus required to learn the ins and outs of the job than for the expatriate's domestic counterpart who might have just taken a comparable position stateside. In fact, most expatriates say it takes three to six months to even begin to perform at the same level as in the domestic operation. Hence, *performance evaluations at the company's normal time interval may be too early to accurately and fairly reflect the expatriate's performance.*

## ▄▄ A Summary of Factors Affecting Expatriation Performance

In summary, an expatriate's performance is based on overseas adjustment, his or her technical know-how, and various relevant environmental factors. Actual performance, however, is evaluated in terms of perceived performance, which is based on a set of fairly complex variables usually below the evaluator's level of awareness. Much of the perceived performance concerns perceptions of the expatriate and his or her situation. Depending on whether the manager assessing the expatriate's performance has had personal overseas experience or is otherwise sensitive to problems associated with overseas work, the performance appraisal will be more or less valid. *The bottom line for the expatriate is that the performance appraisal will influence the promotion potential and type of position the expatriate receives on returning to the United States.* Because expatriates generally return from their experience with valuable managerial skills, especially for firms pursuing an international or global market path, it behooves organizations to carefully review their process of appraising expatriates and the evaluation criteria themselves.

## Guidelines on How to Appraise an Expatriate's Performance

### Human Resource Personnel: Giving Guidelines for Performance Evaluation

Human resources departments can do a couple of things to help guide the evaluator's perspective on the evaluation.

A basic breakdown of the difficulty level of the assignment should be done to properly evaluate the expatriate's performance. For example, working in Japan is generally considered more difficult than working in England or English-speaking Canada. The learning curve in Japan will take longer because of the very different ways business is conducted, the language barrier that exists, and the isolation that most Americans feel within the Japanese culture. Major variables such as the following should be considered when determining the difficulty level of the assignment:

- Operational language used in the firm
- Cultural "distance," based often on the region of the world (for example, Western Europe, Middle East, Asia)
- Stability of the factors affecting the expatriate's performance (for example, labor force, exchange rate)

Many foreigners speak English, but their proficiency does not always allow them to speak effectively or comfortably, so they rely on their native language when possible. In addition, they usually do not speak English among themselves because it is not natural. In Germany, for example, one expatriate said that while relying on English allowed a minimum level of work to be performed, the fact that he did not speak German limited his effectiveness. Secretaries, for example, had very limited English-speaking skills. German workers rarely spoke English together and therefore unknowingly excluded the expatriate from casual and often work-related conversations. And outside work, he had to spend three to four times the amount of time to accomplish the same things that he did easily in the United States. Most of the problem was because he could not speak good enough German, and many of the Germans could not speak good enough English.

Although sharing the same language facilitates effective communication, it is only the surface level of communication. More deep-rooted, cultural-based phenomena can more seriously affect an expatriate's performance.

Countries or regions where the company sends expatriates can be fairly easily divided into categories such as these: (1) somewhat more difficult than the United States, (2) more difficult than the United States, and (3) much more difficult than the United States. Plenty of information is available to help evaluate the difficulty level of assignments. The U.S. State Department and military branches have these types of ratings. In addition, feedback from a firm's own expatriates can help build the picture of the varying level of assignment difficulty.

Rather than having the manager try to subjectively build the difficulty level of the assignment into his or her performance appraisal, human resources could have a built-in, numerical difficulty factor that is multiplied times the quantity obtained by the normal evaluation process (for example, somewhat more difficult $= \times 1.2$; more difficult $= \times 1.4$; much more difficult $= \times 1.6$).

### Evaluator: Trying to Objectify the Evaluation

Several things can be done to try to make the evaluator's estimation more objective.

1. Most expatriates agree that it makes more sense to weight the evaluation based more on the on-site manager's appraisal than the home-site manager's notions of the employee's performance. This is the individual who has been actually working with the expatriate and who has more information to use in the evaluation. Having the on-site manager evaluate the expatriate is especially valid when the on-site manager is of the same nationality as the expatriate. This helps avoid culturally biased interpretations of the expatriate's performance.

2. In reality, however, currently the home-site manager usually performs the actual written performance evaluation after the on-site manager has given some input. When this is the case, a former expatriate from the same location should be involved in the appraisal process. This should occur particularly with evaluation dimensions where the manager is trying to evaluate the individual against criteria with which he or she is unfamiliar relative to the overseas site. For example, in South America the dynamics of the workplace can be considerably different from those of the United States. Where stability characterizes the United States, instability often characterizes much of Latin America. Labor unrest, political upheavals, different labor laws, and other elements all serve to modify the actual effects a supervisor can have on the productivity of the labor force in a company in Latin America. A manager who has not personally experienced these frustrations will not be able to evaluate an expatriate's productivity accurately. In short, if production is down while the expatriate is the supervisor, the American boss tends to believe it is because the supervisor was not effective.

3. On the other hand, when it is a foreign, on-site manager who is making the written, formal evaluation, expatriates agree that the home-site manager should be consulted before the on-site manager completes a formal terminal evaluation. This makes sense because consulting the home-site manager can balance an otherwise hostile evaluation caused by an intercultural misunderstanding.

One expatriate we interviewed related this experience. In France, women are legally allowed to take six months off for having a baby. They are paid during that time but are not supposed to do any work related to their job. This expatriate had two of the three secretaries take maternity leave. Because they were going to be coming back, they were not replaced with temporary help. The same amount of work, however, still existed. The American expatriate asked them to do some work at home, not really understanding the legalities of such a request. The French women could be fired from their job for doing work at home. One of the women agreed to do it because she felt sorry for him. When the American's French boss found out one of these two secretaries was helping, he became very angry and intolerant of the American's actions. As a result, the American felt he was given a lower performance evaluation than he deserved. When the American asked his former boss to intercede and help the French boss understand his reasoning, the French boss modified the performance evaluation to something more reasonable to the American expatriate. The French manager had assumed the American should have been aware of French laws governing maternity leave.

### Performance Criteria

Here again, special consideration needs to be given to the expatriate's experience. Expatriates are not only performing a specific function, as they would in their domestic operation, they are also broadening their understanding of their firm's total operations and the inherent interdependencies thereof. As a result, two recommendations are suggested.

1. Modify the normal performance criteria of the evaluation sheet for that particular position to fit the overseas position and site characteristics.

Using the Latin American example referred to before might serve to illustrate this point. In most U.S. firms, maintaining positive management–labor relations is not a primary performance evaluation criterion. Stabilizing the workforce is not highly valued because the workforce is already usually a stable entity. Instead, productivity in terms of number of units produced is a highly valued outcome. As such, motivating the workforce to work faster and harder is important. In Chile, however, the workforce is not so stable as it is in the United States. Stability is related to constant production—not necessarily to increasing production—and a stable production amount can be crucial to maintaining marketshare. In this case, if an expatriate is able to maintain positive management–labor relations such that the workforce goes on strike only two times instead of twenty-five times, the expatriate should be rewarded commensurately. In other words, while the expatriate's U.S. counterpart might be rated primarily on increases in production, the expatriate in Chile should be rated on stability of production.

How can such modifications in the normal performance criteria be determined? Ideally, returned expatriates who worked at the same site or in the same country should be involved in developing the appropriate criteria or ranking of the performance criteria or both. Only they have first-hand experience of what the possibilities and constraints are like at that site. This developmental cycle should occur approximately every five years, depending on the stability of the site—its culture, personnel, and business cycles. Reevaluating the criteria and their prioritization periodically will make sure the performance evaluation criteria remain current with the reality of the overseas situation. If expatriate availability is a problem, outside consultants who specialize in international human resource management issues can be hired to help create country-specific performance evaluation forms and criteria.

**2.** Include an expatriate's insights as part of the evaluation.

"Soft" criteria are difficult to measure and therefore legally difficult to support. Nevertheless, every attempt should be made to give the expatriate credit for relevant insights into the interdependencies of the domestic and foreign operations. For example, if an expatriate learns that the reason the firm's plant in India needs supplies by certain dates is to accommodate cultural norms—or even local laws—such information can be invaluable. Previously, no one at the domestic site understood why the plant in India always seemed to have such odd or erratic demands about delivery dates. And no one in India bothered to think that their U.S. supplier didn't operate the same way. If delivering supplies by specific dates asked for by their India colleagues ensures smoother production or increased sales and profits for the Indian operation, and if the expatriate is a critical link in the communication gap between the United States and India, the expatriate should be given credit for such insights. This should be reflected in his or her performance review.

To obtain this kind of information, either human resource or operational personnel should formally have a debriefing session with the expatriate on his or her return. It should be in an informal interview format so that specific and open-ended questions can be asked. Questions specific to the technical nature of the expatriate's work that relate to the firm's interdependencies should be asked. General questions concerning observations about the relationship between the two operations should also be included.

There is another, even more effective way this aspect of performance review can be handled. At regular intervals, say, every three to six months, the expatriate could be questioned by human resource or operational personnel in the domestic site about how the two operations might better work together. Doing it this way helps maximize the possibility of noting all relevant insights.

## ▬ *Conclusion*

With the marketplace becoming increasingly global, the firms that carefully select and manage their internationally assigned personnel will reap the benefits. Today, there is about a 20 percent turnover rate for expatriates when they return. Such a turnover rate is mostly due to firms not managing their expatriates' careers well. Firms are not prepared to appropriately reassign expatriates on their reentry. This obviously indicates that firms do not value the expatriate's experience. This further carries over into the lack of emphasis on appropriately evaluating an expatriate's performance. Appropriately evaluating an expatriate's performance is an issue of both fairness to the expatriate and competitive advantage to the firm. With the valuable experience and insights that expatriates gain, retaining them and effectively positioning them in a firm will mean the firm's business strategy will be increasingly guided by those who understand the companies' worldwide operations and markets.

# International Executive Compensation Practices

## MARILYN HELMS

The world is becoming smaller with the development of new technology and the globalization of business. As the old trade barriers melt away, multinational companies are stretching their antennas into every corner of the world. The next decade will be an epoch-making stage for the world economy. In Europe by 1992, the European Economic Community will start to become a single and integrated Common Market. Meanwhile, the Pacific-Rim region, as the upstart of economic development, is trying to extend its economic frontiers throughout the globe. Japan is using more aggressive strategies and approaches to capture global market share as well as to speed up permanence into the U.S. economy. However, the new structure of global competition will also force the Japanese to open domestic markets to foreign goods although they are currently reluctant to do so.

In short, the world today is becoming a global market, and "world economic integration seems to be one of those unstoppable forces" (Reed, Glasgall, and Holstein, 1989). When a company is planning to expand its operation into international markets and establish relevant strategy, it should consider many factors that directly and indirectly affect the success of the strategy. One of these factors is compensation for expatriates who will be sent abroad to work as the representatives of the company. An effective compensation program must provide adequate incentives to encourage the right persons to accept overseas assignments and to do their best in meeting the company's strategic goals. To attract, motivate, and retain high-quality expatriates, the company should make the compensation program not only equitable and compatible to the domestic rate but also flexible and competitive in the world market rate.

For most companies that are about to enter international markets, there is an urgent need to understand how we compensate our domestic executives, how other countries compensate their executives, and how to determine the appropriate compensation package for expatriates. This article examines executive compensation among different countries.

*Source:* This article was written especially for this book.

## ▬ *Compensation, American Style*

Although some experts are concerned over whether the U.S. firms would lose their competitive edge and flexible responsiveness in international market competition, American chief executives are big winners in their compensation. According to *Business Week*'s thirty-ninth annual executive compensation survey of more than 708 executives, the average CEO's salary and bonus reached $1,128,854 in 1988. Including the value of exercised stock options and other long-term incentives, the average total compensation climbed to $2,025,485. Michael D. Eisner, the chairman of Walt Disney, earned more than $40 million in salary, bonuses, and stock options. F. Ross Johnson, CEO of RJR Nabisco, set a record in golden parachutes when he left the company with a package of pay, stock, and benefits totaling $53.8 million (Byrne, Grover, and Vogel, 1989). The tremendous fortunes gained by American top executives eclipses the compensation earned by their international counterparts.

Generally speaking, American executive compensation packages contain four components: base salary, bonus, long-term incentives, and other benefits and perks. Among the highest-paid top executives, base salary is only a small part of total compensation. For example, Lee Iacocca, the chairman and CEO of Chrysler Corporation, earned "only" $1.7 million in salary and bonus in 1986, but he got the other $18.9 million from stock and other options (Much, 1987). The 1988 *INC.* compensation survey stated that a typical chief executive of an average growth-company earned a base salary of $76,000 and a bonus of $40,000 (*INC.*'s 1988 Executive Compensation Survey, 1988).

Although there are still some arguments about whether American executives are really paid according to their performance, a more direct relationship between the performance of a company and its executive pay package has become evident in recent years. A company's profitability, far more than any other factor, determines the executive's paycheck. For instance, Charles Lazarus, the chairman of Toys "R" Us, earned $315,000 in base salary in 1987, but his contract provided an incentive bonus of 1 percent of the corporate pretax profits over $18 million, from which he got $3.2 million in that year (Brown, 1988). It is increasingly obvious that performance-driven systems are particularly appealing because they motivate executives to focus on specific measures of performance such as profit. A *Business Week* survey indicated that sharp performance gains had a lot to do with the big jump in executive pay. Corporation profits increased by 32 percent in 1988, and since most companies paid their bosses accordingly, the average CEO's salary and bonus increased 17 percent (Byrne, Grover, and Vogel, 1989).

Among long-term incentives, stock options are obviously an important source of fortune for American executives. By exercising stock options, they are drawing and accumulating incredible wealth. Charles Lazarus received more than $56 million from stock options. In the United States, options and other incentives can make up to 60 percent of total cash compensation for chief executives of the largest U.S. corporations (Blank and Smith, 1988).

In addition to base salary, bonus, and long-term incentives, there are innumerable benefits and perks in the American executive compensation package. According to the *INC.* survey (1988), the percentages of CEOs who enjoy different benefits and perks are as follows: company car and expenses (82 percent), supplemental life insurance (64 percent), tax return preparation (52 percent), club dues and expenses (43 percent), supplemental medical insurance (40 percent), personal tax and financial planning (33 percent), low- or no-interest loans (25 percent), supplemental retirement benefits (15 percent), deferred compensation (14 percent), first-class air travel (11 percent), and moving allowance (8 percent).

Typically, the American executive salary range depends on the company size, level of management, duties, and responsibilities. In 1986, a department head in a medium-sized U.S. company earned an average salary of only $45,000. The salary of a general manager in a small company would reach $144,000. Then, at the highest level, the average salary of CEOs in the largest corporations would hit $727,000 ("Are U.S. Executives Better Off?" 1987). In a 1988 *Business Week* profile, Mims and Lewis found the average pay (not including long-term bonuses) of CEOs of the 1,000 most valuable U.S. companies hit $760,000, up 11 percent from the year before. Another approach to analyzing salary range is to group CEOs according to the annual revenues of their companies. *INC.*'s (1988) executive compensation study on 1,700 average growth companies provided the following statistics:

| COMPANY ANNUAL REVENUES | CEO'S COMPENSATION |
| --- | --- |
| $10 million or more | $181,000 |
| $5 million–$9.99 million | $125,000 |
| $1 million–$4.99 million | $93,000 |
| Less than $1 million | $58,000 |

Since women are making a substantial impact on the employment market and more female executives are successfully managing their companies than ever before, women in managerial roles has become a recent focus of research. It is estimated that among the managers and administrators in the United States, 23 percent are women. Successful female executives tend to be as qualified as or better qualified than their male counterparts. They are deeply loyal to professions and are committed to their careers even though many have to cope with the conflict between the demands of home and work life. Statistics show that the earnings ratio between male and female managers and administrators rose from 1 : 0.51 to 1 : 0.67 in the past decade (Stoner and Freeman, 1989). This means that although female executives have made great progress in their quest for equal pay, inequalities in compensation continue to exist.

## Compensation Around the World

Theoretically, international executive compensation should vary among countries that have different economic systems and development levels, distinct political and legal institutions, and particular traditions and cultural backgrounds. It is difficult to find measures that we can use to directly compare executive compensation throughout the world. Executive compensation differs dramatically from one country to another. Below is a brief review of executive compensation practices in some major countries.

### Europe

It seems that European executives are far behind their American counterparts in compensation, just as described by Victor Dial, an American in charge of sales and marketing at Peugeot, "European managers are grossly underpaid" (Blank and Smith, 1988). The disparity, however, is starting to narrow with business globalization.

In 1987, some 300 U.S. CEOs earned at least $1 million, but in Europe fewer than 30 CEOs reached the $1 million mark (Blank and Smith, 1988). The average compensation package of $1 million for the chief executive of a billion-dollar-a-year U.S. corporation is typical, but for most European chief executives, the compensation is half this amount. The CEO in a company of comparable size in France earned only $577,000, followed by Switzerland at $468,000, West Germany at $403,000, and the United Kingdom at $342,000 (Kirkpatrick, 1988).

When comparing smaller companies, the compensation difference between the United States and Europe is less. According to data collected by Business International Corporation from nearly 2,000 companies in the United States and nine European countries, the gross compensation of a general manager of a $30 million company is as follows:

| | |
|---|---|
| United States | $144,000 |
| Switzerland | $140,000 |
| West Germany | $112,000 |
| Austria | $104,000 |
| Netherlands | $96,000 |
| Belgium | $95,000 |
| Italy | $86,000 |
| France | $82,000 |
| Denmark | $76,000 |
| Britain | $62,000 |

The reason for the discrepancies in executive compensation can be partly explained by the way executives are compensated in different countries. In addition to a generous base salary, U.S. CEOs are filling their pockets with bonuses, stock options, and other long-term incentives, whereas European companies are just beginning to introduce the American compensation system. Differences are due to the effect of the personal income tax rates.

U.S. executives are getting more money at a 28 percent tax rate, whereas European executives are staggering under heavy tax burdens. The top marginal tax rate is more than 80 percent in Sweden, 57 percent in France, and 45 percent in Great Britain. High tax rates produce two results: They consume a dominant portion of the compensation pie, and they encourage European executives to pursue additional perks or fringe benefits. Many European companies offer tax-favored perks such as a company car, club memberships, augmented pensions, and entertainment and housing allowances. Perks of various kinds make up from 4 to 13 percent of compensation in most European countries (Blank and Smith, 1988). However, in the past few years, the European executive compensation structure has changed rapidly. Some compensation methods that originated in the United States now are being introduced in Europe. Bonus and stock options are becoming more popular. As a result, the compensation difference between the U.S. and European countries is gradually narrowing.

As in the United States, women in major European countries are assuming increasingly important roles in the top management. Women today are more confident and more conscious of equality than in the past; however, the barriers that prevent women from reaching the top still exist. For instance, in Britain, the number of female managers remains very small, and equal opportunity and equal pay remain a battle.

### Japan

Traditionally, Japanese compensation for both managers and workers is much less than that in other industrialized nations. Japanese CEOs in the biggest companies earn only one-third of what their American counterparts get. However, social and traditional ideas of value and particular corporate cultures make the Japanese compensation system much different from other industrialized countries.

First, the Japanese compensation system is primarily based on seniority. This characteristic is a reflection of the Japanese tradition of respecting seniors. For example, the average wage of a thirty-five-year-old worker is about 32 percent higher than that of a thirty-year-old, whereas a fifty-year-old employee receives three times that of a twenty-five-year-old at the same Japanese corporation.

Second, the Japanese compensation system provides long-term incentives to maintain stable employment. Japanese management advocates team spirit and encourages employees to regard themselves as part of the company, therefore establishing a source of being the master of the company. At the same time, job security comes through the permanent employment system, and companies provide a lifetime income retirement program and an additional retirement bonus. As a result, Japanese employees are very loyal to their company, and they push themselves extremely hard to make a contribution to their company. The turnover both of managers and employees in Japan is much lower than that in other countries.

Third, skill level and performance reviews also determine a small part of the total compensation package, which reflects both the employee's competence and job performance. Finally, Japanese companies provide their employees with a variety of fringe benefits such as life insurance, accident insurance, and medical insurance.

Traditionally, Japanese women were housewives who took care of children and housework. New corporate Japan has discovered the importance of female employees. In 1988, Japanese women made up more than 40 percent of the total labor force, and today, about 50 percent of Japanese women hold jobs. The number of women holding managerial positions increased 50 percent between 1982 and 1987 (Solo, 1989).

Unlike American women, Japanese women take extra responsibility for their family and have a different viewpoint on work. Despite the passage of the Equal Employment Opportunity Law in 1986, a third of the women have settled for a temporary job. This is partly attributed to the traditional idea that women only "want work that will not interrupt their marriage or raising their children" (Solo, 1989).

### South and Southeast Asia

The South and Southeast Asia region includes South Korea, Singapore, Hong Kong, Taiwan, Thailand, Indonesia, and India. Even though each country or area in this region has a different social system, they all belong to a Confucian Oriental culture, which has a clear effect on the behavior of the people of this region. Therefore, they have some similar practices in executive compensation.

First, people in this region advocate a harmonious and collective living environment, and they place much emphasis on the relationships among family members, relatives, and other people around them. Here, family is the most basic unit of society, not the individual. This cultural value and concept of family pervades all aspects of society and is even reflected in government policy. To prevent a large pay gap between lower and upper levels of management and to maintain at least monetary harmony, governments and unions often largely regulate compensation. National governments often dictate minimum wages, vacation pay, maternity leave, sick pay, and other benefits. Second, the reflection of cultural value in business yields companies with a small family style. Besides a few big companies, most local businesses are small to medium sized. Family-run companies usually do not have complex compensation programs. Salary and wages are paid mainly for providing necessities of daily living.

## ▬ Compensation of Expatriate Managers

With increasing globalization, more and more Americans will be sent to work abroad. An overseas assignment is not only a career opportunity but a career challenge as well. Faced with new cultures, traditions, languages, and environments, expatriates need extra energy and ambition to perform their managerial duties. In order to attract competent employees to carry out overseas assignments, a company must develop an effective expatriate compensation program—one that provides an adequate incentive to encourage people to work outside the country by offsetting the inconvenience and hardship of a new environment and maintaining the American standard of living abroad. The program should also consider that the family and social needs of an expatriate (such as relationships and communication with family, friends, and business associates) must be properly satisfied and maintained.

There are two common approaches for a company to set up an expatriate compensation program. One is the international cadre approach, which is applied when the company hires expatriates from different nationalities. The purpose of this approach is to provide all expatriates with the equivalent salaries and benefits of their U.S. counterparts. Another approach is the balance sheet approach, which balances all costs of an overseas assignment and obtains an adjustment index. This index is then applied to the expatriate base salary in order to allow the employee to maintain an economic status equivalent to the one the employee would have if he or she had remained in the United States (Frith, 1981). In practice, the balance sheet approach is the most popular approach used by U.S. companies. The components of a compensation program by the balance sheet approach may vary among different companies and even in a single company with multiple multinational operations. Some of the basic components of this approach are outlined below.

### Base Salary

The principle of determining base salary is that it must be comparable with domestic rates. This means the base salary for an expatriate must be in the same range as the base salary for a similar position within the United States. With this base salary, the expatriate may maintain the same buying power while on an overseas assignment. The base salary usually covers the costs of goods and services, housing, savings, and income tax on an annual basis.

### Foreign Service Premium

A foreign service premium is extra pay provided for working outside the United States. It is compensation for the inconveniences of having to live in a new environment isolated from family and friends, for difficulty in language and cultural barriers, for greater responsibility and reduced access to home-office resources, and for the effort of dealing with different work habits. Most companies pay foreign service premiums as a percentage of base salary ranging from 10 to 30 percent. This premium is usually tax-free to the expatriate (Stone, 1986).

### Hardship or Site Allowance

An allowance for hardships is often paid for less than desirable locations, extremes of climate, or inadequate medical care. It is paid either as a percentage of base salary or as a flat amount. The amount of this allowance is based on a location's degree of hardship. For example, in 1986 the monthly site allowance for Hong Kong was from $0 to $200, but for Beijing, China, it was from $500 to $900 (Stone, 1986).

### Cost of Living Allowance

The purpose of cost of living allowance (COLA) is to allow the expatriate to maintain the same standard of living abroad. It is an additional salary adjustment since it is difficult for an expatriate to find a living environment and lifestyle in a foreign country, especially in a developing country, comparable to those in the United States. The allowance can protect the expatriate's standard of living from cost of living differences in the host country, while providing protection against exchange rate fluctuations. Typically this allowance ensures that the expatriate has reasonable spendable income for food, clothing, and entertainment. The cost of living allowance is normally tax-free and is adjustable according to changing living expenses and exchange rates (Stone, 1986).

### Housing Allowance

Next to base salary, the housing allowance is the largest component of expatriate compensation. Because housing has a big influence on an expatriate's performance, companies carefully consider housing when they set up an expatriate compensation program. Companies usually adopt one of three housing choices: (1) provide a tax-free housing allowance with a maximum limit computed as a specified percentage of base salary, (2) provide housing free of charge, or (3) make a statistical housing deduction based on the home location market rate (Stone, 1986).

### Taxation

Taxation of the expatriate income is a very complex problem because foreign countries have various tax regulations and tax rates. For the expatriate, the dilemma is that income is dutiable to both the United States and the host country. To reduce the tax burden, the company usually makes up the difference in the expatriate's take-home pay when the tax rate in the host country rises. This method is called tax protection. Under tax equalization, the company will pay the host country any amount in excess of the expatriate's U.S. tax rate (Gaffney and Hitchings, 1985).

### Incidental Benefits

Besides the various allowances discussed, companies may provide their expatriates with medical benefits. The practice in some companies is to cover all medical expenses (except optical and dental) either in total or for the excess above that provided by medical insurance. Some other incentives include a company car or a car allowance, education allowances for children, relocation allowances, and vacation leave.

## ▆ Summary

U.S. chief executives are achieving tremendous wealth from their compensation in base salaries, bonuses, stock options, and other long-term incentives. In executive compensation, U.S. CEOs still remain the world leaders, but the pay gap is sharply narrowing with the application of American compensation methods in Europe. Despite being far behind executive compensation in the United States and Europe, executive compensation in some Asian countries is rising. To maintain a competitive advantage in the world market, U.S. businesses must establish long-term strategies with a global perspective and expand economic frontiers throughout the world. To attract and motivate high-quality employees to take overseas assignments, it is vital for a company to develop an effective expatriate compensation program that is not only equitable and comparable to domestic pay rates but also competitive in the world markets.

## ▆ References

"Are U.S. Executives Better Off?" *Management Review*, April 1987, 8.

Blank, B.J. and Smith, A.D. "American Bosses Are Overpaid." *Fortune*, November 7, 1988.

Brown, Paul B. "INC's Guide to Writing Your Own Ticket." *INC.*, September 1988, 80.

Byrne, John A., Grover, Ronald, and Vogel, Todd. "Is the Boss Getting Paid Too Much?" *Business Week*, May 1, 1989, 46, 52.

Frith, Stan. *The Expatriate Dilemma*. Chicago: Nelson Hall, 1981.

Gaffney, C. and Hitchings, B. "How To Make A Foreign Job Pay." *Business Week*, December 23, 1985, 84.

INC's 1988 Executive Compensation Survey. "The Take At the Top." *INC.*, September 1988, 79, 86.

Kirkpatrick, David. "Abroad, It's Another World." *Fortune*, June 6, 1988, 78.

Lizhen, M. "Women: The Debate on Jobs vs. Homemaking." *China Reconstructs*, No. 3, March 1989, 67.

Mims, Robert and Lewis, Ephraim. "A Portrait of the Boss." *Business Week*, October 20, 1989, 25.

Much, Marilyn. "How Much Are Executives Paid?" *Industry Week*, June 15, 1987, 33.

Reed, Stanley, Glasgall, William, and Holstein, William J. "Seeking Growth In a Smaller World." *Business Week*, October 16, 1989, 94.

Solo, Sally. "Japan Discovers Woman Power." *Fortune*, June 19, 1989, 153, 155.

Stone, Raymond J. "Pay and Perks For Overseas Executives." *Personnel Journal*, January 1986, 64, 67.

Stoner, James A.F. and Freeman, R. Edward. *Management*, 4th ed. Englewood Cliffs, N.J.: Prentice-Hall, 1989.

# *The Road to Hell*

## GARETH EVANS

John Baker, Chief Engineer of the Caribbean Bauxite Company of Barracania in the West Indies, was making his final preparations to leave the island. His promotion to production manager of Keso Mining Corporation near Winnipeg—one of Continental Ore's fast-expanding Canadian enterprises—had been announced a month before and now everything had been tidied up except the last vital interview with his successor, the able young Barracanian, Matthew Rennalls. It was vital that this interview be a success and that Rennalls should leave his office uplifted and encouraged to face the challenge of his new job. A touch on the bell would have brought Rennalls walking into the room but Baker delayed the moment and gazed thoughtfully through the window considering just exactly what he was going to say and, more particularly, how he was going to say it.

John Baker, an English expatriate, was forty-five years old and had served his twenty-three years with Continental Ore in many different places: in the Far East; several countries of Africa; Europe; and, for the last two years, in the West Indies. He hadn't cared much for his previous assignment in Hamburg and was delighted when the West Indian appointment came through. Climate was not the only attraction. Baker had always preferred working overseas (in what were termed the developing countries) because he felt he had an innate knack—better than most other expatriates working for Continental Ore—of knowing just how to get on with regional staff. Twenty-four hours in Barracania, however, soon made him realize that he would need all of this "innate knack" if he was to deal effectively with the problems in this field that now awaited him.

At his first interview with Hutchins, the production manager, the whole problem of Rennalls and his future was discussed. There and then it was made quite clear to Baker that one of his most important tasks would be the "grooming" of Rennalls as his successor. Hutchins had pointed out that, <u>not</u> only was Rennalls one of the brightest Barracanian prospects on the staff of

*Source:* This case was prepared by Mr. Gareth Evans for Shell-BP Petroleum Development Company of Nigeria, Limited, as a basis for class discussion in an executive training program. Distributed by the Intercollegiate Case Clearing House, Soldiers Field, Boston, MA 02163. All rights reserved to the contributors. Printed in the U.S.A. Reprinted by permission.

**385**

*potential of brains w/ political connections*

Caribbean Bauxite—at London University he had taken first-class honors in the B.Sc. Engineering Degree—but, being the son of the Minister of Finance and Economic Planning, he also had no small political pull.

The company had been particularly pleased when Rennalls decided to work for them rather than for the government in which his father had such a prominent post. They ascribed his action to the effect of their vigorous and liberal regionalization program which, since the Second World War, had produced eighteen Barracanians at mid-management level and given Caribbean Bauxite a good lead in this respect over all other international concerns operating in Barracania. The success of this timely regionalization policy has led to excellent relations with the government—a relationship that had been given an added importance when Barracania, three years later, became independent, an occasion which encouraged a critical and challenging attitude toward the role foreign interests would have to play in the new Barracania. Hutchins had therefore little difficulty in convincing Baker that the successful career development of Rennalls was of the first importance.

*Baker is cooperative*

The interview with Hutchins was now two years old and Baker, leaning back in his office chair, reviewed just how successful he had been in the "grooming" of Rennalls. What aspects of the latter's character had helped and what had hindered? What about his own personality? How had that helped or hindered? The first item to go on the credit side would, without question, be the ability of Rennalls to master the technical aspects of his job. From the start he had shown keenness and enthusiasm and had often impressed Baker with his ability in tackling new assignments and the constructive comments he invariably made in departmental discussions. He was popular with all ranks of Barracanian staff and had an ease of manner which stood him in good stead when dealing with his expatriate seniors. These were all assets, but what about the debit side?

*good qualities*

First and foremost, there was his racial consciousness. His four years at London University had accentuated this feeling and made him sensitive to any sign of condescension on the part of expatriates. It may have been to give expression to this sentiment that, as soon as he returned home from London, he threw himself into politics on behalf of the United Action Party who were later to win the preindependence elections and provide the country with its first Prime Minister.

*bad qualities*

The ambitions of Rennalls—and he certainly was ambitious—did not, however, lie in politics for, staunch nationalist as he was, he saw that he could serve himself and his country best (for was not bauxite responsible for nearly half the value of Barracania's export trade?) by putting his engineering talent to the best use possible. On this account, Hutchins found that he had an unexpectedly easy task in persuading Rennalls to give up his political work before entering the production department as an assistant engineer.

It was, Baker knew, Rennalls's well-repressed sense of race consciousness which had prevented their relationship from being as close as it should have been. On the surface, nothing could have seemed more agreeable. Formality between the two men was at a minimum; Baker was delighted to find that his assistant shared his own peculiar "shaggy dog" sense of humor so that jokes were continually being exchanged; they entertained each other at their houses and often played tennis together—and yet the barrier remained invisible, indefinable, but ever present. The existence of this "screen" between them was a constant source of frustration to Baker since it indicated a weakness which he was loath to accept. If successful with all other nationalities, why not with Rennalls?

But at least he had managed to "break through" to Rennalls more successfully than any other expatriate. In fact, it was the young Barracanian's attitude—sometimes overbearing, sometimes cynical—toward other company expatriates that had been one of the subjects Baker had raised last year when he discussed Rennalls's staff report with him. He knew, too, that he would have to raise the same subject again in the forthcoming interview because Jackson, the senior draftsman, had complained only yesterday about the rudeness of Rennalls. With this thought in mind, Baker leaned forward and spoke into the intercom. "Would you come in Matt, please? I'd like a word with you," and later, "Do sit down," proffering the box, "have a cigarette." He paused while he held out his lighter and then went on.

"As you know, Matt, I'll be off to Canada in a few days' time, and before I go, I thought it would be useful if we could have a final chat together. It is indeed with some deference that I suggest I can be of help. You will shortly be sitting in this chair doing the job I am now doing, but I, on the other hand, am ten years older, so perhaps you can accept the idea that I may be able to give you the benefit of my longer experience."

Baker saw Rennalls stiffen slightly in his chair as he made this point so added in explanation, "You and I have attended enough company courses to remember those repeated requests by the personnel manager to tell people how they are getting on as often as the convenient moment arises and not just the automatic 'once a year' when, by regulation, staff reports have to be discussed."

Rennalls nodded his agreement, so Baker went on. "I shall always remember the last job performance discussion I had with my previous boss back in Germany. He used what he called the 'plus and minus' technique. His firm belief was that when a senior, by discussion, seeks to improve the work performance of his staff, his prime objective should be to make sure that the latter leaves the interview encouraged and inspired to improve. Any criticism must, therefore, be constructive and helpful. He said that one very good way to encourage a person—and I fully agree with him—is to tell him about his good points—the plus factors—as well as his weak ones—the minus factors—so I thought, Matt, it would be a good idea to run our discussion along these lines."

Rennalls offered no comment, so Baker continued: "Let me say, therefore, right away, that, as far as your own work performance is concerned, the plus far outweighs the minus. I have, for instance, been most impressed with the way you have adapted your considerable theoretical knowledge to master the practical techniques of your job—that ingenious method you used to get air down to the fifth-shaft level is a sufficient case in point—and at departmental meetings I have invariably found your comments well taken and helpful. In fact, you will be interested to know that only last week I reported to Mr. Hutchins that, from the technical point of view, he could not wish for a more able man to succeed to the position of chief engineer."

*Plus* [handwritten margin note]

"That's very good indeed of you, John," cut in Rennalls with a smile of thanks. "My only worry now is how to live up to such a high recommendation."

"Of that I am quite sure," returned Baker, "especially if you can overcome the minus factor which I would like now to discuss with you. It is one which I have talked about before so I'll come straight to the point. I have noticed that you are more friendly and get on better with your fellow Barracanians than you do with Europeans. In point of fact, I had a complaint only yesterday from Mr. Jackson, who said you had been rude to him—and not for the first time either.

*minus* [handwritten margin note]

"There is, Matt, I am sure, no need for me to tell you how necessary it will be for you to get on well with expatriates because until the company has trained up sufficient people of your caliber, Europeans are bound to occupy senior positions here in Barracania. All this is vital to your future interests, so can I help you in any way?"

While Baker was speaking on this theme, Rennalls had sat tensed in his chair and it was some seconds before he replied. "It is quite extraordinary, isn't it, how one can convey an impression to others so at variance with what one intends? I can only assure you once again that my disputes with Jackson—and you may remember also Godson—have had nothing at all to do with the color of their skins. I promise you that if a Barracanian had behaved in an equally peremptory manner I would have reacted in precisely the same way. And again, if I may say it within these four walls, I am sure I am not the only one who has found Jackson and Godson difficult. I could mention the names of several expatriates who have felt the same. However, I am really sorry to have created this impression of not being able to get on with Europeans—it is an entirely false one—and I quite realize that I must do all I can to correct it as quickly as possible. On your last point, regarding Europeans holding senior positions in the Company for some time to come, I quite accept the situation. I know that Caribbean Bauxite—as they have been doing for many years now—will promote Barracanians as soon as their experience warrants it. And, finally, I would like to assure you, John—and my father thinks the same too—that I am very happy in my work here and hope to stay with the company for many years to come."

Rennalls had spoken earnestly and, although not convinced by what he had heard, Baker did not think he could pursue the matter further except to say, "All right, Matt, my impression *may* be wrong, but I would like to re-

Just talking at him?
What about his reasons for his behavior

mind you about the truth of that old saying, 'What is important is not what is true but what is believed.' Let it rest at that."

But suddenly Baker knew that he didn't want to "let it rest at that." He was disappointed once again at not being able to "break through" to Rennalls and having yet again to listen to his bland denial that there was any racial prejudice in his makeup. Baker, who had intended ending the interview at this point, decided to try another tack.

"To return for a moment to the 'plus and minus technique' I was telling you about just now, there is another plus factor I forgot to mention. I would like to congratulate you not only on the caliber of your work but also on the ability you have shown in overcoming a challenge which I, as a European, have never had to meet.

"Continental Ore is, as you know, a typical commercial enterprise— admittedly a big one—which is a product of the economic and social environment of the United States and Western Europe. My ancestors have all been brought up in this environment for the past two or three hundred years and I have, therefore, been able to live in a world in which commerce (as we know it today) has been part and parcel of my being. It has not been something revolutionary and new which has suddenly entered my life. In your case" went on Baker, "the situation is different because you and your forebears have only had some fifty or sixty years' experience of this commercial environment. You have had to face the challenge of bridging the gap between fifty and two or three hundred years. Again, Matt, let me congratulate you— and people like you—once again on having so successfully overcome this particular hurdle. It is for this very reason that I think the outlook for Barracania—and particularly Caribbean Bauxite—is so bright."

Rennalls had listened intently and when Baker finished, replied, "Well, once again, John, I have to thank you for what you have said, and, for my part, I can only say that it is gratifying to know that my own personal effort has been so much appreciated. I hope that more people will soon come to think as you do."

There was a pause and, for a moment, Baker thought hopefully that he was about to achieve his long awaited "breakthrough," but Rennalls merely smiled back. The barrier remained unbreached. There remained some five minutes' cheerful conversation about the contrast between the Caribbean and Canadian climate and whether the West Indies had any hope of beating England in the Fifth Test before Baker drew the interview to a close. Although he was as far as ever from knowing the real Rennalls, he was nevertheless glad that the interview had run along in this friendly manner and, particularly, that it had ended on such a cheerful note.

This feeling, however, lasted only until the following morning. Baker had some farewells to make, so he arrived at the office considerably later than usual. He had no sooner sat down at his desk than his secretary walked into the room with a worried frown on her face. Her words came fast. "When I arrived this morning I found Mr. Rennalls already waiting at my door. He seemed very angry and told me in quite a peremptory manner that he had a vital letter to dictate which must be sent off without any delay. He was so worked up that he couldn't keep still and kept pacing about the room, which is most unlike him. He wouldn't even wait to read what he had dictated. Just signed the page where he thought the letter would end. It has been distributed and your copy is in your 'in tray.' "

# High Technology, Incorporated: The International Benefits Problem

## RAE ANDRE

P A R T    A

At High Technology Incorporated (HTI), the benefits policy for international assignments states that:

> Wherever legally possible, HTI will attempt to provide the employee with Home Country benefits under the Life Insurance, Disability Pension and Social Security Plans during temporary international assignments.

HTI employees typically spend one to three, and sometimes as long as four years overseas. Historically, during this time, many employees have received benefits equaling or surpassing those of the home country. Recently, company policy has shifted toward equalizing benefits across countries. The system has been less than perfect, however, with some employees finding that their stay overseas has reduced their benefits. At a 1984 conference for the corporate personnel managers of local companies, Jack Cooke, HTI Corporate International Benefits Manager, commented on HTI's difficulties in fairly compensating its U.S. employees abroad. During his discussion, he made the following points.

## ■ Home Country Coverage

In 1984 HTI carried out an audit of employees and inventoried people for the purposes of determining offsets—the benefits given to overseas em-

*Source:* Reprinted by permission of the author.

ployees to offset loss of home country coverages for pensions, insurance, and similar benefits. The issue was to examine offsetting benefits to determine (1) if there was enough funding and (2) if the funding was allocated to the appropriate areas.

HTI gathered pension and benefits data for each employee on overseas assignment. A benefits book was published for each individual. The audit revealed that there was a considerable amount of overfunding (in the plans of four countries) and some underfunding—people with no plans at all. Cooke believed that HTI was not fulfilling its promise to provide equitable contracts to employees sent overseas. The audit pointed up the fact that whereas HTI was providing adequate funding, the money was being put in the wrong buckets—it was not being well distributed among the countries and individuals who needed it.

Cooke noted that the employees' main fear concerns the security of their coverage. He vividly recalls the old saying "Don't worry . . . but don't die or get sick on assignment!" and how it applied to a Canadian employee in Scotland. The employee died on the last night of his assignment. When his wife was questioned by Scottish authorities shortly after the death, it was discovered that the man had been covered by Canadian Social Insurance (federal social security), and so was ineligible for death benefits in Scotland. The Scottish social security agency refused to pay a death benefit and returned all HTI contributions to the wife, saying the employee should not have been covered in the first place.

The Scottish case highlights the need to review the current local policy to determine when coverage should apply and what steps should be taken to ensure continuity of coverage. Currently the company does not cover the employee under foreign programs when an employee cannot be maintained in a home country plan. A lack of coverage results in one of two major ways.

First, the home country legal requirements or plan documents may not permit participation by nonresidents. For example, a citizen and resident of Country A is transferred to Country B. Country A does not provide certain coverages, retirement income coverage, for example, to its citizens if they live outside Country A. HTI does not provide this coverage either.

Second, nonnationals in the home country are not allowed to stay in home country programs. For example, a citizen of Country B is working in Country A. In Country A, he is only covered for health insurance for a specified period, after which, unless he becomes a citizen, he will not be covered. Again, HTI has no policy to cover him.

To give a real-life example: "What about my pensions in the U.K.?" is a question often asked by "permanent" British employees living in the U.S. From the company's viewpoint, it may be difficult to decide what "permanent" means. Cooke pointed out that any American citizen on a United States payroll is covered by U.S. Social Security anywhere in the world. This type of problem only arises with HTI employees from nations other than the United States.

## ▄ *Additional Issues*

Cooke identified several other problems that he felt needed to be addressed. One was that the permanent relocation policy did not address past service: What happens if a person relocates permanently out of their home country? How should their benefits, especially their pension benefits, be calculated? Another problem was that the company and employee sometimes differed about how to define home country. If an employee had been in a country other than his or her country of origin for ten years or more, which was the employee's home country? Also, there were some employees with *no* evident home country.

Cooke sent questionnaires to the personnel heads in the various countries concerned, asking them to tell him what problems they would face in attempting to make the international benefits program more equitable. Three major issues were identified.

1. *Legal.* The first issue was complying with legal requirements in the various host countries. Of the three issues, this was considered to be the most serious. For example, sometimes employees found themselves involuntarily vested in host country plans by law, when HTI would have preferred them to be covered in the United States. Cooke pointed out that to date corrective action on this particular problem has involved alerting line management of the situation and developing recommendations.

The home country law sometimes excludes nonresidents from coverage in their home country. As an example, if a U.K. (English) resident is outside the U.K. for more than three years, he or she has to leave the retirement plan. Extensions are possible, but only for the fourth year. The nonresidents can buy back into the U.K. plan later on. But in the meantime, the company has chosen to provide coverage for subsequent years.

2. *Financial.* Two issues arise here. The first is liability for past service. For example, with the case just mentioned, who pays for the uncovered years? The host country? the individual? HTI? Also, individuals may lose coverage due to local fiscal requirements. For example, a country might not have a sliding scale for social security benefits, thus putting the well-paid individual at a disadvantage relative to his home country peers.

3. *Administrative.* Not all HTI facilities even *have* pension plans. And among those that do, there are different requirements. Some have a minimum age of twenty-five, some do not. Some have a one-year waiting period for eligibility, some do not. Some have voluntary participation, some do not. And some are benefit plans, whereas some are contribution plans.

At the time of Jack Cooke's talk, these issues at HTI were far from solved. The policy was that when HTI moved someone permanently, the employee would get the sum of the benefits from the country left and the new country. However, because of high inflation in many countries, this often meant that the employee was losing money.

P  A  R  T    B

# ▬ HTI: Cooke's Recommendations

HTI's Corporate International Benefits Manager, Jack Cooke, feels that the company's benefit policy should be revised. The problem is summarized by him as follows: "If HTI moves someone permanently, they get the sum of the parts, and the money left in the other country is often losing money for them due to inflation. This is all they get and it's not adequate." Cooke recommends that the HTI policy be revised to read:

> Assignments shall not result in loss of retirement and retirement-related benefits to the employee, whether compulsory or voluntary, calculated in accordance with the program in effect in the Home Country.

Cooke believes that for temporaries—people on international assignments of up to four years—the problem should be fixed locally. "Whatever the component—risk insurance, annuity, or pension plan—we should sit down with local counsel to provide substitute coverage that equals what they had at home." This may not lead to double coverage since HTI tries to get temporary people excluded from local plans wherever possible. Sometimes HTI chooses to live with the double coverage.

Cooke weighed the pros and cons of providing the employee with the sum of the parts earned in their different countries of employment plus vesting them and updating them in their home country. The advantages are that this policy:

- Reflects the employee's HTI career in each country
- Updates vested benefits so that total benefits are current
- Provides equitable treatment with employees in the home country
- Allows the company to retain control
- Is understood by employees
- Is simple to administer and provides more company flexibility than the alternative (i.e., moving people from country to country and changing their benefits each time, which employees resist)

The disadvantages of this policy are that it:

- Is administratively complex
- May not recognize continuous service for survivorship and disability benefits
- Will be affected by exchange rates (i.e., severe inflation)
- May not achieve retirement income objectives

Cooke noted that through their research HTI found that other companies had not solved the problem either.

P A R T     C

## ▰ *The Bandits*

HTI faces an additional problem, one faced by most international com-panies. The problem is reclassifying people from temporary to permanent. Cooke noted, "We have thirteen to fourteen American 'bandits' living in Ge-neva, Switzerland. Their kids can't even speak English, and they own ski chalets. They have home leave benefits that are more generous than others. But they are 'temporary,' and they are so powerful we can't get them to change to permanent status." The same problem is found among some em-ployees who live in the United States. Exhibit 1 indicates how many bandits of various nationalities are employed by HTI.

On the other hand, if HTI does change the bandits' designated home country, the new home country must give them benefits as if they spent their entire career there. This can be costly to the company in some instances, but it can also be an inducement: "Come over to Switzerland at age sixty-three and we'll fix you up. If the company does not do this, it reduces its flexibility to move people."

E X H I B I T  1

### *Employees on Extended Assignments*

|  | ASSIGNMENT YEARS | | | | |
|---|---|---|---|---|---|
|  | 4–5 | 5–7 | 7–10 | 10+ | Total |
| *To Switzerland* | 13 | 18 | 11 | 7 | 49* |
| *To U.S.* | 9 | 18 | 6 | 1 | 34 |

*From Germany n = 11, Netherlands n = 8, U.K. n = 17, U.S. n = 13.
*Source:* Sample of 550 expatriates.

# Labor Relations Issues in International Human Resource Management

# Racial Factors in Site Location and Employment Patterns of Japanese Auto Firms in America

## ROBERT E. COLE
## DONALD R. DESKINS, Jr.

W hat does it take for us to get accepted as an American corporation?"
Tetsuo Chino, the President of American Honda Motor Co., asked in late
1987. Chino seemed genuinely perplexed. At a press conference, he announced that Honda—which has been manufacturing cars in Marysville,
Ohio, for six years—was rapidly increasing the local content of its U.S.-made
cars. He also noted that the company was expanding employment at its U.S.
plants. It was also planning to export cars from the United States—thereby
helping to improve the U.S. balance of payments. Yet, he complained, his
company is not being treated as a domestic firm.

On March 24, 1988, the Equal Employment Opportunity Commission
announced that Honda of America Manufacturing Inc. had agreed to give
370 blacks and women a total of $6 million in back pay, resolving a federal
discrimination complaint.[1] This announcment gave rise to a wave of speculation in the media as to whether Japanese firms in general had been systematically engaged in discriminatory activities toward blacks and women.

Governments everywhere have a habit of closely scrutinizing the operations of foreign corporations, searching for areas of non-compliance with domestic regulations, and even devising rules that are designed to hinder such
corporations. Thus, it is dangerous to leap to conclusions, especially on so
sensitive a matter as this one.

What does it take for a foreign firm to be a good corporate citizen? This
is the current hot topic among industry and government officials in Tokyo.

*Source:* Robert E. Cole and Donald R. Deskins, Jr. "Racial Factors in Site Location and Employment Patterns of Japanese Auto Firms in America." 1988. *California Management Review*, 9–22.

Surely, it involves more than being active in local community affairs through philanthropic activities. In the United States, one measure of good citizenship is compliance with the Civil Rights Act of 1964 as enforced by the Equal Employment Opportunity Commission (EEOC). Yet, even when there is conformance with EEOC guidelines, companies can still violate the spirit of the law.

We have been researching the behavior of Japanese auto-related firms in the United States for about a year and a half with regard to plant site location and employment as it relates to blacks. To interpret the data properly, we must make comparisons with American firms. This, in turn, gives us the opportunity to reflect on the behavior of American firms as well.

## ■ *What's the Problem?*

The automobile industry has been, and continues to be, a major provider of jobs for blacks. In 1984, according to reports filed with the EEOC, some 17.2 percent of all workers employed by the Big Three American automakers were black: 8.4 percent of the white-collar workers employed by the Big Three were black.

Although their records are by no means unblemished, there is no doubt that General Motors, Ford, and Chrysler, along with the large number of U.S. auto suppliers, have been major sources of jobs and income for black workers. Just how big is seldom appreciated. General Motors estimates that its 1987 payroll (before taxes) for its 76,792 black employees (64,553 hourly and 12,239 salaried) totalled some 3.03 billion dollars. The March 1988 Current Population Survey estimates that the total 1987 wage and salary income for 12.9 million blacks in 1987 was 178.8 billion dollars. This means that although GM's black employees accounted for only 0.6 percent of all black employees, they received 1.7 percent of all black wage and salary income in the United States in 1987.[2]

Blacks constitute almost 11 percent of the civilian labor force, yet they constitute a far higher percentage of employment at the Big Three. We can speculate that this came about because blacks "overselected" themselves as applicants for auto industry jobs; they saw the industry as providing one of the limited number of opportunities for them to achieve middle-class living standards while requiring modest educational credentials. Conversely, the pool of whites available for employment for auto production jobs is less than what would be suggested by their labor force numbers. Higher educational attainment for whites and lack of racial barriers gave them substantial job alternatives.

Since 1979, there has been extensive displacement of American auto workers because of competition from foreign firms. The membership of the United Auto Workers, for example, has fallen by one-third in the past nine years, from 1.5 million in 1979 to 1 million in 1987. In a recent study of deindustrialization in the Great Lakes region, Richard Hill and Cynthia Negrey found that blacks experienced significantly higher rates of industrial job losses than whites between 1979 and 1984 (36 percent for black versus 27 percent for whites).[3] In keeping with our observation about the lack of alternatives for blacks, Department of Labor studies show that blacks who lost their manufacturing jobs in the 1980s have had lower rates of reemployment than whites.

## The Japanese Factor

Employment opportunities for blacks have been hurt by the shift of American manufacturers and suppliers to more suburban and rural plant locations as well as a southerly drift by American manufacturers and suppliers. These are the same areas that have benefitted most by the establishment of large numbers of Japanese auto-related plants. The Japanese have invested both within the traditional midwestern auto corridor (Ohio and Michigan) as well as the adjacent states of Kentucky and Tennessee (for example, Nissan's assembly plant in Smyrna, Tennessee, and Toyota's in Georgetown, Kentucky). This southern drift of industry—both traditional and Japanese—provides closer access to the rapidly expanding markets of the South, cheaper building and operating costs, and more "virgin" labor supplies from rural locations with fewer union ties.

The Japanese plants in North America make up for only a small portion of the job losses suffered at American companies in the past largely because they are more efficient—thereby requiring less labor—and because more than 50 percent of the value of the cars assembled here is produced in Japan. Apart from the reduced labor requirements, the Japanese firms create fewer opportunities for blacks because of where they are locating their plants. Our study indicates that there is an extraordinary mismatch between the heavy toll on black employment taking place among U.S. manufacturers and the small number of opportunities for blacks being made available at the new Japanese plants. It is important to stress that this raises major policy issues, independent of motive. (The issue of whether the Japanese have a "taste for discrimination" is of only secondary interest in this article.)

## Research Methodology

According to EEOC guidelines, the racial composition of the work force at any plant should reflect the population of the local area, or "laborshed," that surrounds it. This concept is widely accepted, but the definition of a laborshed's boundary is not specified in legislation nor are there firm guidelines. Rather, the EEOC relies on a determination of a "normal recruiting area," based on the experience of firms in the local labor market. This definition is itself quite vague and adds credence to what one EEOC investigator told us: "every case is unique."

Our research methodology, based on the widely used "gravity model," was designed to create a simple but consistent standard for assessing opportunity to enter into the applicant pool. The gravity model allows us to measure explicitly the location of a specific manufacturing establishment (destination) in relation to the diverse location of potential employees (origins) by integrating measures of relative distance with measures of relative population size.[4]

For each of seven Japanese assembly plants and 91 supplier plants in North America, we determined the potential number of black and white workers living within the adjacent ring of counties. For all our categories of sites (excepting Volkswagen), those who had access to each plant site on the average lived within a 26 mile radius of the site (see Exhibit 1). That is to say, they lived within reasonable commuting distance. National census data bear this out by showing that the propensity to commute declines rapidly once one goes beyond 29 miles, with only 6.2 percent commuting to work more than 30 miles.[5] Thus, the population on which we base our analysis covers most of those we would expect to be potentially available for work at each site. Our base data come from Census figures on the population in the counties surrounding each plant. The population by race for each adjacent county was recorded. From this we were then able to derive an employment potential ratio of blacks to whites for each plant. We made the simplifying assumption that whites and blacks living within the adjacent counties were equally available for employment.

We can learn a great deal from these estimates of employment potential for blacks and whites through comparing the data from the laborsheds around Japanese plants with similar data for U.S. automotive plants. In a number of cases, we can also compare the data on the ratio of potential black to white employees to actual racial composition of employment at each plant.

The number and types of plants whose laborsheds we examined are listed in Exhibit 1. The American facilities were divided into three types. "Greenfield" sites are new assembly plants built by U.S. manufacturers since

E X H I B I T  1

| PLANT TYPE | NUMBER OF SITES | AVERAGE DISTANCE FROM PLANT LOCATION TO ADJACENT COUNTIES IN MILES |
|---|---|---|
| Volkswagen assembly plant | 1 assembly plant | 34.4 |
| Japanese auto parts companies* | 91 supplier plants | 25.6 |
| Japanese OEM plants | 7 assembly plants | 25.1 |
| GM greenfield sites since 1980 | 8 assembly plants | 25.7 |
| Big Three retrofits | 31 assembly plants | 22.7 |
| Big Three traditional plants | 21 assembly plants | 24.3 |

*This total of 91 plants represented close to the entire universe of Japanese auto parts suppliers in the United States in operation by September 1987.

1980 (all GM facilities) and are the rough equivalent of new Japanese plants built in the United States. ''Retrofits'' are assembly plants that have been extensively modernized since 1980 (more than $200 million investment beyond normal operational improvements). ''Traditional'' plants are those assembly plants built some time ago that have not been modernized. (For comparison's sake, we included the recently closed Volkswagen assembly plant in New Stanton, Pennsylvania, which had been criticized in the past for its poor record on minority hiring.)

## ▬ What the Data Show

With the exception of the Volkswagen plant, the Japanese scored consistently lower in the ratio of black to white population in the area within the laborshed of their plants (see Exhibit 2). The performance of the 91 Japanese auto-parts plants was particularly weak. With few blacks relative to whites in the areas where they locate their plants, Japanese firms can stay within EEOC guidelines and still hire very few blacks. By siting their plants in areas with very low black populations, they, in effect, exclude blacks from potential employment.

We had expected that the most recently built American greenfield sites would have the lowest employment potentials for blacks, the retrofits (many of which were located in or near older cities with large black populations) would have the next highest potential, and traditional plants (even more of which were in older cities) the highest potential. Data from Exhibit 2 show our prediction was incorrect. The laborsheds of the retrofit plants had the

E X H I B I T  2

### Ratio of Black to White Population
### Within Local Laborsheds by Type of Plant

| PLANT TYPE | AVERAGE RATIO OF BLACKS TO WHITES IN LABORSHED | AVERAGE PERCENT BLACK OF TOTAL BLACK AND WHITE POPULATION IN LABORSHED* |
|---|---|---|
| Volkswagen (Pennsylvania plant) | .074 | 6.9 |
| Japanese auto parts companies | .148 | 11.7 |
| Japanese OEM plants | .163 | 12.8 |
| GM greenfield sites† | .204 | 16.0 |
| Big Three retrofit plants | .193 | 15.2 |
| Big Three traditional plants | .286 | 19.8 |

*For all practical purposes, total black and white population equals total population within the local laborshed with the exception of the West Coast and Texas plants. For these plants we used the ratio of blacks to total non-black population.
†Includes Saturn plant.

lowest black to white employment potential ratio, not the greenfield sites. In keeping with our expectations, however, the traditional plants did have the highest ratio.

The American plants in all categories score higher than the Japanese plants—that is, they are located in areas with higher ratios of blacks to whites. It may appear that the black-white ratios in the U.S. retrofit plants and greenfield sites are not that much better than those in the new Japanese assembly plants. Given that these figures are based on relatively large populations, however, even a "small" percentage difference is important in human terms. The GM greenfield sites at 16 percent may be viewed as "only" 3.2 percent above the 12.8 percent of the Japanese OEM plants. But that represents a 25 percent higher potential black employment, and in a county with 50,000 workers it represents an extra 1,600 potential black jobs! For an assembly plant employing 5,000 workers that would mean an extra 160 expected black jobs.

This leads us now to examine whether there are any differences between Japanese and American firms in actual employment of blacks and whites. Although we don't have data on the retrofit plants, we do have data for the seven GM greenfield plants actually in operation. When the Big Three develop greenfield sites, they often employ workers displaced from older plants that, typically, have larger numbers of black employees. The policy arises from agreements with the United Auto Workers. The GM-UAW agreement, for example, requires the company to give priority in hiring to laid-off employees for 24 months after a new plant opens. It also gives employees the right "to follow their work" when there is a transfer of major operations between an old and a new plant. Consequently, the effects of shifts to new locations can be temporarily softened as displaced employees from older plants are funneled into the new greenfield plants. However, as the transferred employees gradually leave or retire, more local people are hired and the plant may eventually more closely reflect the racial mix of the surrounding population.

The average ratio of black to white *employees* at the seven greenfield sites is .267, or 25.4 percent. (There is another 5 percent of non-black minorities, mostly hispanic.) In other words, the ratio of blacks to whites actually employed is appreciably higher than the average potential employment ratio of .214, or 16.6 percent in the laborsheds of the seven plants. (Saturn is excluded from this list as it is not yet operational.)

Is it possible that the Japanese automakers also employ higher ratios of blacks to whites than would be anticipated from the analyses of their laborsheds? On the face of it, this seems unlikely. Four Japanese greenfield sites were operational during the period of this study: NUMMI, the GM-Toyota joint venture in Fremont, California; the Nissan plant at Smyrna, Tennessee; Honda in Marysville, Ohio; and Mazda at Flat Rock, Michigan. NUMMI has far more blacks (23 percent) and hispanics (28 percent) than one would expect based on the population employment potential of its laborshed. That is because, as a condition of its opening, the joint venture agreed to UAW insistence that it rehire workers laid off from the former GM plant at Fremont. Why the original Fremont labor force had such overrepresentation of minorities relates to our earlier speculation that blacks tend to overselect for such jobs while the available pool of whites is smaller than their absolute labor force numbers would suggest.

For those who would justify avoidance of blacks based on the argument that they are not capable of meeting today's new standards of efficiency and quality, we note that this U.S.-Japanese joint venture has achieved an enviable reputation for quality and productivity. Indeed, it has become a model for American firms striving to learn Japanese practices. It is interesting how seldom the high proportions of minorities among NUMMI's employees are mentioned in discussions of NUMMI's revolutionary impact on American management thinking on the manufacturing sector.

The situations at the Nissan Smyrna plant, the Honda Marysville plant, and the Mazda Flat Rock plant are a better guide to what the Japanese are likely to do when they are under no UAW pressure to hire displaced workers. This is, in fact, the case with most of the rest of the Japanese auto manufacturers and auto suppliers. (In the case of Mazda, displaced Ford workers from the Flat Rock plant did get special preference to enter the initial pool of applicants, but they received no special preference in hiring.)

Based on the population employment potential, one would expect 10.5 percent of Honda employees at Marysville to be black; in fact, only 2.8 percent are. The pattern at Nissan is closer to their laborshed potential: one would expect that 19.3 percent of the employees to be black, and the company reports that 14 percent are. Finally, there is the Mazda plant which reports that 14.1 percent of its employees are black against an expectation of 29 percent based on the population employment potential model. At none of the three plants is the percent of blacks to whites actually employed above the population employment potential; instead it is moderately or significantly below. This is in sharp contrast to the situation at the U.S. greenfield sites.

It is in the Big Three traditional plants that the population employment potential of blacks is the highest. However, the growing U.S. production capacity brought on by Japanese plant siting in the U.S. suggests additional plant closings by U.S. manufacturers and suppliers. Among the Big Three plants, the prime candidates for such closings are the traditional plants that have not yet been modernized. Thus, the jobs most at risk from the Japanese auto industry's continued competitive pressure are in the traditional plants with the highest ratio of black to white population in the local laborshed. Indeed, a number of the facilities that we categorized as traditional have already been closed or have been announced as candidates for closing. We can also speculate with some degree of confidence that a similar situation is going on with the large American suppliers.

From our data, we can also compare the percentage of blacks employed in Japanese auto parts firms to the population employment potential of those plants. As seen in Exhibit 2, the percent of blacks to total black and white population in the laborsheds surrounding these plants averaged 11.7 percent. (We surveyed all 91 plants and received a respectable 60 percent response rate.) Our respondents had an average of 8.5 percent blacks among their total employees. When we look at the population employment potential of only those plants which responded, we find that they record an average 12.1 percent for their population employment potential score (close enough to the score recorded for the entire sample to eliminate any concern about major bias among our respondents; if anything, the data suggest that firms with fewer blacks in their laborsheds were less likely to respond). In summary, the Japanese plants' actual hiring practices lead to fewer jobs for blacks (8.5 percent) than would be expected. We should not assume, however, that their performance automatically would be different from new American auto parts plants. There is some reason to think that the smaller the plant and the company, the more likely it is that blacks are underrepresented in the workforce, regardless of whether the company is Japanese or American. Smaller companies are less subject to public scrutiny and thus less likely to adopt formal affirmative action programs.

In Exhibit 3, the population employment potential for blacks forms the basis of an expectation for the proportion of jobs that blacks will hold. To the extent that actual black employment departs from this expectation, blacks can be said to be either over- or underrepresented. This departure from "population expectations" is a standard measure of different experiences and consequences used to assess disparities by race. We can summarize these data in Exhibit 3 as follows: the Japanese firms consistently perform under the population employment potential of their laborshed while the one U.S. category of GM greenfield sites performs well above it. To be sure, these data should only be regarded as suggestive and we cannot necessarily generalize to all U.S. auto firms. Nevertheless, the data do at a minimum suggest that we raise the caution flag on Japanese practices and they provide an agenda for future research.

Some Japanese companies argue that the racial composition of their employees accurately reflects the racial composition of the counties in which they recruit. Therefore, they maintain, they are clearly not discriminating. This neat formulation ignores the logically prior question: in which counties or communities could or should they recruit? Our data showing the gap between the population employment potential of their laborsheds and actual employment suggest the hollowness of their claims.

## ▬ Do the Japanese Have a "Taste" for Discrimination?

The question of intent, while secondary to our interests, is not trivial. The statistical data do not allow us to clarify motives for site locations. However, our personal experiences lead us to believe that the Japanese plant sit-

E X H I B I T 3

*Comparative Differences Between Percent Black Employees and Population Employment Potential by Company or Type*

| COMPANY OR TYPE OF PLANT | A POPULATION EMPLOYMENT POTENTIAL (in %) | B PERCENT BLACK EMPLOYED | C DIFFERENCE BETWEEN COLUMNS A & B (B − A) |
|---|---|---|---|
| U.S. greenfield sites* | 16.6 | 25.4 | +8.8 |
| Honda | 10.5 | 2.8 | −7.7 |
| Nissan | 19.3 | 14.0 | −5.3 |
| Mazda | 29.0 | 14.1 | −14.9 |
| Japanese auto parts (N = 50)† | 12.1 | 8.5 | −3.6 |

*Does not include Saturn plant.
†Five responding plants are not included because they removed their identifying number. They averaged 5.7% black. Thus, if they were added in, the percent black would decline.

ings reflect a pattern in which avoidance of blacks is *one* factor in their site location decision.

In the course of our research, we heard some Japanese managers specifically explain their decisions on plant siting in such terms. Dennis Des Rosiers, a leading Canadian auto industry consultant, was quoted in an interview to the effect that the Japanese don't want to locate near big cities or to be in "union territory."[6] Des Rosiers, who has carried out several site studies for Japanese auto companies, added: "They ask for profiles of the community by ethnic background, by religious background, by professional makeup. They want to know how many accountants there are in the area, versus how many farmers. Those are key variables. . . . There are demographic aspects that they like. They like a high German content. Germans have a good work ethic—well-trained, easy to train, they accept things. . . .[The Japanese] probably don't like other types of profiles." In a similar vein, a midwestern state official responsible for recruiting Japanese firms to his state in the early 1980s reported to us that "many Japanese companies at the time specifically asked to stay away from areas with high minority populations."

Another clue to Japanese corporate practices comes from an official of the Japan External Trade Organization (JETRO). The Tokyo office of JETRO provides detailed census tract information for the United States to Japanese companies wishing to invest in this country. The official informed us that companies routinely examine these data when weighing possible plant locations. In addition, he said that the racial composition of the population near the sites was one of the things that they usually investigated. JETRO's extensive publications discussing the characteristics of site locations in given states routinely report racial structure (though no specific advice is given to avoid blacks). From the perspective of Japanese managers, these decisions are perhaps not so surprising. As one Japanese executive explained, Japanese managers consider it their job to recreate the successful operations they have in Japan, which implies "how do we get American workers to act like Japanese." One JETRO publication describes California as a good place to site plants because they have lots of Asians and they make "high quality employees."

The Japanese are struggling to make a competitive success of their new plants in the United States and have little experience at managing American workers. Contrary to the impression of many Americans, they have approached the establishment of factories here with great trepidation and caution. They may see blacks as sufficiently different from whites in their work habits as to create additional management problems. They may believe that blacks are poor risks as workers because they have lower levels of education than whites, have more problems communicating due to language differences, are more prone to drugs and crime, or evidence a greater propensity to unionize. A recent study of the portrayal of Japanese overseas businessman in Japanese business novels reports that blacks are depicted as "streetwise, rioting, stealing or drugged."[7]

While such beliefs are often built on prejudice, they may make perfect business sense to the Japanese. Practices based on these assumptions may be legal under a narrow interpretation of EEOC guidelines. However, they are a clear violation of the spirit of the Civil Rights Act of 1964 that underlies them. Nor is it a rationale with which American blacks will sympathize.

## ■ Some Policy Issues

What conclusions can we draw from our discussion of the data? Are the Japanese choices of sites the result of wholly independent decisions based on such criteria as cheaper land, closeness to markets, lower taxes, and union avoidance? If they are, there are still serious policy issues raised by this analysis. Our thrust here is not to establish that the Japanese have improper motives. Regardless of intent, their plant site locations contribute to a drying up of opportunities for black workers in an industry that has traditionally supplied large opportunities to minority workers. Moreover, hiring blacks at a lower ratio than suggested by the racial distribution of their local laborsheds further aggravates the problem.

States have systematically subsidized the location of Japanese auto manufacturer plants in the U.S. Should states be subsidizing with the taxes of all its citizens the location of foreign firms that adversely affect the already unequal employment opportunities for blacks? If we want new plants located in the areas accessible to greater numbers of blacks, what policy options are available? Do we need to revisit "enterprise zones.?" Do states need to reconsider the view that all new jobs are equally deserving of state subsidies? Could not the level of state subsidies be a function in part of the kinds of jobs being created? Moreover, don't we need to consider state subsidies for upgrading older plants, thereby protecting many minority jobs instead of encouraging the establishment of new plants that simply lead to closings of these older plants? These are important policy questions independent of whether the Japanese have any intent to discriminate.

> The evidence that Japanese automakers in America minimize contact with blacks is further supported by the small number of minority-owned dealerships.
> The National Association of Minority Automobile Dealers reports that there is only one minority car dealership among Nissan's American car dealers (0.1 percent of the total) and only three among Toyota's dealers (0.3 percent of the total). Indeed, they reported in 1987 that blacks own just eight of the nearly 5,000 Japanese car dealerships in the country.
> While the record of U.S. companies is not sterling in this area, they are certainly better than the Japanese companies by a wide margin: Ford has 170 minority dealerships (3.4 percent of the total) and GM has 204 minority dealership (2 percent of the total).

There is also the policy issue of how the role of the EEOC can be strengthened to insure that race is not a factor in plant site location decisions. This, in turn, underlines the need to strengthen the agency's traditional role of insuring equal opportunity hiring practices. Perhaps, analogous to the environmental impact statement, we need to consider having an "employment impact" statement for firms building new plants over a certain size. There are some possible models growing out of the current obligations of federal contractors.

## ▬ *Does Japanese Behavior Simply Mirror Our Own?*

Rosabeth Kanter argues that the need for reliability and predictability in times of uncertainty leads to pressure in organizations for social homogeneity.[8] For her, the issue was the impact of this way of thinking on the restriction of opportunities for females in American corporations. This logic, however, would appear to apply equally well to exclusion of blacks by Japanese *and* American companies.

This leads us more directly to consider the behavior of American firms. We have seen that the site location decisions represented both by the GM greenfield sites and by the Big Three's choice of which plants to retrofit work against plant locations in areas of high minority concentrations—though not as significantly as Japanese OEM decisions. Moreover, without contractual obligations in these new sites, the initial employment patterns of American as well as Japanese plants would also likely reflect the lower black to white ratios of local population.

Thus, the Japanese site locations provide a kind of mirror to view our own potential managerial decisions were they less constrained by contractual obligations and sunk costs in old plants. If our own companies were growing rapidly and seeking new plant locations, would they not be building them in many of the same places as the Japanese. Indeed, analysis of data from areas that are experiencing rapid growth (such as the high-tech sector) led researchers Markusen, Hall, and Glasmeier to conclude that black share of a metropolitan area's population is negatively associated with high-tech jobs and plant locations.[9] Industrial development specialists in state government report that they are often asked by American firms in a variety of industries to eliminate from consideration plant sites in counties with 30 percent or more black population.[10] All this ought to provide food for thought for those tempted to use our data for simple Japan bashing.

Even if the Japanese thresholds are lower, all this looks in principle quite similar to the practices we have just been describing. The fact that Japanese managers seem to voice racist sentiments should not be interpreted to mean that they are necessarily more racist than American managers. It is clear that many have yet to learn the American taboos with regard to talking about race. By telling state officials that they don't want sites near minority areas, the Japanese might simply be telling white American state officials what they think these officials would like to hear and what they think is appropriate under the circumstances. White American managers may simply be more subtle in their behavior toward blacks rather than any less racist than the Japanese.

The point of this discussion then is not to suggest that newly established Japanese companies should bear the primary burden of solving an essentially American problem. Given the relatively small number of jobs that the Japanese automakers account for, such an expectation would be ludicrous. The total number of Japanese-affiliated manufacturers in the United States is still below 700 (though growing rapidly).

Race *is* an American problem, and it is Americans who must solve it. Without progress on job opportunities we can expect to continue to move toward the Kerner report's "two societies, one black, one white—separate but unequal" with all the socially explosive potential implied by that situation. The closing down of American plants in urban areas, particularly in response to foreign competitive pressures, and the relocation of American and Japanese plants in more rural and suburban areas feeds the structural roots of the growing black underclass.

> Japanese companies can take their cue from what we may call the Jackie Robinson model. To succeed in baseball in the late 1940s, Robinson had to be better than the average white ball player. To be accepted as good corporate citizens, the Japanese should show us that they, too, can adhere to a higher standard than is called for by law.

While we must recognize the primary U.S. corporate responsibility, it is quite another thing to deny that the Japanese have important obligations in this area. Being the "new kid on the block" does not excuse them from these responsibilities. The Japanese say they want to be seen as American companies. If that is truly the case, then they need to accept that part of becoming American is to recognize American problems and accept responsibility for their solution. In our judgment, making a contribution in the area of minority hiring would be a significant step in this direction. Our data do suggest that the Japanese are worsening an already difficult situation. Their behavior with regard to site location and hiring practices heightens rather than eases the dilemma of blacks who are being rapidly displaced from their traditional American employers.

## ▬ *References*

1. McQueen, Michel and White, Joseph. "Blacks, Women at Honda Unit Win Back Pay." *Wall Street Journal,* March 24, 1988.

2. If we take into account that GM's fringe benefits are far higher than the typical firm and that GM also indirectly provides work for blacks through its suppliers and distribution network, GM's impact on black income may well be higher.

3. Hill, Richard Child and Negrey, Cynthia. "Deindustrialization and Racial Minorities in the Great Lakes Region, USA." In Malcolm Cross (ed.), *Racial Minorities and Industrial Change: Migration, Employment and the New Urban Order.* New York: Cambridge University Press, 1987.

4. See Haynes, Kingsley and Fotheringham, A. *Gravity and Spatial Interaction Models,* Vol. 2. Beverly Hills, Calif.: Sage, 1984.

5. Bureau of the Census. "The Journey to Work in the United States: 1979." *Current Population Reports,* Special Studies Series P-23 No. 122. Washington, D.C.: Department of Commerce, 1982, 5.

6. Williamson, Doug. "Japanese Bias Comes to Light in Hiring Plans." *Windsor Star Special Report: Jobs 2000,* October 29, 1987, 14.

7. Prindle, Tamae. "The Japanese Overseas Businessman in Japanese Literature." Paper presented at the East Asian Investment in Arizona's Future Conference, Arizona State University, Tucson, February 19–20, 1988.

8. Kanter, Rosabeth. *Men and Women of the Corporation.* New York: Basic Books, 1977, 54–55.

9. Markusen, Ann, Hall, Peter, and Glasmeier, Amy. *High Tech America.* Boston: Allen and Unwin, 1987.

10. Stuart, Reginald. "Business Said to Have Barred New Plants in Largely Black Communities." *New York Times,* February 15, 1983.

# The Looming Labour Crunch

## BROOKS TIGNER

Just 47 months remain until the end of 1992. By then, the remaining proposals for the completion of Europe's Internal Market *"will* be on the books" and Europe *"will* firmly be on the road to economic union." Thus spake Lord Cockfield in the waning days of his Europe Commission vice-presidency last December.

What will *not* be on the books by then, however, is comprehensive legislation covering that extra dimension of 1992: pan-EC worker rights. Opposing forces are taking sides over the role and rights of labour in a free-wheeling European market. France and Germany are lining up for a Europe with Continental-style worker welfare programmes and worker participation. Britain and Denmark are adamantly opposed. The British in particular under Prime Minister Margaret Thatcher have taken a tougher stance on labour issues than other EC member states.

"Social Europe," or the labour dimension of the 1992 programme, promises to be one of the critical EC contests of the year, even though it is not directly a part of the Internal Market plan.

French officials are leading the drive for the "social dimension." "The young people of Europe will not be swayed by talk of capital movements and the free flow of goods," argues Edith Cresson, French minister for European affairs. "What's needed is this cultural dimension, a humanistic message."

The issues are fundamental. Should part-time employees throughout the EC get full, partial or no health insurance coverage? Will companies have the freedom to create flexible work schedules on a multi-country basis? When machines replace men, who pays for the retraining? Could investments—and jobs—collapse in northern EC markets as managers move to southern low-wage locales? Finally, will there be collective bargaining at the European level?

Should the two sides of industry and labour fail to agree on a basic ap-

*Source:* Brooks Tigner. "The Looming Labour Crunch." *International Management,* February 1989, 26–31. Reprinted by permission.

proach for defining their future relationship in an emerging single economic zone, the consequences could be drastic. "If no concrete proposals appear in the next year or two that guarantee basic worker rights at the European level," says EC labour organizer Bernadette Tesch-Segol, "I think we're headed for wide-scale strikes and demonstrations within the Community. It's that simple."

Bombast or forecast? That depends on your strategic perspective. Today, organized labour is on the defensive. Union membership has declined in the 1980s. Worse, worker solidarity is crumbling as Europe's baby boomers discover that in no way will they enjoy the same retirement benefits their parents did. Social taxes are still high, while social benefits have declined. Indeed, state pension funds in some member states, such as Spain, are bankrupt. The temptation is strong, therefore, to pave one's own path to the rocking chair via personal pension plans, individual salary packages and, most alarming for labour leaders, participation in Europe's sizeable black market, where both boss and employee dodge the taxman and mandatory work rules.

European industry, on the other hand, is on the offensive. Enthusiasm for the Internal Market is high. Economic growth remains steady, if moderate, while unemployment across the 12 member countries as a whole has declined slightly in the past two years. Moreover, industry's lobbies are well financed and well organized. Their influence with the Commission is strong. The two bodies, in fact, form an alliance that is determined to emerge with a "balanced" perspective on future industrial relations. "We do not support application of the law-of-the-jungle to labour rights," says Carlos Liebana, Commission spokesman for social affairs. "But there cannot be the same working conditions for every workforce in every sector in every country in the EC; that's far too complicated to administer. Were we to accommodate all the 1992 wishes of labour, it would lead to an impasse. We've had no choice but to take a middle-of-the-road position."

Labour, not surprisingly, has condemned such moderation. When the Commission brought forth suggestions last September to create a 1992 framework for social policy, the European Trade Union Congress labelled the working paper "a disappointing and very inadequate response." The pan-EC labour lobby found it "regrettable" that social policy for the Commission means dealing with the social consequences of the Internal Market rather than anticipating and preventing the problems in the first place.

If all this parry and thrust over social "policy" seems perplexing to an outside observer, don't feel alone. Even those familiar with the nuances of Euro-jargon are confused. The subject has generated much heated debate recently in union and industry circles. The dialectics pass under many names: social "dimension," social "cohesion," and social "solidarity." Moreover, there are social "platforms," social "partners," and social "dialogues." It's enough to make some observers antisocial.

The beast itself is actually a collection of some 80 objectives, some new, some old, in various stages of proposal and adoption during the past three years. They are divided into five broad categories:

- Living and working conditions in the enlarged market
- Economic and social cohesion
- Employment and training
- Work organization
- The social foundation (which calls for a European Charter of Social Rights).

Some of the goals, such as the "living conditions" proposal to remove administrative obstacles for residency permits, are universally supported. Others, such as the proposed statute for a European company, are highly controversial: unions want mandatory worker participation on the board of directors. That makes industry in some countries, first of all Britain, recoil in horror.

All these proposals are beginning to force the labour/management dichotomy to the surface. Management wants enough financial and administrative manoeuvrability to respond quickly to the dynamic changes that 1992 is sure to bring to the market-place. Labour wants assurances that its hard-won privileges over the years will not evaporate. Striking a practical balance between the two in a borderless European market will provoke a lively debate.

On the ideological plane, labour and industry are generally in agreement on the following: no one wants the raw employment conditions that exist, say, in the United States, where redundancy rules are weaker and protection of the worker is generally less extensive. Trade unions are intent on maintaining notions of national solidarity, such as guaranteed medical and social security benefits for all, which are deeply embedded in European society. Labour would never accept a U.S.-style formula, and industry would never attempt it.

This convergence means the social partners see eye to eye on such issues as worker safety and health standards, freedom of labour movement, Community-wide residency and employment rights, mutual recognition of diplomas and technical qualifications between member-state authorities, the right to transfer pension benefits across borders, and the removal of technical barriers, especially as much of the latter constitute obstacles to employment and economic growth.

Ideologies diverge, however, when defining the purpose of the social dimension: proactive or reactive? The purpose, in turn, defines the timing. That is, should labour rights be negotiated piecemeal—country by country, sector by sector—thus responding to events as they unfold in the Internal Market? Or should the Community put in a detailed legislative framework governing all aspects of employment before the end of 1992? Clearly labour wants the framework in place before the end of 1992.

The Commission, for its part, sides with industry against the all-encompassing "pre-emptive" approach. "National laws, traditions and industrial relations vary far too much among the Twelve to ever attempt a comprehensive EC platform for worker rights," said Liebana. Observes Johannes Wachter, social affairs expert with UNICE, the Brussels-based lobby for European industry: "The principle of 'subsidiarity' should always be applied to Community legislation—that is the EC should deal only with issues that member states can't do among themselves at the national level. That does not include industrial relations."

Counters ETUC, the European Trade Union Confederation: "A Community framework should be created with full trade union participation at all levels for mastering the industrial and regional changes brought about by the Internal Market's completion."

If all this seems like so much academic *brouhaha,* it is worth considering the real-life consequences of a unified European market where capital, investments and competitive forces start changing the way business is conducted. Unions feat that, in place of an orderly spread of secure employment conditions, there will be pot-shot erosion of workers' rights. Instead of similar working conditions across the Twelve, employees will suffer the vagaries of an ever-shifting legal landscape from one region to the next.

They worry, to take a good example, about technology and redundancies: will there be guaranteed access to re-training programmes? If so, who will pay the cost and for how long? The public or private sector? If the latter, will the employer shoulder the burden or split it with the employee? Will the worker be paid for time away from the job to learn new skills, or docked for his hours?

Elsewhere, labour wonders how benefits for part-time and temporary full-time employees should be based. And what about paid parental and vacation leaves, or job security for women and the young (always the last-in/first-out payroll casualties in times of dynamic change) or the cross-border transfer of unemployment benefits?

Most worrisome for the European labour movement, though, is the spectre of social "dumping." By that is meant a post-1992 Europe where firms in countries with high employer taxes run south to Portugal or Greece where not only wage rates are lower but so are living standards and, *ipso facto,* social costs for the employer.

This could in turn exert backward pressure on northern countries to lower their social costs (i.e., worker benefits) in order to compete for investments. The end result, says labour, would be an eventual lowering of all worker benefits via corporate exploitation of variable workshifts, variable payrates, variable lengths of employment, with no guarantee of job security.

Both EC and industry representatives scoff at such reasoning. Commission President Jacques Delors, a Socialist politician himself, has gone on record repeatedly to allay labour's anxieties. "The fears of social dumping are totally unfounded," he says. "Apart from the fact than most labour-intensive industries are declining in importance, all Community countries share one important feature: democratic political systems in which the legal framework is determined by freely elected representatives and which fully accept workers' freedom of association."

Translation: each of the Twelve has firm traditions of industrial relations in which the right to form unions is undisputed. Another counter argument against social dumping is industry's assertion that lower labour costs alone are not reason enough to head south.

"Let's not forget that companies have always had the freedom to pick up and move elsewhere inside the Community," observes Arnout De Koster, social affairs adviser at the federation of Belgian industry (FEB). "Plant relocation is based on many more factors than just pay scales: local banking rates, national and regional infrastructure, productivity levels, worker skills, access to telecommunications and transport systems.

"For unions to say there will be dislocations simply as a function of cheaper Portuguese wages is too monolithic," he adds. "Besides, even in Portugal and Spain there are mature systems of industrial relations. There will not be an erosion of labour rights in the EC because they are too deeply anchored in the national political systems."

Wrong, says labour. "There's a general feeling among unions that realization of the Internal Market will put downward pressure on employment standards," says Tesch-Segol, Brussels secretary for EuroFIET, the 4.6-million strong federation of white-collar workers in the EC's banking, insurance and retail sectors. "Plant relocation in less developed regions in the EC poses a threat for textile and other labour-intensive industries. Our members' problems, however, lie elsewhere."

According to Tesch-Segol, the post-1992 dangers for clerical and technically skilled employees reside in the conditions of work, as opposed to job availability. At stake are such matters as training, proper contracts, and benefits. "We're already seeing more companies making offers of temporary positions, part-time work with part-time benefits, and difficult work schedules," she says.

The French Banking Association, for example, is refusing to negotiate long-term benefits on the grounds that banks need flexible working conditions to respond to the challenges of 1992. "Flexibility is fine," says Tesch-Segol, "but you can't jerk an employee from one temporary contract period to another without offering minimum security. We don't want our people who've done 20 years of loyal work suddenly shoved aside by a young college graduate."

The reluctance of French banks, as well as the rest of industry, to follow historical patterns of industrial negotiation lies in the fact that history, they feel, is a poor guide to the future. "Training employees to do the same job for 40 years, for example, is dead—times have changed," says Johannes Wachter, social affairs expert with UNICE, the Brussels-based lobby for European industry.

"We completely agree that on-the-job training and continuous worker education are vital and necessary to remain competitive, for both the employee and employer," he adds. "I think most of industry is willing to shoulder the costs, but only if industry sets the terms. We will not accept mandatory rules on X number of downtime days for worker education if we have no control over what, where or when he is picking up the new skills. Flexibility is what the whole Internal Market programme means. If we as employers don't have it, it won't work."

In many ways, talk of a European dimension to social policy—particularly that for industrial relations—long predates the Internal Market programme. Indeed, the principle of worker rights is enshrined in the Community's 30-year-old Treaty of Rome, albeit vaguely worded. Precise definition and enforcement are left to national governments. Steady progress towards pan-EC social legislation was slow during the 1960s and 1970s.

In 1980, however, appeared the Commission's infamous Vredeling proposal. Very pro-labour, the Vredeling doctrine advocated strong worker participation in European companies and, moreover, would have required all EC multinationals to keep their entire workforces informed of all major decisions affecting the company as a whole or subsidiaries anywhere in the world.

The proposal died a quick death, but not before sparking an explosive reaction from business and industry. Lingering reaction against it, in fact, helped spur the opposite movement a few years later: creation of the Roundtable of European Industrialists, a rethinking of the Continent's economic problems, formulation of the 1985 White Paper and its subsequent creation of the Internal Market programme.

In the aftermath of the Vredeling proposal, a new alliance between industry and the Brussels bureaucracy was forged, to labour's disadvantage. As long as the alliance stands, it means that European labour will not achieve two very dear objectives: collective bargaining and worker participation at the European level; industry rejects both out of hand, as do some member states.

But while labour may be down for the moment, that doesn't necessarily imply it's being kicked by the other side. There are simply too many unknowns about what the Internal Market will bring to predict what the social dimension should or shouldn't be.

One thing seems reasonably sure, though. If unemployment, investment distortions and disparate working conditions grow too large across the Community, so will the pressure towards the traditional European solutions for labour problems: protest and strikes. If that happens, calls for collective bargaining and worker participation can only increase. And yet, EC-level collective bargaining, says Liebana, "is the rock on which the whole social dimension programme crashes."

Instead, industry and labour seem to be putting their faith in the Internal Market's positive side, hoping the momentum will smother the negatives.

# Unlocking a Hidden Resource: Integrating the Foreign-Born

## GARY ODDOU

Two weeks ago, you were a $75,000-a-year, 45-year-old IBM executive. Today, you have just arrived in Malaysia with other American men, women and children. Having suddenly been forced to leave the United States because of a nuclear accident, you are searching for a new life. You speak no Malaysian and have only a small suitcase of clothes with you. After "stumbling" from company to company, you have finally found a job as an assembly-line worker in a small appliance company. Your wage is $1.00 an hour. Your supervisor speaks no English.

Though probably far from your or any corporate executive's thoughts, imagining such an incident might help you understand the trauma many of the refugees from Asia have faced when entering the U.S. and its workforce. Many migrant workers and others from Mexico have experienced similar culture shock. And upon entering the U.S. workforce, foreign-born workers typically are employed at the lowest levels of the organization regardless of their background or current expertise.

However, foreign-born employees have specific culturally based problem-solving and management styles that could benefit corporate America. Certainly, the Japanese have demonstrated the superiority of certain management and manufacturing methods that are deeply rooted in their group-oriented culture. Our ignorance of both Japanese culture and its application in the workplace has seriously hurt the U.S. auto and semiconductor industries. Market share has decreased drastically since the mid 1970s. Sharply reduced book-to-bill ratios during this same period led to massive layoffs or other corporate restructuring. Reputations regarding product quality of some of America's world industry leaders in companies such as General Motors, Ford, Chevrolet, Intel, Motorola, Texas Instruments and others have suffered.

In short, foreign competition has seriously challenged U.S. leadership

*Source:* Reprinted by permission of the author.

in the global economy. Unfortunately, our research indicates that U.S. industry is reluctant to admit that the challenge is culture-based. Rather than ignore it, U.S. industry should seek to take full advantage of the potential benefits of its multiculturally diverse workforce here on our own soil.

It is time, therefore, to look specifically at the reasons why corporate America has still not really taken significant strides to profit from these foreign-born employees' potential intellectual and creative talents, approaches and perspectives rooted in their foreign cultures.

To explore these issues and thus to discover ways in which U.S. companies could more effectively manage their culturally diverse human resources, various personnel officers and numerous foreign-born employees were interviewed. Most of the companies represented in the sample are from "Silicon Valley," where industry employs from 65 to nearly 100 percent foreign-born employees, principally from Asia and Mexico.

## ■ The Barriers to Integrating Our Foreign-Born

### Language

Many foreign-born employees have problems interpreting written documents that deal with training opportunities, safety regulations, benefit policies, etc. Even those Asian employees who have reputations for being technically brilliant are reportedly held back from project and other management positions because others have difficulty understanding their spoken English.

Written English also poses problems. Implementing simple company procedures can be difficult for the foreign-born because their reading and writing skills are underdeveloped. At one large office equipment company, foreign-born employees in a key-punching group work the graveyard shift. They are supposed to leave information about the work they have done so the next shift knows where to begin. However, because of their lack of communication skills, the foreign-born did not know a message was always to be left and because of their lack of writing proficiency, the messages they *did* leave were not understood by the primarily American-born shift starting in the morning. Losses in time, over-runs and under-runs occurred, costing the company some financial loss as well as strained relations between ethnic groups.

Sometimes such problems are hidden from those whose job it is to know—human resource personnel. For instance, personnel officers in two of the largest and most respected U.S. companies reported they have no problems with language proficiency in their respective companies. Such perceptions contrasted starkly with statements by some managers in those same firms who reported definite communication problems between foreign-born and native English speakers. The lack of English skills is sometimes compounded, then, by a misperception that there is no problem.

## Differing Cultural Norms

Cultural differences ranging from culinary and hygiene practices to more work-related impediments, such as orientations toward power structures, also prove to be road blocks to effective interaction with the foreign-born.

*Workers and Manager: The Role of the Patron* In Hispanic countries, relationships between employees and supervisors are much more formal than is typical in most U.S. companies. Hispanics generally expect the supervisor to give orders and set objectives without eliciting employees' ideas or opinions. For a supervisor to solicit ideas from employees would raise serious questions about the manager's own authority. To Latin workers, a supervisor is regarded as the expert—or he/she wouldn't be the supervisor.

Similarly, for a supervisor to raise his/her voice to either Hispanic or Asian employees is very degrading, and is interpreted by both groups of employees as totally inappropriate. For Asians, in particular, singling him or her out in front of peers for a mistake is deeply shameful. Fellow workers interpret such a practice as reflecting a system so imperfect as to have serious consequences for the department or firm. Both the Asian and the Latin would want to quit and join a more "conscientious" company, one that treats its employees as members of a corporate family.

The following incident as reported by one researcher illustrates this point:

> At a company in Santa Fe Springs, California, the 200 Mexicans on the second shift were once threatening a wildcat strike that could easily have spread to the first shift. . . . The problem was . . . that (the anglo foreman) used foul language and "shouted." The Mexicans believed his style ought instead to have been proper, aloof, reserved, and very formal. Shouting, they believed, should be reserved only for animals (de Forest, 1981)

*Task Clarity: The Need for Guidelines.* A related point of difference between people of these cultures and North Americans concerns the need for task clarity. Asian and Hispanic employees, more so than their U.S. counterparts, tend to expect very defined procedures as they relate to a clear objective. As a result, American supervisors who delegate a task without specifying a series of steps to accomplish the goal might well expect poor results. For Americans, who value the Horatio Alger model of becoming independent and taking initiative, having to take the time to "spell things out" seems both time-consuming and demeaning. Perhaps the real issue, however, is creating a more effective employee–manager match and training 1980s managers to adjust their traditional approach to fit that of the foreign-born.

*Group Identity: The Wish to Blend.* Research and experience has also found Hispanics and Southeast Asians to be much more concerned with group identification than Americans. As a result, the Hispanics and Southeast Asians value cooperation, group norms and group success more than competition or individual success as is typical in the U.S.

As has been well documented, publicly rewarding an Asian for superior work can cause him/her to lose face because such attention sets him/her apart from the workgroup. Instead of encouraging continued superior performance, such praise can serve to punish the person's performance. The well-known expression in Japan illustrates this: "The nail that sticks up gets hammered down."

Because the Asians and Hispanics are group-oriented, integration into a new culture can be made more difficult by their communal style of living. In the U.S., most foreign-born tend to live geographically in the same location, starting their own stores and restaurants. As a result, quite often they develop increasingly self-sufficient Southeast Asian (Cambodian, Vietnamese, Laotian, etc.) or Latin American (Mexican, Salvadoran, etc.) islands within a larger U.S. sea.

In most cases, the tight, familial network of these cultures obviates the need, and sometimes the motivation, to integrate closely with the host nationals. These foreign-born employees rely solely on other family members already living in the U.S. to help them "integrate."

Further, most companies who hire Asian- or Mexican-born workers find they are not hiring one individual but, in the long run, a family-related host of Asians or Mexicans. In one company, for example, five unrelated families accounted for 33 foreign-born employees. When foreign-born employees rely exclusively on one another for access into the workplace, they develop few relationships with American employees. Consequently, adaptation to American customs within the work environment is significantly retarded.

This group-before-individual attitude also influences on-the-job behavior. For example, some cultures value interpersonal relationships more than others. Mexican-born employees, for example, have often been culturally very gregarious. As a result, Mexican-born employees are sometimes stereotyped as "goofing off," as more concerned about talking than about the goals of the organization. With the emphasis on "bottom-line" outcomes (i.e., profit) in U.S. organizations, behaviors are supposed to be seen as directly affecting the task. Ironically, however, strictly enforcing rules to reduce conversation among Hispanics at work will usually decrease productivity.

In comparison to Hispanics, Asian-born employees often *appear* timid and unwilling to use their language skills. They are often typed as introverted and uninterested in integrating with the rest of the workforce. For example, in another company, Cambodian employees did not know they were allowed to eat in the company cafeteria. Because they continually ate off-site, American-born employees believed the Cambodians didn't want to associate with them. U.S.-born managers informally concluded that the foreign-born were simply ignorant and, thus, both unable and unwilling to contribute significantly to the firm.

### U.S. Ethnocentrism

Most stereotyping of our foreign-born workforce is based on ethnocentrism—interpreting right and wrong, good and bad behavior by our own cultural background. Often, we ourselves are not aware of the assumptions underlying our praising and blaming. Most present-day U.S. upper managers, for instance, grew up in a Pearl Harbor-generation in which Japanese-born Americans were to be feared and even hated and Mexicans were good fodder for jokes. It is no wonder U.S. top management is not used to thinking in terms of the potential advantages of a multicultural workforce.

Furthermore, because Mexico and most of the Pacific Rim are much less technologically advanced than the U.S., management purportedly tends to believe employees from these areas cannot really advance current technology.

An immigrant engineer educated in the U.S. said this of his company:

> In my company, there are many engineers trained in their own countries. But because they came to the U.S. not knowing any English, they have had to get what jobs they could. Here they are employed as technicians and the company has the attitude that they are not capable of doing more. Many of them speak good English now, but they are still technicians.

In fact, evidence suggests that top management is not really even aware of or involved with the potential impact of cultural diversity on the organization. For example, in one study of Canadian organizations employing English- and French-speaking employees, where cultural upheavals have been commonplace, management believed that gender affects organizations more than culture (Adler, 1983). With perceptions such as these, any significant and real differences among cultures will go unnoticed and unattended.

Despite the difficulties of overcoming old stereotypes, recognizing Latin and Asian cultural patterns, and getting managers to modify their management styles, several specific steps can be taken to integrate foreign-born employees into U.S. companies.

## ▬ Integrating Our Foreign-Born

### Reward Those Who Learn English

Companies that encourage foreign-born employees to attend community English as a Second Language (ESL) programs or sponsor in-house ones report classes are effective in helping the foreign-born become more productive employees. Other options for encouraging their learning English include offering small but symbolic bonuses for ESL class attendance or raises for higher levels of English proficiency. Language proficiency can be tested by one of the several standardized English tests available (i.e., the TOEFL or Michigan test) and can become part of their performance review if shown to be job- or promotion-related.

## Share Cultures

Firms should distribute pamphlets in English and/or their native language which explain company concepts and work values around issues of power, job expectations, the company's decision-making philosophy and procedures, advancement, and so on. Such training could even be expanded to include topics such as American sports, cuisine, recreation, holidays and other information that would aid the foreign-born's adjustment to the U.S.

Company personnel libraries or lounges could house literature about the specific cultures represented in the company and about the organization's corporate culture. Such information could be distributed in hiring packets. More formally, an integral part of a manager's training should include information and training about the foreign-born employees he/she supervises. Two of the electronics companies sampled, for instance, reported they had included cultural sensitivity as part of their management training program. Personnel officers reported the training to be very effective in decreasing departmental problems.

Company cafeteria cuisine could represent the various major cultural groups. Latin and Asian dishes that do not require imported ingredients could be prepared. Such dishes are particularly appropriate on the various national holidays of the cultural groups represented in the firm. All of these practices, of course, would enhance the firm's image as a company-as-family firm in the eyes of the foreign-born.

## Improve Recruiting

Companies can do two things to improve here: First, in the hiring or recruiting interview, attention should be focused on determining any relevant technical expertise the individual had in his/her country. Second, while many Asians are hired because of their technical orientation and skills, more emphasis should be placed on determining their interest in or aptitude for people-oriented areas. The foreign-born should be employed throughout the firm across functions and among levels.

According to deForest, AT&T, Eastman Kodak, and Texas Instruments have successfully used special testing techniques for Mexican-born employees. Bilingual personnel assistants have also been found to successfully aid Mexican-born employees in career counseling at Hewlett-Packard, Kraft Foods, Bell & Howell, and others.

## Initiate Cross-Cultural Mentoring

Probably the most helpful thing a company can do to facilitate work acculturation is to request coworkers to be "sponsors" or mentors to foreign-born employees. These mentors would be responsible for helping to socialize some of the foreign-born into the work culture.

For example, the sponsor might regularly have lunch with one to three of the employees. Besides helping to develop friendships outside their culture group, such a practice would help the foreign-born improve their English. Those who volunteer to be sponsors could also be informally or formally rewarded in the company. If team development is an important part of the firm's objectives, such "sponsorship" could be formalized in performance appraisals. Of the companies interviewed, one was using this method to orient all new employees. Although not directed toward any particular cultural group, the program was reported as being very effective.

Companies can also sponsor "integrated" intramural sports teams (e.g., bowling, baseball, soccer). This can be particularly effective in cases where both native-born and foreign-born share similar sports as is the case with baseball in Japan and soccer in South America.

Within the workplace itself, company socialization for the foreign-born can also include roleplaying various situations that are culture-specific to America and the company (e.g., introductions, giving and receiving instructions, performance reviews, interviews, etc.).

### Take Advantage of the Inherent Workforce Diversity

Recent studies on innovation clearly indicate that an ability to see things from different perspectives is critical to the process of innovation. Companies taking advantage of the inherent diversity of perspectives and novel approaches of their various cultural groups should therefore have a distinct advantage over other firms. Bell Labs formally adopted the practice of strategically diversifying the members of their research teams to generate a more creative, innovative environment.

Psychological tests can be used to determine if certain subcultures have characteristic problem-solving approaches that differ from most Americans. The Meyers-Briggs Type Indicator, for example, is currently being used by electronics and research and development firms, such as Apple Computers and Eyring Research Center, to determine human resource planning as well as the most potentially innovative work group composition. Such tests and others like them need to be used and/or developed to integrate foreign-born employees into task forces, quality circles, and R&D groups.

## ■ Conclusion

U.S. management has a history of suffering from a short-term perspective, and a history of wanting proof before the pudding. However, in highly competitive, dynamic industries, the U.S. cannot afford to overlook any possible advantage in the increasingly competitive marketplace—even if it is a long-term, developmental effort.

Educating managers about cultural differences among their employees has shown promise in building more effective work groups. Using English programs and bilingual personnel assistants and conscientiously matching employee abilities with job requirements have produced greater employee participation in problem-solving on the production line.

Unlocking our foreign-born resources means investing in our mutual future.

## ▰ *References*

1. Adler, N. "Organizational Development in a Multicultural Environment." *Journal of Applied Behavioral Science*, 19, 1983, 349–365.

2. deForest, Mariah E., "Mexican Workers North of the Border." *Harvard Business Review*, May–June 1981, 150–157.

# The El Al Strike in New York

## ARIE REICHEL
## JOHN F. PREBLE

It was a cold and snowy day in late March 1984 when those passing by the El Al[1] offices at 850 3rd Avenue in Manhattan and at JFK International Airport saw picketers standing by the barriers and carrying placards. On a summer day, some six months later, picketers were still there. Was this the same strike or a new one?

From Los Angeles to New York City to Miami to Tel Aviv, potential El Al passengers kept calling the reservation desks expressing concern that they might not be able to fly because of the strike. Reservations agents indicated, rather matter-of-factly, that El Al service had not been affected by the strike.

## ▬ The Situation

After 12 months of negotiations between the management of El Al Israel Airlines, Ltd., New York, and union representatives for the 225 employees of El Al, members of District 100 of the International Association of Machinists and Aerospace Workers (IAM), negotiations had reached an impasse.[2]

---

[1] El Al, the national airline of the State of Israel, was incorporated November 15, 1948. Its charter objective was and remains "to secure and maintain a regular airlink at all times and under all conditions within a framework of maximum profitability" (El Al At A Glance). The principal shareholder is the government of Israel. During the time of the case, the Chairman of the Board was Mr. Nachman Perel, and the President was Mr. Rafael Harlev. The main office for North and Central America, located in Manhattan, is directed by the General Manager, Mr. David Schneider. The General Manager for Marketing is Mr. Adi Zecharia.

[2] According to the Railway Labor Act (which includes employees of airlines as well as trains), a contract is open for negotiation according to a preset date. A contract is in effect either until a new one is signed or until the Federal Mediation Board releases the firm and the union from the mediation process. This release can take place after 30 days of a cooling-off period that is necessary after a failure in negotiations. After this period, the firm has the right to implement its latest proposal for a contract. The union, in turn, has a right to strike.

Source: Arie Reichel and John F. Preble. "The El Al Strike in New York." Journal of Management Case Studies, 1987, 3:270–276. Reprinted by permission.

Subsequent efforts by the National Mediation Service failed to break the deadlock (*Village Voice*, Jul. 10, 1984; *New York Times*, Mar. 17, 1984). After a 30-day cooling-off period had passed, the old contract expired on March 31, 1983 (*AFL-CIO News*, Apr. 7, 1984), and El Al implemented a new contract. The employees then voted on two issues: (1) to accept or reject the firm's proposals; and (2) whether or not to strike. Ninety-four percent of the rank and file voted to reject the firm's proposals, and 89% of union members voted to go on strike. The strike commenced on March 16, 1984, and continues as this case is being written.

Throughout the negotiations, the style of El Al management was some-what inflexible. For example, several weeks before the strike broke out, Mr. Rafael Harlev, the airline's President, visited New York to meet with employ-ees. He asserted that the union would have no choice but to accept all of management's proposals and he added, "if you don't accept these proposals we will close the New York office and move to another city in North America." But labor–management relations turned bitter when El Al, just a few days after the walkout, flew in 90 workers from Israel (many with dual citizenship), housed them at a Manhattan hotel, and escorted them to work and back in armed limousines (*Village Voice*, Jul. 10, 1984; *Business Week*, Jul. 23, 1984). In addition, management made two trips a day to the airport to ensure the smooth operation of incoming and outgoing flights. The manage-ment personnel were seen carrying suitcases and handling agent-related is-sues such as ticketing. It all looked like a well-planned military operation, which, from a management perspective, had been very successful.

Since then, relations have worsened, with charges being made back and forth between the union and the management. The IAM, as noted in a letter dated July 25, 1984, from the Union Label and Service Trades Department (AFL-CIO) to the National and International Unions State and Local Central Bodies Union Label and Service Trades Councils Labor Press, has charged El Al officials with refusal to bargain in good faith, walking out of meetings, and demanding wholesale concessions with a take-it-or-leave-it attitude. The IAM feel that El Al is trying to "bust" the union (*Village Voice*, Jul. 10, 1984). How-ever, management strongly denies what has been said about them in the press.

For its part, El Al has charged in the Israeli press that strikers had anti-Semitic motives—even though almost half are Jewish (*Business Week*, Jul. 23, 1984). In the same article in *Business Week* it was reported that IAM headquar-ters failed to renew a $1 million Israeli bond that matured in June, due to their negative feelings toward El Al's actions. Further, El Al's management stated that some of the strikers who considered returning to work were threatened and harassed by union activists. The AFL-CIO has demonstrated support for the union position with the endorsement of a boycott against El Al Israel Airlines as of July 20, 1984. There were reports of clashes between guards hired by El Al and the strikers. The atmosphere was one of confronta-tion rather than cooperation. One possible solution to the situation was the use of binding arbitration, should both sides agree to it.

With regard to Israeli labor relations, it has been reported (*Business Week,* Jul. 23, 1984) that in the late 1970s eight unions were representing El Al employees. This created a chaotic environment resulting in 69 strikes over a ten-year period. Chronic losses at El Al, a major drop in the Israeli tourist trade in late 1982, and a wave of strikes caused a four-month shutdown of the airline. El Al reemerged in January, 1983, with only one union (Histadrut), whose members would have no right to strike. A two-year wage freeze was imposed, as well as a 20% cut in the workforce and the elimination of many union work rules. Losses were consequently cut from $46 million in fiscal 1983, to approximately $15 million for fiscal 1984. Additional cost-saving measures were then to be imposed on the U.S. employees through a set of concessionary demands mentioned earlier. For 20 years preceding this development, El Al's labor–management relations in the United States had been excellent.

## ▀ *Management Proposals*

The management of El Al in New York had demanded, as part of a larger package to save the ailing state-owned company, that the IAM make a large number of concessions:

1. agree to a three-year freeze in hourly wages;
2. give management the right to contract out commissary and auto-repair jobs (essentially eliminating these departments);
3. make overtime mandatory, at a reduced rate of pay;
4. give management the right to hire an unlimited number of part-time employees (threatening job security);
5. cut vacation days by five days, across the board;
6. allow supervisors to do the work of unionized employees for up to four hours per day;
7. give management the right to impose the concept of crossutilization, whereby workers could be assigned to work in numerous job classifications;
8. give El Al the unilateral right to contract out all the work involving maintenance, catering, and dispatching of aircraft;
9. give the right to lay off various units; and
10. abolish the lifetime employment guarantee given recently to 37 employees.[3]

---

[3]These proposals, as well as the union's reactions and counterproposals, have been reported in the popular/trade press, including *Business Week,* Jul. 23, 1984, *Village Voice,* Jul. 10, 1984, *The Jewish Week,* May 11, 1984, and *AFL-CIO News,* Apr. 7, 1984 and May 12, 1984. Interviews were also conducted with Mr. David Schneider, General Manager for North and Central America, El Al Israel Airlines, Ltd., and Mr. Motti Horovitz, an employee of El Al, and a trustee for Lodge 2656, which represents clerical workers at El Al's Manhattan office.

Mr. Schneider, the general manager in New York, felt that these proposals were fair in light of the severe financial problems of the airline and the sacrifices already made by other union members in Israel and around the world. Further, he emphasized that many of management's proposals were necessary to maintain around-the-clock service to passengers at JFK International Airport in New York.

### Union Response

The IAM[4] was divided in its response to management's demands. Some 80 IAM members have returned to work since the strike began (*The Jewish Week*, May 11, 1984). The union believes that it has compromised a great deal by offering these counterproposals:

1. accept a one-year wage freeze;
2. eliminate the commissary and auto-repair shops;
3. accept a reduced rate of pay for overtime and a maximum of two to three hours of overtime in unusual cases;
4. allow part-time workers to be hired for up to 8% of the workforce as long as this does not cause full-time employees to be laid-off;
5. cut two vacation days per person per year;
6. a "Tour Desk," comprised of employees who will do both reservations and ticket issuing (less rigid job classifications; but the IAM disagreed on the additional demand by El Al that ticket agents be freely transferred from one location to another).

Although the union has offered the above concessions and counterproposals, management has declined to accept most of these and is taking an even harder line with respect to the 140 remaining strikers. El Al is willing to take back only 10–20 of these employees, recalling others only when any of the 70 replacements leave (*Business Week*, Jul. 23, 1984). The union is insisting that El Al take back all 140 members out on strike.

[4]At the beginning of the strike all 225 strikers were members of the IAM. The union headquarters is in Washington, D.C., and the current membership is 600,000, down from 1,000,000. The next level below headquarters is the district level. El Al employees are represented by District 100, where Mr. Gene Hoffman is the general chairman and the union's chief negotiator in the El Al talks. Within the district, El Al employees are in two different locals: 2656 (New York City) and 1894 (airport). Other employees of various airlines and travel agencies are also members of District 100. The main communication between management and the union is maintained through the district representative. Under this representative, there are "locals," who are responsible for administrative tasks such as collecting dues, updating membership lists, etc. Managers and supervisors are not members. Union officials are elected in a democratic way. The general chairman of a district is elected every four years. Each department has one or two shop stewards. A chief shop steward, who is elected every two years, deals primarily with grievances.

## ▬ *Solidarity*

Support for the union came early on in the strike when Lane Kirkland, President of the AFL-CIO, wrote a letter to Mr. Meir Rosenne of the Israeli Embassy in Washington, D.C. In the March 20, 1984, letter Mr. Kirkland asked Meir Rosenne to intervene and to try and do something about the "take-it-or-leave-it" attitude of El Al. Later on, the Executive Council of the AFL-CIO sent a cable to Israel's Prime Minister Shamir and to the opposition Labor party in Israel "to call upon the Israeli government to instruct El Al to enter negotiations in good faith and stop its attack on the union."

On March 29, 1984, Secretary general Yerucham Meshel of Histadrut, the Israeli Labor Federation, sent a cable to Mr. Kirkland expressing solidarity and support with the striking employees of El Al Israel Airlines. The cable read as follows:

> Have cabled yesterday to our minister of transport condemning in the strongest possible terms El Al's handling of dispute with the company's employees in the U.S. and demanded that strike-breakers be immediately called to Israel and that negotiations with the union be resumed in keeping with accepted trade union procedures and in strict adherence to prevailing collective agreement.
>
> Histadrut expresses its full solidarity with striking El Al employees members of the International Association of Machinists and Aerospace Workers and will continue pressing for speedy resolution of conflict in accordance with free democratic trade union principles.

On April 5, 1984, Mr. Frank J. Barbaro, the head of the Labor Commission of the New York Assembly, sent a letter with 59 assembly member signatures to Prime Minister Yitzhak Shamir expressing grave concern over the way in which El Al Airlines was conducting itself in its collective bargaining with District 100. Mr. Chaim Korfu, Minister of Transport for Israel, responded to the letter to Mr. Shamir on May 6, 1984. Mr. Korfu pointed out that El Al has been under receivership in Israel and has been directed by the court to effect substantial cost savings, ensure continuous operations, and, failing that, liquidate the company. The general tone of the letter to the legislators was not supportive, and Mr. Korfu insisted that the company never tried to break the union.

At least two additional requests for support and solidarity were made by high-level IAM representatives. On April 12, 1984, Mr. R. L. Rapp, General Chairman, sent a letter to Mr. Edward J. Cleary, President of the New York State AFL-CIO, explaining the situation at El Al and asking for support and assistance. Mr. William W. Winpsinger, International President of IAM, sent a letter on April 17, 1984, to Mr. Harry Van Arsdale, President of the New York City Labor Council, detailing the actions of El Al management and asking for support and solidarity. Evidence that these calls were heeded is contained in a letter dated April 24, 1984, from Mr. Morton Bahr, Vice President of the Communications Workers of America AFL-CIO, District 1, to Ms. Carol

G. Creamer, President of IAM Local 2656. In this letter, Mr. Bahr indicated that, in response to a request from the NYC Labor Council, he had recently met with representatives of a major U.S. Jewish organization and an Israeli official who had just arrived in the United States and that he articulated all important points, on behalf of the strikers, to these individuals. Additionally, on May 22, 1984, Mr. Martin Lapan, Executive Director of the Jewish Labor Committee, sent a letter to friends of the committee discussing El Al's attempts to break the union and its charges of anti-Semitism against the U.S. strikers. He urged Jewish leaders to call on the Prime Minister of Israel to instruct El Al to settle the dispute before greater damage was done to Israel's image and interests.

As a result of mounting pressure from labor organizations and Jewish organizations, on July 18, 1984, there was a high-level meeting between the employees' leadership and El Al management, including Mr. Rafael Harlev, the President of El Al. He asserted that El Al would not accept back a considerable number of the strikers. This resulted in a deadlock, and soon afterward the AFL-CIO declared a general boycott against El Al, sending cables to numerous labor organizations in Europe asking for their help.

## The Anti-Semitism Issue

The striking U.S. employees have been accused several times of anti-Semitism. These accusations were made in various places, including the Israel daily, *Davar* (the Histadrut paper). The article claimed that El Al employees accused Israel of being ruthless and declared the strike to be part of the Palestinian's struggle for self-determination.

The strikers argue now that it never happened. "We are not leftists, we have been avid supporters of Israel. We have organized many donation parties and bought Israeli bonds."

In an article in the *Village Voice* (Jul. 10, 1984), it was noted that strikers were deeply offended by the charges. During several of Israel's wars, many of these white-collar, middle-class, Jewish employees worked overtime without compensation, in some cases donating their paychecks to the effort. The strikers emphasize that they are not against the country, but rather the tactics of El Al's management. "You have to separate your feelings and know what you're striking for."

Local Lodge 2656 of IAM is so concerned about the anti-Semitism charges that at their general membership meeting held on Tuesday, April 24, 1984, they passed the following resolution:

> We, the members of Local Lodge 2656, District 100, International Association of Machinists and Aerospace Workers, AFL-CIO, hereby condemn El Al Israel Airlines for lying to the Israeli media by labeling our Union and its leadership as anti-Semitic. This is a despicable tactic being used by El Al Israel Airlines to try and justify their union-busting actions.

## ▰ *Recent Trends in Labor–Management Relations*

Yost (*Sunday News Journal,* Sep. 1, 1985) detailed a number of reasons why unions are facing an unsure future in the United States. For the last two years, nonunion pay raises were greater than the pay raises for union workers (3% per year average). Major strikes for the first six months of 1985 totaled 18, down from 235 in 1979. Many believe that unions have priced themselves out of the market, particularly in mature industries. The combination of deregulation in several industries, increased foreign competition with vast, inexpensive labor forces, a conservative president, the recent recession, and a large unemployed labor pool (ready to be strikebreakers) has weakened labor's strength. Management's stance has been problematic, as well, with its demands for two-tier contracts, plant-closing threats, and filing bankruptcy to cancel labor contracts (Continental Airlines). President Reagan's firing of 11,500 striking air traffic controllers only served to emphasize the declining power of unions. This decline is reflected in recent union pay concessions. For example, Braniff airline's unions agreed to a 10% employee pay cut (Pearce and Keels, 1985).

Burdetsky and Katzman (1984) argued that surefire strikers are more than likely a thing of the past. Unions are competing with automation, imports, high unemployment, and public opinion. In order to be successful, these authors argue that a union needs both public support and the ability to inflict pain on the employer. These conditions are rare in today's labor environment. El Al strikers are currently discovering these realities. El Al's ability to hire replacements for the strikers and to fill in where necessary with supervisors and managers has allowed it to maintain all scheduled service on time. Additionally, high levels of public support have been difficult to achieve because of the potential problem of damaging close ties between the United States and Israel. This situation is made clear in the following statement from *Village Voice* (Jul. 10, 1984):

> For some of the Machinists, the strike has been what one called a "rude awakening" to the realities of political life. Despite a number of interviews and visits by the press, no coverage has appeared in city papers or local television—an absence perceived by many as reluctance to criticize Israel.

## ▰ *Current Developments*

The circumstances surrounding this strike and the tactics of El Al were being carefully noted by other offshore airlines (*Business Week,* Jul. 23, 1984). Mr. Martin Seham, A New York lawyer who has been negotiating for El Al, will represent Aer Lingus (Irish carrier) and Varig (Brazilian state-owned company) in demanding future concessions from the IAM. District 100 representative Hoffman is concerned with the dangerous precedent that could be set at El Al. But the question remains, can anything be done to avert these dangerous developments?

On March 3, 1985, Arie Egozi, New York correspondent for the Israeli daily *Yedioth Aahronot,* reported that some 80 El Al employees are still on strike. Attempts to resolve the strike have been met with a strong reluctance to move from initial positions. Additionally, the IAM has introduced new financial demands and ultimatums.

Throughout the strike many people have expressed the opinion that a "political" solution is needed to resolve the strike. This would involve the Israeli government playing a major role in the settlement. A step in this direction took place recently. It was reported in *Davar* (Jun. 19, 1985) that Mr. Amos Eran, the general manager of Mivtachim (Histadrut's pension fund) had been appointed by Israeli Prime Minister Peres to be his personal representative in an effort to end the strike. After meeting with the union representatives, Mr. Eran reported back to Mr. Peres that the American union is prepared to take most of the areas in dispute to arbitration. As of October 1985, the strike continues and its final resolution does not appear close at hand.

# References

*AFL-CIO News,* April 7, 1984.

*AFL-CIO News,* May 12, 1984.

Burdetsky, B. and Katzman, M.S. "Is The Strike Iron Still Hot?" *Personnel Journal,* July 1984, 48–52.

*Business Week,* July 23, 1984, 71–72.

*Davar,* June 19, 1985.

*El Al At A Glance.* Public Relations Department, El Al Israeli Airlines Ltd.

*New York Times,* March 17, 1984, 27.

Pearce II, J.A. and Keels, J.K. "The fall and rise of Braniff." *Journal of Management Case Studies,* 1985, 1, 4–12.

*Sunday News Journal,* September 1, 1985, E1–E2.

*The Jewish Week,* May 11, 1984.

*The Village Voice,* July 10, 1984.

# *Olivia Francis*

## MARK MENDENHALL

Jim Markham did not know what to do. The more he tried to analyze the problem, the murkier it became. Normally, Jim felt confident in counseling his students—both past and present—but this time it was different. Olivia Francis had been one of the best students he had ever taught in the M.B.A. program. She was bright and curious, one of those rare students whose thirst for knowledge was uppermost in her reasons for being in the program.

She had never disclosed much about her family or her past to him, but he knew from her student file and information sheet, and from bits and pieces of conversations with her, that she had come from a poor, somewhat impoverished neighborhood in St. Louis and had earned her way through college on academic scholarships and part-time jobs. Upon graduation from the M.B.A. program, she left the Midwest, taking a job with a prestigious consulting firm in Los Angeles, and at the time he had felt sure she would travel far in her career. Perhaps that is why her phone call earlier that morning troubled him so.

Awaiting him on his arrival to his office was a message on his answering machine from Olivia. He returned her call and wound up talking to her for an hour. The salient portions of their conversation began to run through his mind again. What had struck him the most initially was the range and the depth of her emotions. Never had he spoken to anyone in his life who was seething with so much rage. After she had vented the rage, like air slowly being discharged from a balloon, she became almost apathetic, and her resignation to her situation almost frightened him—her only way out, as far as she could see, was to find another job. Jim could not recall ever being in a situation where he felt he had absolutely no control over what happened to him, where his input was meaningless to the resolution of a problem he faced.

Olivia had stated that her first performance appraisal had been below average, and two weeks ago, her second appraisal was only average. She felt that she had worked hard on her part of the team's projects and believed her work was first rate. The only reason for the appraisals, as far as she could

*Source:* This case was written especially for this book.

see, was that she was black. She was the only black on the team—in the whole office for that matter. Jim believed her when she said that her work was excellent, for her work had always been excellent as a graduate student and as a research assistant. He had attempted to get her to analyze the situation further, but it was like pulling teeth; she seemed emotionally worn out and just wanted out.

"Surely they gave you more feedback about your performance than that it was below average?" he remembered asking. All she would say is that they mentioned something about her attitude, not being a team player, that her work was technically exemplary, but that she was part of a team and that working with others was as critical as the nature of the work she did by herself. Olivia felt that this was a smokescreen for the fact that she had been dumped on the office by a corporate recruiter with an EEO quota to fill, and that they were trying to get rid of her by using subjective criteria that she couldn't really defend herself against. The frustration came back to Jim as he remembered probing her for more information.

"What was the tone of your manager in the feedback session?" "Condescending, false sincerity; there was a lot of talk on his part of 'my potential.' It was humiliating, actually."

"How do the other people in your team act toward you? Are they friendly, aloof, or what?"

"Oh, they're friendly on the surface—especially the project leader—but that's about as far as it goes."

"Is the project manager the person who gave you this feedback?"

"No, she is under the group manager. He is a long-time company guy. But obviously she gives him her evaluation and impressions of me, so I'm sure that they both pretty much see issues regarding me eye-to-eye."

"Tell me more about the group manager."

"Mr. Bresnan? I don't know much about him to tell you the truth. He oversees five project teams, and each project manager reports to him. He comes in and gives a pep talk from time to time to us. Other than that I've never had occasion to really interact with him. He's always cracking jokes, putting people at ease. Kind of a 'Theory Y' type—at least on the surface."

"Do you ever go to lunch as a group?"

"Yes, they go to lunch a lot and they invite me along, but all they talk about are things I don't find very interesting—they're kind of a shallow bunch."

"What do you mean, shallow?"

"They couldn't care less about real issues—their discussions range from restaurants to social events around town to recent movies they've seen."

"Does the project manager go to these lunches?"

"Yes, she comes and even plans parties after work, too. Her husband is in the entertainment industry, a movie producer. Nothing big, documentaries and that type of thing, but they put on airs, if you know what I mean. She is really gregarious and always wants to be of help to people, but she strikes me as putting on a front, a mask—obviously she isn't really sincere in wanting to help everyone 'be the best that they can be'; that's one of her little slogans by the way; after all, look what happened to me."

"Why do you think they're prejudiced against you?"

"Well, the poor appraisals for one thing—those are completely unfounded. They do other less obvious things, too. Twice I've overheard some of them from behind cubicles relaxing and telling racist jokes about 'wetbacks.'"

"Is it just a few of them that do this? I can't believe all of them are racist."

"I don't know, I don't enter the cubicle and say, 'Hi guys, tell some more jokes!' But it isn't just one or two of them. Look, I obviously don't fit in, do I? It's lily-white in the office, and I'm not."

"What do they do that is work-related that bothers you?"

"Well, when project deadlines get closer their anxiety level increases. They run around the office, yell at secretaries . . . it's like a volcano building up power to explode. They worry and agonize over the presentation to the client and have two or three trial presentation runs that everyone is required to go to. It's all so stupid."

"Why is that?"

"The clients always like what we produce, and with a few relatively small adjustments, our work is acceptable to the clients. So, it's as though all that wasted energy was needless. We could accomplish so much more if they would just settle down and trust their abilities."

"How do you act when they are like this?"

"I do my work. I respond to them rationally. I turn my part of the project in on time, and it is *good* work, Professor Markham. I guess I try to be the stabilizing force in the team by not acting as they do—I guess I just don't find the work pressures to be all that stressful."

"Why not?"

"Oh, I don't know really. Well maybe I do a little bit. I don't know if you know this or not, but my mother was a single parent with four kids. I was the oldest. She worked, and I looked after the kids when I came home from school. She worked two jobs to provide for us, so I would be in charge of the smaller kids sometimes upwards of 9 o'clock at night. Doing your homework while taking care of a sick kid with the others listening to the television—that's stressful! These people at work, they don't know what stress is. Most of them are single, or if they are married they don't have any kids. They all seem very self-centered, like the universe revolves around them and their careers."

"What kind of behavior at work seems to get rewarded?"

"I guess doing good work doesn't. What seems to get rewarded is being white, being more or less competent, and being interested in insipid topics. Professor Markham, don't you know of any firms that are more enlightened I can send my résumé to? I'm looking for a firm that will reward me for the work I do and not for who I am or am not."

Jim leaned back in his chair pondering what to do next. He had promised Olivia that he would call her back in a day or two with some advice. He sensed that he didn't quite understand her problem, that there was more to it than what appeared on the surface. But he felt he didn't have enough data to analyze it properly. He decided to go for a walk around the neighborhood to clear his mind. As he opened the front door and gazed down his street, he suddenly realized for the first time that his neighborhood was lily-white.